Apples, Brownies, or **BOTH?**

A Devotional Cookbook

Kathy Hill

5 Fold Media
Visit us at www.5foldmedia.com

My Heart of Gratitude:

I am grateful to so many who have shown great love and encouragement to me along this journey and supported me in this project. There are few words to describe what publishing your first book feels like. Seeing words God placed in my heart come to life in print is both mind boggling and humbling. I never realized when I started sending a morning email to bring a word of encouragement to four people that it would grow to one hundred, be circulated in several countries, and eventually transformed into a devotional cookbook. I am filled to overflowing with love for those who have been such an inspiration to me:

To God, my Eternal Father and Creator, who placed within me a love for His Word, His people, and His plan.

To my mom, who always told me, "You can do anything you want if you are willing to work for it," and who placed a love for cooking deep within me. You never let me settle for anything average.

To my husband Terry, who cooked for me, brought hot tea every night, and gave up *months* of our personal time so I could spend each night working on this manuscript. You are the most patient and kind person I have ever known.

To my daughter Teree, who has been with me at every junction. You have an amazing eye for creativity and you have been a true source of inspiration. You have both sacrificed of yourself and encouraged me in ways I cannot list.

To Mackenzie and Kailey, for allowing me to share your lives. You are more than special to me. And Kailey, keep fighting for your health. You will be an inspiration to many children.

To Pastor Gilbert, who said it was okay for me to try. Thanks for believing in me.

To my Life Group, for two years of sharing recipes, stories, and prayers. I always needed those nights and love you more than I ever said.

To my girlfriends who have filled the pages of this book, allowed me to share their lives with you, and cheered me to the completion of this project. Shelly, Wendi, Linda, and Paulette—you rock!

To Paulette, Cheryl, and Lana, my first circle of three. I will always remember our first healthy meal together. Never quit! You guys were my inspiration.

To Wendi, who agreed to read my manuscript when I was afraid to ask anyone else. God sent you to me at just the right time. You are loved.

To my brother Chip, who called me one Thursday afternoon. That conversation changed my life! I would have never completed the first forty-two days without you. You were my "carrot."

To my health family, who listened, responded, encouraged, and listened again. Keep walking in freedom and choosing health daily.

Contents

Preface

On January 24, 2011, I walked away from the prison of obesity and a lifestyle of unhealthy choices that had engulfed me for most of my life. I am committed to never return to that dungeon. Although I was disciplined and desperately passionate about freedom in many areas, it seemed I could never obtain and maintain freedom as it applied to my health. As an adult, I came to understand that many people battle this same issue. This discovery did not necessarily console me, and yet it *comforted* me in a strange way.

The Lord allowed me to see how many Christians use obesity as their one accepted vice. I lost count of how many times I heard people confess, "Well, you know Paul had that thorn in his side, and overeating is mine. I don't watch pornography, cuss, murder people, or steal. So, if being overweight is my only option as a vice, then it simply is what it is." I can certainly empathize with that reasoning. It has tumbled from my lips more often than I care to count.

I am adamant about not making excuses for our sinful nature. In fact I tell people, "If you make excuses for sin, you keep it." I totally believe we were not called to make excuses for our sins, but annihilate them. Overeating is not a sin, right? Is gluttony? How about totally disrespecting the body God gave us where the Holy Spirit lives? I am not trying to make any of us feel more pain than most of us do concerning our health, but we must always fight for the truth no matter how painful it is. I was constantly hurting when it came to being obese and never seemed to muster the strength to break free. I have discovered I am not alone.

As I meditated on Paul's thorn and people using this excuse for being overweight, the warrior in me awakened. Does the fact that Paul had a thorn mean I also have to accept that fate? If I get to choose, then I say, "No thank you." I definitely have a choice, as do you. I have told many people over the past years of being healthy that they could watch pornography or some "bigger sin" until they are a hundred years old and it will never kill them physically. It will rob them spiritually, yes, but being overweight could destroy someone's life long before other sin issues.

Choosing to be unhealthy could mean that you never accomplish all God purposed for your life. God has great plans for each of us. Are you willing to allow poor health choices to keep you from being available for God? I am not making excuses concerning pornography, but I am not making excuses for poor health either. I am free of making excuses in this area. Please hear me clearly. I stand for freedom across the board. I make a stand and declare, "No thorn!"

So perhaps you think I am not being realistic. My prayer is that by the completion of this devotional cookbook you will understand that freedom is attainable in all areas if you are willing to stop making excuses and start the annihilation process. While that sounds impossible, God's Word teaches me that with Him all things are possible (see Matthew 19:26; Mark 9:23; 10:27; and 14:36).

The Scriptural foundation of this book is built on a particular verse from Galatians. I believe that if we can digest natural and spiritual health at the same time, we can make a stand for freedom that is based upon what Christ did for each of us and not our own works. As you read, cook, meditate, and sculpt, allow God's truth concerning freedom to give you the courage and hope to fight again. "*Stand fast then, and do not be hampered and held ensnared and submit again to a yoke of slavery [which you have once put off]*" (Gal 5:1 AMP). You can do it. I did.

Be faithful to the daily devotionals and experiment with each recipe. I am not a doctor, a licensed healthcare practitioner, nor do I have all the answers. I am passionate, however, about offering hope to others, eating well, and being free. Freedom in the arena of health, for me, equals the ability to eat an apple and a healthy, homemade brownie (the recipe is inside this book) and smile at them both. My prayer is that at the end of this year you celebrate your health birthday, praise God from a deep place, cook brownies and other yummy foods that allow you legal consumption, and never allow excuses in the arena of health to be your yoke of slavery again. Enjoy!

Kathy

Kathy in 2004

Kathy today

Introduction

Galatians 5:1 proclaims, "Stand fast therefore in the liberty by which Christ has made us free, and do not be entangled again with a yoke of bondage" (NKJV).

There are a lot of emphatic components to the above-mentioned verse that have been forever branded in my heart. The words from this verse assist me in forming boundaries that keep me on course when my past life of failed attempts to become healthy beckons for me to return. I will go a step deeper and say that I memorized this verse as if written to me, "I, Kathy, will stand fast in my new healthy life, and never allow myself to be entangled again with a yoke of obesity."

Ultimately, everything comes down to choice. As you read through this book and make notes, remember you and I are traveling on the same path, which is why you purchased the book and entered my story. It is not an easy story, a grand story, or even a short story; but it is my story.

My story has been one of struggles since childhood to deal with the horrible circumstances that came from growing up overweight. Today I find myself celebrating in Galatians 5:1, realizing that some stories can become good stories if they serve as reminders of a chosen place to which we plan never to return.

This book is not about getting into your summer swimsuit, being a perfect size two, looking amazing for three months, gaining weight over the holidays, and repeating the cycle. Rather, this book represents a place of hope, reality, transparency, and fighting for a healthy lifestyle. This book is about freedom and the fight each of us faces—sometimes hourly—to never settle for the prison of obesity again.

"I will stand fast then and never let myself be burdened again with a yoke of bondage." This personally proclaimed confession is truly the altar on which I stand as it relates to my health. Perhaps soon it will be your place as well.

This book developed from a culmination of morning blogs that I sent daily to friends, recipes, journal pages, and life stories that my "freedom family" has shared in the past several years. This family is comprised of a group of people who are "over the moon" tired of being trapped in a cell of flesh that waits patiently for their destruction. Our past common denominators—including poor health, skewed self-images, and undisciplined approaches in the consumption of food—are just a few of the defining lines that have contained our stories. Our future common denominator, however, is fabulous health.

As you begin reading the devotions and trying my recipes, remember you are not in isolation. You now join the ranks of an army forming that will win our war of obesity and use our creative minds to develop new recipes, share life stories, and declare joy while on this health journey. You now belong to a group of others who really know and care.

Do you want to travel with us? If so, start reading, writing, cooking, and smiling as you experience the joy of victory. If you begin a journey of deleting sugar and starch from your food choices, your health will most assuredly improve. I can promise that. I have coached hundreds who do "the victory dance" on a regular basis and lodged within these pages are the instructions for those moves. I absolutely believe that as long as you stand again, you have not failed and there is hope.

The healthy eating plan we follow is very simple—lean proteins, vegetables, low-sugared fruits, and healthy fats. We try as often as possible to eat whole foods and skimp on the processed ones. We combine this basic eating plan with rest, hydration, movement, and meditating on the truth from God's Word. I do better with easy; how about you?

Like following any good recipe, this book has a formula. I believe all good recipes can be tweaked, so feel free to make the pages work for you.

Here is what I suggest:

1. Read the devotionals each day. Sometimes read them several mornings in a row when you need extra encouragement or re-read one when there is a day with a recipe instead of a devotional.

2. Take time to journal and record your real thoughts about this area of your life. I found that creating a blog gave me an opportunity to take from my heart and allow my eyes to send a fresh signal to my brain.

3. Take the recipes and practice. Make your modifications and adapt them to your specific tastes. They only work if they work for you.

4. Meet my friends who are real people, have lived real lives with definite struggles, and are fighting to overcome obesity just like you and I are. I especially love the stories from our younger fighters. Get a cup of coffee and enjoy your new journey. I am glad to walk with you for this season.

Choose freedom and eat to live!

January

I started my journey on January 24, 2011 and have declared that date as my health birthday. It is a special day when my life was forever altered. Maybe you want to take a moment and list the beginning of your journey as a declaration that you have established something new, and each year celebrate life on this special day.

January 1: Scientific Notions

As a middle school science teacher, I had the privilege of studying and observing reactions in many disciplines. I would conduct experiments in class and glean such deep spiritual truths. I believe that God allowed me to teach science so He could teach me about Him.

I am a big supporter of refueling at regular intervals. If you have a fireplace and you need consistent heat in your house, add wood before the coals get cold. It takes twice the energy and twice the effort to get that burning process started again. Skipping meals only tells your body you are being mean to it, so it starts to hoard. For goodness sake, eat! Eat the *right* things at the *right* times and I promise you will feel better, have more energy, be more alert, and lose weight more consistently. Sometimes I get irritated when I am hungry, as I'm sure others do as well. News flash: Irritation should not be the by-product of healthy eating. We are a family of believers embracing health, not starvation.

Speaking of embracing, did you know that hugging could have an effect on your health as well? It absolutely can! There are many people who have blood pressure issues. Hug a few people today. I mean *really* hug them. Then, do it tomorrow and the next day. Studies have suggested that good, honest hugging can lower your blood pressure. It releases those "happy" endorphins. Hugging is cheaper than medicine and a lot more fun. It is my goal today to hug more people, and while I am helping to lower their blood pressure, mine is being lowered too! Isn't that an inexpensive way to overcome sickness?

I pray for our family of believers. Please keep praying for one another. God is true to His Word and He will help us. But we have a definite part to play.

Stoke that fire, hug a few people, and eat to live.

January 2: Cause and Effect Relationships

During the holidays there are a multitude of eat-out opportunities and parties. And while I love them so much, I do better with a routine. I never attend parties without carrying something of my choosing to consume, but how many of you know that too many parties make my scale be the bearer of not-so-good news? The eating-out endeavors are worse. While I do choose a salad, the meats in it are often cooked in butter or heavy oils, as are the vegetables, unless I request them steamed and without butter. All these fun things have a definite *effect* on my health plan.

Do you remember when we were in school and studied cause and effect? As a public school teacher, I always taught my children to examine the sentence and determine which component happened first. That event became the cause and the responding part of the sentence was then identified as the effect (it was always about chronology and not placement in the sentence). For us, we do not gain weight first and then overeat. No, we eat more calories than we need first, and then the scale officially notifies us of the result. That is the principle of cause and effect.

My problem was having so many fun things scheduled in a six-week period that I never returned to the protocol of lean proteins, colorful vegetables, lower-sugared fruits, and healthy fats. I finally caved and said, "Three more parties and then back to the routine." While too many pieces of cheesecake (even my own recipe) with fruit and sugar-free whipped cream is the cause, a few added pounds on the scale is definitely the effect. See how that works?

So, now I am forced to work backward. Going back to planned meals and regular times of daily refueling will be the cause and the scales running right at normal will be the effect. Great principle. Let's always remember that losing five or six pounds is so much easier than fifty-six.

January 3: Stress and Turmoil

Stress and turmoil are key factors in releasing cortisol, which stores fat around your belly. I wish that were not true, but I have spoken with several doctors (not just read articles) and it is true. Especially if you are stressing late and trying to sleep, this interrupts the rest cycle and can produce those bulges we are trying to eliminate. Sleep is critical in our journey of losing weight and becoming healthy, so fight for it. One doctor told me, "If you are stressing about all you have to do tomorrow, make a list before you get into bed each night and then sleep so your body can do what it is supposed to while you are sleeping, which is to regenerate cells." These things are real-life issues.

We all have stress that comes our way. On the following lines, I want you to journal about the most stressful situation you've encountered in the past twenty-four hours.

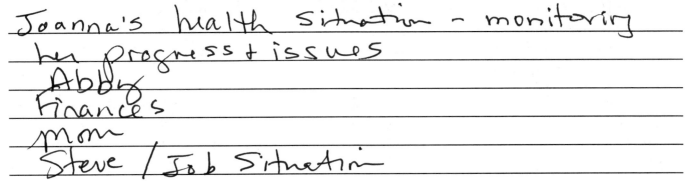

Joanna's health situation - monitoring her progress + issues
Abby
Finances
Mom
Steve / Job Situation

Now, answer truthfully, did stressing and worrying about the above situation solve the problem? I seriously doubt it did. Worry never solves a problem. In fact, the Bible says we cannot add anything to our life by worrying. "Can all your worries add a single moment to your life?" (Luke 12:25 NLT).

No! Worrying does, however, have a negative effect on our long-term health. Also, worrying can be in indicator that our trust in God is being challenged. I have determined that God does not get stressed out or worry, so I am more than willing to pass that baton to Him. I would rather let the one who knows best handle my issues this day. How about you?

Have a great and productive day and pass that stress right off.

January 4: Stick with the Plan

Some scientists believe muscles have memory. I know that for many of us, we lose *successfully* to a certain point. Right? Then, to our dismay, we often begin the "yo-yo" thing. You know, that period where you weigh a certain amount one morning, gain the next, lose the following, and back up on day three. It is as if the scale has remembered that you're supposed to weigh a certain amount and it's not going to move far from that. I used to shake my head at the scale (like it cared) and wonder how it remembered. I have found that scenario to be my plight for the majority of my life. I know some of you are empathic to my struggle.

One person in our group sent me an e-mail recently and joyfully announced that her weight had finally dropped beyond a certain level that she had maintained for years. I was so proud of her. I remember doing the same thing on my journey downward. I weighed a particular number for almost twenty years until I determined that it was costly to my health, both now and long-term. But I really had to push my way to get beyond that "set point" weight. Let that encourage those of you who feel stuck. I believe this is one of the tricks our bodies use to force us to give up and declare failure again. No, our bodies are not the boss of us.

Our mortal flesh may feel comfortable at this set point; however, our spirits are stronger, and we must determine that we will win, regardless. We can no longer make excuses, as our future health is dependent upon the decisions we make today. Our blood reports are really the truest measure of our health, not necessarily our morning weight. If you are healthy at a size twelve, trying to become a size two is going to push you into an unrealistic and unhealthy journey. I always encourage health and do not promote attaining a particular size. Our weight is a by-product of good choices.

When you get close to a set point on your downward journey, be prepared. Your weight could fluctuate for days, as it remembers a number on the scale and determines it will move no further. When this occurs, stick with the plan to eat, sleep, and hydrate well. The plan works. There are enough of us who have followed the plan successfully to declare, "slow and steady wins the race."

January 5: I Am the Boss of Her?

Let's begin today with a reminder of yesterday's devotion, in which I suggested that muscles have memory. I want to propose a scenario I feel reinforces the idea of muscles remembering things we wish they *didn't*. In an eating binge—even one in which we are eating "legal" foods—we always have the potential to stretch our stomach muscles to the point of being overly stuffed. While that muscular organ will quickly notify us that it is being stretched to its maximum capacity, it is more than willing to allow us to repeat the cycle as often as possible, starting with the following meal. Our stomach muscles have no shame.

Subsequently, to accommodate our undisciplined feeding frenzies, those stomach muscles remain enlarged so they can offer their support. Who needs that kind of support, right? Perhaps they are greedy and have adopted the philosophy, "the more the better." I am not certain, but I have experienced trauma at the scale and tried to blame everything but me. How about you?

I wish I could honestly declare that I have never fallen prey to this scenario, but I cannot. In fact, I just jumped aboard lately by consuming a large salad and a small piece of low carb cheesecake. This meal is certainly on my plan, but the simple enormity was not. The tastiness of the food caused me to ignore the warning signs from my stomach. Of course my stomach responded after being awakened by giving me the "gift" of being hungrier the next few days than I have been in months. While I was complaining, "Oh, I am so hungry," the Lord brought to my memory that I had allowed my lack of discipline to awaken those muscles and they were demanding more. I had to literally tell myself, "I have control over you. I am not over-eating again." It had been a long time since I had wrestled with hunger as much as I did in those few days.

Okay, am I crazy? Maybe. But scientifically there are many who believe that muscles actually do have memory. So the moral of the story is to stay away from overeating of any kind. My stomach muscles need to be quiet because *they're not the boss of me*. But I will be more careful to make sure I don't stretch them—even on good stuff—and allow them to think differently.

January 6: Pesto Parmesan Chicken

Yield: 6 servings

Ingredients

- 6 small chicken breasts
- ½ of an 8.1 oz container traditional basil pesto
- 1 cup almond flour
- Salt and pepper to taste
- 1 cup Parmesan cheese
- 6 tablespoons bacon bits (optional)
- 2 cups organic diced tomatoes with garlic, onion and basil

Procedure

1. Preheat oven to 350°F.
2. Place the pesto in a large bowl.
3. Drag the chicken through the pesto and lightly coat both sides.
4. Place into a gallon bag containing almond flour.
5. Turn the chicken over several times to coat both sides with almond flour.
6. Place into a greased 9x13 or 9x14 baking dish.
7. Sprinkle with salt, pepper, and remaining pesto from bowl.
8. Sprinkle with grated Parmesan.
9. Place into oven for 20 minutes.
10. Turn the chicken over, sprinkle with salt, pepper, and grated Parmesan.
11. Sprinkle with ½ cup of bacon bits (optional).
12. Spoon one can of diced tomatoes evenly over the chicken (or you can use a small jar of no sugar added spaghetti sauce).
13. Return to the oven and boost the temperature to 400°F for an additional 20-25 minutes. If it doesn't brown, turn to broil for 5 minutes to obtain a darker color.

Per Serving:
Calories 356.3
Total Fat 24.5 g
Cholesterol 43.8 mg
Sodium 756.0 mg
Potassium 246.1 mg
Total Carbohydrate 10.3 g
Dietary Fiber 3.0 g
Sugars 3.3 g
Protein 24.4 g

January 7: Almond Cookies

Yield: 24 servings

For a variation of this recipe, try combining 1 cup almond flour and 1 cup finely shredded unsweetened coconut for the 2 cups of almond flour. Or 1 cup of almond flour and 1 cup of coconut flour. Or either add 1/2 teaspoon cinnamon or 1 teaspoon cocoa powder to the dry ingredients. There are many different variations to this basic recipe.

Ingredients

- 1 cup light butter
- 1 cup xylitol
- 2 large eggs
- 1 teaspoon vanilla extract
- 1 teaspoon almond extract
- 2 cups almond flour (blanched)
- ¼ teaspoon salt
- 1 ½ teaspoon baking powder
- ½ cup chopped almonds (grind the almonds to small pieces but be careful to not over grind or they will become almond butter)

Procedure

1. Preheat oven to 350°F.
2. Beat melted butter and xylitol. When cooled, add the eggs. Beat in vanilla and almond extract.
3. In a separate bowl combine the almond flour, salt, and baking powder. Stir in the chopped almonds.
4. Gently fold dry ingredients into the egg/sugar mixture.
5. Drop by tablespoon two inches apart onto a baking sheet lined with parchment paper. The parchment paper is very important. (I use a baking sheet with holes to allow evenly distributed heat.)
6. Flatten with a spoon (refrigerate dough for a few minutes if it is too soft) or lightly grease your hands with cooking spray and gently flatten.
7. Bake for 10-12 minutes.

Per Serving:

Calories 99.0
Total Fat 7.9 g
Cholesterol 14.4 mg
Sodium 88.8 mg
Potassium 38.5 mg
Total Carbohydrate 8.2 g
Dietary Fiber 1.2 g
Sugars 0.5 g
Protein 2.7 g

January 8: Stop Looking Back

I have spoken with many who have been really frustrated as they battle obesity. If you are one of them, first know that you are not alone. I applaud those who continue to embrace the plan when everything in you is screaming, "jump ship." I told someone recently that so many times in my life I might lose fifteen pounds, get stuck, give up in discouragement, then sedate and comfort myself with a pan of brownies. The brownies tasted great momentarily but eventually reminded me that failure had been my constant companion. Let us consider a Bible story.

Remember the story of Lot's wife in the book of Genesis? I wonder what could have caused her to turn around and look back to a place of filth, death, immorality, and impurity. I feel the Lord opened my eyes to a possible answer as I was pouring my coffee one morning. What if Lot's wife looked back because of fear? Maybe looking back was easier than fighting for a new normal? After all, at least we know what our past looks like. Right? And none of us know the absolute future.

I am convinced that we cannot focus on our past failures or accept the lie that "this is as good as it gets." We cannot be afraid to live as healthy, thin people. We cannot quit when discouraged and confess, "I was never created to be skinny." Maybe that is true, but you *were* created to be healthy. Fear can cause us to stumble and look back, as moving forward is unknown territory. Failure has been the route for many of us, but we are on a new route. So where can we look?

First, I need you to look up, as that is where your help comes from. God's Word instructs us in this. Next, reach out to our group (via my website), or a similar support group for weight loss, and let us draw strength from one another and encourage each other to not look back because our new life is in front of us. Finally, look at your journey and remember that the new normal is not a place you can define yet, but it certainly beats the prison cell from which you came.

We are leaving a place of destruction and heading to a place of victory. Fear is not welcomed or tolerated.

On the following lines, list the things about being thin and healthy you fear the most.

_____ Looking at past failures _____

_____

Now, take a few moments and find two verses from the Bible concerning fear and write the references on the following lines. Then, memorize and utilize these Scriptures until you are comfortable stating them with authority. God's Word is a powerful weapon in our warrior bag!

_Psalm 23:1_____

_____ 27:1 _____

_____ 91:4&5 _____

January 9: Against All Odds

I want to talk through a situation that one of our group members is experiencing that could be affecting others. She changed shifts at work and found that her health routine became a real challenge. She felt there were few options and quitting her health plan was the easiest. Erase that from your excuse bag. A change in schedule can sometimes affect our food and water schedule; yes it can. However, my encouragement to us all is that "against all odds" we must fight for our health. I realized this truth as I traveled in Europe in the summer of 2011. I quickly discovered that in Europe bathrooms are scarce, and I had to rethink my water intake. I found that my bladder could be re-trained, as I was unwilling to compromise on my daily hydration.

Concerning food, it is critical to remember the fueling we spoke of earlier. You must eat whole meals containing proteins, fruits, and vegetables at regular intervals. Grabbing a quick bite often lends itself to snacking and that usually leads to, "I did not eat much today, so I can eat this brownie." I try not to snack even when I'm at work. I attempt to use my thirty-minute lunch break to sit at a table (away from my desk) and eat on protocol. Trust me, where there is a will, there is a way.

Here is another issue she presented: it is harder to stay on plan when one reaches their goal weight. Some feel the challenge has been answered and the journey concluded. That *can* be true; however, we are not dieting. Our eating plan is our new way of life. *We chose it and we will maintain it.*

When I reached my goal weight, I got tired of the "same old, same old." Unfortunately, I stopped adhering to my preparation plans and soon found I was unprepared a few times and grabbing for nuts or a piece of cheese. While these are not unhealthy choices once your weight is stabilized, they cannot substitute for a meal. I had to really get back to planning and preparing. As soon as I got back on schedule with my water and my meals, I reached my goal weight once again. I don't know why my body responds to the routine, I just know it does. Life is filled with obstacles, but our health commitment must be greater than each one.

January 10: Training Our Children to Be Healthy

I am so blessed by the replies I get daily from my blog posts. Many are experimenting with food prep and teaching their children to eat healthy. I am so proud of you! The other day at work I heard someone say, "Well, you know how kids are? They only love French fries, hamburgers, and pizza." That's a lie we must confront and break in our children, grandchildren, and even ourselves.

One person in our group is experimenting with a wing recipe and relayed that her daughter loves it. I smiled when I envisioned she and her daughter creating and cooking healthy meals together. The Bible instructs us to *"Train up a child in the way he should go, and when he is old he will not depart from it"* (Proverbs 22:6 NKJV). I know we use this verse in every parent meeting at church to reinforce the concept of discipline, but have you ever considered this could refer also to training our children to eat healthy? While under our care, we buy the groceries, as well as create the portions, select the menu, and drive our children through the fast food lines. I know this all too well. The other day I heard a man laugh and say, "I grew up cooking like my mama and that's why I'm so cuddly." While that image says teddy bear and conveys endearment, it also can convey poor health and health-related diseases. I can be cuddly and eat healthy—I promise!

As parents we are charged with protecting our children. Can we protect them from obesity? Yes, by teaching them to choose fruit instead of fries, water instead of soda, and making cookies and brownies with almond flour and xylitol instead of purchasing the sugar and fat-laden ones from the market. Can their pallets be retrained to ask for these substitutions? Mine has been and so can theirs. Can we raise a generation of young ones who are not fighting weight-related issues as many of us are? I think we can. It takes diligence, planning, and training from each of us.

Let us teach our children and grandchildren these health lessons early. Maybe our babies will live to be 120 and healthy. Perhaps we will still be their inspiration at one hundred?

January 11: God's E-vite

Have you ever watched a parched peace lily respond to being watered after their leaves are dragging bottom? Within about thirty minutes of receiving hydration, their leaves begin to stand again and declare, "I am healthy." If you ever need a visual reminder of the power of hydration, try that one. *It works* and it will really convey a message that water is absolutely *life giving*. This is not today's subject though.

John 10:10 is one of my favorite verses in the Bible: "The thief does not come except to steal, and to kill, and to destroy. I have come that they may have life, and that they may have it more abundantly" (NKJV). I don't know about you, but it's good to know someone's plan for your life, even if it's bad. I would *much* rather know the ill intent of a person than be gullible and sucker-punched all the time. As we examine the context of Satan in this verse, it becomes clear that he isn't planning to simply steal everything from us. He methodically calculates how to steal from us so that we *never know we've been violated*. That is really the Greek rendering of the word. And when he steals from us in a manner we don't detect, his intent is total annihilation of our very life—every area! That adds a deeper spin doesn't it?

Can you see Satan viewing you as healthy and stomping his feet, gnashing his teeth, and snarling as *his plan* was for you and I to be trapped in a cell of obesity and despair and eventually give up on God? Satan plans for us to hear the same question he posed to Eve in Genesis, "Did God really say?" He does it in such a way that we begin to really question God—our Father, the Creator, the One who loves us more than all others. He is a crafty serpent, stealing from us the truth we clutch, in a manner designed to destroy!

Today, let's look despair, defeat, poor health, and failure in the eyes and remember that is not what God designed for us. That is the design of the crafty pickpocket who needs to gather a party for his eternal destination. He sent the E-vite and thinks we are naive enough not to see beyond the party decor. He really doesn't care if we attend, but he *does* care that we want to attend God's eternal party and his daily plan includes the destruction of our responding *yes* to God's E-vite. I hope you see this. After this study, I view the term *crafty* in the Genesis story in a different light. How about you? But I choose to *not* have my life stolen and I *choose* health. Let's be keener to the craftiness of our enemy. Praise God for John 10:10, "But Jesus came to give us *life*"!

January 12: Cheesecake

Yield: 16 servings

For a variation, you could bake the cheesecake with optional pecan bottom below.

Ingredients

- 4 pkgs. light cream cheese
- ½ cup sour cream
- 4 eggs
- 1 cup xylitol
- 1 teaspoon vanilla flavoring
- 1 teaspoon almond flavoring

Procedure

1. Preheat oven to 350°F.
2. Beat softened cream cheese and then add xylitol; beat again.
3. Beat in the eggs one at a time and beat well after each addition.
4. Add flavorings and beat until smooth.
5. Pour into a 9-inch spring-form pan and place in a water bath for baking. Check at one hour (mine takes 70-75 minutes. A knife should come out clean when inserted into the center).
6. Cool briefly and remove from the water. Allow to remain cooling for an additional three hours before removing the spring-form pan.
7. Cover lightly and place in refrigerator until the next day.

Strawberry topping:
Ingredients:

- 2 containers strawberries
- 1 cup xylitol

Procedure:

1. Add enough water to cover strawberries about 1 inch. Start on high until full boil, turn heat down several notches to medium, and continue to boil until liquid reduced.
2. Watch carefully as they can overflow if the container is too shallow.

Optional bottom:
Ingredients:

- 2 cups finely chopped pecans
- 1 stick light butter
- 1 cup xylitol
- 1/3 -½ cup almond flour

Procedure:

Chop the pecans, add the melted butter and sugar, and mix well. Add the almond flour and press evenly in the bottom of the spring-form pan and cook for 15 minutes at 350 °F before adding cheesecake mixture. Follow instructions for baking as listed above.

Per Serving: (Cheesecake)
Calories 190.0
Total Fat 14.2 g
Cholesterol 89.2 mg
Sodium 240.7 mg
Potassium 28.5 mg
Total Carbohydrate 12.4 g
Dietary Fiber 0.0 g
Sugars 2.1 g
Protein 5.8

Per Serving: (Topping)
Calories 33.4
Total Fat 0.2 g
Cholesterol 0.0 mg
Sodium 0.4 mg
Potassium 74.1 mg
Total Carbohydrate 11.1 g
Dietary Fiber 1.0 g
Sugars 2.3 g
Protein 0.3 g

Per Serving: (Bottom)
Calories 157.8
Total Fat 14.6 g
Cholesterol 7.5 mg
Sodium 50.6 mg
Potassium 61.0 mg
Total Carbohydrate 10.4 g
Dietary Fiber 1.6 g
Sugars 0.7 g
Protein 1.7 g

January 13: Cauliflower Pizza

Yield: 8 servings

Once the ingredients for the crust are stirred together well, I like to add some Italian seasonings, cracked black pepper, a little salt, and a little Parmesan cheese (a small amount goes a long way). I triple the crust for a regular-sized, deep-dish pizza.

Ingredients (Crust)

- 1 egg
- 1 cup cooked, mashed cauliflower. It needs to be cooked well, as it is very difficult to mash. Drain well before mashing.
- 1 teaspoon garlic salt in the cauliflower
- 1 cup grated mozzarella cheese
- Additional spices to taste

Procedure

1. Preheat oven to 400°F.
2. Stir together all ingredients.
3. Bake the crust for 20 minutes and then add toppings.

Toppings:

- Sugar-free spaghetti or pizza sauce
- Assorted vegetables of your choice (I love grilled onions and mushrooms)
- Pepperoni or other meat. I enjoy turkey sausage.
- I top with grated mozzarella, Parmesan Reggiano, and provolone cheeses. (Optional: to lower the calories you can use only one of the above listed cheeses)

Procedure

Bake pizza at 400°F for an additional 20 minutes. Allow to cool for about 10 minutes so it slices well.

Per Serving:

Calories 183.7
Total Fat 11.5 g
Cholesterol 57.0 mg
Sodium 501.6 mg
Potassium 255.1 mg
Total Carbohydrate 6.9 g
Dietary Fiber 1.7 g
Sugars 0.5 g
Protein 13.3 g

January 14: The Quarry I Came From

I was reading one morning from Isaiah 51:1-2 (NLT) and a real nugget jumped out at me. Consider this:

> "Listen to me, all who hope for deliverance—all who seek the Lord! Consider the rock from which you were cut, the quarry from which you were mined. Yes, think about Abraham, your ancestor, and Sarah, who gave birth to your nation. Abraham was only one man when I called him. But when I blessed him, he became a great nation."

If we have made Jesus Christ our personal Lord and Savior, we come from that quarry. We are cut from the same rock as Abraham. I know sometimes when we have to fight for our health—and some, like me, have had to fight for it from childhood—the temptation to feel forsaken and wronged by God can take root. Our thoughts could say something like this, *What did I do that was so bad that this daily struggle is my punishment?*

As I reread the passage this morning, there are a couple of things I want to bring to your attention:

1. The enemy of our soul will always war against the truth of God's great plan and purpose for each of us.

2. Satan's greatest weapon is to get us to question God, as if He were a man who is prone to lie and disappoint others.

3. The Bible says Abraham was blessed and from Sarah's birthing of a nation we come.

4. If we come from Abraham's rock, and he was blessed, then we are blessed. Like things give birth to like things.

5. If we can begin to view our determination to be healthy as a blessing from God, because we come from a blessed quarry, this could bring an added layer of life to our spirit. It is easier to choose wisely when things are going well and you feel blessed.

We were not cut from a rock of failure, disease, and despair. Absolutely not. We came from a rock of blessing and greatness. May our attitudes in every area reflect that truth. May we choose wisely from the mindset that we are blessed to eat the best foods and enjoy a life of great health because we are mined from the quarry of Abraham.

January 15: God Changes the Seasons

God changes things for specific reasons, but I think that it is amazing that He often allows us to witness such beauty as He brings change. It's as if we are exploring the art gallery of heaven with its brilliant, changing colors displayed for our pleasure. That boggles my mind! Sometimes the changes are subtle, while others are bold and bodacious. I am a girl of color. If we ever meet, you will come to understand that bright red lipstick is a staple in my make-up bag.

I don't know about you, but I get bored easily. I really do. God knew to keep the seasons short so I could plan for them, enjoy their strengths, tuck them away, then plan for their return in a year. Heaven's art gallery is really a representation that things live and die. All life endures these phases of change from the most basic cells that compose our tissues and organs to the highest form of life, the human being.

Some seasons are more brilliant than others. Their brilliance often reflects their response to the variables presented to them. They don't get to choose, they simply respond. These variables could be as simple as, "Is there enough light, rain, warmth, and wind?" When the variables align well, the seasons respond well. That is a basic, scientific fact.

I thought about how we respond to water, warmth, proper nutrition, and other life-giving variables. We are no different from the seasons. We respond to certain variables as they do. However, there is one twist. We get to control the variables that will affect what will be displayed during the seasons of our life. Yes, we do. If we want our *golden years* to be brilliant, then we must control the variables now. Most of God's creations are never allowed to choose. Let's not take that opportunity for granted, but make it count. Then, as our seasons progress from infancy to seniors, people can examine our exterior to determine that we have utilized our health variables well. They will observe the brilliant colors of our health and possibly feel we too are included in the art gallery of heaven.

What a great gallery in which to be included!

January 16: Quit Stepping over the Boundaries

"Trust in the LORD with all your heart; do not depend on your own understanding. Seek his will in all you do, and he will show you which path to take" (Proverbs 3:5-6 NLT).

In our own understanding, we can begin to reason and make excuses for the way we desire to eat. We make such statements as, "The Super Bowl is coming and that's always a huge party. I'm going to eat as I please that night, and I'll start dieting again on Monday." I actually doubt that. I lived there. That one excuse led to another, and eventually five pounds here and five pounds there. FACT: the Super Bowl will occur every year. FACT: we are now seeking to be healthy, as God desires. FACT: we can make our own pizza to take to Super Bowl parties. FACT: we can make our own cookies, vegetables, or no sugar added hot cocoa and have a fabulous time without the guilt and depression from buying into the lie that says, "I'll start again on Monday."

Monday is here. In fact, I have trained myself that every food day is as a Monday. We all need boundaries in our lives and for me especially in the area of food. In Proverbs 23:2, the Bible gives a clear warning about eating beyond boundaries, "Don't gobble your food, don't talk with your mouth full. And don't stuff yourself; bridle your appetite" (MSG). Some versions use the word *gluttony*, which is habitual greed or excess in the area of eating. I can promise you that habitual greed and excessive overeating have definite negative consequences! I wish that were not a fact, but it is. My body was sick and getting sicker. Now my choice is health and I have established clear and definite boundaries in one of my areas of weakness. The consequences have been fabulous.

Where do you need boundaries? The problem with boundaries is that for many of us we see them as movable, which allows us to make excuses as to why we should step over them. My question then would be, are they really boundaries? The person who stated that rules are meant to be broken probably never had a problem with food as I did. If you are going to establish boundaries, then quit stepping over them. Let them serve their purpose.

January 17: Math That Isn't Simple

Here is a quick word that God placed on my heart about math. Logically, when we think about numbers, we know that 1+1=2. No one can dispute that as a fact. But I felt the Lord say this morning, "1+1 does not always equal 2."

As I began to ponder this, I considered that one brownie + one brownie = a lot more than just two brownies many times. One brownie plus another brownie equals two brownies *plus* guilt, cravings for another brownie, hiding the third brownie and whatever else our stomachs say. One brownie may not undo the math, but the addition of another brownie may.

On the other hand, *dividing* the brownie and saving a portion for later in the week may be a great option for some of you. Even for me with a sugar-free version, 1+1 *could* = too many. Perhaps brownies do not throw your numbers off, but I would imagine there is a food item that does. In order to work this equation, simply insert your challenge food. We all have one, right? Maybe you have more than one, as I do, and then the math becomes really complicated.

Each of us is uniquely different, and while I struggled with that for many years, I finally am experiencing some healing. One of my life's sticky notes came when I fully comprehended Psalm 139 and accepted that we were each uniquely created for various purposes. God didn't design me to be you, nor does He expect me to complete your assignments. He had a special purpose in creating me, and I can never be identical to you and fulfill my purpose. That realization has helped me deal with emotional responses to several issues in my life, including my health, for many years now.

Here's the moral of the story: addition is a mathematical necessity. However, but when considering portion sizes that often lead to things we hate to experience, division may be our best choice. Your portion size is different from mine. I understand. You are uniquely you and I celebrate that fact. However, when we utilize basic mathematical equations, I venture to say we are more alike than we know.

January 18: Insight from the Storm

I was awakened by the lighting storm outside my window at 5:00 a.m. one morning. I was not smiling either. However, I am reminded of exactly what lightning storms represent. When two strong forces collide, such as hot and cold, it often generates the powerful storms we see outside. They fight to see who will stay and who will go. In their display, sometimes there is beauty and sometimes violence.

I saw us in that storm that morning. There is often an internal battle that each of us faces, "Do I continue to eat healthy at the party or cheat this once? Do I let the pressures of life push me to give up on my health plans? Do I cave in to my family who doesn't understand why I care so desperately about being healthy?" I totally understand this battle well. The question is: are we stronger than our flesh? We may seem powerless to overcome our will when everyone at the party is choosing the chips and cheese dip and we are eating celery. At that point it is critical to remember that you may not be eating chips, but you *are* eating. Also remember, this is a two-hour party. Your journey is for a lifetime.

Each time you yield and let your circumstances push you to consume sugar or some other trigger food, you not only battle the extra weight, but often you are battling your mind that says, "You really are a failure. You will never lose weight and be healthy." Tell your emotional self to be quiet. You only fail when you fail to get up. I have heard that on numerous occasions and in numerous situations. It is more real to me today than ever.

I do not like bullies. I was bullied in elementary and high school because of my weight. That hits a nerve with me. So when the conflict between my flesh and spirit occurs, I just roll my neck and say, "I can eat what I choose, so let the lightning show between my flesh and my spirit begin."

I pray this brings a word of hope this morning. When tempted, call a friend, eat an extra apple (which is good for your bad cholesterol), stop and determine why you want to eat, and remind yourself, "I can do all things through Christ."

January 19: Frittata

Yield: 12 servings

Ingredients

- 6 eggs
- 1 pkg. turkey sausage crumbles
- Bacon bits (optional)
- 2 cups Mexican cheese
- ½ cup half and half
- 1 container portabella mushrooms (optional)
- Salt, pepper, garlic powder, onion powder, TABASCO® sauce to taste

Procedure

1. Preheat oven to 400°F.
2. Beat the eggs before adding the other ingredients.
3. Mix remaining ingredients well and place in greased muffin tins. Bake for 20-25 minutes.

Per Serving:
Calories 332.8
Total Fat 26.0 g
Cholesterol 167.5 mg
Sodium 671.8 mg
Potassium 67.4 mg
Total Carbohydrate 3.8 g
Dietary Fiber 0.1 g
Sugars 0.2 g
Protein 21.3 g

January 20: Cabbage and Ground Beef Soup

Yield: 12 servings

Ingredients

- 1 large head of cabbage
- 1 large Vidalia onion
- 2 pounds lean ground beef
- 3 large cans organic, fire roasted tomatoes
- 2 tablespoons cumin
- TABASCO® sauce to taste
- Salt to taste

Procedure

1. Brown the ground beef and onions together.
2. Add the tomatoes.
3. Chop the cabbage into small pieces or however you like them in soup.
4. Add the salt and TABASCO®.
5. Cook until cabbage is very tender. This usually takes about 60-90 minutes.
6. Sprinkle grated Parmesan Regianno cheese on the top of each bowl as served.

Per Serving:
Calories 171.2
Total Fat 5.0 g
Cholesterol 43.3 mg
Sodium 766.6 mg
Potassium 278.3 mg
Total Carbohydrate 14.8 g
Dietary Fiber 4.0 g
Sugars 5.3 g
Protein 17.7 g

January 21: The Fire Door

I have spoken with so many people in the last few days about open doors in our lives that draw us in a wrong direction. Sometimes we willingly walk toward them, but often we have no clue as to what opening *that door* will allow.

I remember a very vivid picture from a movie that will be forever imprinted in my mind, although I am not certain of its reality. The scene showed several fire fighters in a house with a roaring fire. A rookie fireman was trying to get out and reached for a doorknob. However, the veteran grabbed his hand from the knob and placed it on the door. The young man immediately drew his hand back as the door was extremely hot. Life-stopping danger stood as a silent killer on the other side.

Certainly any of us might quickly grab and open a door, especially if it appears to be the only way out. Perhaps it is a door with which we are familiar as we have often accessed and utilized its availability. However, when there is a fire on the other side, that friendly door can become a trap. That particular door may be the worst possible route of escape or path to freedom. Why am I bringing this up? These doors exist as realities in our lives in multiple areas. Often, it is not just about starch and sugar. Dangerous doors could be relationships, business ventures, television shows, or many other things. I met with a young man yesterday who needed to be reminded that not all doors are great routes to freedom. When we know where the dangerous doors are, it's best to leave them closed. The problem is that we often do not know.

For years, I thought my problem with my weight was hereditary. I am convinced that is what I *wanted* to think. However, upon close examination (hand on the door) and wisdom shared from the Holy Spirit (who guides us into all truth) I came to the stark and life-changing revelation that some doors must remain closed. Forever.

Can we really determine which doors appear to lead to freedom and yet are the wrong path? Can we honestly consider each door as it relates to our health? Yes, but in order to accomplish this feat we need a *truth infusion*. It is time for an honest evaluation and a real check-up. This is a new year. Let us thank the Holy Spirit who serves as the veteran fighter, knows where the fire is, and when to remove our hand from the wrong knob. That type of knowledge is the difference between life and death.

January 22: A Paradigm Shift

I love the cold, but I love it even more when it's snowing outside and I'm drinking hot coffee in front of the fireplace, which is very unlikely to happen here in Georgia. One of my life-long dreams is to be in a cabin with several feet of snow round about, drinking coffee in front of the fire and reading all day. A girl can dream, right? I have longed for that since I was a child. I can see the picture in my mind's eye, but have yet to see it with my real eyes. When I finally see it, I will know the place. It is vivid in my mind. Until then I'm embracing Georgia's weather, which doesn't know if it is spring or fall. I'm not sure Georgia got the memo that it's still winter.

We all have difficult stories to share about losing weight and remaining healthy. Someone mentioned yesterday that after just three days of re-introducing sugar into their plan, their body was thrown into havoc when they tried to hit the delete button. That's the reality of choice sometimes, is it not? Some things appear to be great for a season, but in reality they are not. Often as children we can eat whatever we please without the penalties we accrue later in life. However, as the years gather around us, we find ourselves laughing as we tell those younger ones, "You better enjoy all that ice cream; you'll be forty someday." I was the worst one. I used to say, "Wait until after you have children. You won't eat like that anymore."

Is waiting the answer? It certainly is not. Waiting only places our body in a position to be affected by diseases and ailments. I wish I had learned the joy of loving to eat healthy and the power of choice when I was twenty. I wish I had fed my children accordingly when they were younger. But my mindset back then was to create the best tasting foods and enjoy them without limits. Today, I still have that mindset but with a new set of dynamics.

In the past I used fat, starch, and sugar to accomplish that goal. Today, I use almond flour, xylitol, fresh fruits and vegetables, and lean proteins, as well as a variety of herbs and spices. I'm still creating yummy foods, but now those foods are bringing life to my body and not early death. Wow, what a paradigm shift!

January 23: The Scream of Starch

Carb is a four letter word for many health-conscious people, but not in the "dirty" way we refer to four letter words. We need carbs because our body converts them to energy in our cells. This is a biological need. However, some have mistakenly interchanged the terms *carb* and *sugar*. But they are not the same term. They function in similar, and yet very different capacities. While we need carbs, our body *can* function quite well without white, refined sugar. Many sugar-type products have simply changed names via the manufactures, but still metabolize and store as sugar does. I encourage you to research the over one hundred names now used to "hide" white sugar.

I want to stop and emphasize that we are not on a carb-free health plan. Our fruits and vegetables have fructose in them, and this is a much-needed form of carbs. As they process through the liver and take a slower metabolic path, they are more beneficial to us than white sugar. When you evaluate recipes and products to determine if they can be used on your plan, you should take into consideration the fiber and the sugar alcohols in combination with the carbohydrates, which both have an effect on net carbs. I always check the sugars on the label as well as in the ingredient list. Then, I examine the listed fruits and vegetables as they relate to the glycemic index and try to avoid those listed as higher within the three groups. While natural carbs are better than white sugar, you can see I am careful with those as well.

What about starchy foods and vegetables? I avoid starch, starchy vegetables, and pastas as they metabolically react as sugar. In fact, starch floods our blood stream with sugar and causes our cells to scream, "I want more." Have you ever eaten crackers or cookies and within half an hour you are craving another six? You might think, "Gosh, I'm still hungry." No, you are not really. The starch has done its conversion duty, and, *like a two year old who wants what it wants when it wants,* it screams, "Feed me more sugar or I'll keep screaming and cramp your stomach until you do." Have you ever experienced that? I have. We know that when children are screaming for our attention the worst possible thing to do is give them what they want. They become undisciplined and demanding. Starch and sugar can behave in the same manner. Ignore the scream and it will eventually change that tune. I promise.

January 24: It's My Heart and Not My Mouth

"If God is for us, who can ever be against us? Since he did not spare even his own Son but gave him up for us all, won't he also give us everything else? Who dares accuse us whom God has chosen for his own? No one—for God himself has given us right standing with himself. Who then will condemn us? No one—for Christ Jesus died for us and was raised to life for us, and he is sitting in the place of honor at God's right hand, pleading for us" (Romans 8:31-34 NLT).

I am convinced that we so easily buckle at the issues that confront our daily walk when God wants us to trust and stand strong. This verse reiterates that life, whatever that looks like for you, can accuse us and even try to cause our trust in God to be questioned. The evil one has been using every weapon known to humankind to penetrate the truth of this verse from the beginning of creation. Satan never really cared *what* Eve ate. He cared that her trust in God was confronted and broken. Can I declare that the same plan remains?

Some of you are crying out desperately, and daily, for God to heal you from the flesh in which you live. God already knows about your situation and the chains that so easily entangle you. He knows. I feel that sometimes our battle against food is not with our mouth, but with our heart. The human heart is the seat of all emotions and will. The desire to be free is lodged there also. Sometimes when our heart is sick from unmet expectations and needs, the broken *voice* asks, "Did God really say?" In that question we never find, "Would you like another brownie?" The intent is never to overcrowd our bellies. The intent is to cause distrust.

The hurt in our heart is usually inflicted upon us as children who were made to endure extremely difficult situations. And often, as children, we never knew how to handle the trauma nor process what occurred. So, as children, we hide. We hide the pain deep within our memory and place heavy stones around that hurt. When that hurt or something similar arises, and we have not determined how to allow the stones to be removed and our hurts to heal, we usually cover it with something again. That covering can be food, drugs, sexual addictions, or any other cover mechanism. God wants His children to be free. Let each of us use our God-given freedom to take the stones down that have covered our hurts, expose the lie that we deserved pain and no one will understand, forgive the offenders, grab God's hand, and walk out of that bondage cell.

Get free in your heart so you are free to choose health every day, all day.

January 25: Food Serves My Purpose!

Today I want to comment on something a pastor said in church yesterday. He stated, "We seldom ask God for a change of character, but always ask for a change in our circumstances." In other words we are asking God to change our marriage and not change us. In our health world, often we want God to change how much our bodies weigh and what they look like in a swimsuit, without our changing the fact that we allow an addiction to rule our life. That realization shook me to the core.

Throughout my life, I would always cry, pray, shout at God, and beg Him to help me lose weight as I stuffed three to four thousand calories of food in my mouth on a daily basis. Occasionally I would ask God to help me be disciplined, but I never meant it. As soon as I would lose five pounds, I headed to the store to get a bag of candy or to my favorite Mexican restaurant for the cheese dip that is so laden with salt and fat it makes my arteries twitch. Get this picture: up 5 pounds then down 5; up 10 pounds and down 3; up 8 pounds only to shed 1 until I was depressed and obese. Can I make a confession? I was mad at God. That sounds horrible, but it was true.

I never really wanted God to change me, only to give me the metabolism to eat what I wanted without the discipline. I never really wanted to delete starch and sugar. I never really wanted to stop eating pizza. I never really wanted to give up chocolate and candy and theater popcorn dripping with butter, but I really wanted God to change my consequence. Can you identify?

Today, my character is being remolded and my addiction to food broken, as well as my excuses. My single-digit jeans bring a smile to my face. But more than that, they are a reminder that change always begins with my character, not my circumstance. Ask the Holy Spirit to reveal to you anything that drives you to overeat, move the boundaries, or make excuses. Then, annihilate each one. In my case, my bottom line was I loved food more than health and making excuses became the "truth" instead of the lie. That is broken in me.

Now food serves *my* purpose, not the other way around.

January 26: Basa Fish

Yield: However many fillets you cook

Somebody thought I was spelling bass; no, it is Basa. Most grocery stores carry this particular fish in the frozen section with the other fish, although it is seasonal. Even my grandchildren love these. They are so mild that all the "non-fish" people really do enjoy it too.

Ingredients

- Basa Fish Fillets
- 1 lemon (more if many fillets)
- 1 lime (more if many fillets)
- Old Bay® Seasoning to taste
- Tarragon to taste

Per Serving:

Procedure

1. Squeeze a lemon and lime in the bottom of a pan, put the fish on the juice, top with the juice of a lemon and lime
2. Sprinkle with Old Bay® Seasoning and some tarragon.
3. Bake at 400°F until most of the liquid is gone and it starts to brown some.

Sugar-Free Breadcrumbs for Pan-Fried Basa Fish

Yield: Coats 2 bags of Basa Fish

I used to fry Basa fish (so mild in taste and amazing fillets) but the Italian breadcrumbs I used contained sugar. Recently, I really wanted a lightly fried piece of fish, so I created my own sugar-free breadcrumbs. My children came for leftovers the next day and asked for the fish. Even my granddaughter snagged a piece from her mom. Baked or fried, this is a great fish for your family.

Ingredients

- 2 boxes of melba toast
- 1 cup of almond flour
- Salt to taste
- 4 tablespoons Italian seasonings
- 1 tablespoon tarragon.

Procedure

1. Combine all ingredients.
2. Half the fillets and place the breadcrumbs in a plastic bag.
3. Coat the fish well, then place the fillets on paper towels on a plate and allow to air dry (This allows the moisture to drain into the towel and away from the breadcrumbs).
4. Heat a small amount of olive oil in a large skillet and lightly fry the fillets on medium heat. To determine if the oil is ready, place a toothpick into the skillet. If bubbles form around the toothpick, the oil is ready (Fish lying in cold oil is not a great scenario for a crispy, light crust). Watch the heat as almond flour will burn easily and the crust needs to form well before turning, as this is not a batter.
5. Place each piece on a paper towel briefly before serving.

January 27: Veggie Mix

Yield: 12

This recipe is easy, creates a large serving, and is a tasty manner in which to add color and texture to your side dishes. These vegetables can be as tart or sweet as you like by varying the vinegar and Truvia®. I never add additional spices, as these flavors were plenty for me. You could use different types of vinegar for different flavors.

Ingredients

- 2 large tomatoes
- 2 cucumbers
- 2 medium Vidalia onions
- Sea salt
- Water
- Apple cider vinegar
- Truvia® Natural Sweetener

Procedure

Layer medium slices of tomatoes, cucumbers, and onions. Sprinkle with sea salt, cover 2/3 of the bowl with water and fill remainder of bowl with apple cider vinegar. Then, add several packets of Truvia®. Mix well and let marinate overnight.

Per Serving:

Calories 34.3
Total Fat 0.3 g
Saturated Fat 0.0 g
PolyunSaturated Fat 0.1 g
MonounSaturated Fat 0.0 g
Cholesterol 0.0 mg
Sodium 6.4 mg
Potassium 249.0 mg
Total Carbohydrate 10.1 g
Dietary Fiber 1.5 g
Sugars 2.8 g
Protein 1.0 g

January 28: A Bad Dream

I had a bad dream last night. I was working in a church office and helping a friend with a new copier when I looked down and realized I had eaten 2/3 of a huge bagel with blueberry cream cheese running down the sides without realizing I had done it. Some of you probably think I'm crazy and that was not *a bad dream*. It was horrifying to me. Now mind you, I watch myself in the dream wrap the bagel quickly and toss the remainder, but could hear people jeering at me saying, "Look at what she's eating." I felt sick to my stomach, embarrassed, and guilty. Then I woke up. How could I feel like that in a dream?

I was lying quietly thinking about the dream and felt very strongly that those feelings seemed so real (even when dreaming) because often that is our natural reaction when we fail. I thought about Adam and Eve. They must have experienced those exact feelings. Often when I was eating what I knew I should not, I tried to hide. Then, the guilt and shame often associated with failure came again. I would eat late when everyone else was in bed, in the middle of the night, and on and on. I can say this today with freedom, I was the "fast food, drive-through queen." Sometimes I would stop on the way home from work twice, as if once wasn't enough, but always found a trash receptacle before arriving home so no one *knew*. However, I could never hide from myself. I would always make a fresh commitment the next day to eat what was right, as my clothes were too tight and my blood sugar level was escalating, only to repeat the cycle on a regular basis.

Eating healthy today means long life, no prison, and freedom for me. That is one of the reasons I still quote my personalized version of Galatians 5:1 on a regular basis, "It is for freedom that Christ came to set me free. I will stand firm and no longer let myself be burdened again with a yoke of slavery." This verse reminds me that freedom came with a price and freedom is worth fighting for. I celebrate our military and our forefathers. Today is a celebration of freedom from a different angle in my life, but freedom nonetheless.

If you are struggling today and want to eat and hide, then eat, but don't hide. Eat another piece of fruit or a little more protein. Fill your body with life-giving foods and weigh in the morning. Always weigh, as it will keep you to your course. And stop making excuses to hide and eat.

Get on that scale and fight for your freedom!

January 29: Just Ask

As we look forward, Valentine's Day candy is everywhere. For my folks addicted to chocolate this is a torturous season, I know. Stay ahead and plan well. I have included a fudge recipe in this book that will keep a little something sweet in your refrigerator—cut in *small* squares—for those times in which you are having a chocolate spasm. But please, plan now that you will not fall prey to the candy isle.

Xylitol and almond flour can be used in almost every recipe with no noticeable difference so remember to give them a try. Make your favorite red velvet cupcakes with the substitutions. Eat one and share the remainder with your co-workers to avoid making the excuse, "But it's a holiday." If you are going out to eat for Valentine's Day, ask the restaurant to accommodate you. They always work with me. But I never fail to ask.

My daughter and I were starving the other day while out shopping and decided we only had time for a quick bite. That is a dangerous position for most of us. However, we stopped at home to grab the red wine vinegar and headed to a fast food restaurant to determine if a salad without all the sugar and starch was possible. As we walked in, the manager greeted us and asked if he could help. We explained our situation and asked for a custom-made salad. He smiled and said, "Certainly." We ordered only romaine lettuce and warmed chicken. That is all. They made us a special plate and even brought it to us. Ask and it shall be given to you.

When in my favorite restaurant recently, Teree and I said, "No fat, no starch, no sugar." The waiter checked on several things and then informed us that our chicken would be grilled with no butter (they usually grill in butter) and we would be allowed to share a salad containing only romaine lettuce. The waiter also brought some grilled zucchini, which had no fat as it was simply seasoned with Montreal Steak Seasoning.

The moral of the story: ask. We can eat out if we ask the correct questions. The Bible teaches that we "have not because we ask not." I am asking.

January 30: Running Errands

I want to comment on a passage of Scripture as we drink coffee together this morning. Romans 6:12-18 (MSG) reads:

> "That means you must not give sin a vote in the way you conduct your lives. Don't give it the time of day. Don't even run little errands that are connected with that old way of life. Throw yourselves wholeheartedly and full-time— remember, you've been raised from the dead!—into God's way of doing things. Sin can't tell you how to live. After all, you're not living under that old tyranny any longer. You're living in the freedom of God. So, since we're out from under the old tyranny, does that mean we can live any old way we want? Since we're free in the freedom of God, can we do anything that comes to mind? Hardly. You know well enough from your own experience that there are some acts of so-called freedom that destroy freedom. Offer yourselves to sin, for instance, and it's your last free act. But offer yourselves to the ways of God and the freedom never quits. All your lives you've let sin tell you what to do. But thank God you've started listening to a new master, one whose commands set you free to live openly in his freedom!"

Freedom is our God-mandate, but freedom does not mean we live, eat, and act in any manner that we choose. I really felt the Lord highlight that truth this morning from these verses. Verse 18 states, "we have started listening." That means we are choosing to turn and embrace the freedom journey and not spend our time running errands on a wrong path. That is a waste of our precious time.

I feel the Lord shared with me a picture of this for today. Often we "peek" into the closed casket door of our past failures and wink at our old ways of eating because we are free. That is hard to fathom, but that is what I saw. Does that make sense? Once we have placed our old eating habits in the death box, we are free to live as healthy people. Absolutely. However, sometimes those old eating habits try to entice us to open the casket lid and "give a peek" at their gestures or run errands with them that are fruitless and empty. Remember, they cannot open the lid by themselves.

The moral of the story: do not peek, listen, or run errands with your past failures. They are failures for a reason. Leave the casket containing your old, unhealthy ways of living closed.

I pray that my visual helps you today. Remember, we walk in freedom because the lid stays shut!

January 31: January Reflection Page

As you are completing your first month with me, are there things you wish you had highlighted or which you had written down? If you're like me, I try to write those nuggets on the front and back cover of my books (along with the page numbers) so I can grab them quickly when I need them. In the following area, write the ones down that you really know you'll need as you journey toward your total freedom.

_____

_____

_____

_____

_____

_____

_____

_____

_____

_____

_____

_____

_____

_____

_____

_____

_____

_____

_____

February

February is "the month of love." This month let us really dig in and concentrate on loving ourselves enough to make the tough calls and "just say no" when our love of food pulls us from our love of self. We deserve to be healthy and have an amazing life.

February 1: Top of the Iceberg

Do you know that changing a habit takes intentionality and time? Sometimes addictions can be broken instantaneously, but more often there is a weaning and fighting for freedom. Sometimes I wonder if some people see the struggle for health as worthless. I really wonder if they see only the top of the iceberg and never really connect with the fact that danger lies just below the water.

When the seamen spotted the iceberg that sank the Titanic, it was too late to turn an enormous ship moving at such a rapid speed. We need to seek and respond to the real truth about what lies beneath the surface of our skin to help force us into a pattern of change before the effects of obesity-related issues consume us. Unhealthy eating takes little effort so sometimes we are not watching for the "iceberg" as we should.

Watching for the "iceberg" means that someone has to be on guard. Many of us never really comprehend this concept because as youth we fantasize of invincibility, which we later come to understand is a myth. Unfortunately, each of us has to be stationed as our own posted guard. At my age, I see this clearly. When examining the importance of living my life in a healthy state, this truth becomes absolutely huge. Actually, it moves nearly to the top of my list.

I feel we live in an age of information and yet, as the seamen on the Titanic, are never really paying attention until disaster strikes. Let me remind you of a saying I once heard, "You can never get insurance when you need it." So, we should never wait until the report from the doctor forces our attention toward health. At that point, it could be too late.

The moral of the story: keep alert and stay on post.

February 2: Multi-level Choices

It's so easy to hit the drive-through as opposed to cooking sometimes, is it not? Sometimes the drive-through has a few options that appear to be less threatening than others and provide a quick bite after a long day. Grabbing a store-bought dessert for a function as opposed to baking something nutritious is sometimes faster and easier too. But how many of you know bad eating is like playing Russian roulette? Eventually, bad choices can lead to a bad ending and sometimes something drastic occurs—like a heart attack—and our eyes are finally opened to the need for change.

I struggled with pain in my body, fatty organs that were struggling to live, and depression for being a failure in the area of health most of my life. I cannot lie, fighting for my freedom was tough. If you have ever battled for your health, perhaps you understand. However, I discovered that fighting to not return to my old habits was much harder. The chocolate called to me, sweetly, but emphatically for months. Every pizza parlor near my house piped the smell of yeast and cheese toward me relentlessly. What is a girl to do? The only reason I finally stayed on course was a strong desire to live. I kept choosing correctly one month, another month, and another month. Eventually it got easier and I started enjoying the benefits of wise choices. But my journey is still a daily choice. I can always return to the life of wrong choices. That is my choice. But for me, that choice leads to death and I choose life.

We must remember that God allows us to choose life or death. That is a multi-level choice. In the area of health, we cannot say we choose life and continue to choose wrong foods that we know do not promote great health. Well, yes we can. But diabetes and high blood pressure are more than willing to offer us their hands and smile as we consume the pizza and promise to do better tomorrow. Eventually their destructive forces invade our bodies and their long-term effects consume our future. I will no longer hold their hands and walk blindly with either of them.

Keep fighting and living today correctly. Make yourself live tomorrow correctly as well.

February 3: Go for the Gold

I see myself as a coach who is leading a team of all stars to the Olympics. Training can be intense, fast-paced, and without the applause of men. But without intense discipline, the journey toward the final prize could end without the gold medal. Perhaps that is good for others, but not me. I have never been one who settles for average, except in the arena of my health. I hope the journey of these devotionals allows you some insight into the reality of settling. It's not God's best for any of us.

I want our family of healthy trendsetters to take the gold medal for health. I realize those athletes winning the silver or the bronze medals have worked hard also, but there is something about winning the gold. We can never settle for "average health." I want us to press toward the mark as if we are rounding the end of the race, victory is in sight, and nothing less than the gold medal will satisfy.

I always try to be transparent. A few days ago I was tired and whiny. I shared with my daughter that sometimes I get fatigued with being so hard-core about always choosing correctly. Did that feeling actually enter my thoughts? Yes, and it proceeded from my mouth. My whiny-self was revisiting the truth that sometimes being healthy is more work than pleasure; and I prefer pleasure. The struggles and daily battles sometimes feel as though my body is at war with my spirit. Does that sound familiar?

I tried to reason with myself recently that "Perhaps it is time to go back to a less drastic menu; I'm close enough to my goal weight; I do not want to be OCD about this." Oh my goodness, I hate to admit those thoughts! But something grabbed me and I declared to my husband, "That is an old mindset still trying to rise up, but in a different form." I reminded him that I am not a quitter. I quickly reminded myself of that as well.

I know what my goal to be healthy is all about, and I know the last few steps for all athletes require the most energy. We cannot quit; the gold is in sight and determination pays off. Let us stand on the platform together.

February 4: Ask the Right Question

Have you ever really asked yourself why you want to lose weight and gain health? What is the real motive? I wanted to overcome depression, sleep better, stop hurting, feel better in my clothes, and live to see my grandchildren grown and married. Yes, and at the bottom level of the pyramid was my appearance. Yes! But quite honestly, I came to understand a greater truth. After losing my first thirty pounds, I became acutely aware that I loved being healthy. My first doctor's report after losing the weight shouted, "Much improved." And it sparked something in me to categorically proclaim, "I choose life."

Now let me ask you a few probing questions. Are you really trying to lose weight to please someone else? Maybe you feel your spouse would love you more if you looked differently? Loving someone is not about his or her outward appearance. Please do not be trapped by that lie. Are you trying because you want to prove to others you can finally bring your life to a place of discipline? You can give that notion up as well. The real bottom-line answer is that we choose life. Being motivated by anything else will probably mean "one day on and one day off." Maybe you are different, but I tried escaping the obesity cell using all the wrong motivations, and when God allowed me to arrive at a place of total desperation, I chose life.

Can you stop for a moment and really ask yourself, honestly, why am I doing this? Is it for the swimsuit? For my spouse? To gain a spouse? To get a promotion at work? To have a new wardrobe? Or simply because I just want to? Often those variables really do not change our long term health or we would not be where we are on this journey. Can someone say, "yes ma'am"? (Remember, I'm from Georgia.) In reality the motivating factor for success has to come from a deep longing within each of us to be healthy. We cannot get to that truth unless we come to a true realization that health is not an option. I read somewhere once that for every ten pounds we carry above our normal weight, we must subtract a certain number of years off the end of our life.

I don't know about you, but I want every year that was appropriated to me by the Father above (see Psalm 139). My answer to the question of why am I choosing health will forever remain, "I want to live."

February 5: Secrets

I hate to feel like everyone in the room knows something I do not and they are deliberately keeping things from me. To me that seems harmful somehow. I always prefer the truth. I may not understand or like it, but I would rather have the truth than a secret. I can always tell when something is being hidden from me. I quickly find myself asking, "What do I not know here?" In my opinion, having to decipher and uncover the truth is wasted energy. My life is busy, as is yours, and trying to unravel the truth costs me time, and often a lot of time.

One of my health goals at the beginning of 2013 was my *Back to Basics* campaign. The more I read labels and check ingredients listed on the internet, the more I am convinced that the food industry has secrets. They need to increase shelf life with chemicals. But we really don't know what those chemicals do in our bodies long term, do we? Unfortunately, I cannot pronounce half of them either. We actually have no idea if they are friend or foe.

In contrast, real turnip greens cooked with water and seasonings or fresh herbs have no secrets. I cooked them, they are real foods, and I know exactly what is in them. To me, that's the safest journey of choice. I really feel that as the cost of food rises, the secrets in food will as well. It is all about the shelf life, remember? I realize some of the products I love are going to need to be replaced and some of my restaurant experiences watched more closely, but I am convinced that food production is being infused with fillers to offset the cost. I would venture to say those fillers may not be the best options for us either. I could be wrong, but I doubt it.

Maybe you feel I am on a campaign to bust manufactured and processed foods. Not necessarily, but remember God created food in its natural form for our bodies to bring us health. Manufacturers are not as concerned with our health as they are with paying their employees. Have I reached the goal of never using processed and manufactured foods yet? Certainly not, but I am on the road. I cannot eliminate all processed foods just yet, but I can start to evaluate the ones I consume most and quickly make the necessary changes.

Repeat after me, "Whole foods have no secrets."

February 6: Red Velvet Cake

Yield: 24 servings

Ingredients

- 1½ cups light butter or oil
- 1½ cups xylitol
- 3 eggs
- 1 teaspoon vinegar (white distilled)
- 1 bottle red food coloring
- 2 teaspoons vanilla extract
- 3 tablespoons unsweetened cocoa
- 2 ½ cups almond flour
- ½ teaspoon sea salt
- 1 teaspoon baking soda
- 1 teaspoon of baking powder
- 1 cup buttermilk

Procedure

1. Preheat oven to 350°F.
2. Beat butter and sugar and add eggs one at a time while beating. Once all lumps are gone, add the red food coloring, vinegar, and vanilla.
3. Combine all the dry ingredients in a second bowl. Stir thoroughly until all dry components are mixed well and set aside.
4. Add the remaining liquid ingredients and beat into the egg/xylitol mixture.
5. Mix in the dry ingredients in thirds and pour into a greased 13x9 baking dish. (I did not use a metal pan.) This batter also bakes 20-24 cupcakes.
6. Bake for 40 minutes (or more) and test with a toothpick, which inserted in the center comes out clean. (Jiggle the pan at 35 minutes to determine the firmness. Be gentle so the cake won't fall. Almond flour is dense and the edges cook before the center.) Cupcakes take less time. Check at 25-30 minutes.

Per Serving:
Calories 221.2
Total Fat 20.1 g
Cholesterol 15.8 mg
Sodium 21.0 mg
Potassium 42.7 mg
Total Carbohydrate 11.8 g
Dietary Fiber 1.7 g
Sugars 1.0 g
Protein 3.6 g

Cream Cheese Frosting: (optional)

Ingredients:

- 2 8 oz. packages light cream cheese
- 1 ½ teaspoon vanilla flavoring
- 1 cup powdered sugar by Whey Low® (for diabetics) or xylitol.

Procedure:

Beat cream cheese well; add the sugar and finally the vanilla. Mix until creamy. Frost the *cooled* cake and top with 1 cup of pecans.

Per Serving:
Calories 95.0
Total Fat 7.6 g
Cholesterol 13.3 mg
Sodium 73.4 mg
Potassium 20.7 mg
Total Carbohydrate 7.4 g
Dietary Fiber 0.5 g
Sugars 0.9 g
Protein 1.8 g

February 7: Almond Flour Pancakes

Yield: 6 servings

Ingredients

- 1 cup almond flour
- 2 eggs
- ¾ cup buttermilk or half and half
- 2 tablespoons oil
- ¼ teaspoon sea salt
- 2 teaspoon baking powder
- ¼ cup xylitol
- 1 teaspoon maple or vanilla extract

Procedure

Mix the above ingredients and add to a hot skillet greased with additional oil. Watch for bubbles on top and flip carefully. The almond flour doesn't always flip easily. Also, be mindful that almond flour burns quickly. You will need to cook your pancakes for a longer period at a lower, moderate temperature.

Per Serving:

Calories 198.0
Total Fat 16.0 g
Cholesterol 61.7 mg
Sodium 30.0 mg
Potassium 23.3 mg
Total Carbohydrate 10.8 g
Dietary Fiber 2.0 g
Sugars 0.7 g
Protein 7.1 g

Maple Syrup

Ingredients

- 1 cup water
- 1 cup xylitol
- ½ stick light butter
- 1-2 teaspoon maple extract

Procedure

If possible, make the day before and allow to remain in the refrigerator over night to thicken. If you like it warm, and you don't care that it's extremely runny, place all the ingredients in a container on the stove and boil for 15 minutes. Serve warm.

Per Serving:

Calories 86.7
Total Fat 4.0 g
Cholesterol 10.0 mg
Sodium 66.7 mg
Potassium 0.0 mg
Total Carbohydrate 21.3 g
Dietary Fiber 0.0 g
Sugars 0.0 g
Protein 0.0 g

February 8: Joy or Happiness?

I know each of us is in different stages of our lives, but I pray you are happy. I do recognize there is a huge difference between joy and happiness and that joy is the deep center that holds us when life has slapped us in ways we wish it would not. Sometimes it is just good to be happy and laugh even if we cannot tap into the joy of the Lord for a short season. Maybe you have never struggled with this, but I have.

Laughter is good; helping others is really good and often can perpetuate laughter; and making healthy changes "just for us" is better than good. However, sometimes we are stuck in a bad situation so long we do not know what a good one looks like.

I never thought I would be free from my weight prison, and to this day I still catch myself not seeing me as others do. I find myself, on occasion, still wrestling with a few old mindsets and having to "stand firm then and no longer let myself be burdened again with *that* yoke of slavery." More often than not, however, I smile more, laugh more, play more, run more, and enjoy life so much more as a healthy adult. Making a stand for my health definitely has taken me to a place in life I had only dreamed of.

Being in prison does not bring a smile for most of us. But many would say that being free does. Jesus Christ handed us the keys to the cell of obesity and shouted, "Be free." And if I have the keys, does that mean I have the freedom to leave and never return to the cell that plagued me most of my life? Absolutely. Again, who has the keys? I do through Christ. It is my choice to go, stay, or never return again. For me, joy in this health journey solidified when I locked the door to the obesity cell and threw the keys away. If I ever decide to open that door again, it will require more than keys. Get that visual.

Smile today, family. We are changing one bad habit at a time for the good of our health. I am proud of you!

February 9: Agape Love

As we approach Valentine's Day, I am reminded of three kinds of love—phileo, eros, and agape. Agape, the "top of the pyramid" love, is wrapped around the concept of sacrifice (see John 3:16). It is a love that gives even to those who have wronged you. It is a love that places others first, is patient, and doesn't speak when it can. Get the picture? We should all strive to follow God's example when He gave the best gift, knowing we didn't deserve it. Can you think of someone who has wronged you? Can you pretend for one moment in your heart that you are going to give one of your children over to die so this rotten person can live? I'm so glad I am not God and more glad that He loves me enough to offer agape love to me. How about you?

In thinking about agape, sacrificial love, I want to utilize the essence of that type of love as we consider ourselves for a moment. What? Sacrificial love is about others, yes it is, but I find we make sacrifices for many people and sometimes never for ourselves. I want to challenge each of us to agape our health enough to sacrifice for it. I know that consuming water gets to be a nuisance, and having to chop vegetables for the week every Monday is a pain, and weighing when I do not want to is burdensome, but if I do not agape myself enough to make some sacrificial choices, who will? My husband cannot drink water and have it flush the fat out of my body. My daughter cannot weigh in for me each morning. My friends cannot grocery shop and cook healthy for me (unless they owe me a favor).

I don't feel that it's wrong to extend some agape love toward my health. Do you? This morning I want to encourage you to be mindful of healthy sacrifices you make today that offer your body life. If you only make one agape choice today for yourself, it's a great start. Celebrate that. If it is a great, agape day filled with sacrifices that bring life, do the victory dance!

Challenge: while you are sacrificing for yourself, please do not forget to agape others by being patient and not speaking when you feel you have the right to do such.

February 10: Leave My Heart Alone

Happy pre-Valentine's Day week.

Telling and showing others that you love them is critical, and really should be done daily. However, Valentine's Day is that designated day to make someone joyfully happy with something extraordinary. Might I suggest a healthy dessert? I love being creative. I am making a red velvet cake and expressing my extraordinary love in this manner to my office staff.

Thinking about hearts, how about our physical heart? The heart is the strongest muscle in our body, and as such, needs to be protected and well-taken care of. Eating and drinking properly is a great start to heart health, but managing stress is another vital key. Stress takes such a drastic toll on our health. Search any article on stress and start writing. Devastation awaits those who handle stress poorly. I want to really bring that forward today.

We cannot claim that we desire health for our bodies and allow stress to consume us. That still represents a prison cell. Sometimes choosing to deny myself a brownie is easier than saying to my life, "I choose no stress today." You know it is. Do I really think life cares? Certainly not. It is not the circumstances; it is my response to the circumstances that often needs help. Some things cannot be changed in our life immediately, but our response to them can.

Stress adds plaque to our arteries, which in turn stresses our heart. Stress can also cause our heart to beat out of rhythm and that is dangerous as well. In addition, stress adds fat to our bellies, and that stresses our heart in a big way. I read frequently how fat on our bellies is a far greater risk to our *heart* than anywhere else. Just reading and talking about all this negative stuff stresses me, but it also challenges me in a unique way as well. How about you?

So this Valentine's Day let's give ourselves a present by eating and hydrating well. Then, let us speak to the stress in our lives and remind it that God is big, His Word never lies, He has good plans for us, and He will never leave us nor abandon us. Just typing that sent my stress level down several notches. Stand on God's truth today and tell that stress to find someone else to harass.

February 11: Make a Fist

Sometimes I wonder if I will ever get to a place where I don't have to deal with being hungry. I am a big eater; I love to eat and that sometimes is a bad combination. I wish I had one of those *little girl* appetites, but somehow when those were assigned I must have been in the food line singing one of those crazy songs we sang at summer camp that declared our impatience as we waited for breakfast to be served.

Having a tiny appetite or being one of "those people" who have to remind themselves to eat would have been so beneficial to me. Yes, it would. But again, not only do I remember to eat, I have to fight the urge to consume abundantly. Even great foods can be consumed in extravagant proportions and cause us issues. Just recently I ate so much fruit at one sitting that I almost got sick. That's just wrong. The whole time I was smiling and thinking, *These fruits are rare, native, and scrumptious. I may never eat things like this again and they are only fruits. Right?* Then, I proceeded to act as if I had never eaten before (even though I was really hungry due to missing dinner the previous evening) and quickly realized I had pushed the boundaries and my body was responding negatively.

Now maybe you're thinking, *Really, it's just fruit.* True, and in another season of my life it would have been brownies or a candy bar, but our stomachs are only designed to hold a limited amount of whatever. Did you know your stomach is about the size of your fist? Try it. Make a fist and get a picture. Then think of the last meal you consumed fitting into that pouch. Does it work? Does it fit easily? Eye opening isn't it? So when we use the phrase, "I'm so stuffed," what we mean is our pouch is crammed full and our stomach is screaming for us to stop.

Let us use the fist visual to help keep us from reaching the stuffed phase, which absolutely stretches our pouch and allows more food and calories to be ingested. This can ultimately lead to increased weight. Remember also that we *can* eat again, there is plenty, and our stomachs are really fairly small. Maybe as a means of not overeating, we make a fist before each meal and determine if the items on our plate will fit easily. If not, remove a few things.

Discipline 101 this morning: Enjoy the sunshine and choose well this day. Let the fist be your guide.

February 12: My Fitness Pal

This week is one of real self-denial as our church is embracing a seven-day fast, as a church family, as we endeavor to move closer and deeper in our intimacy with God. While the days have not been easy, it has been powerful in that when I feel hungry, I stop and pray. Even more amazing is how much stronger I feel spiritually when not bogged down with food. Do you want to know why? Food takes a lot of energy to digest. It pulls from available resources to try and convert the solids we have ingested into energy and nutrients for our body. And if we have swallowed our food whole, it takes even more energy to digest. Fasting, therefore, means I do not feel drained or tired following a meal. That's often very beneficial.

Sometimes we view the process of fasting as a four-letter word, don't we? However, there is a principle behind denying our flesh. When fasting, we actually remind our bodies that we are in control. Fasting is a discipline that many of us rarely access but whose benefits are undeniable. It is wonderful that bringing our fleshly appetites into a place of control offers benefits on many levels. But can you name one person who enjoys the process?

God created us with the ability to choose, and with that gift comes a need for discipline. I would love it if my internal appetite would shut off at the exact amount of calories daily that were needed to maintain my goal weight. How about you? Then no struggle, no hunger, no feeling deprived. But that is not what happens. God allows us to choose our foods, our portions, and our poison (if you will) with the expectancy that we will choose well. He gives us the Holy Spirit, who guides us into all truth (not just spiritual truth), but we must access Him and ask for help.

What about this? I know several weight management programs have great calorie/point counting computer/phone apps that allow you to track everything. What if we thought of the Holy Spirit as our Spiritual Fitness Pal? Let's submit to Him all our foods, exercise, and health journey throughout the day and when we have exhausted our points, we simply stop. How about that?

I see this time of fasting as helping me hear more clearly and gain better control of my health. And since my new Spiritual Fitness Pal (the Holy Spirit) speaks in a still, small voice, it's a good thing to start listening more closely.

February 13: Fudge

Yield: 16 servings

Ingredients

- 16 ounces light cream cheese, softened
- 3 unsweetened chocolate squares (1 ounce each) melted (in microwave-safe container) and cooled (for about 5 minutes)
- 1 cup xylitol
- 1 teaspoon vanilla extract or peppermint
- ½ to ¾ cup chopped pecans (optional)

Procedure

1. In a small mixing bowl, beat the cream cheese and xylitol well until there are no lumps.
2. Add the slightly cooled chocolate and vanilla and mix until smooth.
3. Stir in pecans.
4. Pour into 8-inch square baking pan lined with foil. Cover and refrigerate overnight. Turn the fudge out onto a large platter and peel the aluminum foil from the back.
5. Cut into 16 pieces and return unused portion to a sealed container.
6. Serve chilled, as the cream cheese will soften at room temperature.

Per Serving:

Calories 157.6
Total Fat 14.0 g
Cholesterol 20.0 mg
Sodium 110.0 mg
Potassium 30.5 mg
Total Carbohydrate 8.5 g
Dietary Fiber 1.5 g
Sugars 1.3 g
Protein 3.4 g

February 14: Kathy's Ketchup

Yield: 60 servings

Ingredients

- 2 cans (10 ¾ oz.) plain tomato paste (no sugar)
- 1 can (15 oz.) plain tomato sauce (no sugar)
- 2 teaspoon xylitol
- ¾ teaspoon all spice
- 1 teaspoon cinnamon
- 1 ¼ teaspoons yellow mustard
- 1 ½ teaspoons sea salt
- ½ to ¾ teaspoons onion powder
- 3 cloves garlic, minced finely
- 1 cup apple cider vinegar
- 1 cup water
- 1 teaspoon rosemary
- ¾ teaspoon black, fresh-ground pepper
- ½ teaspoon oregano
- 1 teaspoon cumin

Procedure

Mix all ingredients in a heavy pot and cook over medium heat until the mixture begins to bubble, stirring well. Reduce the heat and allow cooking until thickened to your liking. Watch this closely as it splatters. Reduce the heat and continue to cook until the liquids have reduced and the desired consistency is obtained. Also, the spices can be adjusted depending on how sweet you prefer ketchup. I really enjoy the cinnamon taste, but add it slowly, it can overpower the others.

Per Serving:

Calories 16.9
Total Fat 0.2 g
Cholesterol 0.0 mg
Sodium 111.2 mg
Potassium 135.8 mg
Total Carbohydrate 4.2 g
Dietary Fiber 0.7 g
Sugars 1.8 g
Protein 0.7 g

February 15: The Power of Chocolate

I hope you are enjoying being on this side of a chocolate holiday. I had so many people confess they had no power to say "no" to chocolate. I contemplated that. What type of inanimate object has that much control over us? Have you every thought about it? I used to say that chocolate was "calling my name and I could not resist." Yes, I said it in fun, but after this past holiday with the multitude of comments about the power of chocolate, I really shook my head. Does chocolate really have that strong of a voice? No, not the object, but the taste.

Taste triggers our mind into feeling a sense of pleasure, like we are being treated to something amazing. Have you ever watched someone bite into a piece of chocolate, close their eyes, take a long, deep breath and smile? I have. We must remember that sugar sedates and comforts. So chocolate candy is a three-fold bomb. It sedates, comforts, and tastes great—that can be a deadly combination.

The problem is that chocolate tastes good for a season, but quickly settles on our belly and thighs. Then, often we feel bad and opt for more chocolate to comfort us, only to begin the process again. It can be a vicious cycle with seemingly no end. Once we have made that tough decision to never return to the sugar wheel, often every issue in life straddles our resolve and screams, "You need sugar. It's the only way to endure this issue and no one is watching. It's okay." The only problem with that thought is that it's a lie. The Bible says knowing the truth sets us free (see John 8:32). While we know the sugar in chocolate is not amazing for us, we rationalize with all our friends that "everything in moderation is okay." How about a drop of poison? Are you willing to place that in the pot of soup on the stove?

When we continue to rationalize truth and make excuses for our weaknesses, we weaken the boundaries of success. Slowly we return to the old way of obesity thinking, which now holds the keys to our past cell. While chocolate has a *voice*, it is still an inanimate object. Remember that! We must realize that we consciously give power to the voices in our lives. So let us shout with a clear voice, "Chocolate candy, I will no longer recognize the sound of your voice nor give you any power over me." When that voice is silenced, the voice of apples may actually sound clearer.

Moral of the story: After a couple of years without candy, the taste of apples or watermelon causes me to close my eyes, take a deep, long breath, and smile. This will be you in just a few short months.

February 16: Readers Make Great Eaters

I am still in the "check every label mode" and am certain this phase will never stop. I was eating some dry roasted almonds last night thinking they were on my approved list when I got this little "tap" on the shoulder to read the label. Upon doing so I realized there were some not so friendly ingredients included with the nuts. For example it read, "Seasoning, maltodextrin, contains 2 percent or less of the following: salt, modified potato starch, sugar, a bunch of other things and then corn syrup solids." Who knew that? I quickly grabbed a bag of my 100 percent natural almonds (roasted in sea salt) with no added oils and read its label. The ingredients listed were: almonds, sea salt. That is a huge difference while on our health journey.

Just because we assume dry roasted almonds will not have sugar does not mean that is true. I just shook my head and realized that I still have to be so careful. The problem is that sometimes we rationalize that almonds are almonds are almonds. (You could actually substitute anything.) But just like people create dishes differently, companies do the same. I find that every time I am in a hurry and grab for something at the store without checking carefully, I end up in trouble.

Life is a lot like that. Isn't it? We make so many assumptions only to discover that we were off base. My advice is that you find products that are whole foods, work with your plan, and stick with them. I have always heard it said, "Variety is the spice of life." However, I'm a busy person, so it is necessary for me to know what brand of tomatoes or which brand of nuts make my body smile and be able to access them quickly. For me that is the *real* "spice of life."

Keep those labels in front of your eyes. I am a great reader and someone once said that "readers lead." So I will read well and lead myself right to the age of one hundred in great health. If you will make the commitment to start reading for your health, I am certain you will find the same confidence.

February 17: Fight Your Way to Victory

Some of you contact me regularly asking, "How do we overcome the boredom of eating lean proteins, fruits, and vegetables?" Let us be honest, the answer lies within us. Creating new dishes, eating at a different restaurant, eating a different style of food are all venues for each of us to explore. I must admit that during the winter it is more difficult for me to be creative with the recipes as the fruits and vegetables are not as plentiful and are fairly expensive. Versatility is critical right here. Some days it is a meal-by-meal challenge to explore various colors and textures, but that often helps me with boredom. Other days, replacing those "boring" meal options with a fresh passion to take a walk, shop, or redecorate my bathroom changes my focus.

I suggest you not waste time and energy sitting around thinking about all that you cannot eat. Feeding denial can sometimes create a monster. Have you ever been fueled by the passion of denial? Let us be honest—when I know I cannot have something, I am often propelled toward that forbidden fruit. Most of us are. Most of my life, I planned my meals the day before and spent all day thinking about those brownies I was making or the chicken I was frying. Food consumed the airwaves of my mind.

I still think about food a lot, but now I am creating, reading, and asking questions. In essence, I am fighting for my long-term health. I know that as quickly as I lost weight, I can start the mindset of relaxing the standard and I will find myself sick again. So I fight daily. I watched a movie on Sunday that was set in the time period when kings and kingdoms fought to obtain and maintain the land upon which they lived. There seems to be one main character in each of these types of films who has the courage and charisma to foster victory. Against all odds, often their voice brings such inspiration. I imagine fighting daily for change was not easy for them. I feel that way myself sometimes. Their determination inspires me, and I hope mine inspires you!

February 18: A Three-Fold Cord Is...

I spoke with a friend yesterday who has also had great success with getting his weight down and is walking in health. He said God has really solidified in him that you must have three things in your life to be successful in any area—a plan, passion, and discipline. I emphatically agree with my friend.

A plan originates in our mind (heart) and often, as we have discussed, it is the greatest battle we face. I find that so many are drawn to looking back and focusing on failure as opposed to looking forward to embrace something they have never seen before. Isn't that funny? Our past can be easier to examine than our future that we have not seen, even if our past includes failure. Our plan needs to embrace forward motion and include attainable goals.

Passion is something tricky. It can be an unharnessed force with which to reckon if directed toward the wrong elements. Or, passion can be a life-sustaining force that compels us to never settle for the prison cell of obesity again. My passion to live and be healthy increases daily. I do not ever want to simply exist again; I want to live successfully and arrive at the healthy age of one hundred in great health. I must be passionate about living healthy or being unhealthy could become my passion again.

Discipline takes planning and passion and marries the two terms. I have never seen a person who is determined to be healthy who has no plan and no passion. It just won't happen. Success in this area is not a variable of *maybe*. It is a consistent, planned, passionate endeavor that sets goals, celebrates victories, annihilates enemies, closes certain doors forever, and listens to the voice of our Spiritual Fitness Pal. Being healthy, as we know, is the best choice. But it is not the only choice. Can we be real?

My prayer this morning is threefold:

1. That each of us sticks with the plan to embrace health no matter what variables invade our lives.

2. For us to stir the passion to live when we get tired of the same vegetables, the negative comments, and the scale that gets stuck occasionally.

3. That we seize the concept of discipline, an unpopular word, but one that may add years to the end of our lives.

That is a three-fold cord worth fighting for.

February 19: Fractions

Fractions have been on my mind lately, and as you know they represent a portion of the whole. Our health is only a portion of the whole life God has given us. But can I just say it is a huge portion? We all recognize that the top part of the fraction indicates the portion of the whole while the bottom encompasses the whole. How does this relate to our health? Say that our concern for our health was 1/8 last year, meaning that seven other things, out of eight, were more important to us than the condition of our health. However, after being in our health family and walking with others who are fighting from freedom of obesity, your fraction has changed from 1/8 to 4/8. That is massive progress. Where would you say you are today?

I realize that portions of our life fraction have to be our spiritual, family, and social life. However, if our health is failing, we are constantly unhappy about our daily journey, and we keep going around the same mountain of excuses, there is a chance that our portion of the fraction related to health will steadily decline until we see no hope. Here is a critical news flash: as long as you are still breathing, there is hope. I am proof of that.

Maybe as you consider your health fraction, you might say, "There's really no change over the past couple of years." I operate best with honesty. How about if you begin today with 1/8 as your baseline and every day see in your mind 4/8? Let us increase awareness, accountability, and actual results. How about if we don't settle or let each other settle for 1/8 or smaller yet? How about if we don't allow the bottom number to continue to increase (meaning we are sub-dividing our lives into smaller segments) to cover the pain of how we feel about ourselves? How about if we eat an apple, drink our water, and weigh every day for thirty days and increase the portion size of our health (the top number) to something greater so we feel fabulous and that increases our hope?

I never liked fractions in school, but I am feeling the love and seeing the need to understand them in relation to my health. What about you?

February 20: Spaghetti Squash in the Microwave

Yield: 4 servings

If you didn't know it before, spaghetti squash can be used as a healthy substitute for starchy pasta noodles. Here is a quick and simple way to prepare it to go along with your favorite Italian meal.

Ingredients

- 1 medium sized spaghetti squash

Procedure

1. Poke about 25 holes in the squash with a sharp knife.
2. Heat spaghetti squash for 3 minutes in the microwave.
3. Cut off both ends.
4. Cut spaghetti squash length-wise in half. I lay both pieces on a long plate, skin-side out for the remainder of the cooking time. The juice will fill the plate so make certain it is large enough.
5. Microwave for an additional 10 minutes.
6. Allow to cool for 25-30 minutes.
7. Scrape out the guts. These look like webbed, cantaloupe seeds.
8. Use fork to scrape out spaghetti squash strands and enjoy. Scrape all the way to the skin, as you don't want to waste any of that fabulous "pasta."

Per Serving:
Calories 41.9
Total Fat 0.4 g
Saturated Fat 0.1 g
Polyunsaturated Fat 0.2 g
Monounsaturated Fat 0.0 g
Cholesterol 0.0 mg
Sodium 29.7 mg
Potassium 181.4 mg
Total Carbohydrate 10.0 g
Dietary Fiber 2.2 g
Sugars 3.9 g
Protein 1.0 g

February 21: Clam Sauce for Spaghetti

Yield: 8 servings

I usually triple this recipe, as my family loves it with the spaghetti squash "pasta," although you can serve this sauce with the noodles of your choice.

Ingredients

- 1 28-ounce can diced tomatoes (I use organic, fire roasted)
- 5 cloves of garlic, minced
- 1 large Vidalia or sweet onion (chopped well)
- Olive oil (I use between 2-3 tablespoons)
- 2 large can clams
- ½ teaspoon sweet basil
- 3 tablespoons Parmesan Regianno cheese (optional, but quite tasty)

Procedure

1. Sauté onion, garlic, and basil.
2. Add juice from clams (only) as well as tomatoes. Reserve clams to be added *after* sauce has cooked, as this will render the clams tough.
3. Simmer for 20 minutes.
4. Take off and add the clams as well as the cheese. Stir and allow to cool. Serve when you're ready. This stores well for a couple of days.

Per Serving:

Calories 109.4
Total Fat 5.7 g
Cholesterol 13.4 mg
Sodium 543.3 mg
Potassium 162.6 mg
Total Carbohydrate 9.2 g
Dietary Fiber 1.4 g
Sugars 4.0 g
Protein 5.5 g

February 22: It's Good Enough

You know sometimes when we say, "That's good enough," we are simply tired of doing something, or we are not pressing any further toward excellence. Right? Average is "okay." I have to really challenge that thought in my life so as to not accept average when I know there is something better. I live by the principle, "Good is the enemy of best." But there are times when even our committed clichés can be challenged.

Here's a scenario we all probably know too well:

It was a weekend filled with parties and experiences that could have been disastrous. But, I made a plan and stuck to it. I had a bag filled with healthy goodies and was determined to smile as I ate my apple. However, there are always *those* people who are determined we are emphatically going to *try* their (insert whatever). And if we choose to disobey, they will humiliate us in front of everyone. You know the ones with that taunting voice who say, "One small bite won't hurt anything. Come on, try just a bite." One bite, for me, can open a door that I prefer remains closed.

While attending a party recently, my hostess knew the previous me was addicted to sweetened coffee extras. My motto was: "The more the better." It was my delight and joy to begin every day with coffee, sweetened creamers, and a shameful amount of whipped cream. When guests came to my house, they were always forced to try my coffee, as I was certain mine was the best around. It's horrible when our sins catch up with us, isn't it? Anyway, in the course of this party it was apparent the tables were turned on me. When I tried to convince the hostess that I no longer used sugar, the comments came. I then found that I had to defend myself and justify why I simply now use a natural sweetener and plain cream. I retorted to those listening and prodding, "My new way is really *good enough for me.*" And might I add, I snarled as I spoke.

The good-enough phrase shifted from "I'm tired of this project and average is okay," to "I have the power of choice on my side and my flesh will have to understand it doesn't always get what it wants." The phrase "that's good enough" in this case was really not settling. It was defense with an attitude. But can I really remind you that we do not have to defend our health? We simply live our health and it defends itself. Great point.

February 23: Friendly Foods

Sometimes so many things push against us from all directions and life seems to spiral. Inappropriate eating, for some, can be a response to that. I understand completely. There have been times where eating to hide my pain was easier than confronting the issues. Soon, I decided eating was the enemy and I had to attack it. So I stopped eating altogether. Eating was never the enemy. Let us be clear. But years would pass before I came to the place of inner healing and discovered this truth.

Last night I was tired, frustrated, and hungry. I had several choices but I made myself eat an apple, as it was the best available choice. Let me be honest though, I said best choice but not my first choice. Unfortunately, my family eats foods that I still do not include and there were a myriad of other choices that really appealed to my eyes, which seem to be attached directly to my stomach. This struggle reminded me that I must be determined to surround myself with great, healthy choices so that in a weak moment, where the real issues of life are pushing against my resolve, I can make the appropriate choice because I *can*. The items needed to facilitate the best choice were present and readily available.

If you were to go right now and take an inventory of your pantry and refrigerator, what would you find? Have you given yourself every possibility to succeed, or have you laid your own snare? For the first year of my health journey, I often shopped several times a week and hid healthy foods so that I was always prepared. I called them my friendly foods. I surrounded myself with them in the event that an unfriendly day tried to hurt me. That was my best plan against the enemy of self-indulgence. And guess what? It worked!

I learned to not use food as my comfort and to turn my hurt toward the One who always comforts best, God the Father. I learned that food was not my enemy and that I could eat and live. What a divine revelation.

February 24: Act Now

As many of you know, I stand squarely on Galatians 5:1. It is one of my foundational pillars. While attending a financial series at church last night, I saw a different variation of this principle that really applies to our health journey also: truth + action = freedom.

I was contemplating several of the basic, introductory ideas in this financial class and they were great. But each one required action, and the speaker was very firm that action should not be delayed. We worked through a comparison chart for two men who both invested their money. Unfortunately, one of the men waited several years to start. While they both reaped a reward for their actions, the one who started earlier and kept to the plan reaped the greatest benefit. I smiled as I thought about our health family. I could see a direct correlation. Also, each of the men had a responsibility to their specific journey. That applies to each of us as well. Don't you love seeing yourself in someone's story? I do.

It is not enough that we know that overeating, being overweight, and being dehydrated cuts years of health from our journey. It's not. We can know that truth all day, but if we never act on that knowledge and stay to the journey, the result could be devastating. You know I love the whole *no excuses rule* and wanted to share this morning that each of us has the opportunity on a daily basis to choose health. Let us not allow the variables of our lives to keep us from doing what is best for us today—right now—while there is time. This is not a selfish decision; it's a selfless decision. Let me explain.

Some days it is extremely difficult to say "no" to the comfort foods. But our future—and in many cases, the future of our children and grandchildren—is often affected by our choices. The Bible teaches that a good man leaves an inheritance to his children and children's children (see Proverbs 13:22). I want you to consider your health as part of the inheritance you leave your family.

Moral of the story: Act now. The sooner we pursue action, the greater the return. Don't wait one minute longer. Consider every second as another investment in your future.

February 25: Protect the Truth

"Don't copy the behavior and customs of this world, but let God transform you into a new person by changing the way you think. Then you will learn to know God's will for you, which is good and pleasing and perfect" (Romans 12:2 NLT).

Have you ever wondered and asked yourself, *What is God's will for my life?* Has anyone other than me ever had that real conversation? Sometimes I wonder if we feel the postcard will show up in the mail next week and simply tell us what to do. That would be easy. However, just because I feel like I cannot hear God at times, or I don't know His will for my life in a particular area, does not mean He is not speaking clearly or that He is the least bit confused and does not know His plan. God does not reason like we do. He does not have to explain His thoughts. He is always in control and always has a plan. God wants the best for us every day without exception. Even on a bad day, when humankind may have disappointed us, God will not.

Maybe you are saying, "I have begged God to get this weight off of me and He hasn't." Are you disappointed in God? I understand; I was there for years. I prayed every prayer, got in every prayer line, spoke to my flesh, spoke to the refrigerator, and was still obese. Did God's plan to provide healthy foods for my life change? No. Did God's plan for me to be healthy and live in victory change? No. Was God's purpose and plan for me to be unhealthy and feel like a failure? Absolutely not. God was consistently speaking and offering help, I just wanted to be thin without being disciplined and blamed God for "giving me bad genes."

Freedom, for me, came when I was desperate to live and in a place to really listen. The kind of listening that changes people's destiny. You know that kind of listening? God didn't change—I did. The cycle of excuses in my life became the quiet voice and God's voice moved to the forefront. Is there an area in your health journey that you are still excusing? Today is a great day to silence the flesh and allow God's voice to speak. Then, build that wall, protect the truth, and proclaim freedom.

February 26: The Changes We Face

Most of you know I love science-related things. I know God allowed me to teach science because I am a visual learner. He desired to convey messages to my small brain that allowed me to visually connect and find meaning.

As we approach the change of a season, there are certain patterns and colors that enable us to evaluate and determine, in fact, that a new season has arrived. We depend on that, don't we? And yet, even though change comes and goes like clockwork, there are variables that are solidly consistent that allow the changes to be celebrated. Stay with me, I'm going somewhere with this. Once our health plan is concrete and established, it must become the constant to which change, for a season, does not cause us to revert to an unhealthy lifestyle. There are variables that must remain constant in order to offer our bodies the best opportunity to embrace health—water, rest, non-sugared/non-starchy foods, a balance of lean proteins, vegetables, fruits, and motion. We know this, yes?

But there are *seasons* that come into our lives, some of which we did not provoke nor can we order. The loss of a loved one, a change in our occupation (which often changes our daily schedule), or a sickness that lasts longer than we anticipate can all pull us from the daily routine of choosing health. Often people confess they were doing well with their health until an outside force knocked them down and they never recovered. That can happen to us all.

I want us to embrace change because it is coming and will never stop. However, the variables of our health must be what we consistently return to, whether comfortable or not. There are four seasons that we experience every year as humans. God allows those changes to occur every year so we are not shocked or unprepared. We can always rest assured they are coming. So are the obstacles, which would desire to pull us from choosing health. Let us plan for them, watch for their signs, understand that change happens to us all, and not use change as an excuse to be unhealthy.

I know some of you are struggling in bad marriages or with bad reports from the doctors, etc. In times of difficulties, let us choose health more and offer our organs the best opportunity to not complicate the unfortunate changes. Change comes and goes, but God's Word is constant and His desire for us to be healthy is unchanging. Thank You, Father.

February 27: Taco/Chili Seasoning Mix

Yield: 1 serving

You can make this in large quantities and store for a variety of Mexican dishes.

Ingredients

- 2 teaspoons paprika
- 1 teaspoon of sea salt (this can vary according to your taste)
- 1 teaspoon onion powder
- 1 teaspoon chili powder
- 2 teaspoons cumin
- 1 teaspoon garlic powder
- ½ teaspoon coarse ground black pepper (optional)
- ½ teaspoon jalapeño powder

Procedure

Mix all the ingredients and use immediately with one pound of lean ground beef.

Per Serving:
Calories 93.9
Total Fat 2.3 g
Cholesterol 0.0 mg
Sodium 83.8 mg
Potassium 459.2 mg
Total Carbohydrate 19.3 g
Dietary Fiber 6.3 g
Sugars 5.6 g
Protein 4.0 g

February 28: Taco Salad

Yield: 8 servings

If you need to save the calories by not adding the dressing, serve with your favorite salsa. This adds a lot of flavor without all the calories.

Ingredients

- 3 large bunches or 2 bags Romaine lettuce
- 2 lbs. lean ground beef
- Taco seasoning (previous recipe)
- 4 Roma tomatoes
- 2 cups four blend Mexican cheese
- 2 tablespoons sour cream or bacon ranch dressing (each person, but is optional)
- 2 avocados

Procedure

1. Wash, chop, and dry the romaine lettuce.
2. Fill a large plate with the lettuce.
3. Brown your meat and add the taco seasoning (refer to the previous recipe).
4. Place the seasoned meat on top of the lettuce.
5. Add the cheese.
6. Add the tomatoes and avocado wedges.
7. Add the bacon ranch and serve.

Per Serving:

Calories 490.6
Total Fat 38.3 g
Cholesterol 107.0 mg
Sodium 375.1 mg
Potassium 565.9 mg
Total Carbohydrate 7.3 g
Dietary Fiber 2.1 g
Sugars 0.6 g
Protein 29.3 g

* If this is a Leap Year, please read a few extra chapters in the Bible of your choice, and pick up on March 1st as scheduled.

February Reflection Page

As you are completing February, are there things you wish you had highlighted or which you had written down? I am so proud that you made it through this candy month, but did you try the desserts for one of your parties? Maybe it's time for you to modify a family recipe.

_____

_____

_____

_____

_____

_____

_____

_____

_____

_____

_____

_____

_____

_____

_____

_____

_____

_____

_____

March

*March brings us Leprechauns and the "luck of the Irish."
Maybe? But there's no luck involved in being healthy.
It's hard work and diligence.*

March 1: Lightning Says, "Warning!"

We had a pretty intense storm recently and it reminded me again of how powerful our fight for health can be. Just when we feel comfortable in our new regime and start to enjoy some of the extra calories—pow. The scale sends a powerful message and it's like lightning. The scale shouts, "Extra pound, two pounds, slow down, make the change." When lightning occurs we can rest assured that a positive and negative have collided. And while some collisions are moderate, some absolutely rattle everything we hold dear.

Sometimes our flesh has to be jolted back to the reality that our new weight is not eternally permanent. We must continue to do what we know is correct, which helped us achieve our health goals for the remainder of our lives. If we relax our resolve, we could see the scale change. Somehow I was absent when that truth came out. Maybe you were as well. I don't mind suffering for a season, but come on. I know others who take pleasure in knowing they have suffered "for the cause of being healthy." Again, I didn't get that badge. And, while I would love to make a huge declaration about how I enjoyed losing weight and denying my flesh with the same robotic smile, I cannot. It is like lightning to me—reality versus famous quotes.

You know I'm playing of course, but sometimes unhealthy foods taste so amazing and I could reason that a bulge from eating a Philly cheese steak can always be hidden under a big shirt. Nevertheless, long term that *lightning* needs to keep me alert and watchful. Those blood reports come every 6 months and they do not lie. If cheating is the negative and diligence is the positive, these bi-annual confrontations can certainly make a show.

We are making a lifestyle change, not simply a weight loss change. That should mean we will not be as quick to relax when we arrive at our goal weight because we understand what foods brought us to this place. And we can rest assured that our friend, the scale, is going to conflict with our hopes if our reality has been tampered with. Be alert to the lightning potential in those morning weigh-ins. Do your part to keep the positive choices of healthy living flowing, which allow those powerful lightning demonstrations to remain in the heavens above.

While I love lightning in the sky, I am cognizant of its power and motive. It can be both deadly and beautiful. I hope you see this picture today.

March 2: A Place of Remembrance

Don't you love days when everything is going great—the sun is out, the birds are singing, and your calorie consumption is in check? I am thankful for those days when all the water gets consumed, the meals fall together perfectly, and I rejoice over an apple. Those days need to be burned in our memories because there are some polar opposite days on the radar. We all have them.

Creating a place of remembrance is critical in life, period. As I told someone recently, make certain to record your weight. Then, when you are struggling, you can return to your record sheets and have a visual reminder that you did make a stand for your health and have experienced success. Having a visual of where you want to be is not bad; but, for me, having a place of remembrance is crucial. One looks forward, and one looks back.

We all need places that are safe where we can return and see a victory—a place to remember where someone helped us or stood with us. Many need a place where we remember the exact obstacle we overcame. That is another reason to keep our before and after photos current. Some issues, or people, in our lives want to tempt us to return to our old mindsets about food. These mindsets sometimes dragged us into the obesity trap, didn't they? However, having the photos to serve as a place of remembrance of where we came from and where we plan to never return often places us on stable ground. People mean well, but many of them have not been in a fight for their lives and do not understand our desperation.

Let us serve as reminders to one another. All of you need a support group or a partner who knows you, is not afraid to be honest with you, does not mind offending you if need be, and who can remind you of the little victories (which in the end become the big victories). Stop today. Stop and look at your photos—celebrate where you have come from and celebrate that you have chosen a different path. If you have strayed from the path, dance your silly self back on the path and do what you know is right. Let's remember together this day. I can just see you doing the victory dance as I type.

March 3: My Stomach Gets My Attention

Don't you love cold, rainy mornings? I do, except when my husband wakes me up at 7 a.m. wanting to go to the nearby town of Senoia and drink coffee. Not good. I was in the middle of a beautiful dream (which I never am) and then could not find my way to the story again. My husband did get up and make some coffee though. He is special. We opened the front door to listen to the rain and the birds while drinking our coffee. It was a great start to the weekend.

True confessions though—I went to bed sick to my stomach last night from eating too much. I ate all legal stuff, but too much. I was out of my routine due to a work issue and the interruption was near fatal. In a starving moment, as well as a *have the grand babies over* moment, I just grabbed too much—and too much of a good thing is still too much. I inhaled meat, salad, no sugar added ice cream, root beer, and fruit. Sounded wonderful, but felt not so amazing. When my husband put his arm around me last night for a final hug, I felt sick from eating beyond the boundaries. How many know that is a stomach that is too full?

I have decided, though, that occasionally we need that stuffed feeling to remind us that the boundaries of our stomach can be a good thing. Even though I felt sick last night (I lay awake trying not to scurry to the bathroom), I found a weird way to compliment myself by thinking, *Wow, my stomach is smaller and praise God I need to listen to my stomach.* We have to listen don't we? Listen to our stomach, to the scales, to our clothes (reminder that when your clothes speak, you are probably up ten pounds already), listen to the mirror, to each other, and to our families. Let us open our ears and listen.

Sometimes listening means we have to change, and often change is not easy. But listening and submission are critical to our journey. You would not be reading this book if you didn't want to listen. I know this. So let us agree to listen at a deeper level today. What did the scales say to you this morning? Your jeans when you put them on? Did your stomach try to speak during breakfast? When the boundaries are saying, "Stop," are you willing to obey? I absolutely did not last night and I paid the price. If I don't learn to listen quickly, I will stretch my stomach, push the boundaries, and see the scale start to increase. So today, my stomach gets my attention and I am listening carefully.

Is your stomach speaking louder than your desire to eat as you please?

March 4: The End Is the Beginning

The last few days of winter get so long for me. The last hour of a trip nearly turns me around. The last leg of a twenty-four hour trip to another country and back seems unbearable. But the end of one journey is usually the beginning of another. Right? And the way we embrace the end can really influence how we begin the next chapter. I see this all the time in people's lives. While the past does have its place, there is a time for the old leaves to be swept away by the winds of change and new life to begin. That is the pattern established by God, and we see that repeated over and over before our eyes.

As we approach the week of St. Patrick's Day parties, the real draw for some of us could be to look back to the patterns of our past and allow that "cheat" for a special event. There were certain times where it was *legal* to cheat (at least for me). It was the *accepted cheat*. I know this sounds almost laughable, but I think if we allow a cheat here and a cheat there the word *cheat* becomes familiar and could easily become the excuse. Can I propose something different? What if this St. Patrick's Day we blessed everyone with an all green salad or a tray of all green fruits? And, let us add a jug of green tea to share with the team at work? The combinations are endless.

Let us allow the end of our sugar-filled holidays to cause us to embrace a new way—a new journey. Let's teach our kids to be trendsetters with no fear of the backlash. Somebody has to. I don't know about you, but some people still want to buy me candy every holiday regardless of my "no sugar policy." I have not been able to wrap my brain around that yet. But if we start now and decide to *not* buy candy for our children at every holiday, perhaps they won't equate holidays and parties with food, but will link the holidays to fun and relationships.

Breaking the cycle of taking traditional foods to traditional parties will take some effort, could be a long process, and might cause some frustration as you re-purpose those specific recipes. But, once the old tradition has expired and the new embraced, the next season will be easier. Our kids will grow up realizing that great health is not just a seasonal option that comes and goes. They could learn to appreciate a simple journey of health with no mention of the word *cheat*. Great health is a lifestyle of choosing those things we want to eat and enjoy because we *know we can*.

This is the beginning of something new and the end of our prison-cell experience.

March 5: Never Embrace the Enemy

I know as spring is fast approaching and the clothes we wear are getting less and less, sometimes we have a confrontation with our self-image that is often not pleasant. Remember this—thoughts are empowering, whether negative or positive. A negative attitude can set processes in motion that make losing weight difficult, if not impossible. Slamming yourself every time you eat the wrong foods, constantly focusing on what you cannot eat, and approaching your exercise plan with dread are all ways that negative thought patterns can sabotage your weight loss efforts. When you hold a negative image of yourself, you rob yourself of much-needed energy. When feeling powerless, depressed, or unmotivated, it is easy to cheat on your daily routine or eat a bag of potato chips to relieve the pain.

However, dealing honestly with how you feel, acknowledging those feelings, and transforming those thoughts into something more positive can actually help you achieve your health goals faster. Instead of eating the candy bar or the chips (depending on if you are a sweet or salty person), take the time to make a healthy substitution and then celebrate the positive effect. Substitute jicama with salt for the chips to get the crunch and some strawberries with xylitol if you are craving something sweet. It's really that easy. Try it.

I don't want unhealthy shame to hang on any of us. We are all going to have a bad day here or there, but accepting failure and allowing food to win only cheats our families of our quality time with them. When I was heavy, depressed, and shaming myself (while in the same breath comforting myself with candy), I was not kind to my family. I never wanted to attend outside activities because I had nothing to wear, which was a lie. I had clothes that fit me, but they exposed my weakness and made me feel like an overweight, undisciplined person. It was horrible.

Please fight to never be trapped by that manner of thinking. Continue to fight for your health and always remember it is not about what size you wear. It is about how healthy you are. Feeling regret from eating that doughnut is not a bad thing if you can turn that around to make it positive. You could talk to your accountability partner, go for a walk, or drink more water the following day. Feeling shame when you eat the doughnut and turning to embrace failure only fuels the cycle. It actually becomes an enemy.

Let us never embrace the enemy. That's a destructive plan.

March 6: Pork Roast in the Crock-Pot

Yield: 8 servings

Ingredients

- 5-6 pound boneless Boston butt roast (leave the string on)
- 1 pkg. dry onion soup mix
- Sugar-free, whole berry cranberry sauce (my recipe follows)

Procedure

1. Spray the sides of your Crock-Pot lightly.
2. Place the roast inside.
3. Sprinkle with onion soup mix.
4. Cover with the cranberry sauce.
5. Set the temperature on high. It should take between 4-5 hours. You will know it's done when the meat is tender and pulls apart easily.

Per Serving:
Calories 489.5
Total Fat 24.1 g
Cholesterol 164.6 mg
Sodium 279 mg
Potassium 104 mg
Total Carbohydrate 3.1 g
Dietary Fiber 0.1 g
Sugars 0.3 g
Protein 64.0 g

Cranberry Sauce Ingredients

- 2 bags whole, fresh cranberries
- 2 cups water
- 1 cup xylitol
- ½ teaspoon lemon extract

Procedure

Mix all ingredients together and boil on medium high until the liquid is completely reduced. This takes about 45 minutes. The mixture will thicken, but will not congeal as store bought. The berries do pop while cooking, so don't be alarmed by the sound.

March 7: Carrot Cake with Buttermilk Glaze

Yield: 24 servings

Ingredients

- 3 cups almond flour (not packed)
- 2 cups xylitol
- 2 teaspoons baking soda
- 2 teaspoons ground cinnamon
- 1 teaspoon sea salt
- 4 eggs
- 1 cup vegetable oil
- 3 cups fresh, grated carrots
- 1 cup black walnuts or chopped pecans (optional)
- 6 oz. unsweetened coconut (I used the frozen)

Procedure

1. Preheat oven to 350°F.
2. Grease a 14x11 ceramic pan.
3. In a large bowl, combine flour, baking soda, cinnamon, and sea salt. Stir well and set aside.
4. Using a mixer, combine the oil and xylitol. Add eggs one at a time. To this mixture, add the dry ingredients in thirds to allow complete blending.
5. Add carrots, nuts, and coconut and pour into greased pan.
6. Bake for approximately 40-45 minutes (clean toothpick test).
7. Remove from oven and cool for 15 minutes before adding buttermilk vanilla glaze. You do not have to add the glaze, as it does add calories, but it makes a yummy, thin layer between the cake and the cream cheese icing and yields a very moist cake.

Buttermilk Vanilla Glaze: (optional)

Ingredients

- 1 ¼ cup Whey Low® brown sugar (for diabetics)
- 1 ½ teaspoons baking soda
- ¾ cup buttermilk
- ½ cup light butter
- 1 ½ teaspoon vanilla extract

Procedure

1. Bring first 4 ingredients to a boil in a large container over medium-high heat. Stir often for 3-4 minutes or until it begins to thicken and change color.
2. Remove from heat and stir in vanilla. This will become a dark, rich caramel syrup.
3. Once cake is cooled, use a toothpick to place holes evenly throughout the cake.
4. Drizzle the glaze over the cake and transfer to the refrigerator to completely cool before adding frosting.

Frosting:

This frosting is best when made two days ahead. It tastes great room temp, but I like it better right from the refrigerator as the flavors deepen as it sets.

Ingredients

- 2 (8-ounce) packages light cream cheese, room temperature
- 1 stick salted light butter, room temperature
- 1 ½ cup Whey Low® powdered sugar (for diabetics, optional)
- 1 teaspoon vanilla extract
- 1 cup black walnuts or pecans (again, optional)

Procedure

1. Add all ingredients, except nuts, into a medium bowl and beat until fluffy using a hand mixer.
2. Frost the *cooled* cake. Top with nuts if desired.
3. Keep refrigerated.

Per Serving: (Carrot cake)
Calories 223.2
Total Fat 18.8 g
Cholesterol 30.8 mg
Sodium 79.3 mg
Potassium 103.3 mg
Total Carbohydrate 15.4 g
Dietary Fiber 2.3 g
Sugars 1.3 g
Protein 4.6 g

Per Serving: (Vanilla glaze)
Calories 42.4
Total Fat 2.1 g
Cholesterol 5.0 mg
Sodium 85.8 mg
Potassium 0.5 mg
Total Carbohydrate 5.8 g
Dietary Fiber 0.0 g
Sugars 5.4 g
Protein 0.3 g

Per Serving: (Frosting)
Calories 109.4
Total Fat 9.1 g
Cholesterol 18.3 mg
Sodium 106.8 mg
Potassium 27.5 mg
Total Carbohydrate 7.2 g
Dietary Fiber 0.4 g
Sugars 0.7 g
Protein 2.6 g

March 8: Permission to Burn the Bridge

I was reading in Luke 4 this morning about how Jesus was filled with the Holy Spirit and immediately tempted. I thought about us. Sometimes we have a revelation about our health and our journey to walk in victory and we declare, "I'm going to be successful no matter what it takes. I'm going to do this." And in the next moment temptation shows up in the form of our favorite food. I think it was cool that Jesus was first tempted by food. Satan knows how weak we are in this area. But the truth that confronted the temptation turned the appeal around. Godly truth triumphs always.

When the temptation comes to grab a third cookie or two more pieces of chocolate, stop and ask yourself, "What is the truth here?" The truth is that we *do need food*, but food cannot be our master. It cannot control our impulses and gain victory over our emotions. Jesus did not say, "Man shall never eat bread." No, He said, "Man shall not live by bread alone, but by every word of God" (Luke 4:4 NKJV).

There are a lot of spiritual applications here. We cannot read into the Scriptures and make them say what we want, but Jesus confirms that we need natural food. However, it cannot be what our lives are dependent upon. Eating a cookie or a piece of chocolate for some of us may be okay. For me, it's not. I have chosen to delete sugar and starch from my life as long as possible. The more I read and understand about their influence on my health journey, the more committed I am to stick to my simple health plan, which does not include them. They serve as the lock and key to my prison cell of obesity. For me, I had to smash that bridge to sugar and starch, demolish the crutch, and batten down the escape hatch. If there's no way to return to that place of ruin, then it is easier for me to walk in victory.

I am not certain what that looks like for you, but perhaps it is something worthy of consideration. If the bridge still exists, there is always a possibility to journey across it once again. Take that application into the various areas of your life and see which bridges need to be destroyed. Maintaining victory requires diligence, and that means I am responsible for myself. Remember, relational bridges should be slow to be burned, as people can change. We did, right?

March 9: The Wonderful Wizard of Oz

So often we grab at every new diet plan that makes its name known on the big screen. Many of us spend thousands of dollars trying to embrace the world's way of getting healthy. Why is this? Perhaps because we *know* everything presented on television is true. So many long for the easy route because the troubled route often costs more than we are willing to pay.

Remember Dorothy in *The Wonderful Wizard of Oz*? She longed and dreamed for the land she knew and really never embraced a land she found herself living in. It wasn't her home. It was someone's home, but not hers. She dreamed of going home. But how many of you know we can dream of being healthy and still not be healthy? Dorothy had to fight her way to the realization of her dream. There were obstacles, but she would not accept them as her answer. In the end, as many of you know, she was successful.

I love people who are not afraid to dream extravagant dreams, but I firmly believe that dreams need feet. I am one of those "realistic" type of people who moves dreams forward by creating a strategy for seeing the dream become a reality. Creating a strategy takes initiative, planning, and intentionality. Without these components and our adherence to them, we find ourselves living in the "wishful thinking" society. We don't have the ability to click our heels three times and repeat, "There's no place for extra pounds and physical illness," do we? Nope. We cannot wish our way to health. But we do have the ability to follow a few simple rules—eat well, hydrate well, rest well, and keep moving. Now there's a dream with a strategy for success.

I do not know about you, but I like stories with happy endings. *The Wonderful Wizard of Oz* is one of them. The good thing about *our* story is we get to write our own ending if we will choose a healthy journey and make that our priority. I am clicking my heels and repeating, "I will live to one hundred; I will live to one hundred; I will live to one hundred."

March 10: The Life Is in the Blood

I had dinner last night with my family outside on the deck and it was so nice—baked wings, sweet potato tater tots (I did not eat these as they contain a little sugar, but my family loved them), mixed vegetables, strawberries with xylitol and chocolate whipped cream, which were all sugar-free. It was glorious.

Those of you who know me well know that I emphasize going to the doctor and having my blood tested regularly. The results of the test are cousins to my scale (in spite of my whining) and they are rarely wrong. I feel it is critical to know the levels of various components in our blood as they display the health of our internal organs. If our organs are sick, so are we, even if we are non-symptomatic *yet*. And, as with the scales, the results of my blood tests give me the bold confidence to make changes that I might often dismiss. How about you?

Before I got to the desperate state of health that finally perpetuated my complete life reversal, I had absolutely no plan or energy to make changes. Although I knew I was unhealthy, I kept a regular check on my blood (it is horrible to pay money to be stuck with a needle and confirm you are unhealthy). The Bible says in the book of Leviticus that "the life...is in the blood" (Leviticus 17:11 NKJV). The word for "life" can sometimes refer to the mind, being, desires, passion, and appetite. Now I know that this reference in Leviticus is speaking of the cleansing power of the blood pointing toward the cross, but I really feel that for us our blood is a great indicator of how clean and healthy our life really is.

It is a proven fact that sugar raises our triglyceride levels and affects our liver. And I am certain we have all read that fatty foods will raise our cholesterol and clog our arteries. I'm also certain our doctors have conveyed that sugar and starch raise our blood sugar level and promote diabetes. We have been informed through various sources and yet sometimes what we cannot see, we deny. Or at least we pretend to deny. However, our regular blood tests allow no lying. They reveal our desires, passion, and appetites, don't they? No one knew how much sugar and fat I was consuming until I had my blood tests done every six months. Then, all was revealed as the results clearly indicated that my passion was food, and a multitude of the *wrong foods*. However, after losing over sixty pounds and learning how to eat properly, my blood now reveals my new desire and passion, which is great health.

So yes, my *life* is revealed in my blood and my blood is saying, "Well done."

March 11: Desperate for the Light

I hope the sun is shining where you are. It is shining here and I love the light. Light does great things for us, doesn't it? We need it desperately. One of the greatest benefits of light is giving directions. I think sharing new recipes and giving words of hope helps us all with illumination. It's like this: when you share your victory stories and pictures, I feel light coming into the window of my health journey. This helps me visualize the victory path and remain on it. I really believe that we need a connection to others who are opening our eyes and hearts. When one of you shares your blood results and rejoices in the victory, I rejoice. That opens my eyes and shows that there's victory in the camp. I just love all these victory stories.

I lived in depression and a hidden cave called obesity for so long. Often prison cells have few windows and little natural light. For those in solitary confinement, light may be obscured for days at a time. I feel like that picture adequately depicts who I was for many years of my life. I was trapped in my own body, screaming for help, and never finding a window. Can you picture this?

I love windows, the lights turned on, and brightness; it is part of who I am. I only really discovered this in my health walk in January of 2011. I am blessed that so many of you are finding it also. Keep going and do not accept failure! We are created in the image of God to win. Continue to confess out loud the truth that "I can do all things through Christ who strengthens me" (Philippians 4:13 NKJV). Maybe you need to do that when walking down the aisle hosting the chips and crackers at the grocery store? Maybe you need to make that freedom confession as you reject the birthday cake at your own party? Or maybe, like me, it is when there's pizza on the counter and I try to reason, "One slice won't hurt me." I can scream right now just revisiting that scenario.

There are times even today when I still feel like my flesh wants to drag me to a dark, hidden cave. But the confession from my mouth, knowing God's Word is true and that He will never fail me, gives my sliding feet traction.

Try this: half of the times that you open your mouth to insert food today, either declare God's truth or praise him. Both options are powerful and bring life and light, especially if you are discouraged and feeling defeated.

March 12: God's Mirror

There is a lot to be said for carrying the spirit of joy everywhere you go. I do realize there are times when we cannot be happy. I have experienced tragedy, as you have, and laughter would be fake at best. Happiness and joy are really two different things. When life's unfortunate experiences are shoved in our face, tears usually flow but not laughter. And that is okay. God knew we would cry, but His Word reminds us in Psalm 30:5b, "Weeping may last through the night, but joy comes with the morning" (NLT). That means that joy arrives and is carried somehow into our situation. We know that to be the work of the Holy Spirit. It is amazing that in the middle of the most unfortunate circumstance, our spirits can be at peace and have a steady place where joy, sometimes not happiness, resides. I am confident this is totally God and has nothing to do with me. My emotions change, but God's character is steady. I depend on that.

Many leading researchers have substantiated the fact that stress can produce hormones that cause extra fat to store around our bellies. At first I was convinced that it was another ploy for vitamin companies to abuse we "overweight" folk and taunt us with the next carrot. I do not know about you but I spent hundreds and hundreds of dollars on those *carrots* only to come back to the basic foundation of discipline. And, what is worse, I continued to confess that I had none—*no discipline for Kathy*. I laughed at myself, made fun of myself, and cried behind closed doors. Will the real Kathy please step forward? Ever done that?

Laughing about the most desperate, broken place within me was a wretched attempt to make light of a deep place of hurt. I could act happy, make jokes about being fat, and go home, only to stare in the mirror and confess that I hated myself. My life walked this road for many years, and while I could laugh with the best of them, I had no joy. What is really sad is that I actually believed I had no way of ever gaining joy again.

Let me inform you today that joy is attainable, even for the brokenhearted. I am proof of that. And so is laughter. Now that I am healthy, I laugh constantly, but at real things that deserve laughter and not my broken health. Joy requires that you allow God to take those broken pieces and make them into a mirror that will reflect that you are fearfully and wonderfully made (see Psalm 139). That's the truth in God's mirror.

Toss your old mirror of poor self-image and use God's as it portrays your real image.

March 13: Brownies

Yield: 24 servings

You can add nuts to these brownies if you like, but remember to re-adjust your nutritional facts.

Ingredients

- 1 ½ cups vegetable or canola oil
- 1 ½ cups xylitol
- 2 eggs
- 7 tablespoons cocoa
- 2 ½ cups almond flour
- 1 teaspoon sea salt
- 1 ½ teaspoons baking soda
- 1 cup buttermilk
- 2 teaspoons vanilla extract
- 1 cup chopped pecans (optional and not included in the nutritional information below)

Procedure

1. Preheat oven to 350°F.
2. Beat oil and sugar; add eggs one at a time while beating.
3. Combine all the dry ingredients in a second bowl. Stir thoroughly until all dry components are mixed well and set aside.
4. Add the remaining liquid ingredients and beat into the egg/xylitol mixture.
5. Mix the dry ingredients and pour into a greased 13x9 baking dish.
6. Bake for 40 minutes (or more) or until a toothpick inserted in the center comes out clean. Let the brownies cool completely before cutting, as the almond flour is dense and will fall.

Per Serving:

Calories 221.2
Total Fat 20.1 g
Cholesterol 15.8 mg
Sodium 21.0 mg
Potassium 42.7 mg
Total Carbohydrate 11.8 g
Dietary Fiber 1.7 g
Sugars 1.0 g
Protein 3.6 g

March 14: Five Flavor, Cream Cheese Pound Cake

Yield: 16 servings

Ingredients

- *1 stick light butter
- *1 8-oz. pkg. light cream cheese
- *1 cup xylitol
- 5 eggs at room temperature
- 1 teaspoon baking powder
- 1 teaspoon baking soda
- ½ teaspoon each extract: lemon, coconut, almond, vanilla, and butter
- 3 cups almond flour

  * at room temp

Procedure

1. Preheat oven to 350°F.
2. Cream together top three items.
3. Add eggs one at a time beating well after each addition.
4. Add extracts and blend.
5. Add dry ingredients and mix well.
6. Spray a 9 x 13 inch baking dish or Bundt pan and bake for 50 minutes. Use a toothpick placed in the center to determine if firm. Completely cool before cutting.

Per Serving:

Calories 204.3
Total Fat 16.3 g
Cholesterol 75.3 mg
Sodium 163.7 mg
Potassium 23.1 mg
Total Carbohydrate 12.9 g
Dietary Fiber 1.9 g
Sugars 1.2 g
Protein 6.7

March 15: Finding My Rhythm

Have you ever tried to reason why the concept of being disciplined, for many of us, is such a difficult concept to embrace? Maybe the deep-rooted negative connotations are buried deep within our childhood. I don't know of anyone who loves discipline. But the Bible has a lot to say on the subject, which we will leave for another teaching.

I am disciplined in most areas of my life. I really am. But everyone has that one area that causes the most pain, and mine is knowing what to eat and when to stop. Most of my life I had no control over my appetite. I continued to petition God to reveal to me how I could have discipline in some areas and not in the area that I felt affected all areas of my life—food. How, God, how? The answer does not take a college degree. I did not *want* to be disciplined. It is like needing a shot, but refusing because you hate needles.

Discipline broke free in this area of my life when I set a small goal and promised my brother, Chip, my partner on this journey, that "with God as my witness" I would not cheat once in the forty-two days we established as *the journey*. We made a pact, a promise before God, and I knew it was serious. After those days were checked off, I had every intention of cheating again. Here is my secret weapon to success: I started counting backward *(critical in the journey)* and saying to myself, "I can do anything for forty more days; I can do anything for twenty-seven more days; I can do anything for six more days." That is exactly what I did.

When I finally reached forty-two days, I had lost a great deal of weight and gained a new level of discipline and joy in my life. I discovered that when I denied myself certain things, contained my appetite, pressed down the temptations, and embraced discipline there was a place of joy that I had never experienced in my adult life. Go figure. I know that sounds simple, but it really happened just like that.

Then, once I found my rhythm and could be honest about where I came from, God allowed me to set boundaries around certain foods that cannot be moved. They cannot. I came to understand the value of being disciplined and that I needed it desperately. For the first time in my life being healthy was attainable and staying healthy worth fighting for. That was the beginning of the blogs in April of 2011 and this book is the culmination of that victory dance.

March 16: Life without Sweating

I went to water aerobics last Thursday night. It was a sight. I was determined to not get my hair or my makeup wet. Can anybody go to water aerobics without getting their hair wet? No. But in my trying, I must have conveyed to everyone that I was pitiful, could not swim, and needed a lot of help. In order to "save face and my hair" (I am a very good swimmer, but a prissy one who didn't want to re-straighten her hair that night), I smiled and did all the modifications *so I wouldn't drown.* I was extremely thankful that no one had a hidden camera, but I could not help but laugh at me too.

Let us talk briefly about water aerobics. You now know I was playing a role due to my prissy self, but really the routine in the water was awesome. To me, it was a perfect workout. It was hard (I could hardly move my legs the next two days), but I did not even sweat while working out, burned a ton of calories, and had fun too. Man, I love scenarios like this! The hour went by quickly and while I knew I was working out, my knees never once screamed. Again, big plus for me.

I wish all of life were like water aerobics! The water itself actually shields the force exerted on your body while enhancing the force needed from your muscles to push against the water. What a great thing—all this energy transferring without sweating. Life would be amazing if all our issues were solved without sweating or directly bringing us pain. But that often does not happen in that manner. We have to be willing to endure "whatever" for the sake of a long life laced with great quality.

I also want to remind each of us that when choosing a method of exercise, we do not have to be tortured to reap the benefits. Some people feel because they do not have two hours a day to spend exercising that there's really no need to do it. Not true. My doctors have repeatedly told me to get thirty minutes of exercise at least three days a week for my heart and brain. So I picked an activity that my family loves, and when it is time to head to the pool to *exercise* I ask, "Who wants to swim with Nina?" and the car fills quickly.

March 17: Did My Clothes Shrink?

The spring birds are singing so beautifully and frogs croaking. I wondered if they needed a sweater this past Saturday as the cold wind howled through our city? I must admit I don't know if I have ever heard the bullfrogs croaking in the winter or during the day as much as I have recently. It is so weird that even my husband asked, "Have you ever heard a bullfrog croaking on a cold, winter day?" Well, the only resemblance of that I have is my own voice when I have a sinus situation rolling, but not with the papa frogs. The spring birds started singing in early January and I knew the winter was to be short. But the bullfrogs?

The season of change is coming; are we ready? When I was younger, getting ready for spring meant we would put away our winter clothes. The only problem with packing them was usually my spring wardrobe had shrunk in size from inactivity, I think. Or, maybe mom had washed them all in hot water before they were packed. I have used that excuse on more than one occasion. You? I had to allow myself a calculated window, usually as the spring birds started singing, to have my jaw wired shut so I could quickly shed the Christmas ten. (You know what this is, right?) Unfortunately, I am telling you, the older I get, the earlier those birds sing. So as you can imagine, that train of thought soon imploded.

Several years ago I began to loathe hearing the spring birds, as I knew I had to "face my closet." Isn't that silly? In light of my greater understanding of the world in general, I should have realized if I had enough clothes that I needed to pack some, I had too many. There are people in the world who wear the same clothes daily and I have two closets full! Anyway, this spring is my second one of not dreading the confrontation with my closet. Either I learned to wash clothes correctly, or I learned to keep that mouth shut a little more during the holidays. I would imagine you know which one occurred. This morning as I listen to the birds sing, I can celebrate their efforts. They want me to know some good news and I want you to know some good news. Making health your choice all year means no more closet confrontations (no mirror confrontations either). That is great news for me as I have enough confrontation in places of wickedness.

I don't need to kick my closet in sheer frustration ever again. Praise God!

March 18: I Awakened a Sleeping Giant

I hope you survived the Saint Patty's Day celebrations. I made green velvet brownies (sugar and starch free, of course), which were a huge hit with some funny "after experiences." The green food coloring not only caused the brownies to be green, but other things as well. My son came for the weekend and laughed so hard after eating almost the entire pan of brownies at the "green after effects." Enough said.

I try not to watch horror flicks or movies with huge scary creatures—giants if you will. It disturbs me when the main character approaches one of these monsters who is unaware or sleeping and suddenly the plot takes a drastic turn. It makes me want to grab the character and say, "Don't do something stupid...let sleeping giants sleep!" However, my comments never seem to stop the progression of destruction. Here is what I want us to keep in the center of our choices today—while eating two cookies, our favorite double cheeseburger, or a candy bar may not show up too terribly on tomorrow morning's weigh-in, the greater picture is the awakening of the *sleeping giants* of heart disease, diabetes and other weight-related issues. I could make a list.

These are not possibilities; these are definite issues that bad food and living choices awaken. Regretfully, no one forces us to make those bad choices. We must choose the correct refueling items and leave those food-induced diseases sleeping. Just because my family struggles with cholesterol issues does not mean I have to. My family lived for the next gathering and eating ritual. The more decadent and unhealthy our recipes, the better. We would laugh and pat each other's bellies after stuffing ourselves and make jokes about how fat we were (while our children watched). And yes, I awakened "sleeping giants" and found diabetes, arthritis, reflux, high cholesterol, and high blood pressure had bombed my life and were destroying me.

But God, whose Spirit is bigger than any sleeping giant, gave me the courage to fight back. Losing weight, keeping it off, and choosing to eat right daily keeps these sleeping giants sleeping. We are bodies of flesh and these enemies lurk and wait. Come on family, let's choose health and keep these giants from stealing our lives. We can win this battle. However, we cannot be asleep and look the other way while eating that doughnut and not expect these giants to position themselves for our destruction.

Enjoy the sunshine, add a slice of lime to your water, take a stroll in your neighborhood tonight and continue to affirm yourself by saying, "I am worth it."

March 19: Chain Destruction

"Whatever I tell you in the dark, speak in the light; and what you hear in the ear, preach on the housetops" (Matthew 10:27 NKJV).

This Scripture really spoke to me this morning. There have been seasons of my life where I felt as if God, my family, and my friends had all forsaken me. Those seasons were periods of darkness to me. I felt as if no one really understood how deeply I was hurting. I was totally wrong because God always knew my real heart.

When I first started making a stand for health and was really determined to eradicate certain foods, the breaking of chains was not pleasant. Sometimes hunger would keep me awake at night or during the day. I would be hungry, weak, and a headache would attach itself to the hunger. Imagine that. There were times at restaurants when my favorite foods taunted me in addition to well-meaning friends reminding me that I had never been *really* heavy, that I was just a "big girl with big bones." At first that was easy to accept, but eventually made no difference.

In the past, I had stepped through some chains, jumped around some chains, and dragged some chains. On January 24, 2011, I began the process of chain destruction. And I must be honest, sometimes I felt alone and in darkness. But I was determined to outlast that pocket and win. I had no choice. When awake at night from hunger, God graced me with the ability to pray and listen. As I steadily shattered the daunting hunger during the day, God spoke to me. The longer I endured and displayed my tenacity to never quit again, the weaker the darkness became and eventually it began to dissipate.

I never really understood what that period of darkness really presented to me until I found this Scripture. During those times of intense darkness, God was feeding my resolve and my soul. He was speaking loudly and replacing my hunger with a sustaining word and campaign for health that would be shouted from the housetops. I wonder if you are in a place of darkness in any area of your life today? Instead of feeling forsaken as I did, perhaps consider that God has allowed a period of darkness for you to build His proclamation in you. That happened for me. When I emerged from my prison cell, I could see health finally and was able to speak to God's people concerning the value of health to their bodies as a component of serving Him well for the duration of their lives.

Perspective shift? You bet!

March 20: Chili—Xtreme Low Carb

Yield: 8 servings

Ingredients

- 1.5-2 pounds lean ground beef
- 1 small onion
- 2 large cans organic, diced fire roasted tomatoes
- 1 container portabella mushrooms
- 1 large bunch cilantro, de-flowered and chopped fine
- Seasonings: salt, pepper, garlic powder, onion powder, chili powder, red pepper flakes, paprika, cumin, jalapeño powder

Procedure

1. Brown the meat and add the onion. Cook until onion is tender.
2. Add the seasonings and the chopped cilantro.
3. Add the canned tomatoes and cook for about 90 minutes on medium heat until some of the liquid is reduced.

Per Serving:

Calories 324.1
Total Fat 19.4 g
Cholesterol 78.2 mg
Sodium 857.6 mg
Potassium 397.3 mg
Total Carbohydrate 14.0 g
Dietary Fiber 2.1 g
Sugars 7.5 g
Protein 21.9 g

March 21: Italian-Style Meatballs

Yield: 30 servings

These may be added to your spaghetti sauce or after cooled, frozen for another project. I like to use them from the freezer in a crock-pot with grape jelly (all fruit type –no sugar) and sugar-free BBQ sauce. You can place the meatballs in first, cover with BBQ sauce and then grape jelly. I cook them for a couple of hours on high until the sauce and jelly have melted and combined. I continue to stir and mix until ready to serve.

Ingredients

- 2 pounds lean ground beef
- 1 onion (finely chopped)
- ½ cup almond flour
- 2 large eggs
- ½ teaspoon sea salt
- ½ teaspoon garlic powder
- ½ teaspoon fresh, ground pepper
- 1 cup Parmesan Reggiano cheese
- 3 cloves garlic, minced well
- 1 teaspoon tarragon
- 1 teaspoon thyme

Procedure

1. Preheat oven to 350°F.
2. Mix all ingredients well.
3. Form into small balls.
4. Place on a large baking sheet lined with parchment paper, which has been lightly sprayed.
5. Bake for 45 minutes. Depending on the size of your meatballs, the time will vary. Continue to pull one apart with a fork until well done.

Per Serving:

Calories 95.9
Total Fat 6.8 g
Cholesterol 34.2 mg
Sodium 48.4 mg
Potassium 111.5 mg
Total Carbohydrate 1.4 g
Dietary Fiber 0.4 g
Sugars 0.1 g
Protein 7.2 g

March 22: A Liquid Brownie

I love it when everyone in the family wants the same thing to eat at a meal. It is so much easier. And even though I prefer for everyone to eat healthy, sometimes not all of my family is willing (we are still working on that). In those times, again, I have to remember as I make the mashed potatoes with cream and butter that freedom does not look the same for everyone and I am not the controller of the universe. Sometimes my husband wants something that I cannot eat; I have to be okay with that. His past isn't mine.

When I first began my journey, there were foods I had to bring to the *altar of sacrifice*. You know that place of grieving as you accept the realization that this item must die? I knew there were foods that needed to be sacrificed, but does that mean my eyes were sacrificed as well? Certainly not. I still see the bread and dipping oil at my favorite Italian restaurant. And even though I look at it and proclaim, "Beets," it is still bread and oil (ever tried that?). I would love to claim permanent amnesia concerning some of my previous life's recipes, but go figure, I still remember how to make real brownies. That can present a challenge. My solution follows.

If a food choice that someone wants is really in my old, favorite group, then I often buy it. I do not make it from scratch any longer. Just recently I tried making brownies for an event, real ones, and a wrestling match took place in my kitchen between the spoon and my mouth. "Maybe it's okay to lick the beaters or the spoon, as there is not too much left in the bowl after being scraped. After all, one taste won't matter. Right?"

In my old life I made certain there was at least one brownie's worth of material remaining in the bowl that I could consume and tell myself I had not eaten a brownie. *Oops, so they don't count if they're not cooked, right?* You know the answer. The real dilemma, as I see it, is—are we strong enough to make the brownies and then wash the beaters, bowl, and our fingers immediately so none of it enters our mouth and causes us to trip?

Am I the only crazy one in this family? Are you laughing at me or with me? If your family needs a real brownie, buy enough for that meal and make yourself a small pan of almond flour ones. Or, if you are not a bowl licker, go for it. I would rather not toss that coin in the air as I have a 50-50 chance of losing.

Have a great day and remember, our past may remind us of weakness, but it doesn't mean we are weak. I am strong through Christ.

March 23: Bloopers

I love watching the end of some movies or the bloopers posted from certain shows. They are raw and uncut. I think it's good to really see the nature and actual person of the character I've been watching. Most of the movie or video displays are controlled and practiced segments. Some of these segments have been filmed and re-filmed up to one hundred times for a thirty second segment. There are several insights that can be gleaned from this truth:

1. Perfection takes time and energy

2. Life happens.

Real life really happens and it does not matter how long I walk this health journey, I still have times when my past life of failures on the healthy trail want to manifest.

I was sitting at a nice lunch with a group of people one Sunday and the hostess had prepared a meal with several things which allowed me to eat. I went prepared just in case, but she knows me and planned a couple of things specifically with me in mind that were great. Then she announced, "However, I have no sugar-free dessert." I smiled and answered, "It's okay, I brought an apple." That is the movie version with all smiles and a beautiful response. No worries. *Blooper number one.*

Then she starts stirring a big bowl of brownies with decadent chocolate and pecan pieces. Yes, then I really smile. "You're not bothered by all this, right?" she inquired. "No, no... never," I respond. *Blooper number two.*

I could imagine myself licking that bowl, her finger, and the spoon. Sound familiar? But the amazing part of this story is that I *really* understand I cannot. I would love to say, "Aw, I never want chocolate again." That would be lying. When those brownies came out and were served hot with chocolate chip ice cream to everyone at the table but me, I had to practice my labor and delivery breathing. *Blooper number three.*

What was going on in my head as a smile eked from my face? Torture. Then, I remembered the apple in the car and finally settled back to enjoy my coffee and stuff napkins up my nose so I could pass the plates without licking each one. *Blooper number four.*

But that is the real me. I did get to the car, eat my apple, and feel such a sense of relief that again God had helped me face a real issue and real feelings with His real strength.

So while I was rolling a blooper in my mind, the crowd was watching the film. The ending turned out great in spite of the blooper I was viewing. So how about you? Any bloopers lately? It is okay...remember we are walking this journey together. I had to endure thirty minutes of watching everyone eat those brownies and giggle, but it saved me from twenty-four hours of guilt and shame. And let me tell you, those self-loathing, long mirror talks I used to have were a blooper to behold.

March 24: To Drink or Not to Drink?

As most of you know, one of our health imperatives is water and more water. However, sometimes I feel the consumption of water will simply be the death of me. How about you? I can assure you, if you're stuck at the scales, pull back on the calories and throttle the water.

Recently I had a friend who discovered blood clots in both lungs. We knew something was wrong as his breathing was compromised and he was so tired. Lack of oxygen—possibly, but we didn't know why. Here is what we discovered. His blood was thicker than it was supposed to be and one of the doctor's first directives was increased hydration. They suggested that every thirty minutes he needed to be up, walking, and hydrating himself. That is a lot of hydration pockets during the day. It is better, however, than promoting the formation of blood clots.

While I am certain we are in agreement that water is critical to our health, I am pleased to discover *early* how critical hydration is in the process of keeping our blood flowing and at the correct consistency. When our blood is thicker than normal, it causes our heart to have to pump harder to circulate that thick blood, and then an enlarged heart can develop as well as a host of other serious maladies.

I used to laugh and tell people, "I'm not fat, just thick." In this case, both can cause our lives to be affected. If you look at the real value of water to our health, it's probably the most critical key. Our planet is 75 percent water, our body is 75 percent water, and then somehow we get confused and convince ourselves that we "don't like the taste of water and therefore we don't consume any during the day." This is really not about whether we enjoy drinking water; I don't.

When I pick up my water bottle I make myself take ten to twelve gulps at a time. I also try to not drink anything else until I have met my water requirement for the day. But after hearing my friend's report, I start repeating over and over, "I will drink all my water; I will drink all my water; I will drink all my water." Grab your water bottle, keep it close, and set that timer. Let us move and drink every thirty minutes.

We could create a little dance routine. Ah, a fresh idea with which to play.

March 25: God Feeds the Sparrows

When I sat down to write today it was late because I had gotten sidetracked reading in preparation for my trip to Thailand at the end of this month. I was moved by vast and raw emotions as every chapter of the book I was required to read before departure that detailed the lives of suffering children who were trapped in the clutches of human trafficking. After reading one of the chapters and re-reading the lead Scripture from Isaiah 61, I was gripped and said to the Lord, "I am honored that You would send me to smile and touch these children. Help me, God, to prepare my heart to see as You see and love as You love."

I must confess, though, I have been worried about several things concerning my trip, one of which is what to eat and how to prepare for meals in a country that I have never visited. After reading this morning of the food journeys of these children, I felt horrible for even worrying about something so insignificant. You know that I stand on the pillar of being prepared, but there are times when preparation cannot override the mission to which God has called us. I know that food is our fuel, but it can also be our sole passion and consuming thought. We can quickly get out of balance.

I remember the years when I used to plan two days of meals at a time and get everything lined up so I would not miss a meal, as that would only cause me to go into *starvation mode*. What a joke. No, food was my passion, and I simply fueled that passion with a lie. I'm being honest here. It is perfectly okay to have foods prepared and ready so we are not being scavengers and falling prey to the peanut butter, but preparation cannot be our every waking thought. Our thoughts and passion cannot focus on our food. For years that was a huge distraction for me.

Now I plan for the week, cook for the week, have my food ready, and don't spend time worrying about meals. It is such a freedom pocket! Whatever is in the refrigerator is getting cooked, and when it runs out I will return to the store. God's Word instructs us not to worry. It does not say do not plan. Big difference.

God clothes and feeds the lilies and the birds, and it brings Him pleasure to take care of us. So today, plan and get things ready, then let go of the stress and worry of "doing it right, finding the right combination, and eating enough fruit." Do the math, get the right quantities, eat the right portions, and enjoy your life and family more. That concept is so freeing to me. I hope it brings a smile to you as well.

March 26: The Voice of German Chocolate Cake

Holidays and social gatherings with family and friends bring many opportunities to cook new things, bake, and drink hot coffee, which for me are crazy fun. Some days, however, all these additional social gatherings get me off track. That might seem odd as I have never wavered in the past several years, but I am a "stick to the plan" girl, so when I socialize I must maintain the portions and balance I have established.

I used to reason, "On days when I choose to consume a piece of healthy German chocolate cake, I cannot eat my fruits or all my vegetables. After all, the cake does contain calories and there are only so many calories this body can handle in one day." I would actually substitute one for the other. And, while the taste of German chocolate cake trumps lettuce any day in my book, this plan is not good. It may work for a holiday meal or other special event *for a minute*, but we must always return to protocol.

Our body needs a certain number of calories each day for fuel, but it requires the correct fuel to function properly. Our bodies need lean protein, fruits, vegetables, and healthy fats (in the right proportions) daily to feed our cells. Could you imagine only feeding our children meat and baked goods? They wouldn't be very healthy or live productive lives. Are we any different? No. While some foods are *legal*, they must climb aboard our plan, serve our purpose, and offer our cells life. If my food choices cannot comply, then I have to make some tough choices and they will lose.

My taste must come second to my health. It took me a long time to get here, but I refuse to allow disease to strangle the life out of me again.

German chocolate cake, I can partake of you in combination with my protein and vegetables for a day or two. After that, you will not make the line-up until I have had many days of successfully followed protocol. Then, I will send you a postcard and invite you to my party. But, *I* am the one sending the invitations. You may call, but I choose to ignore you.

March 27: Steamed Cabbage with Onions and Bacon

Yield: 12 servings

Ingredients

- 1 pound bacon with no sugar or corn syrup added (difficult to locate, but I did)
- 1 large Vidalia onion
- 1 large head of cabbage
- 2 cups chicken stock and water to cover the cabbage by half
- Salt and pepper to taste

Procedure

1. Cook the bacon in a large, heavy container on the stove (medium heat).
2. Remove the bacon (reserve) and dispose of the grease. Add a tablespoon of olive oil.
3. Add the onions and sauté until they are tender and browning.
4. Add the chopped cabbage. (I prefer mine moderately chopped as opposed to large chunks.)
5. Add the chicken stock, as well as the salt and pepper.
6. Continue to cook on medium heat until tender. I cover the pot while cooking and remove the lid the last 10 minutes so remaining liquid will evaporate (this is not a soup but a side dish, so you want the chicken stock to reduce and evaporate).
7. Before serving, crumble the reserved bacon and sprinkle on the top.
8. Serve hot with the grilled meat of your choice.

Per Serving:
Calories 50.7
Total Fat 1.9 g
Cholesterol 3.5 mg
Sodium 229.6 mg
Potassium 362.0 mg
Total Carbohydrate 6.9 g
Dietary Fiber 2.6 g
Sugars 0.2 g
Protein 4.6 g

March 28: Stewed Apple and Blueberry Crumble

Yield: 12 servings

Ingredients

- 6 medium apples, I prefer Honeycrisp
- 1 pint blueberries
- ½ stick light butter
- 1 bottle black raspberry flavored water (optional) OR 1 cup water
- 2 tablespoons pumpkin pie spice
- 1 teaspoon lemon extract
- 2 cups almond flour (topping)
- 1 cup xylitol (topping)
- ½ stick light butter (topping)
- 1 cup chopped pecans (topping)

Procedure

1. Preheat oven to 400°F.
2. Core and spiral the apples. Place in a large Dutch oven on the stove.
3. Add the blueberries, ½ stick of butter, water, xylitol, and pumpkin spice.
4. Bring to a boil and then lower the heat until the liquid reduces and thickens well.
5. Place stewed fruit in 9x9 baking dish sprayed with butter flavor spray (coat well as this is sticky).
6. Assemble the crust: Crumb flour, 1/2 stick of butter, and xylitol.
7. Cover top of stewed apples by pressing into the fruit mixture.
8. Sprinkle with additional pumpkin pie spice (optional, but encouraged).
9. Top with pecans.
10. Bake for 40-45 minutes or until the juice is bubbling through the crust, around the edges, and in the center. This is a rich dessert, but very tasty.

Per Serving:
Calories 283.3
Total Fat 18.4 g
Cholesterol 10.0 mg
Sodium 75.8 mg
Potassium 178.3 mg
Total Carbohydrate 34.9 g
Dietary Fiber 6.4 g
Sugars 13.4 g
Protein 5.3 g

March 29: Visitors

I love when people come to my house for a visit. The term *Hospitality Queen* comes to mind here. I love planning, cleaning, and cooking for the masses; it's basic Hospitality 101. I have always prepared large quantities of food in preparation for anyone who *might* arrive for dinner. This notion is a carry over from my teen years where my brother's friends could arrive at any time and were big eaters, as most teenage boys are. However, extra food meant we always had plenty for the meal, extra for lunches if needed, and a remnant for every dog and cat in the neighborhood (you might guess they were all pleasingly plump).

I wonder if planning for guests had anything to do with my unhealthy portion sizes? I am not certain, but blaming something other than me allows a smile for a second. Have you ever blamed someone for your unhealthy lifestyle? While planning for guests to eat at your table is important, accepting *guests* to the scale is not.

It is amazing to me how we conveniently plan and make room for those extra *visitors* to come into our lives for holidays. I honestly know people who plan to gain ten pounds each year from Halloween to January 1st. They speak of this with a laugh and acceptance that makes me shake my head. For me, I never planned for them. I never weighed, so that meant I wasn't accountable for the *guests*.

As I said earlier, I love guests; but a guest is not usually expected to become a legal resident in my house. And, if they need to stay longer than planned, they are expected to submit to the journey of my life and my family. Gaining weight and trying to "pet those pounds" (as if they were a new kitten) can be a monster in the closet. We cannot allow *those* guests to become legal residents.

How do we avoid this? Every morning we must force ourselves to have an honest discussion with our accountability partner—the scale. Sometimes I would weigh myself three times, stand on the corners, and balance on one foot. Ever tried any of those to justify the allowance of your unwanted *guests*? Stupid scale, right?

Moral of the story: never pet the extra *guests* that arrive around certain holidays begging for clothes and a space to live. They have an agenda. They take you places you never planned to go and make you stay longer than you planned.

March 30: The Broccoli IV

Don't you love commercials? I am watching a football game currently and a fairy is asking a family to make their favorite wishes and she will grant them. The wife says to the fairy, "I wish I could eat all the chocolate I wanted." Then poof...she finds herself standing in front of the doctor who is reading her blood reports and informs her that "her chocolate levels are dangerously low and she needs a chocolate transfusion." You immediately see an IV bag filled with chocolate as they are preparing to transfuse the wife. I do not believe in fairies, but I certainly smiled and allowed myself to "be the mom in that vision" for a few seconds. Am I the only one who wishes that sometimes life were that easy? Am I the only one who needs a chocolate IV occasionally?

I have the answer. Anytime I am having that fantasy, I am always capable of baking a pan of sugar-free brownies or making a sugar-free hot chocolate with cocoa and Truvia®. I have to stop the whining and start the cooking. Chocolate IV's are simple, but so is a pan of brownies. Stop now and find a new recipe in this book that you haven't cooked yet, gather the supplies, and smile as you realize you can have the apple and the brownie if you are willing to make a healthy version.

I am a stickler for food tasting good, as well as being appealing to my eyes. My mom was always an amazing cook (she still is) so my love of cooking comes from the great memories she offered me as a child. Mom always made our meals an adventure and I am grateful that she filled our home with the smell of yummy things. I find I am passing this legacy to my daughter and granddaughters. But now my heart's desire is to see my girls not only embrace the art of cooking, but the foods I know bring health to our bodies.

All of us love the chocolate IV, but how about the broccoli IV? Maybe we love to cook, but do we love to cook the correct foods? We *can* change and we *can* leave a legacy for our children and grandchildren so that if asked by the TV fairy for a wish to be granted, they will ask for broccoli.

March 31: March Reflection Page

As you are completing March, are there things you wish you had highlighted or which you had written down? Spring is coming and shorts and bathing suits are right around the corner. But we are prepared and ready. Bring it on!

_____

_____

_____

_____

_____

_____

_____

_____

_____

_____

_____

_____

_____

_____

_____

_____

_____

_____

April

April showers bring May flowers, right? How about spa waters bringing color to our cheeks and life to our skin. That's a big "yes."

April 1: All Things in Moderation?

As we approach Easter, it is a time for celebration once again and that normally means a large family gathering. I love opportunities to have a meal with my family, and Easter, with its warmer temperatures, offers a lot of possibilities. However, Easter is another holiday that finds itself in the back pocket of sugared Easter eggs, chocolate Easter bunnies, marshmallow chicks, and a list of candies all decorated to celebrate this special occasion. I am not opposed to celebrating holidays, so please don't hear that. However, I am seriously frustrated that every month another batch of chocolates and sweets finds themselves at the end of each aisle and the front counters by the registers, calling loudly to our babies who have no idea of their real agenda.

I was describing to someone yesterday at church that changing to a healthy style of eating brought my blood sugar down 120 points and keeps it there. He asked, "Really? Is that really true?" Oh my goodness, yes. Type 2 diabetes, in most cases, can be controlled with diet. In fact, a lot of our health issues can be controlled with diet. Maybe more than we think. I know someone who has overcome Type 1 diabetes with a food shift. It can be done. Not easily, but I have personally witnessed this.

Sometimes, though, there is so much information that we are not certain what to believe. It often appears that one camp contradicts the other. Some promote meat and others deny it. Some allow sugar and all carbs while other plans restrict or eliminate the use of either. All things in moderation or some things need to remain untouched? Who knows which path is best?

There are numerous alternative, healthy food choices now and *living* in a health-conscious world is definitely attainable. I noticed at a meal we provided recently at church that the baked chicken went first while there was fried chicken remaining. I was shocked. And the mac and cheese was left over while the green beans were totally consumed. That speaks volumes to me. I told my pastor, "We need to start rethinking our menu for events." Maybe we *all* need to reconsider our events and offer to plan the menus to reflect the changing trend.

Healthy living is happening all around us. You are reading this book, making changes, and becoming a trendsetter. I applaud you! Keep reminding yourself you are worth the struggle. I would rather wrestle with hunger than fight cancer. How about you?

April 2: Enduring the Cross

I have been reading this morning about Jesus preparing for His final week upon the earth. While He was a man acquainted with sorrow, He was also a man who was filled with joy in the core of His being. The Bible says in Hebrews 12:2, *"for the joy* that was set before Him [He] endured the cross" (NKJV). Have you ever really considered what joy that would be? That joy would be you; that would be me.

Jesus' mission upon the earth was to seek and save the lost. His crucifixion was one of the necessary components to fulfilling His mission. I would imagine the only joy one could experience at such a time would flow from a sense of obedience to the will of God. I also feel, when Jesus thought of enduring this week, our names were in His core, and when He saw us free, joy welled inside of Him. His sacrifice would not be in vain. Our salvation was His purpose. But I believe that our freedom is deeper than just escaping eternal punishment. I believe that Jesus' enduring of the cross offers freedom from our torment, diseases, weaknesses, guilt, iniquity, and pains (see Isaiah 53).

I believe Jesus' death gave me the opportunity to choose health as part of my freedom package. That brings tears to my eyes. There is a price for freedom and a value that we often disregard. Jesus saw us free and endured. I love that thought. As I receive that challenge, I realize that my freedom from obesity contains a high value. While I am now free from the torment of fifty years of unhealthy living, I am not free to return to my past eating habits. Returning to my past ways removes the value from the sacrifice of freedom. Freedom is not cheap, and my health is more valuable than my past failures.

Jesus endured for our freedom and we are His prize. That brought Him joy. Remember, your sacrifice to live healthy could give your family and friends the hope and courage they need to fight for their own health. Does that bring *you* joy? It does me.

Watch the chocolate Easter bunnies and jelly beans. Choose the food of the bunnies (carrots and lettuce) as well as the beans, minus the jelly. Enduring means to continue or last a long time. For us, that means that we continue our often sacrificial journey for the joy of living well for a very long time.

April 3: Say Yes to the Plan

In the Garden of Gethsemane, the Bible recounts a very transparent question posed from Jesus to God. Jesus had seen men be crucified. He absolutely knew the cost of following God's plan. Was there another way? Was there another plan? This journey was initiated before the establishment of the earth and Jesus was well acquainted with the strategy. Without Jesus' journey and sacrifice, we had no hope.

Our health journey is not often easy. Being hungry, denying our flesh, fighting for our health at parties when no one cares, falling down, and being confronted with options that are often easier can all make the journey intolerable at times. I'm convinced there is that moment for each of us where the battle for our health is so intense and choosing life or death becomes a reality. At that point, our submission to God's plan for our health needs to be "not my will but Yours be done," and we never look back.

That date occurred for me on January 24, 2011. I finally came to the place in my heart where death to my flesh and my old excuses were no longer an option. I know this is incomparable to the garden experience for Jesus, and yet in a small way it allows me deeper insight. Are there some of you who need a garden experience? It is certainly not fun and requires the ultimate submission, which is death to our flesh. However, when I submitted to God's best plan for my health I gained *life*.

My prayer is that you stop the discussion phase with your flesh and have that real garden experience. This is a great week to say goodbye to certain things forever. On the other side of total submission, with no escape and try-again routes, there *is* life. Make your list of things that must die, lay them down, find a strong accountability partner who will not give in when you need a candy fix, start eating healthy every day whether you feel like it or not, and start living as a healthy, free person. God's plan is best and gives us our best chance of long, healthy years to serve Him.

Say yes to the plan!

April 4: The Weight of Jealousy

I have a friend who announced to me every time I saw her, "Hello, my name is Cheryl, and I am losing one hundred pounds." She made this proclamation for almost an entire year as we walked closely together. She never gave up and never gave in. I know that her faithfulness and tenacity will eventually get her to the size and health status she has established for herself. I am confident in her resolve. I rejoice this morning to know she is about to do that "final victory dance." Well done, my friend! That gives all of us hope, doesn't it?

When people's victories can give you hope, you are in a good place. Sometimes when I was struggling, someone's victory only made me jealous and I would eat to cover the pain. That is my honest confession. Jealousy is a terrible, torturing giant. I hate to admit that, but maybe it gives you a place to be honest as well. It is not that I was unhappy for others, but I was so angry with myself and unwilling to do what was necessary to make a change. Jealousy, for me, was an additional bar on the cell door. I was angry about being unhealthy as well as jealous, which were intolerable weights dragging the joy from every area of my life. Not good!

The ability to be healthy lives within us all. I am certain of that confession. However, I never realized this fully until I embraced a health plan that was not simply a fad. Living well takes courage and determination. Once those elements are secure, a passion to really live begins to grow. Living beyond the pain of simple existence brings such bliss to me now. I never knew life could be so fun. I desired and longed for a life I thought only existed in my dreams. I am no longer dreaming, and being healthy is now my reality.

God helped me realize that jealousy *never* solved my problem. In fact, it only compounded the hurt. I was jealous of so many, and their success was another reminder of my failure. The truth is that jealousy never moved the scale one ounce in my favor, but always in a direction I hated. Today, when I feel jealousy trying to make an entrance again, I remind myself of the victories from the past several years and that the enormous weight of this sin is not one I will carry. I don't have to be a smaller size than others, and there is plenty of room on the health trail for everyone. Victory looks different on different people. I am finally okay with that.

April 5: Fighting Forward

I do not think in any of the seasons we see the signs of change as vividly as from winter to spring. This year, the spring birds were singing, the warm January temperatures prompted the flowers to peek their heads through the soil, and the trees started budding early. I shook my head and said to the flowers, "You're going to freeze when those 'ole winds and bitter temperatures return. These weeks are just tying to fool you." But none of them listened.

As I went outside yesterday, the hyacinths were standing beautifully, and while I love them, cold weather is quickly returning. They will soon fall and that is sad to me. Do they not watch the weather announcers? Anyway, when they emerge from the solid winter ground, as everything else lies dormant, it appears they know something I do not. Is spring closer than I think? Are the early announcers making a declaration? I don't really count the "vote" of the groundhog in this group, as he is prompted by one single moment in time. But the other signs, they come forth confidently and announce, "It is time for life."

I see the spring announcers' quiet confidence and regardless of how the weather goes, they never waiver. They have had a "taste" of their starting season and they know the plan. They are not afraid to keep pushing forward nor do they care that I bring the warning of bad weather returning in three days. They seem to be untouched by my concern.

As I watched the spring announcers this year, I gained insight from their displays:

1. Know when it is your season to flourish. For us, our season of health is now.

2. Once you commit to life, let nothing keep you from *fighting forward*. For us, there may be a bad weigh-in or a spring storm with the hail, but as the hyacinths, you might be down a minute but stand up quickly.

3. Be determined to have your announcement heard. For us, don't be afraid to smile and say, "I only eat foods that bring life to my body these days."

4. Be grateful that you are choosing health and you can see yourself emerging from death. Remind yourself of the color and sound the spring announcers convey. Your journey benefits you greatly, but you can rest assured your fight for life will bless others who may never tell you.

It is your season to flourish. Proclaim well.

April 6: Dessert Pizza

Yield: 12 servings

Ingredients (Crust)

- 2 cups almond flour
- 2 tablespoons oil
- ½ teaspoon salt
- 2 eggs
- 1 tablespoon half/half
- ½ teaspoon lemon extract
- 1 cup xylitol

Procedure

1. Whisk well all of the ingredients except the almond flour, but don't over beat the eggs.
2. Add the almond flour and stir until well mixed. It will form a sticky ball. Refrigerate for 30-45 minutes.
3. Preheat oven to 350°F.
4. Cover a regular-sized pizza pan with parchment paper and spray the top with cooking spray. When the dough is cooled and ready, lightly grease hands and gently press crust mixture onto parchment paper. Bake for 25 minutes. Remove from oven and cool for 60-90 minutes. Leave the crust on the pan as you complete the recipe.
5. Frost the top of the cooled crust with the cream cheese topping. If you like a deeper cream cheese topping, double the recipe below.
6. Arrange fruit on top of cream cheese topping.
7. Chill for about one hour, cut into 12 slices, and serve.

Cream cheese topping:

- 8 oz. light cream cheese
- ¾ cup xylitol
- ½ lemon extract
- Beat well with mixer until smooth.

Fruit topping:

Dice strawberries, blueberries and kiwi and layer on the cream cheese topping. For Christmas, consider only strawberries or pomegranate and kiwi.

Per Serving:
(for crust, cream cheese, and three fruits listed)
Calories 273.2
Total Fat 17.0 g
Cholesterol 45.1 mg
Sodium 95.8 mg
Potassium 143.6 mg
Total Carbohydrate 33.2 g
Dietary Fiber 4.1 g
Sugars 6.4 g
Protein 7.0 g

April 7: Quiche

Yield: 8 servings

For the crust, I use my almond flour pizza dough recipe found on page 132 (minus the herbs I mix into the base). I usually make two of these at a time. Make sure to allow the crust to cool. After cooling the dough in the refrigerator for about 45 minutes, press into a deep-dish pie pan. Bake at 400°F for approximately 25 minutes or until really golden brown, but not burned, then proceed with the recipe below, which is based on 2 pies.

Ingredients

- 1 pound 93% low fat ground beef
- 3 oz. chopped ham, no sugar, low carb
- 4 large eggs
- ½ pkg. Swiss cheese slices
- 2 cups 2% skim mozzarella cheese
- 1 cup milk
- 1 cup fresh ground Parmesan Reggiano cheese
- 1 medium onion, chopped small
- Salt and pepper to taste

Procedure

1. Preheat oven to 400°F.
2. Brown the ground beef and onions and drain any excess fat. Divide evenly between the 2 pies.
3. Mix all the remaining ingredients except ½ cup of the Parmesan cheese.
4. Divide evenly between the two pies.
5. Sprinkle with the reserved Parmesan.
6. Bake a for approximately 35-45 minutes. Watch to make certain the top doesn't get too brown. Check the center with a toothpick. It should come out clean when the pie has cooked thoroughly. They taste better when allowed to cool for about 30 minutes prior to slicing.

Per Serving:

(Includes the crust and filling)
Calories 608.9
Total Fat 45.6 g
Cholesterol 230.4 mg
Sodium 660.8 mg
Potassium 407.0 mg
Total Carbohydrate 11.5 g
Dietary Fiber 3.4 g
Sugars 2.4 g
Protein 40.6 g

April 8: Take a Number

"But despite Jesus' instructions, the report of his power spread even faster, and vast crowds came to hear him preach and to be healed of their diseases. But Jesus often withdrew to the wilderness for prayer" (Luke 5:15-16 NLT).

You know I have spoken several times about the importance of rest in our health journey. Your cells can only reproduce fully when you are at complete rest, and this usually occurs while you are asleep. I know that "a good night's sleep" is foreign to many of us as we all live tremendously busy lives. Let us be honest, sometimes there is nothing that can be done about our busyness. If we each took a sheet of paper and started listing the things which needed our attention daily and their specific time requirements, most of us would soon discover there are more items than time in the day. That monster will wreak havoc on your health success.

I thought teaching eighth graders was a challenge, and some days it was. But pastoring can be overwhelming as well, as people's lives never stop. I love what the Lord allows me to do daily, but it is a busy pace. Maybe your daily routine is like this? Wouldn't it be nice if when we returned home, there were no more items on the "to do" list? I wish someone would institute an "*if* I want to do" list so those type A people like me could smile at their list and sleep with items still unchecked.

Was Jesus busy? If we consider the above passage, the answer is most definitely yes. How did Jesus handle being busy? According to the passage, not only did Jesus withdraw from the busyness, He did it often. I need to remind myself on a regular basis that no one can withdraw for me and the dishes can wait. I had a pastor once who told me, "Make those problems take a number and limit the number you tackle daily." That was great advice. Can I pass that along?

Jesus rested, the birds rest, our cells rest, and we need to rest. As passionate as I am about food, I am equally as passionate about rest. If we don't rest, we cannot complain when our body begins to rebel. Tell those issues of life to "take a number."

April 9: God's Crook

As I said in an earlier devotion, this Easter I am pondering life beyond the cross. Jesus didn't simply die to give us eternal life, but abundant freedom in this life as well. I am always saddened when people speak of the victory of heaven as if this earth only offers defeat. That is not what God's Word teaches.

I love the 23rd Psalm and memorized it as a young person in church. Recently, I continued to quote a particular portion from that verse,

> "Even though I walk
>   through the darkest valley,
> I will not be afraid,
>   for you are close beside me.
> Your rod and your staff
>   they comfort me" (Psalm 23:4 NLT).

I must have repeated this portion of the passage five times, and each time I felt stronger. I know a shepherd's rod and a shepherd's staff serve different functions with equal importance. I wonder, though, how many sheep feel comforted by them? We know God desires to walk with each of us daily as a Good Shepherd would, but I think that as our heavenly Father, He especially desires this in the toughest times of our lives when we cannot see the peril ahead. God wants us to rest assured that He is walking the journey with us no matter how difficult. We are not abandoned children trying to find our way.

For some, making decisions to stop eating as they please is a tough valley. But God's love and His help are always present. Consider this: what if He is using the scales, your blood reports, your participation in our health family, or the tightness of your clothes as the hook of His staff to keep you from walking off the cliff when we would easily give up? Maybe God placed us on this journey *together* for a definite reason? God's Word teaches that God's thoughts are not mine. I don't know that God uses the scale as part of His crook-system, but it could be a possibility. I am certain that God uses things in our lives in ways we could never understand.

I want you to understand this: God's crook will never allow you to fall beyond where His hand can draw you back to a safe place. Rest in that assurance and feel comforted by the truth of Psalm 23. Be especially grateful that even in that valley God is there. And remember while you may feel you are in a health valley, the mountains are your borders. Look up and start climbing. You can reach the top before you know it.

April 10: The Arrival of Hail

Hailstorms make a statement don't they? They don't come often, but when they arrive, they grab our attention.

My family was having dinner last night and as soon as we heard the fierce hail striking the house, it felt like we became characters in the old Christmas story as we quickly arose from the table to see what was the matter. Actually we were scrambling and running around like a cat that had its tail caught in something. I laughed out loud and screamed as we leapt with our phones to take photos, make video clips, and even open the door to gather pieces of the ice in our hands. If you had watched the scene, we could have been your evening entertainment. Have you ever done this before?

Hail basically exists because it endures a very turbulent procedure but eventually (after being kicked around over and over and turned upside down repeatedly) gains enough stamina and structure to fall through the turbulence and arrive in a unique, round shape at its destination. Let's not concentrate on the destruction for a moment, but on the victory of being formed under intense conditions and outlasting the opposition. Hail arrives because it endured. I want us to arrive at the final stage of our life and smile because we know against all odds we endured. The storms, the ice, the turbulence, and the wind can be destructive forces, can't they? But each of them has their place in God's plan. Sometimes we don't understand why the elements of nature do what they do. Would understanding help? Maybe. There are times when we can't outrun the hail; but we must endure and know that the sun will return.

I want to encourage you to get back in the storm of life. When hail arrives, it makes a statement. When you *arrive* as a healthy person, finally committed to the process regardless of the end that you cannot see now, you make a statement too. Healthy people challenge the status quo. They confront the lie that says aging and sickness are co-laborers. Let that be said of each of us.

April 11: Denying the Truth

I was studying this morning about spiritual fruit as I am preparing to teach tonight at our mid-week service. As you know, there is both good and bad fruit. The condition of the fruit is evidence of internal core strength. We are familiar with the verses in Galatians 5 that describe the evidence and life of the Holy Spirit displayed for all to see. I often say, "This passage is my measuring rod." I do not necessarily like having to measure my life and attitudes against these, but it keeps me accountable.

On our journey, our *fruit* is healthy weight loss, good blood reports, increased energy, a happy attitude, and much more. These things reflect, or indicate, what we are submitting to our bodies on a daily basis. They are the outward evidence to us, and others, that good things are happening. But when we choose to fill our inward parts (stomachs) with things that we know do not lead to great health, there is evidence of that as well. I doubt you need a visual.

I think God established this system, as He knew how weak I would be. I need evidence to help keep me accountable. For me, the basics of being happy about my clothes fitting and not feeling as if I have to hide under layers is a real boost. I refuse to be fueled by comparing my size to others, but I am stoked by the fact that I no longer feel *I need to hide*. A layer of clothes for me was my way of concealing the evidence that I placed bad things in my body on a regular basis.

Evidence is evidence, unfortunately, whether confirming or denying. I tried to convince myself that eating one cheeseburger was not bad. In fact, I could have eaten two. But my clothes displayed a different opinion, as did my blood work. At that point, I had a choice to deny the truth or embrace it. Denying the truth doesn't keep it from being true. Does it?

Let us choose today to allow the evidence of our healthy choices to announce we are embracing health for all to see. Have you inspected your fruit lately?

April 12: If You Make No Plan, You Plan to Fail

Matthew 6:34 (MSG) says, "Give your entire attention to what God is doing right now, and don't get worked up about what may or may not happen tomorrow. God will help you deal with whatever hard things come up when the time comes."

For me, I make a weekly plan and purchase the necessary foods to accomplish that plan. I make a plan for restaurant adventures and I definitely have a plan in place when navigating a party or family gathering. Planning assures that I am not worrying about what happens; I control that. I realize for some of us, making a plan comes easy and for others, not so much. However, I am a firm believer that you really can teach "an old dog new tricks" if the dog still wants to learn. That would be me.

Worrying about upcoming events, in a sense, announces that you have allowed a chance for failure. When I first became healthy, I must admit I did worry about food situations. I think because I had never successfully been healthy and the fear of failure brought worry to my doorstep. The fear of failure is nasty, but I have discovered that establishing a solid plan and eliminating paths to my past have diminished its bite as well as the voices of the worry people.

People were worried that I could not go to Europe, eat healthy, and walk through a German bakery. It became a personal challenge to have a concrete plan in place before leaving, and I did it. I was determined that I would not allow worry or fear of failure to rob me of this wonderful adventure. I did journey inside the bakeries and stare, but only once did I lick the counter (or maybe I just thought about it). I enjoyed the trip immensely and actually returned two pounds lighter. The truth is having a pre-determined plan worked and kept me from worrying about the first morning weigh-in upon my home arrival. Perhaps it was backpacking across three countries that affected the scales? Either way, they were both planned.

Let us live this day in the confidence of Matthew 6:34 and not seek trouble or failure for tomorrow. We are commanded to live in this day and not borrow from the challenges of a new day. Some days are easier to navigate than others as far as our health is concerned, but God promises to help us solve the tough issues as they arise. That is such a great plan to me.

April 13: Yellow Cake

Yield: 24 servings

Ingredients

- *1 ½ sticks light butter
- *1 8-oz. pkg. light cream cheese
- *1 ½ cups xylitol
- 4 eggs at room temperature
- 1 teaspoon baking powder
- 3 teaspoons of vanilla, butter, and nut extract. (This is a new flavor. It is not the extracts separately, but one extract that is the combo of the three.)
- 3 cups almond flour
  *at room temperature

Procedure

1. Preheat oven to 350°F.
2. Cream together first three ingredients.
3. Add eggs one at a time, beating well after each addition.
4. Add extract and blend.
5. Mix the dry ingredients well before adding them to the butter mixture. Add them in thirds.
6. Spray a 9x13 baking dish and after adding the batter, bake for 45-50 minutes. Use a toothpick placed in the center to determine if cake is done. Cool completely before cutting. Frostings are endless. I usually add the Old Fashioned Fudge Icing found on page 139.

Per Serving:

Calories 136.1
Total Fat 10.9 g
Cholesterol 50.2 mg
Sodium 88.8 mg
Potassium 15.4 mg
Total Carbohydrate 8.6 g
Dietary Fiber 1.3 g
Sugars 0.8 g
Protein 4.5 g

April 14: South of the Border Meatloaf

Yield: 16 servings

Ingredients

- 2-3 tablespoons olive oil
- 1 medium onion, diced small
- 4-5 cloves minced garlic
- 1 (14.5 oz.) can of diced tomatoes with green peppers and onions
- 2 tablespoons cumin
- 1 teaspoon salt
- 1 teaspoon garlic salt
- 2-2 ½ lbs. ground beef (8% fat content)
- 2 eggs
- 1 cup almond flour
- ½ cup Mexican four blend cheese
- 1 jalapeño chopped finely with no seeds

Procedure

1. Preheat oven to 350°F.
2. Sautee the onion and garlic in the olive oil until garlic is fragrant and onions are browning.
3. Add diced tomatoes, cumin, salt, and garlic salt and cook for a few minutes. Transfer to a large mixing bowl.
4. Add the ground beef, eggs, almond flour, cheese, and jalapeño.
5. Mix well and place into a greased 9x13 baking dish.
6. Bake for 40 minutes.

Per Serving:

Calories 237.3
Total Fat
Cholesterol 68.5 mg
Sodium 167.2 mg
Potassium 191.0 mg
Total Carbohydrate 3.6 g
Dietary Fiber 1.1 g
Sugars 0.8 g
Protein 14.6 g

April 15: Replaying the Wrong Movie

I love the morning. There is something about being refreshed and calm as opposed to tired and wound up. Do you have a morning routine and a special affection for the morning? I have been reading over and over a passage I memorized as a child as I am walking through a tough experience now. Nothing comforts me like God's Word. While reading the Scriptures in the morning, I hear the voice of a heavenly Father who chose me, picked me out of the crowd, and selected me to spend eternity with Him. His voice brings real comfort to my soul.

When I was so unhealthy, my soul became the recorder of defeated moments and reminded me as often as possible that hope no longer existed. My mind played these hopeless events like one bad movie after another. While dressing in the morning, if my pants were excessively tight or would not zip, the movie began. Off and on throughout the day that scene of defeat repeated in my memory. Every time I went by another mirror, I checked to see if the movie was wrong. I promised myself that I would never eat again. That scene occurred more than I can tell you. My life was consumed with the extra weight I carried and it's control over me.

Is that a scene from your movie? Maybe it is not always about food, but other pictures of failure that seemingly never stop. I can guarantee that God never planned for this to be our movie. He never planned for His creation to live in defeat and hopeless failure. We will experience failure, yes, as we live in a fallen world; but that was not what God intended. His Word in Jeremiah confirms that He has plans to do good by us and not harm us; plans to give us a good hope and a good future.

When the drama scenes of death and destruction ravage your mind, take the movie out and replace it with another. Let your heart hear the truth from God's Word and then replay that over and over. Now that is a great movie choice!

April 16: Climbing Stone Mountain

Daniel 7:25 gives a vivid description of a vision the prophet received regarding the last days: "And [he] shall wear out the saints of the Most High'" (AMP). You can be certain the *he* is not referring to God, but the greatest enemy of God. And where it reads *saints*, you could substitute my name. And perhaps yours? It seems that the circumstances of my journey are not always easy. The fight to be healthy is often a battle, and most of the time uphill. But I tell you it is a strategic plan designed to distract each of us and cause us to give up on our heavenly Father who never gives up on us.

Our health matters to our families, God, and us. Not just us. We were created in God's image and designed to show forth fruit that indicates to others that we are attached to God. In my broken physical and mental health, all I displayed was defeat. I was worn out from trying to climb the mountain for so many years.

Let me encourage each of us today—start again to climb the mountain to a healthy you and when you reach the top, plan to stay and build your new home right there. I remember the first time I climbed Stone Mountain here in Georgia. It was a tough climb for a chubby preteen and when I got to the top we weren't allowed to stay long. I remember thinking, *We just got here. I really want to stay.* I never figured out why we put so much energy in the hard part of climbing only to stay for a few moments. You see where I am going with this?

I spoke with a woman yesterday who really wanted to do something to lose weight and embrace health. I looked at her and said, "Our health plan is just like any other. You can drop the weight, but if you return to your past, you will gain weight again and re-enter the cycle." She just shook her head with that unbelieving look that I have come to realize is most often a "worn out" sign. The more failed attempts, the higher the next mountain to health seems. I get that, but we cannot quit. If you're reading this, I pray you're preparing to climb again no matter what you see in front of you. Remember, mountains are climbed pieces at a time. Gain ground, but keep moving. Victory is just above you.

April 17: A Lesson from a Blister

I cannot remember when I have seen such a dry spring. I miss the rain. I love life, and to me there is something special about the fragrance of the atmosphere after a rain. The rain brings life, cools the air, brings a clean smell, and causes the plants to lift their hands. God created water to be so life-giving. Even when we burn ourselves, we are never to pierce the blister that forms. The blister keeps the fluid next to the skin while the new skin is regenerating. The fluid contains such healing properties. There's a lesson for us here.

Sometimes I sit and wonder how long it took God to create such intricate details for each of our lives? Can you imagine that God actually thought about blisters and cared enough about our healing to make a plan even in that? I cannot fathom that the God who created all life and everything in this world cared about my "boo-boos" before He implanted me into the womb of my mother. He made a plan to heal blisters on my fingers. Who does that? We were not an afterthought.

Knowing that God cares about a blister on my hand deepens my understanding and appreciation that He cares about the health of my entire body. We are the only beings that God created in His own image. Psalm 139 reflects God's intimate knowledge of each one of us. He created certain things on the earth to help us be the best we can be. It's like the two trees in the garden. One of them was forbidden because God knew what it would produce in Adam and Eve. God is not ignorant of the food choices presented to us each day. He knows.

Manufacturers create foods not because they care about each of us, but because they care about their profit margin. This is totally opposite from Father God. He knows and He cares. And given the choice, I prefer to eat the foods He created in their whole, raw form. That's our best bet for fostering great healing.

Some people paint a liquid product that acts like new skin on their blisters. But the flesh of the blister in its natural composition is the best protection offered by our bodies. Nothing beats what God creates! What can I learn from a blister? That God has an answer for everything, and His answer is always best.

April 18: The Fruit Says It All

I was teaching again one night on the fruit of the Spirit (Galatians 5), and while I love these lessons, they continue to point out areas in my life where the Holy Spirit's work is not manifesting as it should. I realized yesterday when I created the Fruit Evaluation Examination for tonight's class, I still have a lot of flesh displaying on my tree. I would love to blame all my flaws, attitudes, and circumstances on someone else. However, I have come to understand that real change always begins with me, and not blaming others. The fruit of my life indicates which *seed* is producing the qualities I display. Are my words and actions saying Holy Spirit or are they saying flesh?

I used to laugh and tell people, "If I don't eat, I get mean." Several things are wrong with that statement:

1. It's a negative confession.

2. It announces that my flesh is stronger than my spirit.

3. It encourages weakness and making excuses.

In 2011 I started asking myself, "What does a size ten look like?" I wrote it out, I proclaimed it, I told people, I made a positive confession, I stopped making excuses, and I stopped watering and fertilizing the wrong seed and began to nurture the right seed. Both seeds of positive and negative confessions live within us, as we are born with a sin nature. I wish that were not so, but it is. And where do these seeds reside? In my heart. While I wanted the good seed to always be evident, my frustration and depression about my weight occasionally prompted a behavior I never wanted anyone to witness.

I am not blaming my occasional wretched attitude and behavior totally on my weight, but I am saying that it is much easier for me to be patient and exercise self-control on this side of good health. My frustration about being trapped in my body after trying everything often caused me to *snap* on folks. I'm being really transparent here. Maybe some of you can join in on this chorus?

It is amazing how love and self-control are the first and last fruits of the Spirit listed in Galatians. Love covers all and self-control helps us love others and ourselves, which brings us to the top of the list again. I'm just thinking about that this morning, having my coffee, and listening to the birds sing. Examine your fruit today and ask yourself which fruit of the Spirit in your life needs more attention. And above all, remember God chose you before the foundation of the world to be in Him. So smile as you inspect your life, knowing that the Holy Spirit is helping us be the best we can be today.

April 19: The Medicine of Laughter

I know that sometimes we vacillate in and out of seasons where we fight for our very sanity, and living a healthy lifestyle either happens or it doesn't. I get that. Sometimes when life is intense and hard hitting, we need to sit down, slow down, lift up our eyes from our circumstances, and realize the real snare that worry and depression are. I see a lot of people in and out of my office who are heavily weighted and tangled in these two traps. And while none of us like to confess that we worry, on occasion we all do. I want to offer a possible solution that is easy and cheap—laughter. The Bible places laughter on the same playing field as medication. It took me years to find the joy and truth in that verse.

The healing power of laughter is waiting to be embraced every moment of every day. Most of the time, however, I find that we have to purpose to laugh. I have had to do that during rough seasons of my life. How about you? I don't like slapstick-type comedy, but I love those funny things where kids get tickled. My youngest granddaughter has the most phenomenal laugh. When she starts laughing it's like a hook that allows me no escape. I literally laugh so hard I cry. And then I feel like a million dollars. Have you ever tried it? Sometimes when she's on a laughter roll, I will record it. Then, in a crisis moment, I play the recording and the atmosphere changes. I take my "laughter medicine." Sometimes I laugh so hard my side aches. Whew, I love that too!

We can laugh at life, our circumstances, and even ourselves. It's completely doable, isn't it? However, in order to really laugh at life when it's slugging hard at us, we cannot take it too seriously can we? We are simply on this earth for a season and life never plays fair for anyone. If we allow ourselves to get consumed with our own human frailty, I am absolutely certain laughter will be of no benefit. Do you take medications for anything? If so, do you take them at scheduled times? Could I suggest you schedule to take your *laughter meds*? I promise the endorphins will be released, you'll feel so much better, and your stomach muscles will get a great abdomen workout.

What could be better?

April 20: Southwest Coleslaw

Yield: 8 servings

Ingredients

- 1 bag of angel hair cabbage (often I put this in the food processor and make the pieces smaller)
- ½ of a medium Vidalia onion, chopped fine
- 1 seeded jalapeño pepper, chopped fine
- 8 petite kosher dill pickles, chopped fine
- Sea salt, pepper, and dill weed to taste (I use probably 3 tablespoons, but start out with one.)
- 3 heaping tablespoons of Duke's mayo
- 2 tablespoons of pickle juice

Procedure

Combine all ingredients and leave for at least 8 hours, overnight if possible.

Per Serving:

Calories 103.7
Total Fat 6.9 g
Cholesterol 5.0 mg
Sodium 540.4 mg
Potassium 459.8 mg
Total Carbohydrate 11.5 g
Dietary Fiber 4.6 g
Sugars 1.4 g
Protein 2.9 g

April 21: Almond Flour Pizza

Yield: 8 servings

Ingredients

- 3 tablespoons light butter or olive oil
- 1 teaspoon salt
- 2 eggs
- 1 tablespoon half/half (optional)
- Garlic, Parmesan dipping herbs, and basil to taste
- 2 ½ cups almond flour
- Sugar-free pizza sauce
- ½ cup each grated Parmesan and Romano cheeses
- 1 cup mozzarella cheese
- Additional topping ideas: pepperoni, mushrooms, ground beef, onions

Procedure

1. Beat the butter or olive oil, salt, eggs, half/half and the garlic, Parmesan dipping herbs, and basil well with a whisk.
2. Add almond flour and stir until well mixed. This will form a sticky ball.
3. Cover and refrigerate for 30-45 minutes. This makes it easier to shape into the pizza.
4. Preheat oven to 350°F.
5. Spray 10-inch deep-dish pan with cooking spray or a regular-sized pizza pan.
6. Lightly grease hands and gently press crust mixture into greased pan. This is easier if divided into thirds and pressed separately.
7. Bake for 20 minutes.
8. Remove and cool for 5 minutes.
9. Top with your choice of sugar-free sauce, cheeses, whatever toppings you like and cook for an additional 20 minutes, raising the temperature to 400°F for the last few minutes to brown the cheese slightly.
10. Cut into 8 slices after the pizza has cooled for a few minutes.

Per Serving:
(Includes topping the pizza with cheese, pepperoni, and mushrooms)
Calories 378.7
Total Fat 30.0 g
Cholesterol 41.6 mg
Sodium 605.9 mg
Potassium 126.7 mg
Total Carbohydrate 10.9 g
Dietary Fiber 3.8 g
Sugars 2.4 g
Protein 19.6 g

April 22: A Miracle Soup

It is amazing that the end of April is close and it seems like it was just Christmas. Time waits for no one, does it? At my age I am keenly aware of this fact.

It is remarkable to me how many weight loss plans people consider and quickly find themselves consumed with. I recently had someone share information on a "revised" vegetable soup diet with me. I laughed and commented that we used this diet forty years ago when I was a teen. Wow, how time flies. The diet now has protein and additional vegetables added to it, but it is still the same premise: eat as much soup as you can and lose weight.

I just smiled when my friend tried to convince me I could lose eight pounds in two weeks with little effort and much success. They tried *really* hard to get me to embrace this *miracle* plan because the article reported "stars and important people" have had success with this plan and "you can too." All these new fad diets simply cause me to wink and smile. I totally do not mean to be disrespectful, and I wink only because I have tried them all. In the Bible, King Solomon reminds us there is nothing new under the sun (see Ecclesiastes 1:9). True that.

I really want to write an article about all of you who have taken a simple food plan, made it a way of life, and are lasting beyond the two weeks. You guys are the real stars. Eating healthy is not about two weeks of denial. The reality is after two weeks of consuming the miracle soup, one is inclined to experience withdrawal and compensate with a cheeseburger. I did. Then, one may be disappointed that one looks as they did before the miracle soup in a relatively short period of time. But maybe the miracle worked better for you than me?

I know people think they can lose eight pounds and that starts the cycle, but if you do not change the "day to day" real food choices, those eight pounds *somehow* often re-appear and bring a few friends. Diet fads do not work—they just don't. I have a million t-shirts to prove that. I am not saying the soup recipe is bad; it is really not. I actually like it. Nevertheless, I would rather eat what I want as long as it falls into a lean protein, fruit, vegetable, or healthy fat category. I prefer options.

Let me say one more time: you guys are the real winners and whatever you are doing is what I want to do. I believe in miracles, but I would encourage you, however, to run from *miracle* diets. Stick with the plan.

April 23: My Personal Prayer Partner

I pray you are comforted and rejoicing this day as you remember God's amazing plan and display of love for you. Nothing can compare to it. I cannot even begin to wrap my small brain around this kind of sacrifice for someone so undeserving as myself. I had a meltdown yesterday, and then while reading in Luke this morning a deeper revelation came that reinforced the concept that even in "melt down phase," God still thinks I'm a great kid. That is amazing to me.

We celebrate the resurrection for many reasons, only one of which is the hope each of us has that we will someday conquer the final enemy, death. Another reason to celebrate the resurrection is found in Romans 8:34 (AMP): "Who is there to condemn [us]? Will Christ Jesus (the Messiah), Who died, or rather Who was raised from the dead, Who is at the right hand of God actually pleading as He intercedes for us?" Can you begin to comprehend Jesus seated at the right hand of Father God constantly praying for you? There is no one I would rather know is praying for me than God's own son. How about you?

Before I left for Thailand, I gathered a team of people who committed to pray for me during the two-week journey. At times when I was confronted or discouraged, my heart remembered people were praying. While they committed to pray for me for two weeks, Jesus has committed to pray for us for an entire lifetime, every moment of every day. Can you get a visual of God on the throne and Jesus beside him interceding and praying, "Father, help Kathy (insert your name) be the best she can be today in every area of her life." Anybody got tears in your eyes?

Jesus never grows tired of calling our name out to the Father and speaking life. He never grows weary of our asking for His help on our health journey. *Never!* He loves each of us enough to give His heart and His life for our victory. He only asked that we give Him every ounce of our heart and allow Him to change us from the inside out.

Jesus is praying for you!

April 24: A Winning Combo, Part 1

Ephesians 3:17-19 reads, "that Christ may dwell in your hearts through faith; to the end that you, being rooted and grounded in love, may be strengthened to comprehend with all the saints what is the width and length and height and depth, and to know Christ's love which surpasses knowledge, that you may be filled with all the fullness of God" (WEB).

I like the way that verse reads, "that I may be filled with the fullness of God." I pray I am never content with a portion of God, but as Jesus dwells in my heart and allows me to be grounded in love, I can be filled to overflowing. I want to be filled with God's fullness every moment of my life. I really do. While this is a great spiritual concept, being filled to overflowing in my belly is not so great a concept.

I'm a big eater and I hate to admit that. I used to joke and say, "I can eat with the best of the men." While I was laughing on the outside, I was dying on the inside. I was taught in many weight management courses to eat slowly, eat small bites, put your fork down, eat only until I was full—all the good stuff, you know.

One of the major challenges to eating slowly came on a daily basis while teaching school. I only had twenty-five minutes for lunch and all I did was cram as much food as I could into my mouth, as fast as I could, and hardly breathe. I have used that scenario as my excuse for many years as to why I eat so quickly. I was always jealous of those people who took long, leisurely lunches and walked in the park tossing half their sandwiches to the birds. I know birds get hungry, but my sandwiches were important to me. I'm kidding about the birds, but not the cafeteria excuse.

There really is something to be said for eating smaller portions as well as eating slowly. Most studies suggest it takes twenty minutes for your stomach to notify your brain it is full. I can consume a lot in twenty minutes. So I had to make a plan to ration my food, make myself eat, and not inhale. I am still practicing that. I bring a lunch that is pre-portioned and check the clock to see how much time I have to enjoy my little bags. I do this consciously as bad habits are hard to break. Learning to eat less and not expect to be filled at each meal with food is hard. But I am learning to replace that physical need with a need to be filled with "the fullness of God," and that brings a whole new level of joy.

Being filled spiritually and physically at the same time is certainly a winning combination.

April 25: A Winning Combo, Part 2

Sometimes there is a sequel, a Part 2 if you will. I felt to follow yesterday's devotion with this revelation: *Stay away from all-you-can-eat buffets!* I always told myself that they offered such amazing choices. Who was I trying to kid? Me, of course. For those who are food addicts and obese, as I was, there should be a sign placed above the door that reads "pick your poison."

I lived for those trips to the all-you-can-eat places and I never understood when people commented, "They make money on me. I never eat my portion." Huh? In my small mind I would always think, *You can shove it on my plate and I will help you feel good about coming.* I wish I were teasing. Can I be honest? I *planned* to overeat. I knew that I would stuff myself until I was miserable, feel bad about myself, stare at myself in the mirror, shake my head at my fat, and then promise myself, "I will fast tomorrow."

The problem was by 10 a.m. the next morning, after three cups of coffee with sugared creamer and whipped cream on the top, I was starving and couldn't wait to find the crackers in my drawer. What a vicious cycle. I had to make some changes. This was a death journey for me. Can you see yourself somewhere on this road?

However, the more I denied my flesh and filled myself with the knowledge that God had a better plan, the easier it got. *But I had to keep walking* toward health and make a vow that I would not *walk* into an all-you-can-eat establishment again. The longer I was healthy, the more I understood how people could announce that they never ate enough to justify going. I calculated that I consumed between three thousand and five thousand calories in a single setting. That is not a typo. Go figure—that is three days of calories for me. I do not know about you, but I would prefer to eat twelve hundred calories for three days as opposed to thirty-six hundred at one meal and starve for two days. That is sheer torture in my book. Our bodies need consistent fueling not consistent gorging. That is a fact.

I like winning, and winning combinations work for me. Thank you God for helping me do the math and determine that trips to the all-you-can-eat establishments are not winning combinations for me.

April 26: A Circle of Three

As I was up late last night, I felt the Lord began to speak to me about long-term friends and their value to each of us. Do you have a friend from childhood who is still a real friend to you? Friendships can come and go, but long-term friends are usually crafted from a mold that does not shatter in controversy or by the pressure of distance. Do you have that friend(s) whom you may not see daily, but you know they would be at your side in a moment's notice if needed? I do. Isn't that a treasure? What you need is to designate your *circle of three*—those "upper level" friends who are going to be your real accountability partners in this next leg of your journey.

I began to list in my mind last night the following "friendships" that are very critical in our quest for health:

1. People who are willing to be honest and encourage us when we want to quit or cheat just a wee bit.

2. People who are willing to hydrate with us at certain intervals simply because they know our water consumption is critical.

3. People who are not afraid to risk our anger and speak up as we reach for the brownie.

4. People who will comfort us when discouraged, but firmly point us to the truth.

5. People who will be honest daily with their fitness plan as it helps us value the struggle of others.

6. People who will continue to offer their hand when we have failed to reach for it recently due to our own failure.

7. People who can be trusted with our feelings and know how to pray and help us fight.

These are just some of the people whom we should gather. My brother Chip was all this and more to me when we first started our health journey. I honestly didn't know if I had the fortitude to break the walls of my cell, escape the prison guards, start over with barely anything, and overcome the many obstacles in my face. I quickly formed a circle of three and we became "fox hole buddies." That group comforted me. We spoke daily for weeks until we started standing on solid ground. You need that.

Why is this important? Because isolation is a huge tool used in the arsenal of discouragement. Once we feel isolated, it is often not long until we feel no one cares and we can begin to return to our past simply because of the *comfort* it provides. How many of you know that sometimes people can be free of prison physically and still be in prison emotionally? That is why I really encourage everyone fighting for freedom from obesity to enlist those friends you know who will grab your neck either with a hug or a yank.

Who are your three, and do they know you have given them permission to help you? Ask today.

April 27: Fish Stew

Yield: 8 servings

Ingredients

- 1 bag Basa fish
- 1 bag Tilapia or Mahi Mahi
- 2 large onions
- 1-2 stick(s) light butter (I use 2)
- 3 quarts 2% milk
- Salt and coarse ground pepper to taste
- Tarragon to taste (I use 2 teaspoons)
- Old Bay® Seasoning to taste (I use 2 teaspoons)

Procedure

1. Melt the butter on medium heat in a large Dutch oven.
2. Add the onions and sauté until tender.
3. Add the thawed fish, cut in chunks, to the mix.
4. Add all the spices.
5. Add the milk.
6. Bring to almost a boil but do not curdle the milk. The stew will continue to cook on low-medium for about an hour to really blend the flavors.
7. Serve warm.

Per Serving:

Calories 194.9
Total Fat 8.7 g
Cholesterol 88.0 mg
Sodium 954.8 mg
Potassium 633.5 mg
Total Carbohydrate 5.5 g
Dietary Fiber 0.4 g
Sugars 3.6 g
Protein 24.5 g

April 28: Old Fashioned Fudge Icing (cooked)

Yield: 24 servings

Ingredients

- 1½ sticks light butter
- 1½ cups Truvia® Natural Sweetener
- 1 cup half/half
- ½ cup unsweetened natural cocoa powder
- ½ teaspoon sea salt
- 2 teaspoons vanilla

Procedure

1. Combine the top five ingredients together in a heavy saucepan on the stove over medium heat.
2. Bring to a full, rolling boil and let boil for 2 minutes.
3. Remove from heat and immediately add the vanilla.
4. Place the saucepan in a sink of cool water and begin to beat the frosting. Beat rapidly until the frosting begins to thicken. This could take 8-9 minutes.
5. Take the round end of a wooden stirring spoon and make holes into the yellow cake (recipe included in this month) in 24 places approximately in the middle of each cut square. (I used a 9x13 baking dish).
6. Pour the warm frosting over the cake (will still be runny) and allow to cool completely. Overnight is great!
7. Cover the top with pecan pieces (about a cup or cup and a half).
8. When cooled, cut into 24 squares.

Per Serving:
Calories 83.2
Total Fat 4.4 g
Cholesterol 11.2 mg
Sodium 54.5 mg
Potassium 40.9 mg
Total Carbohydrate 17.5 g
Dietary Fiber 0.6 g
Sugars 8.1 g
Protein 0.6 g

April 29: Our Organs Have Need of Us

The wind is blowing here and it is going to be a hot one (for those of you outside the US). Maybe you are in a place that is cooler, but not so here. The ten-day forecast shows no rain, and that presents a problem. I can deal with the heat, but minus the water and the drought becomes ominous to me. It hovers over the land, sucks the life out of the earth, and nothing stops it. Sometimes after days without rain I begin to feel cheated. Any sight of a raindrop brings a skip to my step.

I wonder if our bodies feel the same way about the water we drink daily. As our bodies are 75 percent water, why wouldn't they crave it? However, the longer we go without saturating our bodies, the more our natural desire dwindles. This becomes a critical situation with often-unpleasant side effects. However, immediately upon beginning the hydration cycle again our natural thirst makes its return. That is so like God to me.

It really is like the water cycle also. After long periods of drought, there are no evaporated fluids coming from the ground, so there is no moisture to reach the clouds and provoke rain. The cycle stops. However, a system can arrive bringing heavy rain to the dry soil and within hours, minutes sometimes, life emerges. Water from the ground now starts the cycle of rain over the area again.

It is amazing how God shows us pictures in the natural realm of His instituted, spiritual principles for our lives. Our daily water consumption prompts our organs to remain soft and active. In turn, certain organs cause other organs to grab toxins that threaten their existence, pull the toxins from our body, and eliminate them from our bodies. They depend on us to ensure the *water cycle,* which mirrors the natural one, functions properly for them also. When we don't hydrate, our organs go into drought and beg for any ounce of water to give them hope of functioning again. Just as the earth does—they slowly begin to die.

My husband informed me recently of a woman who died and her husband conveyed that she existed with only two liters of coke daily and her cigarettes. Can you imagine what her organs were doing? Get a picture. They were fighting for their lives and trying to preserve hers. Eventually they lost their fight for life and could no longer fight for her's either. I am a picture girl and that really impacted me. Hopefully as we drink our water today, we can smile and pat any place on our body that has an organ and realize we are contributing to their life and compliment them for functioning to their best to sustain our life.

April 30: April Reflection Page

As you are completing April, are there things you wish you had highlighted or which you had written down? Did the refreshing *rains* of truth allow those dusty excuses to be washed away? I hope you heard clearly this month how critical water is.

Keep asking God for the help of the Holy Spirit to make water your drink of choice.

_____

_____

_____

_____

_____

_____

_____

_____

_____

_____

_____

_____

_____

_____

_____

_____

_____

_____

_____

_____

May

This month all the pools open. Are we ready for a healthy, fun-filled summer? Are we feeling great, energized and full of life? That's what healthy eating is all about.

May 1: The Right Fuel

"Don't you realize that you become the slave of whatever you choose to obey?" (Romans 6:16a NLT).

In this verse, Paul is really encouraging the new believer to stop submitting to their own fleshly desires and temptations, as emotions are so powerful. As Paul stated, we can become their slave if we allow them control. The problem occurs when we do not realize their influence as quickly as we should. In addition to this, our desires often portray themselves as always being correct. What a lie.

I want to unpack a situation with which most of us may be familiar. I had been successfully following my health plan for a period of time but little by little I began to relax the boundaries of what I knew was correct. I never ate *off* plan, I simply allowed my routine to decline. For example, I started eating nuts instead of vegetables, as they were quick, easy, and quite tasty. But just that small substitution became a trap. I realized soon that I wasn't cooking as I should and I was okay with nuts and an apple a couple of times a day as opposed to a meal. At first the scale was being a "good boy," but eventually he turned on me. Why? I was thinking, *Nuts and an apple are not a lot of food.* Stop right there—that was my desire not the truth. My preference was the taste of nuts over vegetables, so I reasoned that they could become my meal. Faulty thinking.

I had to immediately readjust my attitude. I returned to the basics of our healthy plan and quickly my spirit lifted. Our cells cannot live off nuts and fruit, even if we don't feel like cooking. I hit a *bump in the road* in my personal life and instead of eating sugar or starch, I simply quit following the plan and started grabbing what was easy. I had gotten to a place of carrying nuts in my purse and not taking my lunch. That procedure does not fuel my cells or give me energy. I noticed by last week I was so tired and sluggish, and felt like I was in a rut. For me, it was like going to a pump and getting bad gas; my *car* responded by running poorly. This accountability helps me.

The moral of the story: Eat your vegetables and fruits daily and vary the color and kind. Do not substitute nuts as a veggie. I have determined that *I will be a slave to the plan of God* for my life and not a slave to my own emotions.

May 2: Sir Isaac Newton

I was thinking last night how difficult it is sometimes to shift from a place of maintaining (in all areas of life) to motion again. Occasionally, the initial outlay of energy may not seem worth the effort. For example, moving the heavy weights through the water at aerobics class is tough. When I start with the weights at class, dread will often flood my mind as I am more than acquainted with the energy required to move them through the water. However, I find the experience quite rewarding once they are moving and I gain my rhythm. Isn't this true about life in general?

Sometimes our stomachs want us to remember only what benefits them. They want us to remember the pain and difficulty of staying on plan when obstacles seem abundant. Once we determine that we are eating on plan *no matter what* and we start the motion, it becomes easier, doesn't it?

The basic laws of physics really do apply to our health journey. Sir Isaac Newton had three laws (basically) that relate to motion. One of those states that an object in motion will remain in motion until energy from an outside force is exerted against it. That is the issue with diets. Often they are strong and in motion at the beginning, but little cheats occasionally slow that motion to a halt. Starting again is even harder and eventually we quit. Have you ever been on this cycle? I have.

We must purpose in our minds and hearts to never stop or slow down, and then we fight against all odds or objects that would challenge our resolve. I know it's hard to make such a stand against obesity when we cannot see the future, but we *really* can. We know that heart disease is real and stems from unhealthy eating in most cases. We know diabetes can be controlled with healthy eating and the effects of "staying in motion." These are just two of the possibilities. Start naming things that doctors are now linking to obesity and the picture is not pretty.

We have an opportunity to start in motion toward a healthy future or we can remain still and hope the statistics and facts concerning the future of those following an unhealthy food plan are not true. I would rather not roll the dice. I would rather get in motion and stay in motion. Starting and re-starting is difficult and I am afraid I will eventually decide starting again is not worth the effort and accept my fate.

How about we get in motion with our food, exercise, and attitudes and then remain in motion? It easier to stay moving and that gets my vote.

May 3: Eating from God's Table

Praise God it is raining. It has been almost three weeks here with no water. I thought about going outside and standing in the rain and just laughing out loud. Earlier this week when I sent out my blog, we had been weeks with no rain and it was predicted that for the next ten days we would remain in a drought. I started calling the water out of the skies and reminding God that we were desperate—I was desperate—for Him to rain on the earth and in my heart. To me the rain brings peace and life to my weary soul.

One morning I was leaving for Sarasota, Florida to speak at a spring women's event. I was beyond excited to meet a new group of sisters in the Lord. I know God protected my marriage, mind, finances, health, integrity, etc. during the darkest of days so He could use my journey to pull the captives from prison and receive magnificent glory all unto Himself. God's like that. Sometimes we feel when we are suffering and struggling that God is absent. That is absolutely not the truth. He is more present than ever, coaching us gently and illuminating the path that brings us to safety. We must return to times in our lives where we built a place of remembrance and remind ourselves that God will never leave us nor forsake us. That does not mean we escape difficulty, but it means in Him we find our rest. The rain always, for some reason, takes me to those places of remembering.

Remember also that God is no respecter of persons and He is more than able to do the same thing in your life. I have journeyed through intense seasons of testing over the past several years and this journey has placed things in me I would never have gotten anywhere else and for that I am grateful. I turn and proclaim God's Word (from Psalm 23:4-5 NLT) that "Even when I walk through the darkest valley, I will not be afraid, for you are close beside me. Your rod and your staff protect and comfort me. You prepare a feast for me in the presence of my enemies." If you are not familiar with these verses, you probably should be.

Obesity is an enemy, and yet God's table is prepared right in front of my problem. I choose to eat from the King's table and not the fast food line at the closest café. Grab a chair, join me, and let the enemy of obesity find its own table. We choose to eat from the table of our King.

May 4: Did God Really Say?

I think some people feel it is easier to fight cancer than obesity. We have to remember this promise found in Matthew 8:17, "This fulfilled the word of the Lord through the prophet Isaiah, who said, 'He took our sicknesses and removed our diseases'" (NLT). That is a promise and God never lies. I consider obesity a disease and therefore I can apply the truth of God's Word and believe Him to be healed in this area.

For us, obesity probably won't manifest as what we would consider a physical healing. Our healing often manifests in our mind, our choices, and the will to make the correct choices daily without compromise. God healed us at the cross and guides us to make the right choices. We must not allow our daily issues to dissuade us from God's truth.

Some people self-medicate with wrong foods and this concept strikes a chord of compassion deep within me. I do take medications when I need them, but self-medicating with food *only leads to the crash and burn scenario*. We feel bad, we grab something sweet, we feel comforted for a minute and then we realize our issue is still painfully present and we proclaim, "I am not free or healed." That is why our health family is so important to me, as well as realizing that Jesus took obesity like a cloak upon His body for me.

Let us thank God for these things today:

1. We are healed according to Matthew 8:17.

2. Our mind is healed and will make the correct choices to maintain that healing.

3. Food is fuel for our body and not comfort for our soul.

4. We will not allow our wants for various kinds of food to bring compromise into our daily choices.

Self-medicating with wrong foods is like playing truth or dare with Satan.

I can hear him whispering, "Did God really say?" Our response, "Yes, Matthew 8:17 does say." God's Word declares my healing and I will make the correct food choices to foster and maintain what His promise provides me.

God *did* say and so do I.

May 5: Who's Running the Show?

Life can be a train wreck when we allow our feelings to run the show all the time. I like running with my feelings on occasion, but *sometimes* they get me in trouble. How about you? Our feelings can change from day to day, hour to hour, even moment to moment. They often lie to us. In short, trusting our feelings is probably not our best platform upon which to stand. But we can choose, as Christ's followers, to ask God to help us to live by truth and wisdom and not simply our emotions. Let me give you some examples.

Perhaps you have found yourself in a crowd of people and felt as though everyone was talking about you. That does not mean they were. Maybe you feel that nobody understands you, but that does not mean they do not. You may feel misunderstood, unappreciated, or even mistreated, but that does not mean you are. Have you experienced any of this only to discover you were wrong? I certainly have. I want to also add to this *feelings group* that just because we feel hungry, does not mean we always are.

Sometimes I have to really stop and ask myself if this is truly hunger or is my flesh running the show? That is a critical determination before eating. Sometimes when I am tired or frustrated, my flesh still tries to drag me to my past. I have to remind myself that I ate an hour ago and have refueled properly. Then, I really have to *listen*. Is this hunger? If yes, and I just ate, water or fruit is a good choice. If I have not eaten in a while, then I eat. There is that fine line that we must examine and ask God to give us wisdom. We cannot eat every time our flesh cries out. Sometimes it is actually just a test. No more prison for us. Right? So listen well today and do not allow your flesh to dictate your future health.

We would never allow a child "testing the waters" to control our lives. Tell that flesh, "You're not the boss of me."

May 6: Apple Salad

Yield: 8 servings

I prefer using Honeycrisp apples for this recipe; however, if you like tart apples you could substitute Granny Smith, or do a combo. Remember that raisins, as with other dried fruits, are high on the glycemic index. So, if you choose to use them, go sparingly.

Ingredients

- 4 large apples
- 2 stalks celery
- 2 tablespoons Duke's mayo
- 1 teaspoon white balsamic vinegar (optional)
- ½ teaspoon lemon extract
- 1 cup English walnut or pecan pieces
- ½ cup raisins (optional, as they are high on the glycemic index)
- Salt to taste

Procedure

1. Peel, core, and chop the apples.
2. Cut the stems off the celery; chop finely.
3. Combine the mayo, white balsamic (optional), and lemon extract and add to the apple mixture. Blend well.
4. Add nuts, salt, and raisins.
5. Cover, refrigerate, and allow to sit several hours before serving so flavors can blend. Best if allowed to sit overnight.

Per Serving:

Calories 237.1
Total Fat 13.3 g
Cholesterol 2.5 mg
Sodium 34.9 mg
Potassium 342.7 mg
Total Carbohydrate 31.4 g
Dietary Fiber 5.3 g
Sugars 19.8 g
Protein 2.9 g

May 7: Savory Asparagus

Yield: 4 servings

The onions in this recipe will give a sweet flavor while the dill a more intense herb flavor. This is amazing!

Ingredients

- 1 large bunch asparagus
- 2 Tbsp. light-tasting olive oil
- 2 medium Vidalia onions
- ½ tsp. sea salt
- Cracked black pepper (to taste, but not too much)
- Dill weed to taste (I use a hearty portion as I love the savory flavor.)

Procedure

1. Cut about two inches of the woody bottom off the asparagus.
2. Peel and slice the onions in rounds.
3. Heat the oil and sauté the onions. Add the asparagus.
4. While the asparagus is cooking add the salt and the dill. Allow to cook to your desired tenderness.

Per Serving:

Calories 121.3
Total Fat 7.2 g
Cholesterol 0.0 mg
Sodium 8.1 mg
Potassium 574.4 mg
Total Carbohydrate 12.9 g
Dietary Fiber 4.6 g
Sugars 0.0 g
Protein 4.6 g

May 8: Watermelon Leaves

What a beautiful, crisp morning it was today. I love the temperature and the moisture on the ground. Many of you know I am a watermelon freak (I eat some every day), so my precious husband has started growing some for me. I go outside every morning to watch the progress as the seeds have pushed through the ground and the leaves are getting stronger.

Of the ten seeds he planted, only three are coming up, but those three are looking fabulous. I am amazed that the leaves look exactly like the skin of a watermelon. Every day God shows me something different in their growth and I love it. This morning I want to encourage us all to look for God even in the tiniest parts of our days. Watching these watermelon seeds come out of the ground and look like watermelons, even the baby leaves, has once again reminded me that God desperately cares about the tiny details of our lives. He created our bodies to respond to food and water in certain ways.

Water is a great conductor of electricity, right? Did you know our hearts use electrical current to keep them in rhythm? They do. So when we hydrate, our heart and brain work much better. Also, when we hydrate well, our feet are not swollen, our eyes not puffy, the fat being burned inside our body can be eliminated properly, and so on. God created our bodies so intricately, as He did that watermelon plant, because He is into the details. How cool that He uses something so simple to keep it running at maximum capacity like water. I would imagine He did that because He knows each of us so well. Water is easily accessible, cheap, easy to transport, and does not require any cooking. You see where I am going? That is a profound simplicity with not so simple ramifications.

When I look at the baby watermelon leaves, I can only smile as I am reminded that God uses the simple things to confound the wise. I am certainly not stating I am "wise," but I am confounded nonetheless. Have you noticed the tiny details of your life lately where God is reminding you of His affection and attention for you? Stop and think about this, then offer a prayer of thanksgiving.

May 9: The Curse of Comparison, Part 1

When I think of comparing, there are multitudes of things that come to my mind. We compare numbers, houses, friends, foods, everything. While at the store this last Sunday, I was selecting Roma tomatoes to go into a salad. Another lady walked up and started examining every tomato as I was. I thought, *What if I were the tomato being mashed, turned over and over, closely examined, and compared to every other tomato in the bin?* Then, for a brief moment, I felt sorry for the ones I returned. Is that crazy?

Where did those feelings originate? *Perhaps* as children we heard such things as, "Your big sister played varsity ball; your brother made all A's on his report card; your friends are all wearing these clothes." *Perhaps* at this level, comparison was designed to foster and encourage the following of a role model. *Perhaps* that attempt actually birthed a nasty giant in us that causes us to doubt our own God-given worth. When those feelings begin and actually take root, jealousy can be a very difficult emotion to conquer.

In my life I was always looking at others and wishing that I could look like them, act like them, be them. I have battled my entire life with wanting to be someone else. Maybe you see yourself in that? Let me remind us all from Psalm 139 that God wonderfully created us and breathed life into each one of us. His stamp of approval is upon us! He sketched our face in His book before He implanted us in the womb of our mothers. He knows and loves us for exactly who He created us to be, not who we covet.

> "You made all the delicate, inner parts of my body and knit me together in my mother's womb. Thank you for making me so wonderfully complex! Your workmanship is marvelous—how well I know it. You watched me as I was being formed in utter seclusion, as I was woven together in the dark of the womb. You saw me before I was born. Every day of my life was recorded in your book. Every moment was laid out before a single day had passed. How precious are your thoughts about me, O God. They cannot be numbered!" (Psalm 139:13-17 NLT).

I wish I had learned this earlier. Do not spend another minute looking at others and wishing. Look at the truth and smile.

May 10: The Curse of Comparison, Part 2

As I said in yesterday's devotion, it is a wretched journey to spend chunks of time comparing what God seemingly has done for others and not for you in the areas of money, your body, marriage, or whatever you feel is inadequate. When we give ourselves to this school of thought, we basically say, "Thanks, God...but what You did for *me* is really not good enough." Just the thought of entertaining that notion makes me shutter. Have you ever considered that?

Instead, we must realize that God has plans to do good by us and give us a good hope and a good future regardless of what our circumstances say at this moment or how we view them. We must remember that certain entities were created to function together while being uniquely different, and that this truth was part of a predetermined eternal schematic. For example, the organs of the body are all different, none identical, and yet all are necessary. Moving from the natural to the spiritual realm, we read in 1 Corinthians 12 how Paul uses this truth to remind the body of Christ that questioning their eternal purpose and comparing themselves with others can destroy the unity of the body. His encouragement in verse 25 serves to rebuke comparison with others, "that there should be no division in the body, but that the members should have the same care for one another" (WEB). Always coveting what others have or how they look can be such a curse in our lives. It is a major distraction. I wonder how many millions of dollars have been wasted trying to be someone else.

I do believe we need to look our best, work as hard as we can, and enjoy life with all that is within us. I have come to realize that my life is best lived focusing on what God's Word says about me and not what my eyes perceive. We are all unique and as such have our own journey.

Truth Alert: We were created to be us—the best us we can be. We were not created to be someone else. I think comparing ourselves and wishing we were different never communicates to God how grateful we really are that He created us. He took the time to uniquely give us the specifics that foster our identity. He did His best when He created us. Sometimes we need to fight for that revelation.

Come on, kill the comparison curse and learn to love yourself and appreciate who you are. Remember: you can never look in two directions at one time. You cannot look at others and compare while also looking at God with heart-felt gratitude. That is not possible. Comparison only drags our eyes in a wrong direction. May we purpose to look God's way and say, "Thanks" instead of asking, "Why?"

May 11: Extra Money in the Envelope

In my journey over the last couple of years, God has been so precious to place me in certain situations to "school" me. He has often done this without the additional cost and given me insight into key components concerning nutrition. I never understood all the hype about those who shopped all natural or cooked everything from scratch. I almost viewed that as wasting time. Boy, I was totally in the dark.

I recognize that we are all busy, and I realize it takes extra time to eat mostly unprocessed foods. Eating whole foods requires more shopping (as the food does not last as long), time to cook the unprocessed foods, and an adventurous nature to explore with herbs as opposed to extra salt and sugar. And if that was not enough, choosing the whole food route is often more expensive, as many of us have discovered. But again, what price can be placed on living a long, healthy life? What is so difficult for me to understand is why companies charge those of us who desire to be healthy more than those choosing poor health. Does anybody know the answer to that? Not me, but I do have a theory. I will save that for another devotion perhaps.

I also have a plan to compensate for the additional cost. Consider this: as the medications I needed monthly decreased (due to increased health), the additional money in my grocery envelope increased. Fewer medications=more money for whole foods=better health and fewer medications=more funds for watermelons that I love. Let us continue with this line of thinking. Better foods, better health, cheating "the system," fewer doctor's visits, increased energy, better overall attitude. Am I saying that healthy living promotes all of these? Oh, yes I am! And, who doesn't want this type of life? In fact, I will take this for the *rest* of my life. If you will commit to a healthy lifestyle and get a brand new grocery envelope, I think you will be pleased with the contents in a matter of months. After my first ten pounds I was able to drop the reflux medication. That meant twenty more dollars each month, which allowed me two or three more watermelons. I love this!

May 12: The Partnership between Salt and Sugar

I was speaking to a chef at a funeral recently and inquiring as to which foods contained sugar. Let me stop and encourage you to never be afraid to ask, even at functions, as to what is contained in the foods prepared. While it may seem rude to some, I have found that it actually encourages people to carefully craft their plates. If I choose not to ask, my scale will inform me later; so I have learned to ask before assuming.

Check this out: a long table was beautifully prepared and several of the dishes appeared to be ones I would place on my plate. However, all but two items had additional sugar and some were vegetables. As I questioned the chef as to why she had added sugar to the green beans, her reply shocked me. She replied, "The sugar helps to enhance the work of the salt. It really brings out the flavor in the food." I never knew that. As I stated earlier, God has been really kind to place the right people in my path to supply the answers to some of my really tough questions.

We have to be so careful on every turn and at every function. And who would not consider green beans safe? While I was shocked that the chef said that most caterers add sugar to push the salt to maximum flavor, I was grateful for her honesty. That is why I encourage my health family that it is best when we cook and season our own foods, carry them to functions, and never allow chance to torpedo our health plan. Planning is so critical to our success. I always find when I fail to plan, I suffer.

I learned early in my health journey that when in doubt, simply ask questions. I do that everywhere I go now and I can't tell you how many times I have been rescued simply because I asked. I really have to smile when I question a server and they cannot definitively inform me of the sugar content within a dish and *they do not realize it would be best to ask too*. In my mind, it is cheaper for them to ask concerning the presence of sugar than for me to return the food. I am getting very proficient at detecting the slightest hint of the white stuff.

May 13: Spicy Chicken Dip

Yield: 8 servings

This dip is nice when served with pork rinds (no starch or sugar), or vegetables such as celery, jicama, and yellow squash.

Ingredients

- 8 oz. light cream cheese, softened
- ½ cup light sour cream
- ½ cup bacon ranch salad dressing
- ¼ cup TABASCO® sauce (adjust to taste)
- 2 jalapeños (chopped finely with no seeds, unless you prefer the heat)
- 1 cup shredded Mexican four blend cheese
- ¼ cup Parmesan Reggiano cheese (reserve some to sprinkle on the top when it comes from the oven)
- 2 to 3 whole chicken breasts

Procedure

1. Boil chicken, cool, and cut into chunks.
2. Beat the cream cheese until smooth and add the remaining ingredients. Stir well.
3. Spray a dish and place the mixture into the container.
4. Bake at 350 degrees for 25 minutes or until mixture is heated through; stir again.

Per Serving:
Calories 322.2
Total Fat 17.7 g
Cholesterol 106.1 mg
Sodium 479.0 mg
Potassium 250.7 mg
Total Carbohydrate 3.2 g
Dietary Fiber 0.1 g
Sugars 1.8 g
Protein 35.0 g

May 14: Crab Salad

Yield: 8 servings

You may substitute shrimp for the crab but keep in mind that the cholesterol will be different. You can also serve this on a bed of lettuce for an amazing salad.

Ingredients

- 3 lbs. bag lump crab
- 3 tablespoons Duke's mayo
- 3 tablespoons light sour cream
- Pinch sea salt
- 3-4 stalks of celery, chopped fine
- Dill herb to taste (about 2 -3 tablespoons)

Procedure

1. Remove the lump crab from the container, and chop it with a heavy spoon to break the big pieces apart. This makes it easier to mix other ingredients.
2. Add the remaining ingredients and chill well before serving.

Per Serving:

Calories 225.3
Total Fat 7.5 g
Cholesterol 39.9 mg
Sodium 483.4 mg
Potassium 267.6 mg
Total Carbohydrate 19.1 g
Dietary Fiber 0.6 g
Sugars 0.0 g
Protein 21.0 g

May 15: Protective Custody

We often discuss the critical importance of making a plan, and I totally believe that concept. You know I do. But how many know that sometimes we look at our lives and wonder if we can sustain the plan we thought we made? We all know that the cost of healthy food increases almost hourly and could be more than our budget can support. At that point it is time for a Bible study on faith.

When I commented about the cost of my groceries, my friend at a local grocery store said, "If I had a place to grow my own food, I would. The cost of food continues to rise. I would put my money in seeds." Well, for those of us non-farmer girls, that will not help. Neither will worrying about how I will continue to eat healthy when it costs more. Even my sweet husband, from time to time, has to be reminded that my health journey is non-negotiable as far as our income.

I have heard from several people that they find it challenging to stay with a healthy protocol due to the cost of food or the limited choices of meals at restaurants. I totally understand. I find myself making choices at the store differently and with more consideration than this time last year. However, the cost of being healthy cannot be the first place we cut corners. We cannot worry about where the money will come from to provide for a healthy lifestyle. Our choices may have to look different, and we may have to make exchanges differently in other areas, but God provides for our needs. His Word makes that promise.

Rest assured, God will take care of you. He knows that we are being good stewards of the body He created, gave to us, and dwells within. That pleases Him. So stop worrying about God's protective care. Think of it this way: We are in God's protective custody and everything is provided for us. I trust God and I choose to not worry. Matthew 6:34 states, "So don't worry about tomorrow, for tomorrow will bring its own worries. Today's trouble is enough for today" (NLT).

That is good enough for me. Let me take one day at a time and rejoice that God has me in His protective custody. Therefore, no weapon of destruction can have the prosperity of destroying my journey to freedom.

May 16: The Wishing Well

For such a long time, I blamed my unhealthy lifestyle and sixty-five extra pounds on everyone and anyone other than myself. We have established that. I spent a lot of wasted time making statements that sounded good with no stability like, "I wish I could lose some weight." I laughed and confessed for years, but I was never serious enough to really look at my responsibility to the destruction of my health. I made all the food choices, cooked all the food, and lived from one meal to the next.

Even though I controlled my eating destiny, I had a place I loved to visit—the wishing well. I continued to stop by the wishing well when I needed my pants to zip, went for a doctor's visit, and when everyone was getting in the pool and I was embarrassed. And of course, it was never my fault. My excuses included genetics, life circumstances, love of cooking, and having no other vices as I was a Christian. Unfortunately, my trips to the wishing well never seemed to free me from the cell of obesity in which I was locked, so I visited often.

One day I came face to face with the truth that the wishing well was just a myth, and if I did not turn my life around quickly, I would eventually eat my way into a disease-filled death. No, no, and no. I had to confront the lies, stare them in the face, and be more determined to live than be okay with obesity. My doctors played the repeat button each visit, saying, "If you could lose just five to ten pounds." Ever heard that? And I would visit the wishing well. They would say again, "We could decrease some your medications if you could lose just five pounds." *And I would visit the wishing well.*

When we are younger, extra weight may avoid us. However, all that fat inside our veins eventually takes its toll and often we never see the results until it is too late. That is why heart disease is often called the silent killer. I don't know about you, but I do not want some *silent killer* pushing me to the lie, which is the wishing well. I want to walk in truth and light. I want to live as long as God has planned, in great health, and serving Him with this body at optimal performance level. Stop visiting the wishing well and throwing your pennies into the water. Instead, make the life determination to choose health and fight every day.

Let us make a pact to never visit the wishing well again.

May 17: My Magic Eraser

Recently I have fallen in love with magic erasers. I know that some people are offended by the term *magic* in any form, but please indulge me and simply examine the word for the visual it brings today. One of my grand babies is raising money for summer camp and I have agreed to help her with the resources if she'll clean all the white surfaces in my house—window frames, baseboards, and door jams. My house is fifteen years old and bears some scars on the white surfaces. So, I opted for magic erasers.

Mackenzie and I both stood with awe as she rubbed the first surfaces and before our eyes the dark streaks vanished and the pure, white surface emerged. It was amazing! What in the world is in that piece of cloth? It requires little effort, has no smell, and erases for a long period of time. In my mind this was a new, amazing discovery (perhaps you have been a fan forever, but I just joined the ranks). Anyway, the longer she used the eraser the more in awe I stood. Finally I had a moment of revelation. My life had dark, black streaks until I allowed Jesus to come into my life. He did an eternal work in my heart that allowed me to stand clean before God the Father. I said over and over again, "Jesus can erase anything! He is my Magic Eraser." Doesn't that make you smile?

While the erasing Jesus does within our hearts is an eternal work, our daily life can often be bombarded with those issues that can create dirty stains. Yes? We need times of meeting with the eraser again and again—this is repentance. James 4:8 reminds me that if I come close to God, He comes close to me. The closer God gets, the more I see my need for His touch (eraser) in every area of my life. Sometimes we get busy and life's storms pull us from the closeness of God, but when the Holy Spirit is allowed to really touch our hearts, through authentic communication and relationship with God, the daily stains so easily are removed and the purity of our life in God shines bright once again.

In our health journey, sometimes we need an eraser experience to get back in the game. We need to see that we can be cleansed from yesterday's catastrophe. Did you mess up yesterday and feel like quitting this whole "healthy thing"? Bring that thought to the One who knows the real truth and let Him rub your mind and thoughts till they shine like new again. Remember, draw near to God. He made the first move via the cross and never gets tired of moving toward us. He gently and efficiently removes our stains better than an *eraser*. He does not need magic—He simply honors His Word.

May 18: The Slap of a Friend

Accountability takes courage, but it also takes humility. Letting someone know where you are weak and having a friend stand with you and pray when the storms of life come to attack the core of who you are is critical. I do want to look at this from both sides though. Simply telling someone where we are weak cannot become our release. I can confess that I am struggling, laugh it off, have someone console me, and keep dancing around the same issue. I did that for so many years with no real intent to fix the problem.

Having someone to confess your issues to is designed to strengthen your resolve. Our health is a battle; you know that or you wouldn't read these each morning. And when in a battle, just absolving someone's mistakes is probably not going to save their life. Your partner, friend, coach sometimes needs to take your confession and then firmly help you make a stand. They need to challenge you to see the truth and stick to the plan. That takes someone with courage who loves you more than you love yourself sometimes.

The Bible speaks about wounds from a friend in Proverbs 27:6, "Faithful are the wounds of a friend, but the kisses of an enemy are lavish and deceitful" (AMP). Their accountability is designed to get the structure of your thinking back to a solid place. Remember, we are not on a "fad" journey in which we choose health for a season. Our expedition is a new structure with all the joints and bolts and foundational components foundationally secure.

The winds of life will blow strong against our resolve, but having the determination to endure has the distinct ability to keep us to our course. I hope you find the courage to embrace the honest help of an accountability partner. I know we can travel this path alone, and often we do, but I am convinced that it is much more difficult flying solo.

I need you, I need God, I need my family, and I need the humility it takes to accept the truth from others without an attitude. We can either be humbled privately or often suffer humiliation publicly. You know which one I prefer.

May 19: Scatter the Buzzards

I cannot watch those animal shows where the mean guys *select* the weak one and eventually take it down for their evening meal. My husband continues to say, "That's just nature." But my heart wants to slap the *mean* guys while the weak animal struggles in those final few moments.

I really do understand the food chain, but that does not mean I have to like it. While at my mom's house recently, we heard this moaning sound behind their property and determined it was a cow in distress. Within a short amount of time, a group of buzzards gathered. Mom would go out and scream, "Let her alone," and I would pace looking for a gun to kill the birds. (This is deep, but I am going somewhere.) The cow was not dead and the mockers/consumers had already arrived for their lunch. The louder Mom screamed and the buzzards wouldn't scatter, the more frustrated I got and the more insight downloaded.

Finally, Mom convinced my stepfather to locate the owner of the land, the sheriff or someone and help this poor cow so these buzzards could not start their cleanup while she was still suffering. I said over and over again, "I cannot believe they arrived before she died."

Isn't that the way life is sometimes? Jealousy, or intense envy, can cause others to look upon our decision to become healthy in a negative manner. Soon, they could become mockers or at least critically negative. I have had more than a few people pronounce that I cannot maintain this type of "diet" indefinitely. I used to try to defend myself (scream at the buzzards) but eventually realized I would fight for life and let my health scatter the buzzards. Eating healthy is not a diet. It is simply my choice for life. The longer I walk in health and the more life I portray, the more scattered the buzzards.

While others may desire to change the way they eat and become healthy, often the journey is too difficult and they eventually give up. We cannot join them in their decision to accept defeat. I applaud many of you who have battled difficult life situations, as have I recently, and fought desperately for your health. I want to encourage you to keep screaming at the buzzards, regardless of whether they look like people or problems. Scream loud! You deserve to live.

May 20: Whipped Topping

Yield: 12 servings

The uses for this basic recipe are endless. I use the variations listed below for coffee toppings, with hot cocoa, to top fresh berries or fruit mixtures, or on top of a slice of pumpkin pound cake.

Ingredients

- 1 pint (16 oz.) heavy whipping cream
- ¼ cup xylitol (more or less depending on how sweet you want the whipping cream)
- 1 teaspoon flavoring—vanilla, peppermint, coconut, or almond (depending on preference)

Procedure

1. Place beaters in freezer while gathering supplies.
2. Place heavy whipping cream in a tall mixing bowl, this mixture will splatter.
3. Add sugar and extract and begin mixing on medium-high for about a minute.
4. Increase speed to high until the mixture changes to whipping cream consistency. Be mindful to not over beat as it will eventually turn into butter. But I like the peaks firm. Store in a sealed container. This will keep for several days.

Per Serving:
Calories 85.2
Total Fat 7.4 g
Cholesterol 27.3 mg
Sodium 7.7 mg
Potassium 16.5 mg
Total Carbohydrate 6.0 g
Dietary Fiber 0.0 g
Sugars 0.2 g
Protein 0.4 g

Try These Variations:

1. **Chocolate:** Use chocolate extract instead of above listed extracts and when the mixture has turned to whipping cream consistency, add one container of no sugar added cocoa mix and blend on low.

2. **Coconut:** I use one can of unsweetened coconut milk (that I have had in the refrigerator for several days) and when I open the can, I scoop the solid part from the top, leaving the coconut water on the bottom. I add the solid coconut milk to the heavy whipping cream, add the xylitol, and use coconut extract. Follow the procedure listed above. The coconut water remaining is excellent for drinking.

3. **Pumpkin Spiced:** Use the vanilla extract, but add a couple of tablespoons of pumpkin pie spice mix to the finish product. This is better the following day, so make it ahead of time and plop on your pumpkin pound cake or morning coffee.

May 21: Stuffed Cabbage Shells

Yield: 24 servings

Ingredients

- 1 regular container ricotta cheese
- 1 regular container light sour cream
- 1 regular container 4% cottage cheese
- 3 eggs
- Italian seasoning (to taste)
- 2 pounds lean ground beef
- 2 large cans fire roasted, diced tomatoes
- 2-3 cups 2% shredded mozzarella cheese (depending on how cheesy you want it)
- ½ -1 cup fresh grated, Parmesan Reggiano cheese
- 1 large head of cabbage

Procedure

1. To prepare the cabbage: Pull the 2 exterior leaves from the cabbage. Prepare the steamer basket in about 2 inches of water in your large Dutch oven on the stove. Core the cabbage and place the cored hole on the center of the steamer basket. Bring to a boil and reduce heat. Allow to steam about 30 minutes. Let cool for a few moments. Carefully remove the cabbage and begin to peel the leaves in whole sections. Place these in a bowl to cool completely. If I find the interior leaves are not tender, I return them to the steamer for additional time. Again, let the leaves cool completely before stuffing them.
2. Brown the ground beef and drain if necessary. Add the 2 large cans of tomatoes and heat thoroughly.
3. Preheat oven to 350°F.
4. Mix the first five ingredients and blend well.
5. To make the casserole, spray a 9x14 baking dish with oil. Add about 2 heaping tablespoons of the cheese mixture to each cabbage shell and fold over to make something that looks like an egg roll. Place these seam side down in the baking dish.
6. Top with the meat mixture.
7. Add the mozzarella and Parmesan.
8. Bake for approximately 45 minutes or until the sides are bubbly and the cheese is really browning on the top.
9. Allow to cool for about 20 minutes before cutting. Best served hot from the oven.

Per Serving:
Calories 260.1
Total Fat 15.7 g
Cholesterol 79.4 mg
Sodium 653.2 mg
Potassium 317.0 mg
Total Carbohydrate 9.2 g
Dietary Fiber 1.9 g
Sugars 2.8 g
Protein 20.1 g

May 22: The Memory of a Rat

Can I say how excited I am that watermelons have dropped in price? They are one of my staple foods (when available) but if funds are tight, I have to ask myself if I really need that watermelon. The answer is absolutely yes. Don't you love that? My weekly mission from May to October is to locate the best melons at the best price. Some people shop for shoes; I shop for melons.

News flash: someone sent a text last night informing me that she found a jam sweetened with stevia and that it was good. She was asking if adding stevia was like adding aspartame? Absolutely not. Head to your local health food store and investigate natural sweeteners that metabolize slowly. You may love the visit. Some of my favorite trips now are to those stores for the treasure hunt to find the newest *weapon* in my arsenal, like a jam flavored with stevia and packed with great taste.

I never knew I loved health food stores until I got healthy. Do you have local fresh market-type stores that offer options that you may not have considered? One of my favorite stores is a little more expensive on most items, but I am scheming as to how to find myself on their payroll with an employee discount. It is all in how you present yourself, right? And remember, learning for us will never stop.

Someone recently told me that rats that are fed sugar water forget more rapidly how to run the maze than other lab rats. Wow, I can just see the little fellas winking as the sugar water gets close to their mouths and faking amnesia so they can participate in the study. Where can I sign up? You know I would not do that, but maybe for watermelon juice? I am not certain of the validity of the experimentation, but I can say that not drinking sugared drinks has made a huge difference in my mental acuity. So, maybe taking less sugar does improve my memory?

As we revisit the health food store journey, there are many options for sugared items that you will find on their shelves. Shop well and see if your memory improves also.

May 23: The Real Enemy to My Success

The Word teaches us that Satan comes to kill, steal, and destroy (see John 10:10). While I personally do not believe he has the power to physically kill us, I do believe he has the power to wreak havoc on our lives. And where does this often occur? Usually within our minds. I feel sometimes the torment in our minds could be worse than physical death.

I have spoken with so many people recently who are caught in the "question trap" concerning the circumstances of their lives. Why, why, and why? Often they question and then blame God for such deep wounds in their hearts that usually occurred when they were children and unable to process the injury. I am not slighting their feelings. What I am saying is that God is not the author of such injuries.

Unanswered questions and unmet needs can often cause adults to experience brokenness that induces the building of walls around their feelings and emotions, which protect hopelessness and foster anger. Unhealthy eating can become a byproduct of such turmoil. As simple as it sounds, sometimes it is easier to eat a candy bar than to explore the issues hidden in our hearts. After all, "we will all be in heaven soon." Come on, I get it. But we have many years of life upon this earth before we reach our final destination, and living in a disease-filled body seems worse to me than being dead. Do you see this? Don't you wish disappointment would play fair?

The truth is that our life is just a short season, and while it may appear to be an eternity for us, it is not. Our battle on this earth is not with flesh and blood, but principalities, rulers, and authorities of darkness that always cause us to fall into the question trap of "Does God really hear me? Does He love me? Do I matter? Does God care?" The battle for freedom is often fought in our minds. Making wrong food choices, hiding chocolate, eating starches and sugar are not the enemies of our soul. But there is a dark presence whose daily objective is to get you to not trust God, not trust God's love for you, and to not trust your love for God or God's intentional help with your daily struggles.

God created us and wants us to *allow* Him to share in every area of our lives, even the hidden hurts of our past. He wants us to forgive the offender, turn to Him and accept His unconditional love, and live our lives as healthy adults and not shackled, broken people.

May 24: A Declaration of Freedom

I know Galatians 5:1 has been a foundational Scripture for us, but Isaiah 61 is as well. While Galatians 5 is my personal declaration, the Scripture in Isaiah puts the extended "spin" on my escape to freedom, as only free people can offer freedom to others. Once I fought my way out of my own cell, God opened my eyes to see His breaking heart for those who are suffering in silence. He allowed me to see that my freedom journey was going to offer hope to many. God always wants to proclaim the good news to everyone. His heart is that none would perish or suffer in captivity.

I do realize this passage in Isaiah is speaking of the saving grace that Jesus brings to each of us, but as I said earlier, I see the Bible as applicable on multiple levels. Yes, God sent his Son to set us free from the punishment of eternal separation and to create a bridge between Himself and humankind. The good news of the gospel confirms this. However, I feel that same relevance applies to our freedom from the torment of obesity. I want to be able to offer words of comfort and help. My desire is to see all the prison doors open and those suffering being renewed. There is a way, and hope is available.

Freedom is a journey and while the concept of freedom evokes pictures of no boundaries, no ropes, no constraints—for us that is not the complete picture. Freedom from the cell of obesity is a wide-open door, but remaining free has a strategy. War can offer people their freedom, but maintaining freedom usually requires a plan. That is okay. I would rather be a free person working a plan than a captive person having no hope. How about you?

Reread this portion of Isaiah 61 and be encouraged:

> "God sent me to announce the year of his grace—a celebration of God's destruction of our enemies—and to comfort all who mourn, to care for the needs of all who mourn in Zion, give them bouquets of roses instead of ashes, messages of joy instead of news of doom, a praising heart instead of a languid spirit" (verses 2-3 MSG).

Now that's quite a declaration!

May 25: Put It in the Ground

So many in the generation in which we live—where money can change things—do not really consider the cost of their actions as I feel they should. Maybe none of us really do. Why is that? Perhaps because we cannot see into the future and capture what our actions will precipitate? Maybe we feel that time will place enough distance between what we do and the consequences of our actions? Maybe?

The Bible teaches that whatsoever a person sows, that also will they reap (Galatians 6:7). Does that mean only money? Unfortunately, we all know the answer to that. My actions, attitudes, responses, etc. can all be sown. Reaping is the consequence. If I am always angry, I sow anger, and guess what I reap? If I am always fearful and worrying around my children and grandchildren, I sow fear; then, I find myself having a difficult time trusting God. And if I constantly make excuses for an undisciplined lifestyle, I sow a compromised attitude toward life and I very possibly could reap negative consequences in many areas.

For example, people who do not floss find that eventually their gums bear the consequence of bad habits. At that point, it may be a long journey to health, if at all. Flossing takes less than a minute but the benefits are great. Low-impact exercise like water aerobics only takes a couple of hours weekly and has great benefits. But the consequences of never moving our muscles and/or never allowing our weight-bearing joints to be challenged may prove to be detrimental in our later life.

If I start allowing small cheats in my health plan again, those *cheat babies* that I sowed will grow up and eventually I could find myself bearing the ugly consequence of obesity and horrible self-esteem again. My prayer is that each of us could honestly examine our lives and have the courage to say, "That one, little cheat has the potential to compromise my entire journey." While I am speaking of food, I felt the Holy Spirit remind me this could apply to any area of our lives. No cheating allowed.

If we sow cheating, I can promise the consequences will not be pleasant. The flip side of this is to sow fabulous hydration into your body and reap beautiful skin, great elasticity, and lack of water retention. Sow beautifully colored vegetables and reap happy cells that make your organs smile. Sow limited portions and reap the benefits of smaller clothes. Sow a smile and reap smiles all around. Put the good stuff in the soil of your flesh and reap the positive consequences and benefits of sowing well.

May 26: A Memorial Day Tribute

As Memorial Day approaches, this is a fabulous time to celebrate the greatness of our military people who give themselves openly for our protection and security. I am so proud to be an American!

I also want to celebrate today the greatest fallen warrior of them all, Jesus Christ, who died for humankind, and whose life grants each of us freedom. I am proud to be His disciple. I know that because Jesus is in my life and resides in my heart, this places me on the journey of love, joy, and peace in spite of anything this world brings my way. How fitting our family Scripture declares freedom and speaks of the sacrifice that secures this priceless concept.

"It is for freedom's sake" means that Jesus knew, understood, and valued freedom so highly that the thought of us in prison prompted Him to give His life for my freedom—our freedom. His value of freedom, His love for each of us, and the price He willingly paid for our freedom are certainly reasons we fight to maintain that freedom. Jesus secured our eternal freedom, but we live in the now—not eternity. We are eternally saved by grace through faith, absolutely, but every day can be a struggle and fight against the sins of our flesh that so easily entangle, and whose purpose is to cause us to turn and walk away from God. I am grateful on a daily basis for the sacrifice that Jesus made, but equally as grateful for the work of the Holy Spirit who was given by God to help assist me with my stand against failure and defeat.

We must also remember that Memorial Day is about celebrating those who not only provided freedom for us, but also for the generations to follow. Each generation establishing and maintaining freedom for those who follow is a foundational pillar. I know my fight has been a challenge, but somewhere in my spirit the frustration turns to a smile as I think that I am establishing a pillar for my family.

This Memorial Day we may not be war heroes or celebrated veterans, but we can certainly be proud that we are freedom fighters and in some small way, we are really making a difference in the physical freedom of our families and loved ones. Let's keep doing our part.

May 27: Deviled Eggs (or Angel Eggs)

Yield: 24 servings

You could refer to these as "angel eggs" since they do not have any sugar. I do not advocate using sugar-free relish because the sweetener used is on my "naughty list."

Ingredients

- 1 dozen eggs boiled
- Several tablespoons Duke's Mayo
- Salt to taste
- Green olives chopped finely
- Paprika (optional)

Procedure

1. Boil and cool eggs. Peel when cooled and cut in half length-wise.
2. Scoop the yokes into a bowl and add the mayo, chopped olives, salt, and a little of the juice of the olives (just a wee bit of juice).
3. Mix well and stuff the empty egg whites.
4. Top with paprika. These are not sweet deviled eggs, so the paprika is a good addition.

Per Serving:

Calories 53.1
Total Fat 4.6 g
Cholesterol 94.2 mg
Sodium 58.4 mg
Potassium 41.7 mg
Total Carbohydrate 0.2 g
Dietary Fiber 0.1 g
Sugars 0.0 g
Protein 3.1 g

May 28: Salsa

Yield: 16 servings

I have an exceptionally large blender so I can use all of the ingredients at once. You may need to divide the recipe in half if your blender is regular sized.

Ingredients

- 2-3 large cans diced tomatoes with sweet onions, or 5-6 of the regular-sized cans
- 2 large or 4 regular Roma or 3 large "on-the-vine" (whatever looks the best) fresh tomatoes
- 1 large sweet onion
- 1 ½ - 2 limes (squeeze the juice of 1 ½ and only add the other ½ if needed for additional taste)
- Garlic salt to taste
- Salt to taste
- Jalapeño and Serrano peppers (In this batch I'll use 3 jalapeños, and two or three of the Serrano. I try to get most of the seeds out. However, if you like the heat, leave some of the seeds, but be careful. It gets hot fast.)
- Cilantro (I put close to half a bunch in this recipe)

Procedure

1. Put all the "must haves" in a blender and experiment with the salt, garlic salt, lime juice, and cilantro.
2. I pulse mine until it's the consistency we like. This stores well for about one week.
3. If it's too hot, make certain you have no seeds in the mixture next time and back down on the Serrano peppers. They really carry the heat.

Per Serving:
Calories 35.4
Total Fat 0.1 g
Cholesterol 0.0 mg
Sodium 337.3 mg
Potassium 65.7 mg
Total Carbohydrate 8.6 g
Dietary Fiber 1.7 g
Sugars 4.3 g
Protein 0.3 g

May 29: The Freedom Yoke

Jesus cares about the little things that we care about, so I know He cares that we struggle to attain and maintain our health. I think one of the hardest things to reconcile for me on my personal journey was that I emphatically knew Jesus could heal my hunger and food addiction so that I could eat everything and anything I wanted without bother. He could. But my story was not that easy.

I have been totally and immediately healed of certain things, but not others. Sometimes I have a compelling desire to know why. I felt God spoke to my heart two weeks ago and said, *I could tell you the why, but it would not change the circumstances. Just trust Me.* So I continue to stand and trust. But wouldn't that be a lot easier if I knew why? However, trust is about standing, believing, and not always seeing the answer. Isn't it?

I have lived long enough to know that life is a journey of highs and lows. Some extreme, some gentle. And even though God adores us deeply, He never promised a life without conflict or struggle. In fact I heard one of my spiritual fathers recently say, "The Bible is just one big book of storms." So true.

I am certain when some people think of these life-storms, perhaps one of the visualizations they contemplate is a yoke. It is certainly one of the pictures I quickly visualize. A yoke is a device placed *on something* to harness its energy and remove any hope of freedom. It binds one to something with no choice of partner. For many of us, obesity is a yoke that offers no pleasant options. In fact, I could begin a long list of deadly things to which obesity harnesses us.

But praise God; Jesus offers us a yoke of freedom! We get to choose whether or not to be yoked to Him and when He is in the yoke with us, His Word says it is easy. I love easy. God give me the strength and wisdom to remove the yoke of slavery and replace it immediately with a yoke of freedom. Jesus, You rock!

May 30: Mosquitoes

I bring to the table for consideration this morning the subject of mosquitos. Does anybody like them other than frogs? They bug the snot out of me. They never give up, they don't care that you hate them and they are determined to bite you. Can you see a picture?

Sometimes I can sense the "mosquitos" in regard to my own, fleshly desires as they relate to food. How about this? I can go to certain restaurants and nothing bothers me, but when I visit certain favorites all the "mosquitos" arrive. For example, the servers smile as they bring the bread and butter for the table (that I love), and everyone is eating and laughing. Immediately the mosquito to remind me of how I am suffering arrives. Then, the waiter brings the appetizers and everyone grabs and laughs while I sit and smile—mosquitos.

On Tuesday, while sitting through this scenario and smiling as I drank my water and dealt with my mosquito attitude, I wanted to swat someone. I did all the right things though, smiled, sipped my water, and confessed that "food was not my boss." But that wretched *mosquito* was hovering over the shrimp and peppers and drawing my attention. Finally, I had to move the plate away. Food is a social event for me, so I love eating with friends, except when I am in a mosquito-swatting frame of mind. Not good.

Then the questions started: How about just one? Is there really anything on there that can hurt me? Aren't these really small shrimp? But how many of you know that just that one little open door could have started a pattern of making excuses. Then I got irritated as I had not planned well, had no snacks with me, was eating late, had purchased my favorite appetizer to bless others, and then was tormented by mosquitos.

The moral of the story: Make a plan. Mosquitos will be with us forever, as irritating as they are, but they too are not the boss of me.

May 31: May Reflection Page

As you are completing May, are there things you wish you had highlighted or which you had written down? With the Memorial Day celebrations, the summer festivities begin. Let us plan at every summer function to volunteer to cook the healthy desserts. You have gotten several now. The only problem is that you will now be expected to supply them for each function. Not a problem. Right?

_____

_____

_____

_____

_____

_____

_____

_____

_____

_____

_____

_____

_____

_____

_____

_____

_____

_____

_____

_____

June

This month the healthy fruit options begin to really explode. Watermelons are plentiful and summer vegetables and fruits abound. Fill those plates with lots of color so your organs smile.

June 1: Walk into the Wind

I walked last night in a strong wind. It presented itself as a force of opposition. I was walking and meditating about things in our health journey that present themselves as forces of opposition:

- Our attitudes
- Our ability to move the boundaries
- Our ability to make excuses to cheat
- Our families and friends who are "scared" that we are not eating enough
- The television
- Various reports of the latest "diet" fads
- Our schedules/events
- Being unprepared
- Not seeing our health as we should and "rolling the dice"
- The cost of eating healthy
- Going out to eat
- Hunger
- Our past diet cycles
- Etc., etc., etc.

We can allow the force of the wind to deter us, or we can walk *into* the winds of opposition and realize that sometimes the opposition causes us to exert more energy, use more muscles, and enhance our health journey. There are two patterns of reasoning, but both have to do with the way we see things. Is the opposition strong enough to push us off course or perhaps cause us to stop? Or is it a challenge and we love the victory of pushing it back?

My muscles are sore this morning, but I smile because I outlasted the opposition. We can do this, family. Outlasting our opposition and our past is critical to our long-term health.

Remember: We only fail when we fail to get up.

June 2: Mirror, Mirror on the Wall, Part 1

As I was meditating this morning, I felt the Lord speak to me about how infrequently we feel we accomplished our assigned tasks well and what bondage that mindset is. Most of the time people are quick to see fault in almost everything. There is certainly a time to see even the smallest issue—the foundation of a mighty building skewed, one malignant cell, money drawn from your account from someone unauthorized. Yes we pray for that "eagle eye" as it is critical to survival. When we spot those things, we quickly move to attack mode. But not everything needs a *critical* eye. Hear me out.

It is okay to try on a bathing suit and blame the mirrors for making you look a wee bit chunky, especially if you have not been moving the boundaries daily. It is okay to laugh and grab another swimsuit, and yes, it is okay to go home without one. You do not have to stand in front of the mirror and slap yourself (like that helps) or proclaim, "I hate standing in front of mirrors. I always look so fat. I never look good in clothes." Have you ever had one of "those" conversations?

For many years, I never tried anything on in the stores because it lead to moments of intense criticism and then quick journeys to the doughnut shop for comfort. If I felt really bad about what the *mirror* reflected, maybe I grabbed two goodies. Have you ever experienced something like this?

It's okay to believe in yourself *and give yourself credit,* even when you have failed. It is even better when you understand the power of trying again. It is okay to realize that failure is a part of life and sometimes so is constructive criticism. It is okay to remind yourself that you missed the mark, but too much dwelling on defeat can lead to prolonged negativity and depression. So many people are caught in that trap. And that is *not* okay.

You need to set some boundaries around those mirror conversations and realize that mirrors are simply reflections and even they can have a bad imaging day. So, give yourself a break.

June 3: Mirror, Mirror on the Wall, Part 2

None of us can escape our reflection forever, but we can change our response to that reflection. Have you seen people walk past a mirror and try to avoid looking at themselves? (It's hysterical!) It's not bad to look, but it is bad to allow the mirror to prompt a negative response. If you are doing everything you can to be healthy, know that you are not moving the boundaries to allow for compromise, and the mirror is still *lying*—then deal with the mirror. I find stores that have *favorable mirrors* that tell the truth and all my clothes come from there. But the real truth is God is not sitting in heaven being critical of our appearance. Can you really hear and accept that?

Sometimes I wonder if God is saddened by the way we feel about ourselves, as He created us in His image. I wonder if He sees that we are being horribly critical of His best creation? Have you ever poured your heart and soul into a project and then had someone criticize it? I have and it is devastating. I wonder if God feels those emotions when I criticize me—the work of His hands—a daughter He adores.

Being critical is a choice. Speaking life to you is a choice, as is choosing healthy foods. As I said in the beginning, God wants you to know today that He fashioned you, never criticizes you, and loves you more than you have words to describe. So as you read this today, can you promise to speak well and not be so quick to criticize? There are plenty of great things about each of us to celebrate, but often we are so busy criticizing we cannot see them.

From now on, when we look into the mirror, let's wink at God's best piece of art and not allow our own critical judgment to taint the reflection He wants us to see.

June 4: The Work of Perseverance

This morning can we speak about perseverance? In a society where giving up is the norm, as believers, however, we are encouraged to continue and persevere. According to the book of Romans, going through trials and tribulations causes perseverance, which in turn produces character and then hope (see Romans 5:3-4). I am watching my watermelon seedlings fight for maturity now and it speaks to my heart about so many things in life where it is easier to give up than continue to fight for what I know is right.

My husband transplanted the seedlings when they were about three inches tall from a pot on the porch that I, personally, could watch, water, and tend to. When he transplanted them, he thought he was placing them in good soil that had been decomposing for a couple of years. I had my doubts, but he "knew." Not to make a point about a wrong decision, but the seedlings went from my porch where the conditions were almost perfect to a place where some of the conditions were certainly unfavorable. They stopped growing quickly. They simply stopped. Their leaves browned, and for a moment it seemed death was imminent.

I checked them daily, prayed over them (yes I did), encouraged them with my words to grow and prosper, but last week I came to the realization that *they* must fight for life. They must persevere when conditions are not always perfect and they must adapt if they are going to grow, mature, produce fruit and live a long, healthy life (in plant terms).

I see our health journey in this picture. For me, I was in a "pot" where I had grown and actually had outgrown my surroundings (jeans, clothes, amount of medications to combat overweight issues, etc.), and life no longer was best lived in this tight container. So I chose another place to start over on January 24, 2011, and there were many times when it was not easy. The convenience of stopping at fast food restaurants, eating anything (and more) that people prepared for me at parties, and living from one meal to the next all stopped. Choosing to live a healthy lifestyle was questionable at times. Many said that it couldn't be done. I am proof that perseverance pays off. Never give up.

June 5: Keep Persevering

I feel as if we should continue our topic from yesterday. There are a few things that really ensure a successful journey, and perseverance has to be at the top of the list. I would imagine if you consulted a gold medal athlete, a billionaire, and a kindergarten teacher, they would all concur that perseverance helped them as much as any other attribute.

Today, I am now in another world (soil structure—from yesterday's devotion) and I cannot go back to that same pot. It no longer exists. I cannot choose health with the option to return to my former lifestyle if healthy eating does not work. It is not allowed. I live in a different place now with its own challenges. I have started to mature (as have my watermelon plants) specifically where I am now planted, and there is no place of return. That option in our lives must be eliminated.

My daily health journey is my new normal. That is what perseverance is all about. The watermelon plants cannot return to their former life (pot) so they must accept their new journey and fight for survival where they are. The good news is that they are doing just that. They are now showing small signs that they are fighting to live. My husband is planning to redo the soil because they are not growing as rapidly as he feels they should.

Now that Terry sees the baby watermelon plants have persevered, he is responding to their dedication to live and now desires to help increase their chances of survival. Until he saw their determination, he was not willing to commit any extra time to assist them. I wonder if our internal organs and our body feel the same? I think they probably do.

We can never return to our old way of living and healthy eating cannot just be a *choice*. We can't say, "I'll eat what I want at this meal and do better at the next meal." If that is our mantra, then we still live in the old pot. Can we be honest? We must persevere and continue to persevere against all odds so that perseverance finishes its work which means we have no options other than being healthy.

June 6: Chicken Salad

Yield: 8 servings

You can serve this with lettuce or low-carb wraps. For a Thanksgiving variation, you can substitute your left-over turkey. I prefer to refrigerate this overnight, allowing the flavors to blend longer. If it's dry the next day just add ¼ cup half/half or a little extra mayo, stir, and place back in the refrigerator for a couple of hours.

Ingredients

- 1 bag frozen chicken breast
- ½ large bag red grapes
- ½ cup mayo
- ½ cup sour cream (light)
- Salt to taste
- ½ container shredded Parmesan cheese (from the deli, not the sprinkle cheese)
- ½ cup chopped pecans (chopped fine)
- Thyme to taste (fresh or dried, I use *a lot* as I really enjoy the taste this gives to the meat)

Procedure

1. Boil the bag of chicken breasts and allow to cool.
2. While they are cooling, prepare your grapes by washing and cutting in half-length wise.
3. When cooled, cut the chicken in chunks and add all other ingredients.
4. Mix well and cool for several hours or longer.

Per Serving:

Calories 421.7
Total Fat 26.7 g
Cholesterol 117.0 mg
Sodium 394.7 mg
Potassium 382.4 mg
Total Carbohydrate 6.1 g
Dietary Fiber 0.9 g
Sugars 4.0 g
Protein 40.1 g

June 7: Caprese Salad

Yield: 6 servings

Ingredients

- 1 large mozzarella ball
- 4 large Roma tomatoes
- 1 container sweet basil pesto
- Fresh basil leaves, sliced long and thin

Procedure

1. Slice the mozzarella ball into 1/3 inch rounds (or whatever size you desire. At this size, the ball should yield about 8-10 slices).
2. Slice the tomatoes in rounds. (1 tomato slices into approximately 4 hearty rounds.)
3. On a plate, stand one tomato round up and place a mozzarella round against it. Continue vertically placing the slices beside each to form a complete circle. Or, you can arrange them as you desire but they should be touching.
4. Spoon the pesto sauce over the salad liberally and garnish with fresh basil leaves if you desire. You can serve immediately, but I prefer to allow an hour or so for the flavors to blend. Also, you can place the basil leaves between the cheese and tomatoes.

Per Serving:
Calories 264.7
Total Fat 21.5 g
Cholesterol 24.6 mg
Sodium 553.2 mg
Potassium 123.5 mg
Total Carbohydrate 6.3 g
Dietary Fiber 1.1 g
Sugars 1.3 g
Protein 9.5 g

June 8: Prayer at the Grocery Store

This morning I am thinking about our Dave Ramsey class last night. We had the task of creating a zero-based budget as our homework last week and then tonight's class was followed with a *plastic-surgery party* to shred some of our credit cards.[1] I really am enjoying the class and learning the new principles is helping me develop and stretch in some areas. It is hard, I cannot lie, but the challenge is really good. There are those things that we must budget first and can I say that I'm glad food is listed in that top four. Yes, I am.

As many of us are focused on the planning of our budgets, discussions of healthy foods and their expense are numerous. My husband suggested a couple of cheaper items last night, but I do not eat most of them, nor do I want to return to boxed foods because they are simply cheaper. They may be cheaper to ingest now, but they will be more costly in the future if they encourage obesity-related diseases.

As I prayed last night I began to thank God for wisdom in this area. The class is challenging, the budget is challenging, and now food selection is getting challenging. That sounds like a recipe for prayer. Asking for God's help along our journey to health and success should not be the last thing we do, but the first. Dave Ramsey is having us create a budget at the end of each month *before* the next month begins. Then, we have our structure for the month from which to work. I smiled last night as I see how he puts planning at the front of the journey as we do. Failing to plan for the week can often cause the drive-through window to scream loudly. The food they are offering is often filled with words we cannot pronounce. The same goes into financial planning. There are voices screaming for our money, but I get to decide to whom I respond. Thank you, Dave Ramsey.

It is God's desire for our bodies to be healthy. And God knows we need proper fuel to be successful. God also knows that we need great wisdom in the grocery stores as they can be trying to hold us hostage. Let us pray as we make the grocery list, as we enter the store, and as we search the isles for God's wisdom. That is more critical than we know. Please do not discount the power of prayer when the numbers in our bank and the numbers at the register are in competition. No stress—prayer works.

---

1. For more information about David Ramsey's ministry visit www.daveramsey.com.

June 9: Rosemary Anyone?

For those who know me, you know I am not really a "garden girl." Well, I didn't used to be. But now that I am walking on the healthy path, fresh herbs have become my second best friend.

My husband and I planted some rosemary over a year ago and what a hearty, sturdy plant it has become. We actually divided it and made two containers and they are now both flourishing. I have started trying to use the herb to add flavor to our foods (be careful as a little goes a long way) and how nice to walk on the deck and grab some sprigs, chop them, and add to whatever.

Last night I took about two and a half pounds of lean ground beef (no added oil), browned it and added three large cans of diced, fire-roasted tomatoes. I let this heat well. Then I chopped a large head of cabbage in small pieces as well as a large Vidalia onion and added both to the beef mixture. I seasoned the entire batch with sea salt and TABASCO®. Finally, I also added two stems of rosemary chopped extra fine (about thirty to forty pieces, but it was too strong). I let this cook together until the cabbage was very tender (your preference). Before serving, I added grated Parmesan cheese. This new recipe was low in calories, made a big pot, and lasted for several meals. It was my first time cooking with the rosemary, and while it was a little strong, it made me smile to think it came from my deck. I was a proud momma.

I said all that to say that as I researched the rosemary herb to find recipes, I discovered that it actually has great health benefits. I discovered that rosemary is beneficial in helping with memory issues and is used in other countries to help treat Alzheimer's disease. I also found that the herb is packed with antioxidants, which are memory enhancing and cancer fighting too. That is awesome to me. I like finding new things that are so beneficial to our bodies. I did use a stem of rosemary on Saturday as part of my marinade for the Mahi Mahi on the grill. If you have never tried it, you should. My grand babies kept saying, "Yum, Nina!" Variety is a key component in our new world, so keep being creative and utilizing those herbs God gave to help keep our bodies healthy.

June 10: Me Time

I love the coolness of the morning, but the warmth of the late afternoon sun on my skin also brings a smile. When we consider the real complexities of creation, how can we help but smile? I know that many times there are formulas for everything and everything seems so complicated. But last night I had such a special encounter with *simple,* and God sweetly reminded me of several things. I was honored to visit with my friend, Tina, and spend some time in her pool. Her backyard is surrounded by trees and secluded from the normal mirage of houses. For that span of time, life came to a resting halt and the complexities of the day melted as we laughed and *simply* floated.

We tried some water aerobics and worked our legs a wee bit, but it was fun and uncomplicated. I drove home realizing how critical to our journey are the moments of peace where our bodies really rest and enjoy life. The psalmist writes that our hearts are to be set "at peace" again. That means set back to their original resting state. God never intended for us to live in such complexities that our heart is racing in competition with our minds and one day simply rolls into the next.

As my body hung in the water with its warmth protecting me from the chill of the wind, I was reminded that God's best plan for our life includes moments like this. I concentrated on the fact that we must stop striving to be, have, do, or perform, and simply rest, even for a moment, and let our bodies regroup. Many times life demands all of us, and then our health, our food, and our water intake are the last items on our minds. In fact, we often give to everyone, make meals for everyone, watch everyone's lives in our protection mode, and don't have enough energy for ourselves. It is time to re-evaluate.

I have heard statements like "Always make time for yourself—you deserve it," and honestly I felt people who spoke things as such were selfish. But I have had to rethink my position. I had to readjust. I challenge you to readjust the budget, readjust your exercise time (get in the pool and laugh), readjust your *me time,* and your heart will begin to laugh. That contagious joy will change the atmosphere where you are—especially your home. I promise. Give yourself permission to take care of you. The dishes will be there tomorrow.

June 11: Restaurant Ally

I have been thinking a lot about planting and what is displayed after planting. Some plants immediately take to their new homes and their leaves and colors quickly display their connection. However, within a few days, others quickly begin to fade, drop leaves, and wither. Their environment is not conducive to bringing forth life. I wonder how many times we actually offset healthy habits by going out to eat too often, reasoning that "its been a bad day and I'll work out twice as long," or perhaps attending too many social gatherings. While each of these are not destructive in singular situations, consistent eating out can often be the beginning of an unhealthy journey.

Please be mindful that dishes at your favorite places usually contain increased amounts of sugar and salt. Then, when we begin to swell or thicken around the middle and our "leaves" convey that something is not right, usually a transplant situation has to occur and that halts the process for a season and places us back at square zero. To me, that is an unproductive repeat behavior and if I am repeating behavior, I want it to count. How about you? My encouragement would be to limit the number of times you eat out or attend social gatherings without packing. Once a week, for a season, could be plenty. Remember, no one is going to select and prepare your best health foods as you will.

This is the season where we normally start grabbing yogurts, ice cream, and quick meals coupled with some fun outside lounging and long conversations. Be mindful of your calories. One of my favorite restaurants has started listing the calories on their menu. I was shocked when I got a tea the other day to discover that one of their sandwiches was almost eight hundred calories. Too many of those "bad boys" and your season of displaying well could be short. I am including a passage from Psalm 1 this morning as an encouragement that we should be planted by places that allow us to produce life. Restaurant Ally five days a week is not good soil. Perhaps consider a transplant (new mindset on eating out) and see if the display of your healthy self is better. I am checking that in my own life recently and thought I would share.

> "Blessed (happy, fortunate, prosperous, and enviable) is the man who walks and lives not in the counsel of the ungodly [following their advice, their plans and purposes], nor stands [submissive and inactive] in the path where sinners walk, nor sits down [to relax and rest] where the scornful [and the mockers] gather. But his delight and desire are in the law of the Lord, and on His law (the precepts, the instructions, the teachings of God) he habitually meditates (ponders and studies) by day and by night. And he shall be like a tree firmly planted [and tended] by the streams of water, ready to bring forth its fruit in its season; its leaf also shall not fade or wither; and everything he does shall prosper [and come to maturity]" (Psalm 1:1-3 AMP).

June 12: What's That in the Water? Part 1

During water aerobics last night we were surprised by a *special visitor* that escaped from a diaper from one of the babies (I guess) at the other end of the pool. I almost lost my dinner. Contamination...ugh.

But the really bad part was that if one of the ladies in my class had not looked down as she was walking laps and tried to grab "the pebble" to remove it from the pool, any one of us could have stepped on it. Am I creating a visual for you? Are you laughing? All of a sudden my eyes were focused on the murkiness of the water and the fact that I was in the "toilet bowl" while the lifeguards were trying to *examine* the substance to verify what it actually was.

This really only took about eight to ten minutes, but I felt like I was trapped in a bad story. I know I could have vacated the pool immediately, but the officials continued to reassure us, "It probably is nothing." They were wrong. I had to really talk to myself as we were asked to transfer to the bigger, lap pool. As bad as this experience was, it actually offered me another "life story" to share with you.

Consider that the pool represents our body (our structure), and the water represents our internal fluid. How many times do things enter our bodies that can go unnoticed for years that can contaminate the fluid that our body requires to live? I wonder how many things we willingly place in our mouths that deeply affect these life-giving fluids. Our instructor told us as the guards started fishing the "visitor" from the pool that we should only be concerned if we had shaved our legs and left an open cut that the contaminated water could touch. Now I was really sick. I shaved my legs only twenty minutes before class and am absolutely certain that I probably had an exposed place somewhere.

Do I need a lawyer, a net, or a crying towel? All I can do now after being in the water for twenty minutes without knowing a "visitor" had been released is pray. If there is damage, it has been done. Now I wait. Part 2 to this devotion follows.

June 13: Avocado Salad

Yield: 8 servings

Ingredients

- 4 avocados
- 1-2 limes (start with one)
- 4 Roma tomatoes
- ½ bunch cilantro
- Olive oil
- Cumin (optional)
- Kosher salt
- Coarse ground pepper

Procedure

1. Slice the avocados in half length-wise and remove the seed.
2. To easily remove the skin, you can use a teaspoon and gently scoop the fruit onto a cutting board and chunk, or take a sharp knife and score the fruit into small squares. Then, gently peel the backing so the squares fall into the bowl.
3. Chunk the tomatoes and add to the avocado.
4. Remove the stems from the cilantro and chop finely. Add to the avocado/tomato mixture.
5. Add the fresh, squeezed juice from the limes.
6. Drizzle about 2 tablespoons of olive oil on the mixture.
7. Sprinkle with salt and pepper to taste.
8. Toss gently and serve.

Per Serving:

8 Servings
Amount Per Serving - **Calories** 166.4
Total Fat 14.8 g
Cholesterol 0.0 mg
Sodium 3.1 mg
Potassium 440.9 mg
Total Carbohydrate 10.7 g
Dietary Fiber 3.3 g
Sugars 0.3 g
Protein 2.9 g

June 14: Baked Jicama Fries

Yield: 12 servings

They will brown, become somewhat crisp and taste good with a low-carb ketchup, but they will not be an exact match for your steak fries. Remember, white potatoes carry a whopping 33g of carbs/1 cup while jicama only has 5. That is a huge difference. My family enjoys these and as I do not eat potatoes at all, this is a great substitute for me.

Ingredients

- 1-2 large jicama (these go a long way, so if you're feeding 3-4 people one large is plenty.)
- Olive oil
- Sea salt
- Paprika

Procedure

1. Peel the jicama and boil for 30 minutes.
2. Dry well and slice into steak fries (I use a mandolin, but a sharp knife works well also. Remember, the jicama will always have a crunchy texture like a water chestnut.)
3. Preheat oven to 400°F.
4. Line a large baking pan with parchment paper.
5. Toss the jicama in olive oil and distribute evenly on the pan with none touching (for best results, they should be at least 1/3 inch apart.).
6. Sprinkle with salt and paprika and bake for approximately 30 minutes. 15 minutes into the baking time, turn the fries and season the other side if you desire. (I do.) Watch closely as they can burn.

Per Serving:
Calories 65.0
Total Fat 2.5 g
Cholesterol 0.0 mg
Sodium 4.8 mg
Potassium 191.7 mg
Total Carbohydrate 10.3 g
Dietary Fiber 5.8 g
Sugars 2.1 g
Protein 1.0 g

June 15: What's That in the Water? Part 2

The other day we spoke of those unwanted visitors that find their way into our bodies that have no intent of bringing health, but could bring long-term contamination. What about all the chemicals and preservatives added to foods to make them taste better and last longer? MSG is at the top of the list of the "not so good for us" category. Our liver and kidneys act as major filters in our bodies. As with filters in our houses, computers, and electronics, if not properly cared for, they stop working and our equipment can be destroyed. The same thing happens in our bodies.

I was telling someone recently that when my triglycerides were so high several times in a row, I was sent for a liver scan and it revealed that I had a "fatty" liver. My filtering system was clogged and I had no knowledge of that except for the blood test. The doctor immediately limited the amount of sugar and fatty foods that I ingested, as well as instructing me to eat a large salad with lots of raw vegetables daily to help "clean the filter." This filter affects my fluid levels and the purity of the water in and out of my blood. But until someone "spotted" the unwanted visitor, I was walking along thinking all was well.

We also need to watch those sugar-free products, which are almost always loaded with sodium as well as aspartame. Aspartame is another substance reported to have long reaching detrimental effects on our bodies and needs to be avoided also. We need to be reminded that some scientists say that aspartame takes as long as ten years to clear our bodies and can make our brains crave sugar. The sugar-free products may make us feel better about not eating sugar, but they may be more of an unwanted visitor than we know. Is there any hope?

We do have options, but they are time-consuming. However, given the choice of sacrificing my time or being visited in my "pool" by an unwanted visitor, I will start cooking today. How about you? The vessel God has given me has to be maintained properly, filters cleaned, fluid levels balanced and refilled, and all systems checked on a regular basis. I have a large part to play in this.

So, try to cook as often as you can and check the labels on everything. Examine the fluid around and make certain we are not the one placing the unwanted visitor in the water. Sorry to be so vivid in this book, but I am a visual girl.

June 16: More than a Conqueror

I woke up this morning with the phrase "more than a conqueror" on my heart. I thought conquering was good enough? For most of us, knowing we win is the best part of the game. Right? Not always. We have to constantly remind ourselves that in this world there are multiple trials, temptations, and battles. It has been this way throughout history. Always. The kingdom was always in need of protection as various rulers saw the political gain of land as another jewel in their crown.

This morning I do not want to focus on conquering, I want to focus on the phrase "more than." Romans 8:31-37 gives a wonderful picture of never being separated from the love of God. That one concept is so eternal some of us miss the real implications. We understand that life is a daily battle but we praise God that even in our failure His love never changes. We often miss that nothing can remove us or separate us from God's love and yet we struggle to accept that truth. How is that possible?

Coming to the full realization of the power of this passage places us in the "more than conqueror" category. There is a place in our heart where we must come to understand the verse in these terms, "Do you think anyone is going to be able to drive a wedge between us and Christ's love for us? There is no way! Not trouble, not hard times, not hatred, not hunger, not homelessness, not bullying threats, not backstabbing, not even the worst sins listed in Scripture" (Romans 8:35 MSG).

Last night I actually got up about midnight and ate some nuts because I was starving. I know that is the wrong time to eat, but I was actually hungry as water aerobics class was so late. I felt horrible when I went back to bed—almost defeated. But this morning the Spirit of the Lord awakened me with "more than" a conqueror. God is so good.

I began to meditate on that phrase, and while looking at this passage in several translations I discovered, "overwhelming victory, surpassing victory, more than a victory" because of the way Jesus embraces us. We are more than, and *more than* means, "above, beyond, not limited by (a defeat, whether one meal or three months), embracing of, and understanding at a different level than the other soldiers on the field." Keep declaring that truth confidently all day, "I am *more than* conquering my health plan." To all my more than conquerors, someday we will feast at the table in our eternal home and smile at each other with that *God confidence* that says, "I was one and so were you." Conquer well this day and live above.

June 17: Living versus Existing

God's love and concern for each of us is beyond description. He never desires that we compromise in any area of our lives, because He never compromises with us. Over and over again while at camp with our young people recently, we heard the cry of God, "Just surrender, quit trying to have your own way, give up, My way is easy."

As I listened, I was reminded that the fight for life is strong within each of us. People cling to life, and I understand that. But in God's economy, simple submission and letting go is really the best way. I realized at camp God was stressing to these young people, "Let go; I've got it." But I really feel that sometimes that "let go" is perched right in the heart of our "But what if I fail...again?" Sometimes, in relation to our health, letting go means we really let go and there is nothing to which we can return. Scary, huh?

My husband and I had this discussion the other day as a follow-up to a discussion I had earlier in the week with a dear friend. We know that choosing health is the best option; each of us really knows it. But our past way of existence is always a possibility. We could say, "If choosing health doesn't work and I don't lose enough weight to be a size whatever by whenever, then I'll go back to eating as I please." We simply cannot do that any longer.

Living and existing are two different concepts. While engulfed in sixty-five pounds of extra weight, I simply existed. I got up every day, did my stuff, and longed for heaven so I could be free from this prison of a mortal body in which I found myself trapped. I worked hard at covering my pain and hiding. A lot of times I did that by cheating. However, as I said to someone last week, I don't look at cheating the same any longer, because I am *living* now and not merely *existing*.

In my old life, cheating was indulging generously in the wrong foods with a promise to do right again tomorrow. That is an existence mindset. Living, on the other hand, does not consider indulging in those things as an option because that old life is gone. Sugar, for me, is no longer a part of the options for life and therefore cannot be used as a cheat for me. If it does not exist as an option, it cannot be revisited as a cheat, right? I do not cheat because I cannot. Cheating is death to me and I choose life. I simply let go and burned the bridge to my old way of thinking about food and there is no place in which to return. I would rather live than exist any day.

June 18: The Bubble Gum Principle

How many of you know there is an art to chewing bubble gum and blowing bubbles? When I learned to create these beautifully round and huge circles with my bubble gum, I felt I arrived. I am not certain why as my jaws would ache and some of the bubble gum always found its way to places on my face, hair, and clothes. Oh well, that is one of the benefits of ice. Right?

I never knew how baseball players kept one piece of gum in their mouths for hours. After I chewed mine for a few minutes, and the flavor was gone, I quickly became bored and often disposed of the remainder in a speedy fashion. I loved the flavor, but when that was gone, the effort was too great even though I loved the challenge of varied bubbles.

It was not until I was older that I realized bubble gum has properties that teach life lessons. One of those a friend deemed the *bubble gum principle.*

What we learn from the above situation is that gum, when chewed, releases its flavor quickly and then has served its purpose. I use this principle often in my life situations. I tell people when hearing difficult information about themselves, "Chew it, get the flavor, and spit it out. In most cases there is a nugget of truth that we need to obtain from the statement. We need to determine what it is and how we need to respond—not react—and then spit out the *gum.*" Sometimes that is easier said than done. So how does this apply to our health journey? Consider these:

1. You get a bad report about your blood. Do not panic, just grab the truth, make the changes, and put the report in the drawer until the next one comes to announce your changes worked.

2. The scale shouts a number you remember from several days ago. Nod your head, record your weight, and rethink what you ate and drank yesterday. Make the changes and weigh again tomorrow.

3. You have a horrible day at work and find your desire to comfort with sugar is uncontrollable. You feel like a failure. Eat two apples or an entire pint of strawberries. That is a better choice than sugar. Eat the extra fruit and return to protocol immediately. If you chew this gum too long, shame and guilt can park at your house and torment you for days.

The *bubble gum principle* works in so many areas. Chew the statement, digest the truth, and spit the remainder out. When you spit it out, do not walk over to it in an hour and try to get additional flavor from it. Bubble gum issues will be coming again soon. Work the principle.

June 19: How Much Can One Person Carry?

Have you ever been carrying something heavy and had someone come and ask to relieve the burden and you refuse to let it go? I have. Sometimes we do that because we don't want to inconvenience someone else. Sometimes it is a balancing act and one slip means everything kisses the carpet. Or sometimes we are just so tired that someone wanting to help is hard to fathom.

I spoke with a friend yesterday who is really tired as life continues to manifest through various trials. We can identify, correct? Sometimes out of desperation we can begin to proclaim, "This is my place in life; this is the best I can expect." Then in defeat, and sometimes shame, we carry those burdens and the weight of life brings despair. Despair can lead to a "why bother" mentality. That is when it is imperative to reach out to someone who knows you are choosing health in all areas of your life. We all need someone who smiles and nods and *gently* will not allow the stupid talk to continue to flow from our mouths.

We are not packhorses. We were not designed to carry heavy loads for long periods of time. Telling someone you are tired, you have been making poor food choices, and carrying this huge burden while your heart is breaking is a good thing. God spoke to me last week at camp about people hating what they see in the mirror and it breaks His heart. He reminded me that as Christians we are not supposed to hate anyone, and yet we hate ourselves most of the time. We cannot do that because it hurts our Father, God. He designed, color coded, and created each of us and He is really proud of His work.

We need to download all the self-hate statements and shake off those negative words. Then we simply look back in the mirror and confess, "I can do all things through Christ," and, "I bring my yoke of obesity to Jesus, for His yoke is easy and His burden light." Come on family, give up today. Drop the burdens, drink your water, smile, and realize you are starting over and that it is never too late. Then remind yourself that we can do this. We can live a healthy life and never grab that extra baggage again. We just have to look into the mirror and decide that this person was never created to carry such heavy, crazy, death-inducing stuff.

June 20: My Spelling Teacher

The sounds from the wind chimes remind me that while I am not on my deck, the wind is still saying, "Good morning." And to that I reply, "Good morning, last week of June." As I was driving to church yesterday and reflecting on my journey to the farmer's market (and it was truly an experience), I was really pondering as to why I still had a twinge in my heart when I had to keep moving past all the bread and dessert samples. When will I see them and not stare, feeling cheated as the swarm of partakers huddle around the tables?

I was having one of those moments and the Spirit of the Lord reminded me that some doors are never meant to be opened again. I grew up in the church and the cliché "our doors are always open" was so prevalent. I thought while I was driving that opened doors are inviting, warm, they say friendship, they speak of trust, they boldly say, "Yes, come in." So while I was talking this through with myself (I know—pay attention to the road), I felt the Lord say, "Unless they are open to the wrong thing." The wrong thing?

I questioned, "Who opens doors to robbers, thieves, and intruders?" In fact, who would ever willingly open a door to something bad? That would be me. The bread tasting counter was an open door experience that said, "Welcome." Had I participated, I would have most likely welcomed a second and third piece, felt guilty, and headed straight to the dessert counter. For me, that particular open door was spelled t-r-o-u-b-l-e. I have years of wrongly spelled doors: j-u-s-t one, o-k-a-y for now, s-t-a-r-t again tomorrow.

I left feeling wonderful that while my husband walked through the open door at both counters, I was able to stand at the door and practice my spelling list. Yea me! I have lived in this body for fifty-six years and have tried every conceivable plan known to humankind to be disciplined with my health. My only victory came when I learned how to spell through the Holy Spirit. He taught me to spell, stay away from the opened doors, and smile while doing the victory dance in the market.

I am thankful beyond measure that the Holy Spirit became my spelling teacher.

June 21: Spa Waters

I love taste and texture. While in Destin one summer and being pampered by my daughter with a day spa package, I fell in love with this water combo. The ladies at the resort said they rotate water flavors every ten days, but when the tarragon and red grapefruit flavored water is the flavor of the day, they are never hungry. That is a great thing when at a spa.

The attendant did inform me that there is a procedure that needs to be followed for the flavors to blend properly and leach into the water. So, every time I make these, I follow the rules. The procedure is the same—layer the fruits and herbs one on top of the other (not mixed) add the ice, and pour the water through it. I use the three-gallon container with the dispenser nozzle for parties and staff luncheons. The lady also told me the drink is best if more ice is used early and a smaller amount of water and the combination is created early enough so the ice is allowed to melt and become the liquid. Also, I only use fresh herbs and fruit. These can be costly, but for a party they are a hit.

I noticed when at the spa, the longer I remained, the more flavor-infused the water became. When making these at home, I have discovered the flavors really pop when the liquid is very cold. So, as it is being consumed, I do not only add water. I add ice as well.

In the following recipes, the first ingredient listed is on the bottom and the second one on top. Then, add your ice followed by the water. Wait a couple of hours and you have a beautifully flavored, refreshing liquid.

1. Red grapefruit and tarragon

2. Strawberries and mint

3. Mandarin oranges (only canned fruit I use and no sugar is allowed) and mint

4. Oranges, lemons, and strawberries

5. Peaches and chocolate mint (can use regular if needed; I grow chocolate mint)

6. Sweet basil and peaches

These are my favorites, but the possibilities are endless. Enjoy.

June 22: Peanut Butter Cookies

Yield: 36 servings

Ingredients

- 1 stick light butter
- 1 ½ cups almond flour (I use blanched)
- 1 cup xylitol
- 2 large eggs
- 1 teaspoon vanilla
- 1 16 oz container all natural chunky peanut butter (You can use smooth. I like the chunks. If using fresh ground, add ½ teaspoon sea salt.)
- 1 ½ teaspoons baking powder

Per Serving:

Calories 108
Total Fat 12.6 g
Cholesterol 28.1 mg
Sodium 132.9 mg
Potassium 9.3 mg
Total Carbohydrate 9.4 g
Dietary Fiber 1.7 g
Sugars 0.7 g
Protein 5.1 g

Procedure

1. Cream together butter, xylitol, eggs, and peanut butter. Mix well.
2. Mix dry ingredients together in a separate bowl and add to the peanut butter mixture in thirds. Blend until smooth.
3. Cover with plastic wrap and allow dough to cool for a couple of hours in the refrigerator before using a teaspoon to gather a small portion and roll into a ball.
4. Preheat oven to 350°F.
5. Place balls on a cookie sheet lined with parchment paper and bake for 20 minutes. This time may vary depending on if you chose to refrigerate the dough.

June 23: Victory Loves Company

I woke up this morning thinking about how confidence is crucial to every person. I was able to minister to one of our youth last week about that statement and how it finds application in every segment of our lives. There is a big difference, however, in having confidence in our own ability, and having confidence in God's ability. I fully understand that self-confidence can easily turn into pride, but the flip side can be equally as disastrous.

For example, we must have confidence that following a healthy plan for our lives will produce long-term benefits. If we are not secure in that, then every other day could bring a day filled with bad choices. We must be confident also that our resolve to be healthy cannot be overturned as we pass the yogurt shop daily. There is something to be said for being certain of what we believe and never being dissuaded from that.

I am a truth girl. Knowing the truth gives me the stability to stand in a difficult situation when I really want to quit. Being confident that God really desires to help me in my struggle to be healthy has been a huge factor in my success. Reading and rehearsing His Word gives me such crazy confidence. The more I hear it, the more deeply I believe it.

Knowing that others are embracing health, enjoying life, and walking in freedom as I am is also a confidence booster. I know that if you are reading this book and trying the recipes, you are walking with me. I have confidence that I am not alone. That helps me. How about you? I have always thought the cliché "misery loves company" was so negative. I would much rather create a cliché that states, "victory loves company."

Remember, we are confident in God's truth and we fight for freedom without making compromises. Let us repeat, "Victory loves company."

June 24: Wisdom versus Folly

I think back, shake my head, and sometimes sarcastically comment, "Was I really ever twenty?" Where in the world did the time go? Someone said last week, "At my age I do not digest food as I used to, and I cannot seem to keep my weight off." I realize some of that statement revolves around the simple process of aging; I get that. As our body ages it responds to certain variables in our food journey differently, whether we like the process or not. Certain meats and sugar-processed foods digest at much slower rates for those of us reaching the senior's qualification status. Steak, for example, can be harder to digest than some other meat and tends to stay longer in the lower intestines. That does not mean we do not eat steak. It means that we eat less, drink more water following, and take a walk after dinner to bless our neighbors with a warm hello.

Has anyone noticed that the older you get, the more certain places on your body want to settle? I tried blaming the drooping skin on synthetic materials, but came to realize that excuse didn't work. *Aging is part of our future, but using it as an excuse is not.* Honestly, time waits for no one and we are all getting older. Hopefully, as the Bible teaches, we are gaining wisdom in our aging. Wisdom says, "Eat another fruit and drop the cookie." Wisdom says, "I you will drink additional water and take an extra lap, you *can* have steak occasionally." I am a carnivore and that is really good news for me.

One of the definite places where wisdom should always trump folly is in our meal selections. We must limit those folly-filled meals and social events where we easily say "Tomorrow is another day." Yes indeed, tomorrow is another day, but your body does not understand that concept and it grabs salt, sugar, and fat and places it in certain areas where we all wish it did not. You know I am right.

When I was twenty, I thought people at fifty were elderly and headed to the retirement home. However, the older I get, the younger everyone else gets. Come on family, let us make a definite plan to age well. We must sidestep folly and excuses, as they potentially make way for illnesses. Also, let's sidestep, two-step, and high step while we have the energy *to* step. Great health is the key to great stepping. Wise people know this and folly people could care less.

June 25: Discipline and Peace Walking Hand in Hand

Hebrews 12:11 reads, "No discipline is enjoyable while it is happening—it's painful! But afterward there will be a peaceful harvest of right living for those who are trained in this way" (NLT).

I categorically wish things like this were not true. Have you ever commented after a really successful health day (eaten on plan, consumed your water, moved your body), "Wow, I feel really bad. I wish I had cheated all day long, eaten everything I wanted, and lay on the sofa stuffing my face." Really? I doubt that.

Usually at the completion of a great day, we feel a sense of peace, a sense of joy, and a sense of victory. During the day, however, while disciplining our bodies and training our stomachs to live with smaller portions and without certain foods, perhaps we snarl and say not so pleasant phrases. But when we've had a victory day, peace often comes. And most of us prefer that, don't we? I certainly do.

I would much rather awaken for coffee and morning quiet time not feeling a sense of loathing and failure. I prefer to awaken every morning with that same peaceful, joyful sense of accomplishment. Here are a few of the key elements to that realization:

1. We **have** a plan. Do you know what the boundaries are for your health? We must establish them in concrete and be confident that this is what our body requires. I know what I need daily, and when my flesh tries to convince me otherwise, I call my flesh a liar.

2. We **work** the plan. Do you have the courage to take your own food to a function or call ahead and ask if there are foods on your plan? Have you trained your body to comply with, "You're not the boss of me"? We must utilize this principle of discipline in our daily walk.

Discipline equals a peaceful harvest of right living. That is worth fighting for every day in my life. Discipline during the day, each day, equals long-term health minus the feelings of guilt and failure. I prefer the happy evenings, the peaceful meals, and the feelings of accomplishment from knowing that I had the fortitude to make correct choices when no one else other than God saw or cared.

June 26: Change One Thing

The watermelon and spaghetti squash plants are growing abundantly now. It is amazing how just one variable can break the chains that were stopping growth. The new soil worked like a charm. If you are stuck today on your health journey and find yourself saying, "I am doing everything as I always have and my body doesn't seem to be responding any longer," then ask yourself what one thing could you change to see if that variable could make a difference?

Maybe that change could be as simple as decreasing your portions, increasing your water, or simply adjusting the amount of nuts you consume due to the salt content. Take one variable away for three days and weigh in faithfully. If no effect is recognized, try another one for three days. The trick is to modify only one variable at a time. The Bible says it is the "little foxes that spoil the vines" (Song of Solomon 2:15 NKJV). I realized that eating nuts daily made my feet swell from the increased sodium. Not only have I limited the amount I consume in a week, I now purchase them raw.

I got the results from my lab work before summer camp and it was really good. While my bad cholesterol was up a little, my good cholesterol was so perfect it counteracted the other. I have received several great blood reports in a row. That alone is such a change for me. Years of opening reports in the mail and seeing the red circles proving I was a failure have now changed. I am deliriously happy to be healthy. If you dread those reports as I did, keep committing to changes and those reports will change.

Remember, if you are not keeping regular checks on your blood, you could be fooling yourself by thinking all is well. You can have no symptoms of critical illness for years. Fortunately, our regular blood screenings as well as our scales are really *bad liars*. Sometimes having them as your accountability partners is the one thing that may never have to change again.

Now see, that's an easy variable to change.

June 27: Healthy (low carb) Smoothie

Yield: 4 servings

This smoothie is chock full of antioxidants and flavor. The Greek yogurt adds the protein. Occasionally if I have some apples that need to be eaten, I will add a few—minus the seeds, which adds to the fiber. This is a wonderful summer snack. Try topping it with a sprig of mint for additional color.

Ingredients

- 1 cup watermelon
- 1 cup cantaloupe
- 1 cup strawberries
- 1 cup blueberries
- 8 oz. plain Greek yogurt or unsweetened soy milk
- 5-6 pkgs. Truvia® Natural Sweetener (adjust to your taste preference)
- ½ lime
- Sparkling water (This is optional. There is enough liquid to make a nice smoothie from the fruits, especially the watermelon. But the tiny addition of sparkling water gives a little fizz.)

Procedure

Combine all the above ingredients in a large blender.

Per Serving:

Calories 106.9
Total Fat 0.4 g
Cholesterol 0.0 mg
Sodium 31.4 mg
Potassium 233.2 mg
Total Carbohydrate 23.5 g
Dietary Fiber 2.8 g
Sugars 15.3 g
Protein 6.1 g

June 28: Cheesy Cheese Balls

Yield: 16 servings

Ingredients

- 1 cup sharp cheddar cheese (I like white, extra sharp)
- 1 cup Swiss cheese
- ½ cup Parmesan Regianno cheese
- 1 pkg. light cream cheese
- 1 tablespoon Worcestershire sauce
- 1 teaspoon paprika
- 1 teaspoon onion powder
- 1 teaspoon garlic powder
- ½ teaspoon chives
- 1 teaspoon dill weed
- ½ teaspoon salt
- 1 cup pecans

Procedure

1. Allow the cream cheese to soften and grate the remainder of the cheese (I prefer to grate mine fresh) and allow to reach room temperature.
2. Blend cheeses well, add seasonings, and form into a ball.
3. Place in the refrigerator for 30 minutes to one hour to harden slightly.
4. Roll the ball with the pecans. Cover in plastic wrap.
5. Allow to cool and seasonings to blend before serving, sometimes 12 hours.

Per Serving:

Calories 168.4
Total Fat 14.4 g
Cholesterol 28.7 mg
Sodium 201.6 mg
Potassium 65.2 mg
Total Carbohydrate 3.3 g
Dietary Fiber 0.9 g
Sugars 1.1 g
Protein 7.5 g

Variations:

Tex/Mex Cheese Ball

This is a spicy recipe if you include the seeds. You may need to modify. Serve with crinkle cut vegetables or other non-starch type crackers.

- Delete the Swiss and Parmesan and use the Mexican blend cheese mixture (3 cups).
- Delete the chives and add 1-2 jalapeños chopped finely (Remember, the seeds carry the heat. If you want the flavor of the jalapeños without the extreme heat, clean the hull of all seeds well.)
- Replace the Worcestershire with TABASCO® (Start with 5-6 shakes and adjust to your preference. I use almost a teaspoon.)
- Add ½ cup of sour cream.
- I used ½ teaspoon of ground cumin to add extra flavor (optional).
- Use the finely chopped pecans to coat the outside of the cheese ball.

Smoked Salmon Cheese Ball

Ingredients:

- 1 large package smoked salmon (I find this in the fish section of my local grocery store in a sealed package.)
- 8 oz. cream cheese (can use light), ½ teaspoon white horseradish, and dill weed to taste. I use a lot. I often add a couple of drops of liquid smoke, but go gently. It will overpower the other flavors quickly.
- 1 cup of chopped pecans.

Proceedure:

Allow these flavors to blend for a couple of hours. You can then roll in crushed pecans.

June 29: The End of the Storm

The cool air here is so refreshing as it bathes the morning in anticipation of close to one hundred degree temperatures. It has been hot since February and I long for fall. The months of heat seem like they will never end, and summer is just beginning. Have you ever been faced with a tough situation for a long time? The battle sometimes seems to never stop. We look around and it *appears* that the storms of life never end.

Let me remind each of us that Satan will use a wrong perception as a tool to keep us from remembering how big God is. Satan is a master at causing us to always see the storm and never the rainbow. The Bible instructs us that things happen first in the realm of nature and then in the spiritual realm. Why? Because the world quickly sees the realm of nature, but only those wearing "God glasses" see in the realm of the Spirit.

When thinking about nature, let me remind you that not one storm has ever lasted indefinitely. Never. All storms come to an end. Following the storms, there are always periods of sunshine. None of us can deny this or offer an opposing statement. We do not always see a rainbow, but we always come to the end of the storm. And for that we must show gratitude and change our perspective. Only seeing the storm can bring depression and added fear, which serve as triggers for those comfort responses. Those responses, for many, include sugar and carbs and by now I am confident that you know they are not our best options. I wish that were not true, but it is.

In order to break this pattern, we must see the truth, walk in the truth, fight for the truth, sleep with the truth, and so on (you get the picture). Read Proverbs 8 today as there is a high price for a lack of wisdom and understanding.

Yes, there are storms. Yes, the storms can be devastating. Yes, the storms can last for more than one day. However, the storms always end. Thank God today that the storms around you will end and ask to see God's rainbow so you can experience His promise of life and hope once again. And while the storm is raging, choose fruit and water as your comfort foods.

June 30: June Reflection Page

As you are completing June, are there things you wish you had highlighted or which you had written down? Which recipes have been your favorites? Have you been brave enough to take one to a gathering yet?

_____

_____

_____

_____

_____

_____

_____

_____

_____

_____

_____

_____

_____

_____

_____

_____

_____

_____

_____

_____

July

July is the biggest BBQ month of the summer. The grill offers much help and options as food choices are numerous. Remember, check your seasoning salts and BBQ sauces, as they normally contain sugar or corn syrup.

July 1: Repairs or Accessories

I love having friends share wisdom from the Scriptures with me. Wendi sent this little nugget to ponder from 2 Kings 12 this morning. Briefly summarizing this passage, we find that the children of Israel were spending money on accessories for the Temple of God and not necessarily to restore it. The leaders finally understood the problem and went to the people and instructed them to basically stop the accessories and provide for the necessities. Cool thought to ponder, huh?

As I read and re-read, looking for the application for my life, here is what I gathered. The Bible teaches us that our bodies are the temple (or dwelling place) of the Holy Spirit. I know the term *temple* is a word we are not familiar with, so we will say *dwelling* or *home*. Wendi said, "When adding things to our lives, we could ask ourselves—is this a temple repair or a temple accessory? Does this food I am about to eat actually help to repair my body, or is it an accessory?"

Accessories are not necessities are they? Necessities are basics that we must have. Accessories may add dimension and color, but are not required. Right? Our temples break down daily as we age and must be repaired. Therefore, the food we bring to the "temple" (our body) should mainly be *to repair* and not simply because we *like* it. However, as you know, I am a big proponent of food being healthy, adorned well, *and* tasting great.

There are a substantial number of foods on the *required* list these days that I do not necessarily like, but they are fabulous at repairing my temple. On the other end of the spectrum are foods that I cannot bring to the temple because they add weight and inches to my middle (thus qualifying them as accessories). Given the choice of building or accessorizing, I would rather build the core value of my health and accessorize the outside of my body with jewelry. Just being honest.

Great teaching, Wendi. Thanks for sharing with us.

July 2: Wave the White Flag

As much as we talk about victory, this morning I want to talk about surrender. During a battle there is much to protect—one's life, one's family, one's country, one's honor. And yet, sometimes, even though you have done all you humanly know to do, there comes a moment of surrender. Do you know how difficult that place can be? It is so difficult to give up our right to defend our actions or defend our feelings.

One of my favorite sayings that I tucked in my Bible is an excerpt that reads, "I don't have to be first, I don't have to be right, I don't have to be in charge, I don't have to be applauded." That statement champions humility and surrender. Sometimes we are called to surrender, and sometimes more than we like. Jesus surrendered His life and we gained eternity. Many of us surrender our position in a fight and gain peace. Sometimes we surrender our old mindset about life and we gain life.

A large portion of dealing with the fight for a healthy lifestyle is an inverted and wrong defending of bad habits. I was encouraging a woman recently who cannot seem to find the strength to break free in her eating and offered every reason for her *right* to be heavy. Is that crazy? But, isn't that what excuses are? I wanted to grab her and say, "Surrender! Just give up and realize you don't need to defend a wrong manner of thinking. Submit to a new way; a healthy life is worth the surrender." But sometimes we see surrender as a bad word.

I shared last night at our Healthy Eating Club that while I am allowed to eat many foods, I have tried a certain bread made with seeds and nuts three separate times only to discover that in each instance I gain weight. I finally had to surrender. It is not a battle I can win. My body immediately responds by gaining. As much as I love it, I cannot eat it. So I *surrender*. I would rather surrender and live than make excuses for its place in my life. While you may be able to eat starch and sugar with no weight gain, I cannot. I wave the white flag of *surrender*. Just think—surrendering my right to always have what I want—now there's a great biblical principle.

Today, are there areas in your life in which you need to surrender? Maybe you need to realize that you cannot fight obesity on your own and you need more accountability. *Surrender.* Perhaps you need to vary the fruits and vegetables. *Surrender.* Or maybe you need to weigh more. *Surrender.* Do you feel you need more water? *Surrender.* Quit trying to defend a wrong mindset and surrender to the destiny of health.

July 3: Prepare for the Fireworks

One of my favorite things is watching fireworks. I am not particular about the where—over the land, over the ocean, or in my neighborhood. I simply am captivated by their majesty and color. I also love the combinations and how they complement each other. I know that in order to create such a grand display, someone spent an enormous amount of time, money, and energy. I still feel like a child when the fireworks begin and always run to the best viewing area to allow their grandeur to captivate my heart.

I was invited once to a gathering of people in my neighborhood who were displaying some fireworks they purchased from one of those rather large shops you see on the expressways. The colors in the sky were beautiful, but their random journey and lack of combination seemed to *tone down* the success of the show. Can you see where I am going with this?

Here is what I know (and I am passionate about this)—food should look good, taste good, speak to my senses, satisfy my body with good things, and make my organs smile. That sounds like a lot. But those expectations are very realistic. After sitting through a mediocre fireworks display, I found a better one next year. If your food does not reflect good planning, you (and your family) could settle for whatever is easy, which could absolutely be the worst thing.

We cannot expect to follow our healthy plan when the world is offering the *better* meal, the *tastier* meal, the *bigger* meal at a less expensive price. I find that many do not invest the time to plan properly and make the color combinations work. Eventually, they change course out of sheer frustration. Work diligently to not allow the world to offer your family a better display than you can. As God's kids we deserve the best display. He has given us the creative minds to make this happen. Let us make each meal the grandest display of creative cooking talents and let the world have the second best. Then your family will always run to be at *your* table for the fireworks.

July 4: Independence Day

Happy 4th of July! This is an important holiday for our country *and* us. As you know, this is a day when we celebrate freedom. I don't know about you, but freedom is priceless to me. I am one of those patriotic "babies" who still cries when the *National Anthem* is sung. There, I said it.

Just a brief word today and a sincere prayer that the Holy Spirit would bring His help to each of us so that we can enjoy the sun, our families, a day of rest, and not culminate the day feeling like a failure.

Before the first piece of meat touches the grill, recite our family Scripture verse, "It is for freedom that Christ came to set us free." Obesity-inducing foods offer no freedom, only failure and depression. I am praying right now that we will desire the best foods today, resist those that contribute to obesity and obesity-related diseases, and smile—knowing that we are no longer trapped.

Our founding fathers made a declaration and were willing to give their lives for its truth. In fact, Benjamin Franklin commented, as he encouraged the others to stand for freedom against severe opposition, "We must all hang together, or we most assuredly will all hang separately."

Let us "hang together" today knowing that each of us is choosing life amidst the challenges of another food-filled holiday. I love a good challenge; how about you? But I also love winning, and choosing well means I win. Bring it on.

July 5: Never Give Up!

Yesterday, the storms stole power from the community next to us and yet we had no rain, no storm, and no interruption in power. I soon would realize, again, that I take things for granted like electricity. We were invited for dinner to a friend's house who lived in one of the communities with no power. We had no clue how difficult it would be to get to their house that evening, but we were determined. We had planned this holiday dinner for days and the steaks were marinating. As difficult as the journey was, the next obstacle was more challenging! While we could cook on the grill, no power meant no flushing the toilet as they draw water from a well. If you are a boy, things like that are barely significant. But being a girl meant we gathered all our dinner supplies and transferred back to our house where having power equaled flushing toilets. And that was great for me!

While on the way to our friend's house, there was a visually clear path indicating the journey of the storm. The storm moved through that specific area quickly and furiously. It seemed to establish the exact path of its choosing with no obstacles to deny its success. I was thinking *Isn't that like life?* I always wondered why some people were gifted with metabolic "powers," which enabled them to eat whatever and whenever without limit. I always saw that as so unfair. I also never understood why some people were born with perfect bodies and I was always chubby.

Was I in the wrong place at the wrong time when body types were given out? The vision of little, skinny girls with tiny waists compared to my "thick trunk" danced merrily in my head. Was that fair? Honestly, I fought with that vision most of my life. However, in reality, some receive rain, some receive storms, and some receive nothing. Life gives each of us a different set of circumstances. Some people are born thin; I was not. But God has given me (us) a sound mind and we have the freedom of choice.

When thrown a bad set of circumstances last night, we had to try three different routes to get to our friend's house, but we never gave up. We had to change our location to prepare dinner, but we never gave up. We had to drive over branches and debris, but we never gave up. And while dinner was late, we had a lovely meal *because* we never gave up.

The moral of the story: No matter how your day was yesterday or the last seven days, keep trying every possible route until you experience victory in your health. Never give up.

July 6: Zucchini Muffins

Yield: 12-14 servings

Ingredients

- 2 ½ cups almond flour (blanched)
- 2 teaspoons baking powder
- 1/4 teaspoon sea salt
- 1 teaspoon pumpkin pie spice
- 1 stick light butter, melted
- 4 eggs
- ½ cup buttermilk
- ¾ cup xylitol
- 1 teaspoon vanilla
- 2 cups zucchini, washed and shredded. Pat the extra moisture with a paper towel.
- ½ cup chopped pecans (optional, and are not included in the nutritional data below)

Procedure

1. Preheat oven to 400°F.
2. Spray the muffin tin of your choice. This makes 12-14 regular sized muffins, 24 minis, or about 16 muffin tops.
3. Mix dry ingredients together with a whisk to ensure the baking powder is evenly blended. Set aside.
4. Cream the butter and xylitol. Beat the eggs in a separate bowl and add to butter mixture. Mix but don't over beat.
5. Add the dry ingredient mixture. Blend. Then add the buttermilk and the extract.
6. Fold in the zucchini. I don't beat too aggressively as I don't want the pieces mushy. This really depends on how tender the squash is when you begin.
7. Put in muffin tins (about 1/2 to 2/3 full) and bake for about 15-20 minutes.

Per Serving:
Calories 193.0
Total Fat 15.2 g
Cholesterol 72.1 mg
Sodium 189.6 mg
Potassium 98.9 mg
Total Carbohydrate 13.9 g
Dietary Fiber 2.4 g
Sugars 1.6 g
Protein 6.6 g

July 7: Zucchini Squash and Mozzarella Melt

Yield: 8 servings

Ingredients

- 6-7 large zucchini squash
- 3 tomatoes
- 1 large sweet onion, sliced in rounds
- ½ stick butter
- 2 cups mozzarella cheese

Procedure

1. Melt the butter and add the onions.
2. Sauté until the onions are clear and browning.
3. Add the squash and diced tomatoes.
4. Sprinkle with salt and pepper.
5. Cover and simmer on medium heat for 20 minutes.
6. Remove the lid and place the cheese over the mixture. Replace the lid and turn the stove off. Leave until the cheese melts (this takes about 5 minutes). Serve warm. This will get runny the longer it sits, so time the presentation of this side dish well.

Per Serving:

Calories 125.0
Total Fat 7.7 g
Cholesterol 23.9 mg
Sodium 188.2 mg
Potassium 349.8 mg
Total Carbohydrate 7.4 g
Dietary Fiber 1.9 g
Sugars 1.5 g
Protein 7.9 g

July 8: Those Yummy Yeast Rolls

I do not remember as a child hearing my teachers discuss nutrition. I remember taking health in my fifth grade class, but I think they talked more about personal hygiene and never emphasized the value that healthy eating played on my heart, skin, or hair as a child. I am certain they did, but I must have had my fingers in my ears. And even if I did study nutrition in elementary school, I am not certain our lunchroom ladies did. How do I know? I remember vividly how yummy our lunches were each day. Our lunchroom ladies were excessively proud that their yeast rolls were the "best in the county." And might I say, there was never a shortage of them.

There are reports daily to support the value of changing the eating habits of our families. Talk show hosts, prime time reports, and articles abound offering us little to no excuse for "lack of knowledge." Recently I heard on a news report, "Just losing five to ten pounds can make such a big difference in diabetics, and *so few can lose that.*" The journalist went on to report a staggering statistic that somewhere in the neighborhood of 65 percent of all children are in the heavy and obese range in the United States. I wonder what the statistics are for adults? I know we cannot change everyone's perspective, but we *can* foster change within our own families. You might not lose a hundred pounds, but five to ten pounds to help with diabetes is certainly attainable. The majority of the people I speak with are battling high blood pressure and type 2 diabetes, the effects of which can be devastating. Both maladies, however, can be greatly impacted by dietary changes.

I think the hardest issue for me to resolve, though, is children who are battling obesity. Sometimes I realize they may demand food and their parents have no plan in place to help. Others, however, depend on adults to purchase and prepare life-giving foods, and that may include us. That is why I am grateful my little ones have options at home and at school. I am very committed to offering my thoughts on health to my granddaughters, Mackenzie and Kailey. I am really pleased to see that salads and fruits are offered as choices for both of their lunches at school now. Applause to all the cafeteria workers—keep smiling as you hand those apples to our young people.

I love a good yeast roll, as do we all. But for the past several years I have not allowed them to enter my journey. And guess what? I'm still alive. There is life beyond yeast rolls.

July 9: Eating with Our Eyes

Last week a member of our family responded to a devotion I posted on my blog and remarked, "We really do eat with our eyes." She had brought several colorful vegetables from the garden, washed and prepared them, and while arranging them on her plate marveled at the colors which were so vibrant. I immediately thought about how much I love color. I really enjoy sitting in a room with life, warmth, and color as opposed to a black and white or sterile surrounding. I am so grateful God allowed my eyes to work well, as seeing beautiful colors always stirs those "warm fuzzy" feelings. Okay, I am being a girl right now; I know it.

When my plate is filled with colorful foods that I know are healthy, I feel differently about the meal. Maybe you feel the same? There is almost a sense of joy before I start eating as I recognize and reward myself for giving my body the best choices. In turn, these great choices refuel my organs and keep me at optimum efficiency until my eternal birth date. That *really* is true and *really* does bring a deep sense of joy to me. My challenge daily is to count the number of colors on my plate. Are they different from yesterday? Have I challenged my creative abilities to use fresh herbs and spices to add color when needed? How many colors did you eat yesterday? How many are planned for today?

Speaking of eyes, I wanted to remind you that those beautifully colored foods often help ensure eye health. A poor diet can lead to inflammation and increased risk of cataracts, macular degeneration, and other "eye-related" problems. On the flip side, some foods, like blueberries, can actually promote eye health. Can you say yes to deep, rich color? Blueberries are rich in antioxidants that help in a host of areas, especially keeping our cells fighting those bad guys that try to act rebellious and mutate as they divide. We call those *cancer cells,* which are often rebellious, mind-of-their-own, sneaky cells. We can feed our bodies with whole, healthy foods and actually help our healthy cells fight the rebellious ones. Now that is a great thing.

So, as you approach your meals today, count the colors of your fruits and vegetables and vary them meal to meal so that the differing vitamins and minerals are incorporated throughout the day. If my eyes see the colors, my mouth smiles as it recognizes life. Count well, friends.

July 10: Letter of the Law, Part 1

I have been reading in the book of Romans about the law this morning (referring to the law given to Moses in the Old Testament) and what really made someone a Jew or a Gentile. Some people could only see that following the law made them God's chosen. The apostle Paul is challenging this philosophy and reminding them that being circumcised has value only if you never break the law, and we know that no one is without sin. That is why we need a Savior. That is why we are grateful for grace through faith; yes, we are. Paul's response at the conclusion of chapter 2 speaks directly to a conversation I had with someone recently about eating.

Romans 2:29 reads, "No, a true Jew is one whose heart is right with God. And true circumcision is not merely obeying the letter of the law; rather, it is a change of heart produced by God's Spirit. And a person with a changed heart seeks praise from God, not from people" (NLT). The person I was speaking with recently shared about the diligence and self-restrictions they impose on themselves in relation to certain things that have been stumbling blocks to them in the past. I wanted to shout. Sometimes we need diligence and self-restrictions, not from others, but from our changed hearts.

I, personally, cannot go back to my old way of eating and living, as it produces death in me. When I first adopted my new health plan it was very strict—legalistic in fact. In order to achieve success I followed it to the "letter of the law." However, I cannot enforce that "law" on everyone around me or get frustrated when they choose to do something different. The joy of being healthy can sometimes push us toward being dogmatic with others. That attitude is unhealthy for everyone. If I am being honest here, I was overly critical and judgmental at times. My attitude was "I have come into *the light,* and those choosing not to walk in *my light* are destined for darkness." I hate even typing that, because it sounds horrible. But transparency helps.

After watching the response from some, I finally realized that I was trying to *convert* people with no grace. My understanding and truth was not their truth. I had to recognize that the Spirit of God best precipitates change in us all. My determination to be healthy came from my own epiphany. God opened my eyes and gave me courage. I am healthy today because of Him and not me. Stay tuned for part 2 tomorrow.

July 11: Letter of the Law, Part 2

Continuing my thoughts from yesterday's devotion, I do recognize that God gave me the epiphany of my own unhealthy state. But I also had to burn the bridges to my past so that moving forward was the only option. I could no longer gravitate to the laws that had governed my health for years. They strangled me and never really produced health.

Years of following the *diet laws* had produced so much failure, as "sin did much abound," that my spirit was at a place of total destruction. I did not have the energy or the desire to ever try again. I had accepted the *fact* that I was a failure.

Today, I am convinced the long-term success of my health journey is not about the law of dieting and the "I cannot syndrome." My heart (this word is often translated in the Bible as mind, will, or emotions) has changed to now see what life as a healthy person looks and feels like. I am happy here; and when others eat things around me that were part of my past, but are not part of my future, I cannot legalistically impose my way on them or look back with regret.

I refuse to walk this journey out of fear or compulsion. It is simply my way of life. It is my new heart—a changed heart—a healthy heart (both spiritually and physically). This conversion is so like my walk with Jesus—such a cool parallel. At first the applause of people was an encouragement to me as I walked toward health and the size of my body made a display. Now healthy blood reports, healthy joints, no depression, and a healthy life really bring me joy. It is a total mind shift. It happens daily in my heart. That is such a good thing.

Let us diligently strive to delete the "I cannot" from our health journey and confess, "I can eat what I want, and what I want to eat is healthy." I can make this freedom statement not because of the law, but because of freedom from the law. I can eat anywhere and anything that I choose.

Finally, freedom!

July 12: Attached to the Right Thing, Part 1

You know that I have been gleaning from my watermelon plants all summer, and yesterday another revelation arrived in my inbox (maybe you know this, but I just discovered it). As the plant or vine grows, it creeps out away from the main source and travels everywhere. They spread out like untamed kudzu.

Last evening, as I was watering my healthy plants, I noticed one of the vines had maneuvered to my rose trellis and started climbing upward. That sight appeared strange and I thought, *No watermelon can hang on this trellis and grow. They are too heavy.* So, I decided to simply move the vine. Easier said than done.

The vine sends out tentacles every couple of inches that attach and coil themselves around *whatever* in order to stabilize and ensure its survival during a windy storm. I actually had to forcibly rip those little anchors and redirect the vine to a place where it could produce healthy fruit. I see the truth here, do you?

We can be traveling along life's journey, growing as we should, throwing out anchors to seemingly support ourselves, only to discover that we have anchored to the wrong thing. The vine had no ability on its own to get off the trellis. It was stuck. Something bigger and more powerful and with some wisdom (me) had to dislodge and redirect its attachment or the vine would have looked pretty, been colorful, but unable to support life.

I wonder how many times in our daily experiences things are not as they appear? Simple appearance can be deceiving. The really wicked part of this is that often we attach ourselves to a wrong support and have no concept of its inability to assist in our journey. As I talked about in yesterday's devotion, we all probably have had interactions with the "laws of dieting." They seemed good, but never offered us true, long-term success. The diets, in fact, often became the trellis to which our hopes were attached. Wrong attachment=projected doom.

To be continued...

July 13: Turkey Breast in the Crock-Pot

Yield: 12 servings

This makes a great meal for any special event.

Ingredients

- 5 to 6 lbs turkey breast
- Olive oil
- Fresh mint
- Vidalia onion
- 2-3 medium apples
- 3 large celery stalks with end leaves
- Tarragon
- Salt and pepper

Procedure

1. Spray the Crock-Pot.
2. Place the stalks of celery in the bottom as a support on which to rest the turkey.
3. Place the turkey breast skin side up and coat with olive oil.
4. Inside the cavity, place the peeled onion and if room the apple halves. If not, place the apple halves along the edges of the turkey.
5. Sprinkle the turkey with salt, pepper and tarragon.
6. Place the fresh mint alongside the meat as well.
7. Cook on high for approximately 5 hours. The turkey will be very tender and *very* flavorful.

Per Serving:

Calories 162.6
Total Fat 5.4 g
Cholesterol 40.4 mg
Sodium 55.4 mg
Potassium 324.8 mg
Total Carbohydrate 10.3 g
Dietary Fiber 2.1 g
Sugars 5.2 g
Protein 17.9 g

July 14: Mardi Gras Wings

Yield: 8 servings

Ingredients

- 1 bag frozen wings (3 pounds) or the same amount fresh
- 1 bottle wing sauce
- Spices: Grill Mates® Montreal Steak Seasoning, salt and pepper, rosemary, thyme, and seasoning salt
- ½ stick light butter (optional)

Procedure

1. In a gallon-sized freezer baggie, cover the wings with the wing sauce and place in the refrigerator. I marinate mine for several hours, flipping the bag every 30 minutes or so to evenly distribute the wing sauce.
2. Drain the wings and bake for about 30 minutes on 350°F.
3. Heat the grill to medium and place the wings in rows. Sprinkle with seasoning salt, Montreal, and remaining seasonings. Reduce to low heat and close the lid. Cook for about 10 minutes. Turn the wings and repeat. After about 20 minutes, I leave the lid up and turn often until they are crispy and the color I want. I like mine dry and crisp.

Per Serving:
Calories 118.6
Total Fat 2.4 g
Cholesterol 36.3 mg
Sodium 447.3 mg
Potassium 150.6 mg
Total Carbohydrate 0.8 g
Dietary Fiber 0.5 g
Sugars 0.0 g
Protein 12g

Variations:

Hot Wings

Before transferring to the grill, sprinkle with TABASCO® (go sparingly). While on the grill, only use seasoning salt. When really crispy and coming off the grill, toss with a fresh batch of hot sauce and sometimes ½ stick of butter. Serve hot.

Teriyaki Wings

Marinate the wings in a teriyaki sauce made with ½ cup of teriyaki and a stick of melted butter. I mix the sauce, coat the wings and leave out for ½ hour, turning the bag frequently. When ready for the grill, I add a touch of salt and baste with a fresh batch of teriyaki butter sauce (discard original as it will have the juice from the wings). Grill to perfection.

July 15: Attached to the Right Thing, Part 2

In our journey to live a healthy life, we must try to anchor our focus on healthy truth, which gives us the best chance of sustaining life. Sometimes the next diet pill, the next specialist on a talk show, or a friend's dramatic weight loss tosses us about. We often run and attach ourselves to that "truth" out of sheer frustration and not wisdom. That can be dangerous. In fact, the longer I walk this journey and the more I learn, the more I absolutely know I am correct in my belief that frustration drives us *from* the truth and not *to* it.

Instead, let us attach ourselves to truth that gives us the best chance at life. When we experience life-giving truth, I suggest we wrap our tentacles around it tightly so that when circumstances come to dislodge us and try to influence us, like those who jeer and say, "Living without sugar is stupid; you cannot do that the rest of your life," we are grounded and unmovable. Can we be honest—we need these types of truth anchors in many areas of our lives. In fact, I have a deep stirring in my spirit that many are being led astray in areas of godly truth, not just concerning health, in this day in which we live.

Are we anchored to the right thing this morning? Let us find supported truth, not dramatic promises that sell products, and let us fight to be grounded there. The Bible says in John 8:32, "And you will know the truth, and the truth will set you free" (NLT). God's foods in their whole forms are our best choices. Send your tether to that truth, find your local fresh market, and choose life for you and your family.

Free to live, grow watermelons, and feed others. Yes.

July 16: Retirement Plans

We have spoken a lot about destroying our old ways of thinking concerning a healthy lifestyle and how difficult that can be. But thanks be to God, He can take our discipline and concerted desire and use it to restore life to our bodies. He created natural vegetation on the earth to feed us—and feed us well. But sometimes our own desires for sweetened, processed foods cause moments of temporary insanity. I can't tell you how many times I grabbed a candy bar and used that as my excuse. The only problem is that my sane mind always returned, as did the fat on my thighs. I finally realized pleading insanity did not keep the scales silent, and I was simply playing games.

Sometimes we roll the dice with our health, don't we? It too becomes a game. I don't know about you, but a 50/50 chance of survival in a broken down container does not seem like the ideal life to me. No, not for me. Each of us will exit this life someday, but I would like to be a sassy, one-hundred-year-old, healthy person, leading water aerobics, cooking lean protein, and consuming tons of brightly colored fruits and vegetables. Then I will someday sit down to take off my shoes and close my eyes, only to open them and behold my heavenly Father. (That makes me smile.)

I cannot guarantee that my exit from this life will be that easy, but I can plan for that. We spend years planning for our retirement, putting away funds, and making a portfolio to give us a great future. I am doing the same type of planning for my future health. Have you ever heard someone say, "You can never get insurance when you need it?" Well, I feel the same way about my health. It is the wrong time to scramble and try to be healthy when disease manifests. We need to start today and do whatever we must each day to plan for a healthy future.

Unless God touches us with a miracle, it takes years sometimes to bring our bodies back to health following years of abuse. That is why I want my grandbabies choosing healthy foods now. Healthy planning needs to begin as soon as possible so we are not caught scrambling. No rolling the dice for me as I am building my health portfolio.

July 17: A Visual Learner

Some of you know I was a public school teacher for twenty-five years. I loved using hands-on activities as a means of conveying and concreting information. I am truly a visual learner. Let me draw on a white board or play with my hands and I can remember the process in my "mind's eye."

God allowed me a teachable moment using an old water hose with one of my granddaughters recently. The bulge in the old and worn hose was a great picture of how certain things can cause a build-up of plaque in our arteries and eventually trigger them to balloon and perhaps burst. It was dramatic. She was amazed at how clamping off one end caused a bubble in the middle of the hose. It actually almost burst right in front of her eyes. I love it when a prop responds as it is supposed to. What a great opportunity to convey the critical importance of heart-healthy foods to a nine year old.

I wonder today what visualizations convey ill health to you? Maybe you could start a list? I have several pictures that immediately pop into my head. Do you think the pictures you retrieved happened by chance? I doubt it. Remember, these are ill-health pictures, not accidental-health pictures, and there is a big difference as you know.

What normally happens is this: when we are younger we can never envision ourselves as growing old. Honestly, did you? Some youth believe that those who are advanced in years come from a *planet to which being young does not belong and to which they will never enter*. They often embrace the "live for today, for tomorrow may never come" philosophy. Eventually, we all discover that tomorrow *really* existed all along.

I found a beautiful photo of a yoga instructor with snow-white hair and a beautifully tanned and healthy body who epitomizes health to me. I am keeping that image in my mind as I move toward my golden years. She is one of my visuals for choosing life right now, my *carrot* so to speak. Closer to home, I have a beautiful woman at my church, Jane, who has survived cancer, takes water aerobics three days a week, works out with weights, cares for her family well, and is always smiling. She is such a godly example to me. She is another visual of what I desire to be as I embrace health for my future.

Both women make me smile. Find your visual and fight for it.

July 18: Where My Help Comes From

When I was so heavy, my health care providers were kind and spoke to me gently about the importance of losing weight. I think I needed a water hose and a demonstration (previous devotion). Just losing ten pounds never seemed too critical to my ears. Maybe they should have given me a ten pound weight and asked me to carry it for a week without ever setting it down, and then allow me to drop it. Maybe then I could have grasped how important their words were.

To me, losing ten pounds was the same as losing a million; both were unachievable. Occasionally, I could lose this "little fox," but my inability to see years down the road and my addiction to food caused me to reward myself. Soon I discovered I was up fifteen pounds. Anybody understand? After seeing my mother-in-law suffer with several issues that I know to be food-related and hearing her cry for help for many years, I am more committed than ever to not be swayed by a future I cannot see. I do not have to *see* my future, as there is enough data from others' lives to speak loud and clear.

I bought every diet pill known to man, tried hypnosis, and even wrapped bands around my body with no lasting results. Did my help come from them? Certainly not. I wanted to live, I wanted a slim body, *but at no physical cost to me.* I could spend the money, but I couldn't change my eating. Did my help come from a longing to be thin and healthy? Again, no.

I prayed and begged for God's help and He was always willing but I wanted Him, or someone, or something to do all the work and let me reap the benefits. It just does not work that way. I wish it did. I like easy and you probably do as well. My "help" came when the epiphany that I was eating myself to death, as evidenced by the number of pills I ingested daily to feel decent, caused a desperate cry within me that ignited action and health finally responded.

I am too big of a sissy to get a tattoo, but if I were to ever consider having it done mine would read *standing firm.*

July 19: Asking for Help

"Praise the Lord! Let all that I am praise the Lord. I will praise the Lord as long as I live. I will sing praises to my God with my dying breath. Don't put your confidence in powerful people; there is no help for you there. When they breathe their last, they return to the earth, and all their plans die with them. But joyful are those who have the God of Israel as their helper, whose hope is in the Lord their God. He made heaven and earth, the sea, and everything in them. He keeps every promise forever. He gives justice to the oppressed and food to the hungry. The Lord frees the prisoners. The Lord opens the eyes of the blind. The Lord lifts up those who are weighed down" (Psalm 146:1-8a NLT).

Oh my goodness, I feel better already!

I love reading the Word of God. I know each of us have our favorite authors for various reasons, as do I. But God's Word is filled with such hope. Just reading this psalm communicates so much. God is our helper; God gives food to the hungry; the Lord frees prisoners. Every line conveys the power and majesty of my God.

Sometimes on our journey we can become self-absorbed. I hated so much of my life and was consumed with how bad things were. I seldom stopped to show any gratitude to God for even the smallest victories. Whining was my portion. I rarely saw God for just who He was and not what He could do for me. God never opened my mouth and inserted the food, nor did He consume thousands of calories daily on my behalf. I did that all by myself.

Psalm 146 begins with praise. Let's begin there today. We should never place our confidence in powerful people, but in a God who always keeps His promises. Thank Him that He sees our day and let us ask for godly wisdom in every area of our life. His Word declares that if we ask for wisdom He gives it. Check out the beginning of the book of James.

So have you asked for help today? I have. God will honor His Word. Tomorrow, before our feet hit the ground, let's ask for wisdom again, and then follow the plan of the Lord.

July 20: Turkey and Smoked Sausage Soup

Yield: 12 servings

Ingredients

- 4 cups turkey breast, use more if you like meaty soups
- 2 pkgs. smoked sausage, cut in chunks
- 1 large onion
- 1 bag frozen carrots
- 2 containers portabella mushrooms
- 2 large cartons chicken stock (99% fat free, no MSG)
- Olive oil
- Salt and pepper to taste
- One sprig fresh rosemary
- Tarragon
- TABASCO® to taste (6-8 splashes)
- 1 cup quinoa (uncooked)

Procedure

1. Heat the olive oil and add the onion chopped in larger chunks. (I prefer the texture of the larger pieces.)
2. Add the mushrooms and allow tenderizing. (While these are cooking, cut your cooked turkey breast in chunks. The flavors from the mint and apples add a nice touch if you chose to try my turkey breast in the Crock-Pot, page 218.)
3. Add the remaining ingredients and bring to a boil. Reduce the heat and simmer for about an hour so the flavors blend. Remove the sprig of rosemary before serving.

Per Serving:
Calories 222.9
Total Fat 12.1 g
Cholesterol 64.4 mg
Sodium 887.6 mg
Potassium 463.8 mg
Total Carbohydrate 9.8 g
Dietary Fiber 1.5 g
Sugars 2.3 g
Protein 19.5

July 21: Spinach Salad with Strawberries and Blueberries

Yield: 8 servings

I purchase the bags of pre-portioned spinach, which makes it easier to tell how much you have.

Ingredients

- 2 bags baby spinach
- 1 carton strawberries
- 1 carton blueberries
- 1 carton feta cheese
- 1 small red onion
- Poppy seed to taste
- Sweet pecans (recipe and nutritional info listed in August with the Chocolate Trifle)
- 1 bottle lite raspberry walnut dressing (depends on how wet you like your salad. Start with ½ bottle and toss well before adding the remaining)

Procedure

1. Wash and half the strawberries; wash the blueberries.
2. Slice the red onion into rounds extremely thin (a mandolin is great for this).
3. Place everything in a large bowl except the dressing. The spinach will appear huge, but will shrink with the addition of the dressing. The salad may be assembled up to an hour prior to adding the dressing.
4. When you are prepared, add the dressing, toss, and serve.

Per Serving:

Calories 157.6
Total Fat 7.1 g
Cholesterol 16.7 mg
Sodium 404.2 mg
Potassium 548.2 mg
Total Carbohydrate 19.3 g
Dietary Fiber 4.2 g
Sugars 12.3 g
Protein 5.5 g

July 22: My Prayer for You

We ended July 19th's devotion talking about the need to ask for God's wisdom each morning. How many of you know we would be better off with His wisdom as we execute our day as opposed to our own? That was my first prayer this morning. I also thought about the psalm featured in the previous devotion and how it began with praise. What I'd like to do this morning is pray for you and speak blessings over you.

Good morning Father, and thank You for this day. You are loving and kind and always steady. You always have our heart close to You, and we praise You for thinking of us when we are going through our day. Thank You for living in us and keeping us on the right path throughout some tough places that we will journey before this day ends—that comforts us. Thank You for loving us more than we understand or deserve. Thank You for never leaving us alone because we know You are always present and know every thought and word that we speak and do not speak. We know that You desire for us to live according to Your plan and we ask for Your help and wisdom. Father, we thank You for Your Word, which is always true, and the hope it gives to each of us. God, You know that our heart's desire is to be healthy and strong so we can accomplish Your will in the earth. We confess our weakness in this area at times, and Holy Spirit, we ask that You guide us into truth. We ask You to speak loud and clear to us as we make food choices this day. Help each of us to eat what we need and not just what we want. Help us to feel Your strength when we want to default to bad habits that we know lead to death. We give You thanks in advance for Your support. Thank You, too, that Your Word is filled with promises of goodness and for that we are grateful. We love You and are grateful to be Your children. We expect the blessings of the Lord to chase us down and overtake us this day. We love You more than life.

I pray this over each of you today. Stop and ask the Holy Spirit before you consume even one bite of something that will clog your arteries or continue to propagate wretched stuff in your body. Stop and ask—stop and listen.

July 23: Switch on the Light

Have you ever thought about how much easier it is to walk without stumbling, tripping, or breaking things when light is present? Walking at night in my neighborhood, even when the streetlights are on, can be a challenge as the shadows are not clear nor are the cracks in the pavement easily visible. I much prefer the light.

I know we *can* walk without the light, but it is much easier and safer when we can see. I was discussing with someone about the choice we have daily to walk in the light. If I get up at night and the house is totally dark, I have the choice of stumbling or turning on the light. Even a small amount of light is really beneficial. You are probably asking how this applies to our health? Well, light often symbolizes the concept of truth. When we choose to do what we know is correct concerning our health, it is like we switched on the light.

When I am unsure about a food product or how my body responds to a certain food, I start doing research. Here is what I know. The closer to all natural we live, the better. When we have the choice of a 100 calorie snack (totally processed food) or an apple (about the same amount of calories) and we choose the apple, we switch on the light.

Can you imagine what our cells are thinking as we consume the contents of the 100 calorie snack bag? "Anybody know what this is? How do we digest something we cannot pronounce? Is this real food? Because I'm having trouble breaking this apart to grab the nutrition. Is there any nutrition in this?" Can you hear them?

Given the choice of a pre-packaged, 100 calorie container of *whatever* (which are easy to pack, eat, etc.) or an apple, your better choice is the apple. They are the same amount of calories but processed so differently. While it takes hours for our cells to turn the small amount of nutrition from the 100 calorie snack into energy, the apple gets switched on quickly. That is light for my body. I see that as truth. May we no longer walk in the dark and say, "calories are calories." Switch on the light and realize an apple and a processed snack may have the same amount of calories, but they function in our bodies very differently. I will take the one that gives me good fiber, great energy, feeds my cells properly, and does it quickly.

Your morning test: Apple or processed snack?

July 24: Mr. Armadillo

I am having coffee, reading the Word, re-reading Psalm 18, and reminding myself how much I love God and am so grateful for His rescue procedures at various times in my life. If you have not read this psalm lately, try to take a moment and read it in the New Living Translation. When I read this, I smile and feel so protected.

This morning, let's talk about those armadillos that invade your territory while you sleep. Now maybe you live in a place where no such creature has dominion, but I cannot say that. The Word teaches us that what happens in the natural can absolutely be a picture of what can manifest in the realm of our spirit. So I was pondering (although I saw some armadillos in an online video marching through the yard during the day) how wretched that armadillos wage war on my yard while I am resting. I'm supposed to be sleeping peacefully and dreaming of almond flour pancakes and bowls of watermelon, only to discover that my yard has been impaled by one creature. That is not fair.

The capture and removal of Mr. Armadillo has become almost a joke, and yet a problem that seems to escape every trap, every plan, and every attempt at removal. How can something so small win this war? Are these creatures intellectually brilliant and I on the opposite end of the spectrum? No—but they do have the advantage. I cannot see them while they wage war, because I am asleep. How many of you know it is easier to fight something you can see and have the correct tools to defeat? Often when we make excuses for our unhealthy habits, we actually equip them to defeat us. Think about that.

Here is my new insight: I feel that many of our excuses are not visible, "in our face," tangible enemies. Many of our excuses are generational, lack of correct information, defeatism monsters that love to hide in the shadows of our reasoning. "Is that really true?" "Could that really be that bad for me?" "Just because my doctor says ten pounds makes a difference, another doctor probably would tell me something else." Do you know what that is? It is called being asleep while the armadillo destroys our yard. Making excuses about your health can eventually create an ugly and messy "yard" that seems to have no hope of stopping the intruder. Stay alert and informed. Just because you cannot see the armadillo doesn't mean he is not destroying your property. I'm like a crazy "attack the armadillo" person right now. I check every morning to determine his path and make my new plan. I have eyes wide open and am reading and trying everything.

I will defeat Mr. Armadillo as well as my excuses.

July 25: Asking Special Questions

It is a wonderful thing to be able to eat anywhere, as well as eat *whatever* I choose. I will say, however, it is a bit more challenging at the nicer restaurants that cover all foods with sauces and cheeses and have limited items on the menu. It can be done nevertheless. I would suggest that you cook as often as possible, but those special times that require a special French restaurant require special action. After reviewing the menu, I simply start asking *special* questions. I quickly inform the server that I choose to eat foods that are not accessorized.

How many of you know that we wrestle not against flesh and blood? (See Ephesians 6:11-13.) Sometimes that means we have to remember *we are not wrestling against ourselves either.* While Jesus came to give us abundant life, the destroyer came to kill, steal, and destroy. Part of what he intends to destroy is any confidence we have that we can, in fact, live in freedom. Have you ever questioned everything you do? Have you ever made any of these declarations before? "I am always going to struggle with my weight. Vacation is always the struggle for me and I never win. I can never eat out because I always make the wrong decisions." Have you ever questioned yourself in such a manner?

Let me remind all of us that if we have the Holy Spirit within us; we have the mind of Christ. That means we do have victory over our flesh, as well as victory over our desires and emotions. However, we must determine which voice is speaking the loudest at this meal, during this vacation, at this restaurant. As many of us have dealt with extra pounds at the scale and an unhealthy journey most of our lives, winning this battle is unfamiliar ground. We must deliberately recalculate our response and reaffirm the truth. We are free to enjoy any special restaurant because we are free to ask questions. And, if our questions and needs cannot be addressed properly, another establishment can and will work with us. (I have learned that as well.)

I had to talk to myself yesterday and bring a word of encouragement while at a very expensive restaurant with my grandbabies. Their menu was quite a challenge and at first I considered leaving, but this was a special event. I took a deep breath, put a smile on my face and started asking *special* questions. Good news: I left declaring, "I did it." I find that most people are willing to work with our needs if we are willing to share them kindly.

July 26: The Window Unit

Here we are in the middle of summer and most everyone loves the long days of sunshine. Me too. But I tell you this, the heat can sometimes make me feel like doing crazy things. Given the choice of hot or cold, most of the time I prefer the cold. I can always add more clothes; but how many of you know there is only so much that can be taken off?

As a child, the air-conditioned buildings we enjoy today were non-existent. Our home was not air-conditioned and I wonder sometimes how I lived through such an *atrocity*? Maybe a hundred years ago, when I was little, we were in the ice age? No. Seriously though, we had no air-conditioning until mom bought a window unit for their room. My thoughts were, *what about us poor children?*

As I recall those days, I remember the lack of air conditioning never bothered me until the window unit went in. Why? Because I did not expect it, was not accustomed to it, never really knew the benefits of it until that window unit started functioning. Isn't that the way it is with most conveniences? We would never know of their existence or how we would come to love them had we not been introduced to them. How would one know the joy of having a window unit without the pleasure of having one?

The moral of the story: Let's plan to feed our young ones healthy foods from the beginning and fight to keep from introducing them to the junky stuff (the window unit). On the other side of that, for those of us who installed the *window unit* and must now be reconditioned to live without it, keep going. Your body will adjust, and once it does, remember how difficult the transition was and let those feelings serve as reminders that keeping it clean and simple is not so bad. And if our kids never become accustomed to the *window unit*, they will never have the fight for freedom that we have experienced.

July 27: Herbed Spaghetti Squash

Yield: 8 servings

Ingredients

- 1 large spaghetti squash
- ½ stick light butter
- ½ teaspoon garlic salt
- Salt to taste
- Fresh chopped parsley

Procedure

1. Follow my recipe for preparing the "spaghetti" noodles from page 67.
2. Melt the butter over medium heat in a skillet. (Be careful to not let it burn, it will change color quickly.)
3. Add the salt, garlic salt, and stir well.
4. Remove from the heat, add the "spaghetti" noodles, and toss well.
5. Stir in the fresh parsley.
6. Serve warm as a side dish. You could add grated Parmesan before serving.

Per Serving:
Calories 51.7
Total Fat 3.3 g
Cholesterol 7.5 mg
Sodium 67.5 mg
Potassium 114.7 mg
Total Carbohydrate 6.4 g
Dietary Fiber 1.4 g
Sugars 2.5 g
Protein 0.7 g

July 28: Red, White, and Blue Trifle

Yield: 16 servings

Ingredients

- 1 recipe of my Five Flavor Cream Cheese Pound Cake from page 92
- 1 recipe of my coconut whipped cream from page 163
- 2 large containers strawberries (washed and chopped)
- 2 large containers blueberries (washed)
- Chopped pecan pieces (optional)

Procedure

1. Bake my pound cake recipe in a 9x13 baking dish.
2. When completely cooled, use star cookie cutters (if you can locate them) and cut the cake into various-sized stars. The extra cake is good for crumbling and using as the base for the trifle.
3. Make the whipped cream.
4. Assembly: Put some of the cake crumbles into the bottom of your container for the trifle. Line the side of the glass container with some of the stars. Make a layer of strawberries, then blueberries, then more stars, and whipped cream. Continue layering. The final layer should be whipped cream. I did have 2 stars left over that I used on the top of the whipped cream. Add the nuts if you like. Allow to set over night for best taste. The flavors blend nicely.

Per Serving:

(Just the fruit and nuts, see serving info for pound cake and whipped cream on pages 92 and 163)

Calories 92.9
Total Fat 5.5 g
Cholesterol 0.0 mg
Sodium 3.5 mg
Potassium 149.3 mg
Total Carbohydrate 11.3 g
Dietary Fiber 3.1 g
Sugars 7.8 g
Protein 1.3 g

July 29: Solving Problems

When I hear the chimes ringing on the porch, I know that the wind is moving outside. I do not actually *see* the wind, but I know it is pushing the chimes. There are things we cannot *see*, but we "see" their effects. There are deep, spiritual truths here for us all.

When considering vision, we really get to choose how we see our life and the circumstances that are presented to us daily. I do not know about you but sometimes I get ruffled being around people, who always find the negative, confess the negative, and embrace the negative. It depresses me and I have to limit my contact with them. Just being real. Sometimes I have been accused of "not being realistic." To that I say, "If being realistic means always being negative, I will live in a fantasy world." I absolutely feel we have the opportunity to see the cup half empty or half full. Confessing the half empty side of the picture does not mean the half full side is wrong, does it? It is a matter of perspective.

I love crime scene shows on television and my husband hates them—difference of perspective. Why do I love them you ask? The fixer in me desires to solve problems. Within a one-hour program, some problem is solved. From my perspective that is a good thing (although in real life, I am positive it took more than an hour). I love watching the process of how issues are solved, and I love helping others solve problems.

I think that is one of the reasons I enjoy writing these daily devotions and sending them out on my blog. It gives me joy to help someone see things differently. I am simply a person who loves people, understands the journey of hiding my unhealthiness behind bad jokes, realizes that freedom is attainable no matter how we view the cup, and longs to see people live on the side where the cup is full and not empty.

If I can share a recipe or some hope, maybe that helps you see your journey to a healthier you. That makes my heart smile. Maybe you can do that for others?

July 30: Chipmunks for Real

As this month comes to a close, let us take a minute and reflect upon the holidays we have already walked through and hopefully have some amazing testimonies to share with the groups we are forming as another big group of holidays is approaching. Here are the ones we have conquered *so far*:

- Valentine's Day
- St. Patrick's Day
- Easter
- Mother's Day
- Memorial Day
- Father's Day
- 4th of July

How about that? I can proudly say that I journeyed through each one in complete health. How about you? If not, no worries. Get the recipes down and create some new ones that are specific for you before the beginning of next year. Remember, the recipes are your baseline. You should use them as a tool and never give up. Make them work for you. This is your life and you should enjoy the food options given to you.

But while you do that (and you have about five weeks until the next holiday), try some vegetables and fruits that are about to be phased out as the summer closes. They are more costly during the winter and we have fewer and fewer choices. At this point of the summer, I feel like the chipmunks that have that internal instinct to hoard and prepare for the winter.

But for now, choose from lots of colors and enjoy the summer abundance. I vote to celebrate the previous victories and prepare for the upcoming ones. The fall and early winter holidays are sometimes the hardest ones. I will not be defeated. Planning together with you to be victorious.

July 31: July Reflection Page

As you are completing the July devotions, are there things you wish you had highlighted or which you had written down? Which recipes have been your favorites? Did you volunteer to have the 4th of July celebration and make a declaration of freedom from sugar?

_____

_____

_____

_____

_____

_____

_____

_____

_____

_____

_____

_____

_____

_____

_____

_____

_____

_____

_____

_____

August

The "dog days of summer." I never really knew what that phrase meant, but I know August is long and hot. That means a lot of grilling and swimming. Those are both great choices for us.

August 1: A New Trick

As I mentioned in a previous devotion, I have never endorsed the phrase "you cannot teach an old dog new tricks." That has such a wrong connotation to me. The older I get, I find this is just not true. In fact, it is actually wrong. There are many seniors who continually learn new things no matter what phase of life encompasses them. Take me as an example. I have learned to text, use a touch-screen tablet, unlock wireless passcodes, fly over tall mountains, and handcuff robbers. Aren't you proud of me? Therefore, it stands to reason this has nothing to do with age and everything to do with attitude. I feel that if the *kids* can learn it, I can.

Would you be willing to experiment with a new trick to determine if you are actually hungry or not? I like new tricks and especially one that works. Consider this: If you desire something to eat, then the questions to consider are, "Am I really hungry?" and, "Do I need to eat?" I know that often we eat as it is time or everyone else is eating. I am not talking about these re-fueling times. I am trying to address snack times.

Try this: perhaps you want an afternoon snack, a doughnut. To determine if you are hungry or just bored, ask yourself, "Would I eat an apple instead of the doughnut?" If your response is yes, you know you *would* eat the apple, then you are probably hungry, so find something healthy to eat (skip the doughnut though). If your answer is no, and you would not eat the apple, you are not hungry. So, skip the snack and wait to refuel at the next meal. This really works.

At whatever age you find yourself today, this is a great trick. You can learn and apply this or if you like your afternoon snack, you can say you are too old to learn new tricks. That made me smile. The only problem is the scale is not too old to report your weight gain.

August 2: Lessons from My Mouth Guard

This morning as I am brushing my mouth guard (worn at night to keep me from grinding my teeth) I felt the Holy Spirit began to speak to me about the importance of the guard I wear. I really detest it, but would like my teeth to be nice when I turn one hundred years old. When I began to think of my mouth guard, these thoughts emerged:

1. It protects my teeth from being destroyed.

2. It works while I rest.

3. It serves a purpose that I cannot see.

4. It could save me a lot of time and money in the future.

Can I tell you eating healthy does all the above? Yes, it does. Healthy eating protects my teeth and gums, regenerates my cells while I sleep, works from the inside out to allow my body a long life, and keeps those doctor bills to a minimum. Then I began to really consider how nice it would be if a mouth guard miraculously appeared every time we were about to consume a food which offered no nutritional value. Or, if a guard would appear when our portion size had been met. That could be good or bad. As much as I hate my mouth guard, somehow this sounds appealing.

If the mouth guard is not efficient enough, what about talking food? "I'm sorry, these French fries you are about to consume are loaded with fat and salt which eventually will lead to heart disease." I'm laughing, but sometimes I need this. How about you? That is why we have a support group. The food cannot talk, but the scale and our health family can. I have a choice each night as to whether the mouth guard is placed or not. No one reminds me of its importance and sometimes I am too tired and stressed to even fit the device in my mouth.

But as I begin my morning routine, I am certainly aware of my bad choice the previous evening. This is such a picture of our journey, our health. No one is with us when the temptation to "remove the guard" for a season occurs, but our jeans remind us quickly that consistent, bad choices lead to consequences that we were hoping to avoid. So today, whether we like it or not, let's place a guard around our food choices and portion sizes. It may not be comfortable today, but it will be easier tomorrow.

I am starting this month off making great choices and saying thank you to my mouth guard.

August 3: Do You Really?

I watched a pastor from Atlanta preach last night on television a very hard-hitting, "in your face" message. He continued to hammer his congregation with, "So, you want to be a world-class athlete? You want to be a super star?" He went on to exclaim, "No you don't. You're not willing to change what you eat, work out three hours a day, and drink those muscle drinks they drink. No you ain't' gonna be no world-class something." I felt like I got kicked in the pants. I appreciated his boldness and honesty. Challenge me, brother.

"Oh, you wanna be more like Jesus, all that Jesus was? No you don't." He continued his challenge with, "You're not willing to get up in the middle of the night and pray three hours, live a life of extreme purity, and die on a cross." How many know that at this point I was looking for the remote? He continued, "Being great sounds great but it has a great price. Some are willing to do whatever and pay the price. Many simply "talk out loud," not "wish" they could become something else."

That really hit home with me. I know so many people who say, "I wish I could be more disciplined like you. I just cannot do all that cooking you do. I can't live without sugar. I have to eat at work functions." My reply is simple, "If you are desperate to live, you can do a lot of things."

My choice to make a radical change came in response to a cry for life from deep within me. *People can change, but can they change with no intent to go back to their former place?* I tell people all the time, "Anybody can be good for a little while." That is not real change. Real change is the new path we choose and the old path is no longer an option. I want to commend many of you for choosing health when it cost you dearly and for continuing to choose health when your flesh is screaming for a slice of pizza. We all know how loud our flesh can scream. Unfortunately, mine still screams, but a lot less these days. Being radically healthy is a not a fad, it is a way of life. Pizza is for the crowd, but health has its price and is only for those who are willing to make a real change.

Real change=long life. That is my choice.

August 4: Lessons from a Postage Stamp

One of the things I admire most about certain people is their ability to cope with and endure extremely difficult situations. For example, I admire people who are closers and unwilling to quit mid-stream when fatigue and an easier path appears. I am not speaking of the scratch-your-nail or stub-your-toe experience. I am speaking of those who have struggled against cancer and are well, lost limbs and learned to walk again, lost hundreds of pounds and continued to walk in the freedom of a healthy body. Those experiences take great determination and endurance. Those individuals know what it is to have a passionate desire to live again, not simply exist, and stay with the plan until the manifestation of their determination emerges. Their patient endurance gives me hope.

I have been thinking a lot about purpose and completing my God-given assignments. Sometimes our health journey seems to find itself in challenging places. I have heard from several of you who are eating healthy, and yet still struggle with cholesterol or gaining around your belly when you absolutely know you have stayed within the boundaries. Sometimes our bodies have their own agenda and stress can cause responses we cannot account for. Ever been there? I have. During those times it is easy to pull out the "this plan does not work" card or the "nothing ever works for me" card. That is the easy path. But can I encourage you today to use the "I will stick to my health plan no matter what" card.

Can we examine the life of a postage stamp for a moment? I found some stamps in my wallet that were two years old last month and yet sticking to the book as if they were first placed on the paper. I wondered exactly how long those little guys would keep to the task of sticking? They really have no options if they are going to complete their assignment, do they?

The stamps remained attached through various temperatures, being tossed from bag to bag, and being transported across the ocean. Years may pass and we find the postage still attached. Hebrews 10:36 speaks of patient endurance. Patience is not one of my best virtues, but my determination to be healthy regardless is developing that patience muscle within. I cannot buckle under today's weigh-in or yesterday's issues. Being healthy is not an option, therefore I am stuck to my health plan until I go to heaven. Today, I am seeing myself as a postage stamp fulfilling my assignment against all odds. Our verse in Hebrews declares there is something waiting for those who endure patiently. The little stamp never quits. *God, give me the ability to stick like that.* Continue doing what is right—it will pay off.

August 5: A Sincere Prayer

I love reading the prayers of those in the Bible, as they are familiar to me and give me a sense that my heart can also need consolation. I can identify with many in the verses that are lifting their hearts to the Lord. They suffered through difficult life situations as we do. No one escapes, do they? Out of our desperate prison cells of unhealthy ways, we cry out to God and eventually come to realize that He always answers. Sometimes God says yes, sometimes no, and sometimes He says, "Not now."

God is not slow of hearing or distracted by the journey of His creation. I believe He absolutely hears and is touched by every prayer, but His plan must be executed at the right time. There are things we learn in those waiting periods. I am convinced that I will never understand God's reasoning in the manner in which He responds to my prayers. That is okay. It never changes my love or undying devotion to Him. I know He heard and He knows best.

As you read the following Scripture, let it bring hope and encouragement to you today as you deepen the understanding that God listens and God performs great wonders. As I read it, there was such peace that rested in my heart.

> "Bend down, O LORD, and hear my prayer; answer me, for I need your help. Protect me, for I am devoted to you. Save me, for I serve you and trust you. You are my God. Be merciful to me, O Lord, for I am calling on you constantly. Give me happiness, O Lord, for I give myself to you. O Lord, you are so good, so ready to forgive, so full of unfailing love for all who ask for your help. Listen closely to my prayer, O LORD; hear my urgent cry. I will call to you whenever I'm in trouble, and you will answer me. No pagan god is like you, O Lord. None can do what you do! All the nations you made will come and bow before you, Lord; they will praise your holy name. For you are great and perform wonderful deeds. You alone are God. Teach me your ways, O LORD, that I may live according to your truth! Grant me purity of heart, so that I may honor you. With all my heart I will praise you, O Lord my God. I will give glory to your name forever, for your love for me is very great. You have rescued me from the depths of death" (Psalm 86:1-13 NLT).

Is that powerful? Did you pray as you read? I did.

August 6: Italian Stuffed Chicken

Yield: 8 servings

Ingredients

- 1 pkg. prosciutto ham
- 4 large chicken breasts
- 1 regular container of ricotta cheese
- 1 tablespoon of Italian spices
- 1 small container of sugar-free spaghetti sauce (your preference)
- 2 eggs
- 1 cup 2% mozzarella shredded cheese
- 1/3-1/2 cup Parmesan Reggiano cheese

Procedure

1. Preheat oven to 350°F and spray a 9x9 baking dish.
2. Slice the chicken breasts lengthwise, but not completely through. Open the two halves to lay flat. They should still be connected.
3. Lay 2 pieces of ham across the 2 halves.
4. Mix the ricotta cheese, the eggs and the Italian seasonings. Spoon 2 tablespoons of the mixture in the center of the halves.
5. Beginning on one side, roll the breast halves into the shape of a log. (If they are small breasts, the two halves may simply overlap. This is fine.) Place these in the greased pan seam side down.
6. Cover with the spaghetti sauce and cheeses.
7. Bake for 35-45 minutes to allow the meat to cook thoroughly and the cheese to brown.
8. I cut the pieces directly across the middle and serve 2 people with one piece.

Per Serving:

Calories 397.6
Total Fat 18.0 g
Cholesterol 164.3 mg
Sodium 1,086.8 mg
Potassium 310.2 mg
Total Carbohydrate 9.7 g
Dietary Fiber 1.5 g
Sugars 5.1 g
Protein 47.5 g

August 7: Taco Bake

Yield: 16 servings

I like to serve each slice of this taco bake with sour cream and guacamole, or for a healthier meal, serve with shredded lettuce and chopped tomatoes.

Ingredients

- 3 cups almond flour
- 2/3 cup melted butter
- 2 teaspoons salt
- 3 eggs
- 2 pounds ground beef
- 1 large onion, or two medium, chopped fine
- 2 cloves minced garlic
- 1 teaspoon of the following: salt, pepper, cumin (I use 2 teaspoons), paprika, red pepper flakes, jalapeno powder (or 2-3 tablespoons of my sugar-free taco seasoning mix)
- 1 regular jar mild or medium salsa (your choice)

Procedure

Crust:

1. Preheat oven to 350°F.
2. Mix together the almond flour and salt.
3. Mix the eggs and cooled butter in a separate container.
4. Combine the eggs and butter with the flour mixture and blend until a ball forms.
5. Press into a sprayed 9x13 pan. The dough is extremely sticky. I suggest you spray your hands or lightly grease them as you evenly distribute the dough over the bottom. I don't put any on the sides.
6. Bake for 25 minutes. The crust should be light brown.

Meat Mixture:

1. Brown the ground beef.
2. Add the onion and garlic and cook until the onions are tender.
3. Add all the seasonings and stir well.
4. Place the meat mixture on the baked and cooled almond crust.
5. Sprinkle with 2 cups four blend Mexican cheese and the jar of salsa.
6. Bake for about 25-30 minutes until the cheese is melted and browning. Allow to cool for about 15 minutes and cut into 16 servings.

Per Serving:
Calories 394
Total Fat 31 g
Cholesterol 94 mg
Sodium 324 mg
Potassium 326.5 mg
Total Carbohydrate 10.3 g
Dietary Fiber 4.1 g
Sugars 1.7 g
Protein 21.5 g

August 8: Head Knowledge or Heart Knowledge?

Do we wish making the right decision took no real effort? I do. But that's not the way life is. Some days, choosing correctly all day long is easy. But most days, if we are honest, it takes dedicated focus. Simply knowing the right things to do is not good enough. That is not where the battle is.

Constant consumption of calories beyond what our body can digest and utilize causes many difficult issues. That statement is a fact and yet many ignore the truth. Ignoring the truth only delays the inevitable and never solves the problem. While at dinner tonight, one of my granddaughters asked, "Nina, why are so many people really heavy?" It was a wonderful opportunity to speak with her about the difference between head knowledge and heart knowledge. I also found a couple of pieces of fat trimmed from my meat and brought this as a visual into the teaching moment.

I told the girls that everyone in the restaurant has been exposed to the knowledge of the effects of poor eating. No one is a stranger to the reports. But, *comprehending and believing* the truth is a different subject. It must move from our brains (knowledge) to our hearts (understanding). I picked up the fat and allowed the girls to see the effects of bad choices and told them this is exactly what collects on our thighs and the inside of our hearts. I asked them if they would like to hold the pieces of fat? They both freaked as if I had asked them to touch a rattlesnake.

Here is the story of someone with heart knowledge: I went to the eye doctor Monday and his senior partner is eighty-eight years old, still working, driving over one hour to work, looks sixty-eight, is the picture of health, still exercises, etc. I said to my doctor, "How is this?" His response, "For the thirty years we have worked together, he has always eaten well, watched his fat content, exercised, and kept his mind sharp." He told me, "I promise you everyone thinks he is in his late sixties. He is as sharp as a tack and so healthy." I smiled as I considered that could be said of each of us one day.

If we make a stand for truth, *truth* will eventually make a stand for us. Let us transfer our head knowledge to heart truth.

August 9: The Voice of a Candy Bar

We need to return to the cross of Jesus Christ on a daily basis and bring our wandering thoughts back to the captivating concept that a high price was paid for our freedom. I will never understand God's love for me in that He would give His only Son and watch Him die just to have a long-term relationship with someone as wicked as me.

When we think of the "gifts" of the cross, we could make a list. We certainly pray and confess that Jesus took our infirmities and diseases upon Himself and "by His stripes we are healed." I stand on that truth in my own personal life. Sometimes, however, I wonder if we firmly accept that Jesus heals diseases like cancer, diabetes, and things I cannot pronounce, but cannot heal our eating disorders. You will never convince me that Jesus' death was only for certain select issues.

Jesus' death brought us freedom on many levels, including the freedom of choice. As I told a friend the other day who was ingesting a large double cheeseburger and a bucket of fries, "You are free to eat that now, but you are not free to choose the consequences that eating this could bring to your arteries in a few years." His response, "I'll worry about it later." How sad that often when "later" arrives, it doesn't come empty-handed. Our bad choices rarely ask if we are concerned with the consequences, they simply demand to be accommodated.

I wonder how often our freedom to eat as we wish hinders God's best desire for our body later in life? Perhaps our ability to be healed of certain diseases could be directly hindered by the freedom to make healthy choices in the areas of food, hydration, and rest? Is the cheeseburger encouraging healing within my body? Are the French fries serving to cleanse my arteries? Does the candy bar scream louder than the strawberries at the market?

I would rather eat to live and use my freedom of choice to fill this body with great substances which produce life, than endure heart disease and cancer and find myself in need of a miracle. I cannot guarantee that healthy eating will prevent all diseases, as I cannot see into the future. But I can promise that healthy choices will improve your quality of life, perhaps for a long time.

Let the candy call to whom it chooses and you choose to say no. You'll thank me later.

August 10: The Top of the Food Chain

When we think of the food chain, often the phrase "survival of the fittest" emerges. My mom taught me that concept early. And while the concept points to one winning through some type of competition, for us as healthy people it is so true. We must win our battle against obesity or the wages of weight-related diseases will prepare to destroy us with a vengeance. In my own strength, I am totally a loser. I have learned that valuable lesson in some desperate battles throughout the past several years.

I tried on my own to arrive at the top of the health food chain, and failed more times than my tally sheet could contain. Eventually I was weak and willing to be consumed by the multitude of illnesses that had ravaged my body. But in a final attempt to live, God, my family, my accountability partners, and my renewed strength gave me the courage to make a stand that changed the course of my life forever and renewed my quest to survive as a fit person. Hope is so powerful, isn't it?

Perhaps as you read this you feel hopeless and have consented to the illnesses as I did. God is the only hope of life-long success I can offer you. I want you to see the truth in John 15:5 (NLT) this morning and let it encourage you again. The verse declares, "apart from me you can do nothing." This truth resonates within me. It can resonate within you as well and give you strength, when quitting would be easier, if you will accept it as God's Word to you today.

John 15:5 also speaks of a dependent relationship where we abide in Jesus and His Spirit abides in us. We must choose to remain connected to Him in every area of our life (including our health) as if being removed from Him yielded immediate death. When we abide in this manner in Jesus, He alone gives the strength to reach the top of the health food chain. While I hate the concept of the competition that phrase evokes, I am encouraged and challenged to think of this in a plural manner. I am not competing *against* you to get to the top. I am competing *with* you so that together we will achieve our health goals. I am grateful to be on your team!

August 11: The Trampoline Park

A couple of weeks ago, my daughter and I took the girls to the newest, hottest playground around—a trampoline park. I am a bit leery of trampolines at any level, as my daughter broke her ankle on one as a teen. But my granddaughters really wanted to go. What an experience.

As I opened the entry door and looked up, my eyes focused on a huge room filled with various trampoline experiences and wall-to-wall people. At first I was a bit overwhelmed. But the energy and excitement of the jumpers sucked us into the adventure. After the completion of the necessary paperwork, the craziness arrived. The girls were timid at first, as people were jumping from one trampoline to the other with no seemingly determined pattern or reverence for other jumpers. I was not even jumping and my heart started pounding as little people were jumping around big people and from mat to mat like a swarm of bees.

My girls jumped onto their first mat and slowly found their rhythm. Within minutes, however, they joined the jumping frenzy and were bopping from mat to mat along with the crowd. Quickly, something grabbed my attention. One of the jumpers left the floor, jumped on the wall, flipped back to the floor and back to the wall. I was thinking, *Is that some kind of super hero?*

I stood for seconds looking in amazement at all the variations of jumping offered. It was craziness at its finest. Although there were a multitude of trampoline experiences in this arena and the jumpers varied in all shapes and sizes, there was a common denominator running throughout. Contagious fun and spontaneous energy rolled from mat to mat and jumper to jumper. The jumpers were having a great time while sweating like tiny water faucets. Their cheeks were bloody red while they scurried from mat to mat with joy in their journey.

Many times our daily routine bounces all over the place, tosses us against the walls, and causes our faces to be red and dripping with sweat. The question is can we still find a way to laugh? No matter how much difficulty life bounces our way, let us bounce back, bounce on the wall, bounce in the easy squares, and keep moving. Even the kids who hit the mats hard were back to their feet and jumping wildly in seconds, smiling as they began again. My life is a trampoline park experience and my health is only one of the mats. I pray God help me, and you, be fabulous jumpers and come to trust that His strength will help us bounce against life and smile as we bounce again.

August 12: Am I Honoring God?

I want to share a passage of Scripture this morning as we round out our week. The context is found in 1 Corinthians 6:19-20 (NLT): "Don't you realize that your body is the temple of the Holy Spirit, who lives in you and was given to you by God?" That is a very familiar passage isn't it?

It is the next part of the verse to which I would like to direct our attention: "You do not belong to yourself, for God bought you with a high price. So you must honor God with your body." If I read that correctly, it implies that one of the methods in which we convey our high regard for Father God is by the things we do with our body. I wonder how many of our daily activities actually pass through this filter successfully?

That is a powerful and challenging thought. Do I really even consider that my fight for great health honors God? I understand that the verse is actually speaking of sexual immorality, but I really believe that God is well pleased with our concerted effort to take amazing care of our bodies in many areas.

Question: If you gave two of your children fabulous, brand new cars that were very costly and one child took really good care of it and one let it rot, never washed it, and ran it into trees, which one would bring you more honor? Great question, huh? I have never thought about that part of the passage in those terms until this morning and I am simply asking myself to be honest.

I applaud each of you for doing the best you can to walk in health each and every day. Give God the biggest shout out that your body belongs to Him and He gives you the ability to make the right choices and do the right things this day. When the end of the day arrives, let us evaluate our health journey and decide if we did our best to honor God with our body. As we arise in the morning, may we choose to make this our personal challenge.

August 13: Chocolate Trifle

Yield: 16 servings

Ingredients

- 1 recipe of my Chocolate Pound Cake (found on page 278)
- 1 recipe of my whipped cream found on page 163 (Add chocolate extract and 3 packages of no sugar added hot chocolate mix.)
- Sugared pecans (recipe following)

Procedure

1. Bake the pound cake in a 9x13-baking dish. When completely cooled, cut into squares.
2. Make the chocolate whipped cream. Set aside.
3. Make the sugar-cinnamon pecans. This takes time, but the taste is worth it.
4. Place 1/3 of the pound cake squares in the bottom of your trifle container. Add 1/3 of the whipped cream followed by the sugared pecans. Repeat. So you'll have three layers of cake, whipped cream and layers of sugared pecans. I added sliced strawberries to the top and someone asked if next time I could add more. Perhaps I may add sliced strawberries to all three layers next time.
5. Chill until ready to serve.

Per Serving:
(This nutritional data is only for the sugared pecans. Refer to nutritional information for cake and whipped cream.)
Calories 136.5
Total Fat 13.7 g
Cholesterol 7.5 mg
Sodium 50.0 mg
Potassium 61.0 mg
Total Carbohydrate 5.6 g
Dietary Fiber 1.4 g
Sugars 2.3 g
Protein 1.4 g

Sugar-cinnamon Pecans:

Ingredients

- 2 one-pound bags pecans
- 1 stick light butter
- 6-8 tablespoons Truvia® Baking Blend
- Cinnamon to taste (don't be stingy)

Procedure

1. Preheat oven to 250°F.
2. Place both bags of pecans in a 9x13 baking dish.
3. Cut the sticks of butter into chunks and place on the pecans.
4. Cook for 30 minutes.
5. Make sure the butter has melted and stir from the bottom up as to coat the pecans with the butter.
6. Sprinkle 1 heaping tablespoon of Truvia® Baking Blend on top as well as a good sprinkle of cinnamon. Blend well and put it back in the oven for 30 minutes. Follow this procedure for 5 additional 30-minute segments for a total of 3 hours baking.
7. After the last stir at 3 hours, turn the oven to 500 and place them in for an additional 10 minutes, "jiggling" them often to really crisp but not burn.

August 14: Yogurt Dessert Variations

Yield: 1 serving

Ingredients

- Plain Greek yogurt (fat free and sugar-free). I purchase the 3 oz. individual containers. (100 calories)
- 2-3 pkgs. Truvia® Natural Sweetener (depending on how sweet you like the yogurt) or sometimes I use 2-3 teaspoons of xylitol.
- ½ teaspoon vanilla extract

Procedure

1. Blend the above three ingredients and return to the refrigerator for approximately 15 minutes. This will allow the sugar to dissolve.
2. This can be eaten as vanilla yogurt.

Per Serving:

(The nutritional information only reflects the yogurt, Truvia® Natural Sweetener , and extract. There are so many variations.)

Calories 85.4
Total Fat 0.0 g
Cholesterol 0.0 mg
Sodium 40.4 mg
Potassium 159.5 mg
Total Carbohydrate 12.5 g
Dietary Fiber 0.0 g
Sugars 8.5 g
Protein 10.0 g

Variations:

1. Add the juice of ½ lime for a key lime pie yogurt.

2. Add ½ cup of strawberries and substitute almond extract for the vanilla. Add 2 tablespoons of chopped pecans.

3. Add ½ cup of blueberries.

4. Add ½ cup of peaches and freeze for about 30 minutes (optional). Sometimes I eat it without freezing.

5. Make a layer of strawberry yogurt (number 2 above) and freeze for about 30 minutes in a shallow dish. Then, add a layer of blueberry yogurt and return to the freezer. As an option, you can also add a final layer of vanilla and return once again to the freezer. After a couple of hours, allow to sit for 10 minutes at room temperature and cut into squares. Serve immediately. This is a colorful dessert.

August 15: Is God Your Diet Pill?

Many of us know that God's Word teaches that He answers prayer. We know that God hears our requests and that His heart is tender toward each of us. The real issue is not if God hears, the issue comes when He does not answer the way we feel He should or in the time frame we desire. I am convinced that many people have no real understanding of what prayer is, and often misunderstanding leads to disappointment. That was me.

For many years I begged God to release me from the prison of obesity in which I found myself. I prayed and I begged while opening my mouth and ingesting over four thousand calories each day. Sometimes I became angry with God. I really expected Him to be my *diet pill*. Can we be honest?

For those of you who have never taken diet pills, they are designed to help with self-discipline and be the answer to the obesity issue. For many, they are an "answer" to prayer. However, their power to control our fleshly desires are momentary. As soon as their term is completed, our flesh begins to scream again. Diet pills are never the answer to long-term change. They always made me irritable and jumpy, which was amplified even more once I stopped taking them. So back to God I would turn in prayer and petition.

I felt like God did not want to help me and I even sarcastically commented, "Well, God must want me to be fat." Can you hear my frustration? That was irritation and anger speaking because I desired to be thin and eat as I wanted. My attitude conveyed that I expected God to be my "magic" diet pill. Guess what? I would have stayed right there for the remainder of my life if I had not turned that agitation and desperation into something positive. Perhaps God's answer was to allow my frustration to develop to a place where He knew I would irreversibly fight my way out of that dungeon and turn to offer a hand to others.

God does answer prayer; God does hear every prayer; and God does really care for us. But God never promises that our life will be void of discipline or restriction. He does promise to never leave us or forsake us. He does promise to guide us beside still waters, *but He never promised to be our diet pill*. I hope you see what I'm trying to say. Pray without ceasing because you love God and want a relationship with Him. That is awesome, and there are no strings attached. After your morning prayer, plan a healthy day and stick to it.

August 16: Living beyond the Fast Food Lane

As I listened last night to a report on the terrible plight of our country due to the drought and the effect of the failed corn crop, I was shocked at some of the statistics. I had no clue that 75 percent of everything we purchase has corn or high fructose corn syrup in it. The reporter continued to elaborate on the importance of corn as a filler even in some of our toothpaste. I actually pressed the DVR rewind button and that is actually what he reported.

Then the reporter began to challenge the viewers to consider where we could possibly see the greatest, immediate impact of this failed crop—the grocery store and gas pump. For a wee bit I was concerned, as I know food cost for healthy eaters can be higher than normal anyway. I slowed down and started processing what they were actually saying. They were essentially communicating that processed foods contain these corn fillers and were going to increase in cost as a by-product from the drought. Those fast lane choices are pumped with a corn product so the cost can remain low. Ah...I began to see this beautiful picture.

The reporters announced that meat will increase, as most animals are fed with corn, but fruits and vegetables may go down. Shelf foods will increase while whole foods may actually decrease in cost so that markets can remain in business. I started smiling. That is great news for us, as we should remain in the whole food lanes as often as possible as opposed to the fast food lanes. While everyone else is scrambling to pay their additional food costs, we can be a beacon of hope.

My suggestion is you gather a group of three people as a life group and meet for a healthy cooking party. All participants can bring the same ingredients, share the responsibilities of preparation, cook the meals to be frozen when taken home and assist with cleanup. A house filled with whole foods, cooking, and great aromatherapy. That sounds both fun and efficient to me.

August 17: The Punching Bag

I have always been amazed at those folks who workout with the *punching bag*. I would probably have a broken nose within seconds as dodging the bag takes an enormous amount of energy and rhythm. Notice I said dodging. I do not know about you, but that thing seems to fly quickly and certainly does not seem to be kind. I do not like round objects flying at my face.

I have observed, however, that people who practice with these creatures seem to master a flow and rhythm that allows them to strike the bag with authority. Let us discuss the journey. Punching bags punch back. Brilliant statement, right? I was thinking about how fiercely they strike back and how there is no one to defend you, but you. The bag always responds; and the greater you strike the bag, the greater it strikes back. I feel this is unfair, especially when learning how to use the device as a means of working out. I do not imagine tapping the bag works very well, so perhaps I will stick to water aerobics. But there are some who *love* the encounter.

As I was thinking about the punching bag yesterday, I thought about our lives. When we first commit to a healthy lifestyle change, we begin punching the bag, only to discover it punches back. When I first started, I would pray for an easy meal, easy day, easy anything. The journey was difficult at times and I felt as if I had been punched in the stomach. I never knew how to "work the bag." So there were those trials and attempts at hitting my rhythm on the bag, but slowly and methodically—because I never quit trying—I learned how to strike the bag and keep striking. I finally began to look like one of those boxer dudes at which we all marvel.

Here is the moral of the story: in the book of John, chapter 17, Jesus is praying to our heavenly Father as He knows His time on the earth is short and the disciples are about to "enter the ring with the bag" for themselves. Jesus never asked God to remove them from the punching-bag experience, but to allow them to experience the closeness that He and the Father enjoyed which allowed Jesus to strike the bag effectively every time and gain our freedom. We are never going to escape the punch of life, but with Jesus as our coach and trainer, the voice of the Holy Spirit as our encourager, and God the Father nodding as He knows the outcome, we can learn to punch the bag of life with such God confidence that the rhythm and flow of the experience is effortless. Do not be afraid to punch the bag.

August 18: The Drama Mama

I do much better in certain situations than others. I wish I responded the same way each time to all situations. Sometimes I find that I am extremely calm, and other times I wonder who has invaded my body. Have you ever had such an experience? Some people refer to that as drama. Drama happens to the best of us and I like to always blame the invader. You know you do as well. The worst part about drama is that it seems to always show up at my house when I'm hungry. And a hungry me is not always tolerant of drama.

While drama arrives, it also leaves; and for that I am most grateful. I am not certain if my hormones equalize or if eating a meal calms the drama, but I prefer life drama free. We need to remember, however, that in those seasons where drama is a regular visitor, the book of Proverbs declares that to everything there is a season. While some of us are fighting desperately with a low number of calories right now, some are resting and working the plan. Some are wrestling with the "last ten" while others are cruising toward their goal weight. Some phases are drama free while others are not.

Being faithful to weigh, eat, rest, and hydrate properly will ensure that some of these drama seasons conclude on schedule. However, making excuses to take a bite of this or a bite of that may actually prolong the season. While we have no control over the seasons in nature, I am convinced we do have some control over the seasons in our lives, especially as they relate to our health.

I was looking at some photo albums two nights ago and I almost cried. I had no idea I was that heavy. My daughter asked, "Mom, does that make you want to cry?" Yes. My husband then commented, "You look so unhappy." I was and I never seemed to find a way out, a change, a new season. I was smiling on the outside and screaming on the inside. My smile is different now; it is genuine. I smile not simply because I weigh less, but because I am healthy. And a healthy me is so less likely to be the drama mama.

August 19: Healing in the Fluid

I woke up yesterday morning with fluid running from my left eye. As I opened my eye, I realized it was hurting badly and perhaps I scratched it accidentally in the night. As I sat trying to get the water to slow down, I remembered that when we have a blister, from whatever, it is important to never puncture the blister but allow the fluid to remain around the wound until the blister releases on its own. There is healing in the fluid. The fluid protects the new growth and shields it from the harshness it may encounter until new skin, or cells, have brought new life to that area. I imagine the fluid running from my eye was doing the same thing but in a different manner.

If we are going to obtain and maintain a healthy weight, our water intake has to be at the top of the list of things we must do. And can I be honest? My greatest challenge to hydration is busyness, which can become an excuse if I am not careful. I wish that sometimes I could blame my hydration issues on something colossal like availability. Come on now—it's free and available, and I have issues. That is the honest truth.

As we have discussed on numerous occasions, our organs need water for health. Fat that metabolizes must be flushed from our system or within twenty-four hours it will reconstitute and store again as fat. This is what I have been taught. Fat leaving our body is fabulous, reconstituting within a day, not so. This is a totally bad consequence to inefficient hydration. God created the variables of our life to often co-labor whether they like it or not. There is a deep spiritual truth in this.

Best of all, on a spiritual level, the Holy Spirit is often represented as water and His heart is always to bring healing to areas of our lives. He is called the Comforter, Healer, and our Advocate, just to name a few. I can so get a visual of the Holy Spirit being our shield like the cover over a blister. He protects and allows us to heal from the inside out.

Let us hydrate ourselves today both in the natural and the spiritual realms. Healing, here we come!

August 20: Healthy 4 You Choice Salad

Yield: 1 serving

This recipe is a winner when you really want a lot of flavor with a few calories. You could add banana peppers, or you could use steak strips from the grill as your meat.

Ingredients

- 2 cups romaine lettuce
- 3-4 Roma tomatoes
- Grilled chicken breast, cooled and cut in chunks
- Grill Mates® Montreal Steak seasoning
- Honeycrisp apples, cored and cut in chunks
- White Balsamic vinegar

Procedure

1. Wash and cut the romaine lettuce. Allow to dry for about 20 minutes. (The extra lettuce will keep well in a baggie for lunches for the week.)
2. Slice the Roma tomatoes into rounds.
3. Grill the chicken with steak seasoning. When cooled, cut into chunks.
4. Top the lettuce with tomatoes, grilled chicken, apples, and vinegar to taste.

Per Serving:

Calories 483.1
Total Fat 7.4 g
Cholesterol 145.9 mg
Sodium 159.7 mg
Potassium 1,604.3 mg
Total Carbohydrate 49.2 g
Dietary Fiber 10.4 g
Sugars 23.9 g
Protein 58.1 g

August 21: Cinnamon Squares with Pecans

Yield: 16 servings

You can make soft cookies with this recipe if you prefer. Take a teaspoon of the dough, roll into a small ball and bake on parchment paper. They won't be crispy and they taste better the next day, but they are easy. They will flatten as the almond flour is dense and shrinks as it cools.

Ingredients

- Use a double recipe of the almond flour pizza dough (page 132) substituting ¼ cup xylitol for the Italian spices.
- Xylitol (about ½ cup) for topping the dough when cooled.
- Cinnamon to taste
- Pecan pieces (about ½ - 1 cup)

Procedure

1. Follow the instructions for creating the dough for the pizza. When formed, place in the refrigerator for 30 min.
2. Preheat oven to 350°F.
3. Lightly grease a large cookie sheet.
4. Lightly grease your hands and evenly press the cool dough onto the cookie sheet.
5. Sprinkle with a combination of xylitol and cinnamon. (You could use pumpkin pie spice for a variation.)
6. Sprinkle with pecan pieces.
7. Bake for 30 minutes. Watch the time as almond flour burns easily. When cooled, cut into squares. These will be flat like pita bread and not crispy, but they are very tasty.

Per Serving:

(The following data reflects only the xylitol, pecans, and cinnamon. Use the listed nutritional value for my almond flour pizza on page 132)

Calories 49.7
Total Fat 4.0 g
Cholesterol 0.0 mg
Sodium 0.1 mg
Potassium 25.0 mg
Total Carbohydrate 5.1 g
Dietary Fiber 0.8 g
Sugars 0.2 g
Protein 0.5 g

August 22: A Big Hit

I just returned from a wonderful experience with the *Fabulous Four* who happen to be our interns from church. I love going to orientation to cook for these young people and count it my honor and privilege. But this year I decided to experiment with them as they are young adults and often eating healthy is "just not in their budget."

I cut peaches into slivers, with the skin remaining, and sprinkled them with Truvia® Natural Sweetener as a snack *for me* and within seconds, the whole bowl was gone. My snack was consumed as the snack chips lay upon the counter in the same vicinity. I did not provide the fruit as a choice. One of the interns saw I was munching a peach and asked if they could try one. Within 4.5 seconds piranha had invaded our cottage. It made me smile. The interns were amazed that real peaches, with the skin, tasted so good. Go figure.

I laughed as they devoured a fruit, not a sugar cookie, and were fighting over the last one. Someone asked, "Those are not real peaches, right?" Yes, they were real, whole peaches that brought life and health and offered an incredible taste also. It is amazing how these healthy foods are often hidden behind processed milk shakes and desserts from boxes. The flavor really popped and that entire bowl was consumed with pleas for more. Again I just laughed— kids eating healthy and fighting over a real peach.

Another big hit was the spaghetti squash. Most had never seen one and were amazed at how they flaked like angel hair pasta. But the biggest hit was the coconut whipped cream with xylitol, which I used over fresh strawberries and blueberries for dessert Sunday night. I normally make brownies, but not this year. They ate it like ice cream. I did buy some cookies and a few other things, but there were healthy options and they ate those just as quickly. You know *young people will eat anything*. That is the cliché and if it is true, which it is, why not feed them the good stuff all along.

The moral of the story: Our families can be trained to enjoy whole foods and perhaps come to a place of choosing them. Cooking for the interns proved that young adults, who are sometimes the most picky, will correctly choose the healthy food options if they do not appear to be from an alien land or if they do not taste like cardboard.

August 23: Never Fuel the Attack of the Enemy

During Bible study last night, we were talking about how the enemy of our soul targets certain sheep and they become easy prey. We then discussed how certain types of people actually fuel the attack of the enemy—discontent, discouraged, downcast, and depressed. I want to use that and talk about our journey for a moment.

Have you seen the animal shows where the stalker lies quietly for a season of observation as dinner plays gingerly in the field near by? While watching, I desperately want to shout, "You need to stop acting oblivious to the danger waiting to attack." But none of my squirming or stomping my feet notifies the animals that they are about to be the "Thanksgiving turkey."

Finally the predator narrows the field to the smallest, weakest, or most isolated one and then baby, "it's on." I usually scream and grab for the remote as my husband cheers and celebrates that the predator has managed to conquer. That is such a guy thing. Terry continues to remind me that God established the food chain. Please, no Sunday school lessons as I change the channel. I get it, but my heart is filled with compassion. Anyway, back to the Bible study.

The longer we walk around in brokenness and failure, the easier prey we become to death and disease. The additional fifty pounds of extra body weight we gathered over the past five years (some studies say most people gain an average of ten pounds a year after age fifty) only wink to the predator and announce, "I am yours." I do not know about you, but that will no longer be me—no way.

Here is a ray of hope though. One of the shows actually filmed the rescue of the lame animal as it was being dragged to the river for consumption. The pact banded together and returned to defend and rescue the weak one. The sheer magnitude of courage rattled the stalker and eventually the prey was released. I am here—we are here—to rescue each other. But if I had my pick, I would prefer to be the rescuer and not the one being rescued. How about you?

August 24: The Yo-Yo Principle

In my life, I have been the poster child for the "yo-yo" weight management program more times than the law allows. During years when life was perfect, it was easier to control my weight and make fairly decent choices. But when the dark clouds came, fighting for my health went out the window. The next year, however, another gimmick would surface and I would try again. It worked for a season and then my desire to eat as I pleased would gain momentum. Say, "yo-yo." But let us be honest, you loved them as a child, right?

I think the area that seems to be the funniest participant in my yo-yo journey was my closet. At one time I had four sizes of clothes so that no matter where I found myself on the yo-yo trail, I had adequate clothing. I developed terms of endearment for them—my skinny clothes, my happy clothes, my sad clothes, and my fat clothes. Do you think I am crazy? I wonder just how many of you have named your clothes?

My closet became my hidden shopping mall. I think I heard someone refer to this as, "shopping in my closet." While that makes me laugh, it really is horrible. The various sizes allowed me to move food boundaries season by season and event by event. No worries... yo-yo up and yo-yo down. The actual variety of sizes encouraged me to cheat, as there was always a pair of black pants available in various sizes to coordinate with any top.

I remember the day when I decided I was going to be healthy forever and burn the bridge to my past. I started bagging my clothes to be given away. I was elated and horrified all in the same sixty-minute period. Yo-yo principle here, too. My emotions were reeling and lots of fear flooded my heart. After all, over fifty years of "shopping in my closet" was about to come to an abrupt end. The yo-yo principle was concluding its stronghold and I was going to embrace a new me and never look back.

Two years later, my sizes are still the same and instead of shopping in my closet, I shop at nice department stores. No more "yo-yo" for me!

August 25: Fighting on This End

Yesterday I heard from a couple of people who are extremely tired of dieting, tired of always having to cook, and tired of fighting. After hearing some of these, I went to my office and I felt the Lord bring a word of hope to my spirit. Here is the truth: We can either fight for life on this end or we fight obesity-related illnesses on the other end. Let me explain.

While fighting to find time to cook or denying our flesh that cinnamon roll, we can grow tired and convince ourselves that the fight is "simply not worth it." Let me tell you this, I would much rather fight for new recipes, fight to get my water in, fight to stay on plan than fight cancer, diabetes, or heart disease later in life. Somebody shout, "Amen."

Getting our water in daily is a whole lot easier than losing a foot. Isn't it? Sometimes we all need a reality check. Life is a series of battles, but occasionally we get to "pick and choose" where our battles lay. I choose to fight on this end and not against disease. We need to really put that truth in the front of our thoughts.

God designed the vessel (our bodies) and He placed around us the tools needed to keep us healthy. We have a responsibility to our Maker to do the best we can to watch over the vessel. (I'm preaching again.) Let's give our bodies and cells a fighting chance. Stop confessing things like, "Well, you don't understand how busy I am." Listen, we are all busy, but I am never too busy to fight for my life. Can you tell I am passionate about this?

If you are tired of the fight, I want to encourage you to speak truth into the atmosphere of your life today. I want you to make declarations into the air so your spirit hears the truth and you are renewed in your passion to fight on this end. Repeat this verse (I have listed it from two different translations so you can recite from one or both):

> "I've found the recipe for being happy whether full or hungry, hands full or hands empty. Whatever I have, wherever I am, I can make it through anything in the One who makes me who I am" (Philippians 4:12-13 MSG).

Or:

> "I have strength for all things in Christ Who empowers me [I am ready for anything and equal to anything through Him Who infuses inner strength into me; I am self-sufficient in Christ's sufficiency]" (Philippians 4:13 AMP).

Same great passage, two different ways to fight. Use them both as weapons. God's Word is sharp and powerful. Let us learn to use it well.

August 26: Driving with the Top Down

Many of you know that I cannot stand to be confined. That is odd to me sometimes as I am a rule follower, but I need space, light, opened doors, and the sunroof peeled back when at all possible. I love sticking my hand through the roof and into in the air to feel the rushing breeze grab my fingers. I hate tight clothes and tight spaces. Just the thought of being confined causes me to twitch. I need options and lots of them.

However, in the area of eating, I have learned to eat the same thing and be perfectly content. In this area, too many options can cause me to not check the labels carefully or take a second bite when I know the first one contains sugar. I think it is a real blessing from God that He allows me to detect even the slightest hint of sugar as I have been free of that addiction for over two years now.

I never appreciated how the apostle Paul could write, "I know how to live on almost nothing or with everything. I have learned the secret of living in every situation, whether it is with a full stomach or empty, with plenty or little. For I can do everything through Christ, who gives me strength" (Philippians 4:12-13 NLT). I used to reason that I could never view my life through this lens, as did the apostle Paul. But I certainly can if I learn to use his secret—doing all things through the strength of Christ.

How many of you know that driving through life with the top down and your hands in the air, with no regard for the variables, can be dangerous? The steering wheel requires hands placed around the wheel and not in the air. Following this rule provides me the freedom to live, while breaking this rule can have severe consequences. Healthy living is much like this and requires strength from God to allow us to maneuver through all phases of life as a healthy, content person.

We can do it though, if we learn Paul's secret.

August 27: Grilled Vegetables

Yield: 6 servings

Ingredients

- Yellow squash
- Zucchini squash
- Vidalia onion halves
- Green and red pepper halves
- Greek salad dressing
- Grill Mates® Montreal Steak Seasoning

Procedure

1. Wash and prepare vegetables.
2. I use a mandolin, but you can use a sharp knife. The trick is to cut the pieces into thicker slices. If they are too thin, the heat of the grill will cause them to fall through.
3. I use Greek salad dressing as the marinade. Place the vegetables in a large baggie and pour the dressing over them. I use ½ bottle of dressing per gallon baggie of vegetables.
4. Place the baggie in the refrigerator and flip the bag every hour for 4-5 hours.
5. Place the vegetables on a medium heated grill and lightly sprinkle with steak seasoning.
6. Grill on both sides until the color reaches your preference. I flip mine a couple of times to cook thoroughly. Serve immediately while warm and crunchy. Occasionally, I will dust with Parmesan Reggiano before serving.

Per Serving:
Calories 116.7
Total Fat 7.7 g
Cholesterol 6.7 mg
Sodium 379.0 mg
Potassium 558.9 mg
Total Carbohydrate 12.7 g
Dietary Fiber 3.3 g
Sugars 4.8 g
Protein 2.4 g

August 28: Peanut Butter Dip for Apples and Peanut Butter Coconut Balls

Yield: 1 serving

Ingredients

- 1 cup natural, chunky peanut butter (no sugar added and you can use creamy peanut butter, but I prefer chunky)
- 2 squares baking chocolate melted in the microwave
- ½ cup xylitol (more if you prefer sweeter)
- 1 teaspoon cinnamon (optional)

Per Serving:

Calories 290.0
Total Fat 16.5 g
Cholesterol 0.0 mg
Sodium 145.0 mg
Potassium 0.0 mg
Total Carbohydrate 29.0 g
Dietary Fiber 3.0 g
Sugars 1.0 g
Protein 8.7 g

Procedure

1. Mix the oil into the peanut butter.
2. Melt the chocolate squares and stir well. When cooled slightly, add the xylitol and mix well.
3. Add the peanut butter.
4. Add the cinnamon if you like or try pumpkin pie spice. You can also delete the spices and use the dip as it is. The spices are nice in the fall, but the in summer by the pool, no spice required.

Variations:

1. Core an apple and stuff the dip into the core. This makes a great, healthy snack as well as a cool centerpiece for a table decoration. Use different colored, stuffed apples for your fall party.

2. Add 2-3 tablespoons of sugar-free coconut (I use the frozen brand) to the above recipe and roll into a ball. Keep cool as the peanut butter will run if too warm.

August 29: Frozen Cookies

Do you know anyone who does not love cookies? I do not. I am not certain that person exists. I do absolutely enjoy the taste of *several* varieties, unfortunately. Chocolate chip, peanut butter, and oatmeal raisin were always my favorites. Well, if I am being honest, you would not need to try too hard to force any cookie down my mouth. That was a real issue, yes it was.

I do not know if you have ever tried this trick, but I would buy boxes (plural) and plan to give them all away (because I was a great person) and then consume probably two boxes before the others made it to the teacher's lounge. There is nothing like trying to deceive myself. I knew exactly what the journey for those boxes was going to be and so did my various jean sizes.

But all was not lost; I developed a plan.

Plan #1: Freeze them. That worked until I hit an emotional meltdown and then I learned to consume them frozen. My teeth ached but I was comforted.

Plan#2: Ration them. I hid one box, ate one box on Wednesday going to church, took one box on Thursday to share at choir and ate half on the way home. Is that what rationing looks like?

Plan #3: Give the money for the cookies to my favorite charity and declare a fast from cookies for a great cause. Really? That never happened one time.

Maybe you feel this is an emotional disorder that requires sincere counseling, but it is honestly the truth. I can tell you I still love cookies, but I cannot purchase them nor are they allowed in my house. I know the boundaries and I know that one cookie, for me, will open a gate that I may never shut again. I have no clothes to support the yo-yo principle and no bridge upon which to journey backward to being unhealthy. Some things are triggers and this happens to be one of mine.

The wonderful part of this blog is that God has creatively shown me how to make cookies that are yummy to my taste and allowable on my journey. Several are listed in the recipes and I hope you love them as I do.

August 30: Being Dad's Nurse Just for Fun

I never got the fishing *anointing*. My whole family loves to fish, except me. Dad, Mom, and my two brothers are all great fisherman, but me—I am the fisher girl of the brims. As a child, I remember making the dough balls and laughing as the fish grabbed for the bread as if they did not realize there was a hook in the center. Did they not get the memo? Did they not see Uncle Joe being dragged off to the cooler?

As I was not a great fisherman, I suppose I never developed that love for the taste of fish. My family all loves fish, but I only like fried fish with tarter sauce. And you know, that is not the healthy choice. It was always a challenge on fish night when my family was destroying the plate of fish and I was wishing it were a steak. How many of you know simply wishing fish was steak does not make it so? In fact, if I had my way, everything would taste like steak, although I realize we need to seriously limit red meat.

The one thing I did enjoy about fishing was the game dad and I played with the fish. He was the surgeon and I was his nurse. He would inquire, "Nurse, what seems to be wrong with the patient today?" To which I would reply, "Doctor, it has a headache." His solution was to simply remove its head. The fish would be scaled then and prepared for dinner. If there was a large catch of fish, I had to be really creative with their "issues." But it never mattered what I said, their end was always the same. Funny how we remember those details from our childhood.

I am a picky fish-eater. If it tastes fishy, I have to pass. The problem though is that fish has such great health benefits we really should include it several times a week in our health plan. So many of my blogs encourage color and texture. But let me remind you, adding fish is a critical element as well. I have had to learn, as I did with smaller portions, that I do not always get my way. Choosing fish for me is really a discipline. But it is something I do simply because I know it benefits me. I am creative with the spices and herbs to flavor the taste, but it still has not fallen into the "natural" category.

It is okay, I am not there yet, but I am better than I used to be. Hopefully my disciplined life will keep me from the journey of the fish. You get it, right? And that is a great thing.

August 31: August Reflection Page

As you are completing the August devotions, are there things you wish you had highlighted or which you had written down? This month begins our real walk away from summer. School started, football games started, but did you start? What was your favorite recipe this month? Keep experimenting and building your healthy cookbook week by week.

_____

_____

_____

_____

_____

_____

_____

_____

_____

_____

_____

_____

_____

_____

_____

_____

_____

_____

_____

September

The official kick-off of fall happens this month. And we all know that the big holiday season is drawing close. Start planning now to be victorious.

September 1: Funny Foods

You know I totally believe that we need color and texture at each meal. We have established that, I hope. I am also stoked when friends bring new things I have not tried to our Healthy 4 You Life Group.

One of my sweet friends, Linda, is a great cook. That is actually an understatement. I can always count on Linda to bring the recipes that are unique and flavor-filled. So when I see she and Don approaching, the child in me leaps, as I know goodness has arrived. One night as I opened my door she smiled as she handed me a bowl filled with dried leaves. "Taste them," she enthusiastically suggested. I remarked with a funny look, "What...are they?" (Let me share a secret. While I was addicted to food I ate everything I *wanted*, however, there are some "healthy" foods that I have tried to keep from my radar—dried leaves being one of them. But when Linda smiles, the room stops. How will I get out of this?)

I shrugged, grabbed a dried-leaf chip, and man was I shocked. Kale that had been baked and salted was really yummy. One chip turned into several and for a minute I felt proud that I could tell someone I actually enjoyed kale chips. To my surprise, even my granddaughter Kailey loved them.

That evening opened the door to a new food for me. I now can make chips with kale, but I also use it in my veggie/fruit smoothie. Adding kale, spinach, and some carrots to a whole food smoothie is very filling and makes a great lunch option. It is low in calories and yet offers a real infusion of energy. I do not like to drink my calories, but in this case, the healthy benefits and fabulous taste make this exception a real treat.

Have you ever tried to disguise food for your kids? I made a smoothie the other night for my family that included two varieties of kale and everyone was raving about the taste. When I eventually informed them of the ingredients moaning and louder moaning erupted. When I produced the kale for inspection, they really freaked. But in the end, Nina wins. They loved the taste of the fruits and vegetables and we promised to never again have a "visual" of the kale.

September 2: Something New

Sometimes we feel that one day rolls into the next, one season into the next, and that time gets lost, don't we? Some feel their lives are a blur with no definitive borders. But this is simply not true. Every twenty-four hours marks a new day. The date changes; we either lose or gain one minute of sunlight (depending on the season); a new name christens the day. It is really different.

However, sometimes we are too busy or too stressed to pause and acknowledge the fresh start. Sometimes due to our oppression, we have no ability to see the newness of the day. Sometimes we try to carry yesterday's struggles and failures into the next segment of time. But today is new. What can you do today to let go of yesterday and embrace a new day?

Do you need to find a new recipe, buy a new shirt, find a new place to celebrate, create a new memory, taste a new food that will bring life to your body, embrace a new motto, do a new exercise video, make a new friend, have your family eat dinner in a new place? Man, just typing new so many times brought a smile to my face. It actually did. Let us thank God that He created each day with a new start and let us do just that—start new.

I feel some of you really need to stand up, shake off the heaviness, and drop all the yucky stuff from yesterday. Reach up, smile, and grab this new day. It is yours, my friends. It is mine. Thank you, God, for knowing I needed a new start today.

September 3: A Bad Tank of Gas

I am horrible at car stuff. I know I drive a black car but that is about it. My husband is the car pro and keeps our vehicles running in great condition. I know he has explained certain things to me about what makes the car run, and in my small mind I hear him, but I do not always connect with his lesson. Although I have learned a few things, like how bad gas causes the car to respond, I never have the correct diagnosis.

I do not know what makes gas bad, but I do know how my car acts when that yucky stuff finds its way into my tank. My car begins to display flu-like symptoms. It slows down, stutters, makes noises, and basically responds unlike my normal car.

While I may feel the car is dying and God is trying to send me a new vehicle, my husband is always the gas detective and knows when to encourage me to wait and let the bad gas run its course. Then, he will place a container of gas additive in with the next tank and voila—it's as if new life appears.

That is like the journey of our lives many times. We need the good stuff to do the *good stuff* God assigned to each of us. If you are placing non-healthy foods in your body, that is like placing bad gas into a car. Eventually, your vehicle will begin to show the signs. Then, you may require an extra additive to assist you with your daily routine. I know this well and it is called weight-induced medications. I had to allow sometimes ten minutes to take all of mine each morning and not choke. But without these "additives," my day was destined for trouble.

In the previous blog I mentioned a fruit and veggie smoothie that I make with three vegetables and five fruits. After I drink one cup of this, I normally get such great mileage out of this 'ole body. While I do not understand the boost that the smoothie brings, I do know it works. I can definitely feel the effects. Maybe this is my new "gas additive"?

The bad thing is I never know if I have gotten a bad tank of gas until the signs manifest. Let us chew on that truth for a couple of days.

September 4: Rubber Bands and Stretchy Pants

I remember how I hated Mondays because it followed a three-day eating binge. Monday was always a "fast day," which most assuredly made me feel horrible after tons of sugar from Friday through Sunday. What a horrible and unhealthy cycle! It was bad enough to buy larger clothes year after year, but the worst part was the way I felt physically. We may hide our emotions sometimes, but physical illness shows on our face often when we wish it would not. A weekend filled with thousands of heavy calories linked to Mondays where I tried to compensate by starving was never a great combo. By Monday afternoon, as I suffered with stomach cramps and often a headache from not eating, I would console myself and say, "Friday is coming." Vicious, right?

Part of the frustration was this internal battle between my soul and spirit. I felt as if the real Kathy was always being stretched beyond capacity. On top of this conflict, add the daily struggles of life and the issues of work. The rubber band would get to the edge of snapping then somehow the road would smooth out and the rubber band would return to normal. However, that period never lasted as long as I wished and eventually the rubber band was tested again to determine the exact capacity to which it *could* be stretched.

Have you ever felt as if everything in your life was being pulled back and forth and maybe one day the boundaries could never be restored? That is a wretched journey. Seemingly, at the farthest point of being stretched, life was done. But there it was—the next bigger size of rubber band. While that may seem a good thing, just start thinking about stretchy pants. Maybe you have never owned a pair. I have only lived the past two years without some.

Rubber bands and stretchy pants have a purpose, but each one has its breaking point. God never designed us to live on the edge emotionally, spiritually, or physically. He really never did. If something needs to get stretched, let it not be my stomach, my waistline, my emotions, or frustrations. Stretching my faith, my resolve, my confidence that I can live life as a healthy person is much better than the rubber band experience. My stretchy pants have gone the way of all flesh.

September 5: Are Your Doors and Windows Open?

This morning I want to share from Proverbs 25:28 "A person without self-control is like a house with its doors and windows knocked out" (MSG).

Sometimes self-control is easy and other times not. I do also realize that we must always go back to the basics of healthy eating and remind ourselves on a regular basis that even if we can have a particular food, it cannot be without limits. People always say, "Eat all the rabbit food you want." Right? Have you ever seen a skinny rabbit?

When I first baked a chocolate pound cake (no starch, no sugar) and it tasted so amazing, I ate four pieces at one time. I paid the penalty for that on the scales. And as the Proverb just described, I was a house without doors and windows indicating no boundaries. When the windows and doors are always open, everything (including the unwanted) is welcome.

Perhaps you might be saying, "One time is not going to hurt anything." But if we cannot see that as a breach, then tomorrow it could be four pieces again and the next day whatever. Here is the preferred line of thinking—stop, realize we can have a piece of cake again (when the scales come into submission), and decide ahead of time that one piece is good enough. Too much of a good thing can still be too much. I think my overeating sometimes was prompted by the misconception that there was going to be no more food forever. That is a lie. Slowing down to remind myself that food will be available tomorrow allows me to stay within the boundaries.

Today, if you are wrestling with the "formula" for regaining self-control and replacing the doors and windows in your house, I say simply go back to the basics. Ask the Holy Spirit to give you strength and courage to close the doors and windows of your house and secure your emotions, which are often scrambled by a simple breach. Satan always wants something simple to seem catastrophic. Let us secure the house, our hearts, and our health. God wants us to live in a secure place in Him, and often our lack of self-control in the area of eating causes a lack of self-control in our responses, reactions, and other areas, and our households pay the penalty.

Close those windows. Secure the boundaries.

September 6: Stewed Apples

Yield: 8 servings

I like to serve these warm with a tiny bit of half and half, or simply by themselves. Some have added sugar-free vanilla ice cream to make a delicious dessert.

Ingredients

- 8 medium-sized apples or 6 large (I prefer Honeycrisp apples, but have used others as well.)
- ½ stick light butter
- ¾ cup xylitol
- 2 tablespoons pumpkin pie spice
- ½ bottle black raspberry flavored water
- ½ teaspoon lemon extract (optional)

Procedure

1. Wash the apples. I use a spiral-coring device and crank the apples through the handle to peel and core. I leave the apples in spirals and place them in a large Dutch oven over medium high heat.
2. Add the remaining ingredients and bring to a boil. Reduce the temperature and continue to cook until most of the liquid is evaporated and the apples become a beautiful red color and are tender.
3. Continue to stew the apples, without stirring, as the liquid reduces. If you used a spiral coring device like I do, you don't want to break the apple rings as they serve beautifully in that shape. Lift the slices to ensure the butter and liquid has infused the apples, but be very careful not to mash them.

Per Serving:
Calories 186.5
Total Fat 3.5 g
Cholesterol 7.5 mg
Sodium 50.8 mg
Potassium 253.9 mg
Total Carbohydrate 45.4 g
Dietary Fiber 6.0 g
Sugars 21.4 g
Protein 0.4 g

September 7: Chocolate Cream Cheese Pound Cake

Yield: 16 servings

Ingredients

- *1 stick light butter
- *1 8-oz pkg. light cream cheese
- *1 ½ cups xylitol
- 3 squares unsweetened chocolate
- 5 eggs at room temperature
- 1 teaspoon baking powder
- 1 ½ teaspoons vanilla extract
- 2 ½ cups almond flour
  *at room temp

Procedure

1. Preheat oven to 350°F.
2. Cream together the butter, cream cheese, and xylitol.
3. Add eggs one at a time, beating well after each addition.
4. Melt squares in microwave and add to above mixture and blend well.
5. Add extract and blend.
6. Add dry ingredients and mix well.
7. Spray a 9 x 13 inch baking dish or Bundt pan.
8. Pour the batter into the pan and bake for 50-55 min. Use a toothpick placed in the center to determine if cake is done. Cool completely before cutting.

Per Serving:
Calories 239.0
Total Fat 18.9 g
Cholesterol 75.3 mg
Sodium 163.6 mg
Potassium 22.3 mg
Total Carbohydrate 18.4 g
Dietary Fiber 2.6 g
Sugars 1.2 g
Protein 7.4 g

September 8: The Simplicity of Being a Child

Sometimes the simplicity of being a child never leaves our heart. Do you long for those easy days? I certainly do. We were so clueless and never appreciated how simple life really was. Our responsibilities as children were—do not bite, share your toys, be good for mom, do not create a mess, and be potty trained early. Life was easy. How did we get so complicated?

Then with each passing year, life changed. It was supposed to, but sometimes I feel we make things a lot harder than they should be. Here is a simple plan—eat lean proteins, drink eight to twelve cups of water daily, eat fruits and vegetables that are varied in color and texture, sleep eight hours daily, and move your body. That seems simple and yet our busy lives often stand in direct opposition to that simplicity.

The older I get, the more deeply I value simplicity. As you work through my recipes, you will find I am a simple girl. I did not use herbs I cannot pronounce; I did not utilize fancy cooking techniques from culinary school, but I did use basic household items in my recipes. Why? I think if things are simple, people will try them and perhaps experience success. I find that if success is simple, people want to try it again.

As we go through the journey of our lives, it will flow into seasons of complications. We can count on it. When that happens, look for the simple answer, the simple recipes, the simple path, and do not easily settle. Sometimes we get sucked into the vortex of complicated because we refuse to make a stand for simple. I watch movies occasionally of simple times in small towns where families ate together, worked and played together and life seemed to be filled with authentic relationships.

We can have a simple life—we can. We have a simple plan and I vote we *simply* follow it with childlike obedience and joy.

Honest question: What do you need to simplify in your life so that you experience success today?

September 9: The ABC's of Having a Great Day

1. **A**lways try to find the good in every situation. Sometimes in a really bad place, this is hard to do. But if nothing else, smile and remind yourself God never allows us to be tempted beyond what we can endure. He also sets the boundaries and knows our final breaking point. God's strength enables us. In God I find my strength. In Him I move and breathe and have my being.

2. **B**e slow to speak and react. Consider your words carefully, because once they are in the airwaves, they never dissolve. Responding is a much better avenue than reacting. Responding indicates contemplative processes. Reacting, on the other hand, is usually our mouth conveying the wounds in our heart. Slow down. Allow your words to bring life and not death. We choose to get angry, so it stands to reason we can also choose to be sweet.

3. **C**are for others with the same passion you care for yourself. This initiates the sowing and reaping principle. We do not care for others in order to get anything, but in doing so our harvest is being established. Treating others as we want to be treated and becoming the servant of all takes willingness to not always be first, right, or in charge. It is okay to let someone else get the glory on this side. God claps His hands at the things we do in secret where no one, except Him, knows the truth.

Those are basic, simple statements, but how much easier life would be if we could pause long enough to utilize them. I pray that God uses you today to richly bless the lives of others and in return that your life, heart, and spirit will soar. Living a healthy life is more than simply ingesting the correct kind and portions of foods as well as drinking tons of water.

As children we learned our ABC's early. As adults, let us practice them daily.

September 10: Give 'Em What They Need

Someone mentioned this week how much more hungry this time of the year makes them feel. I am absolutely convinced that it is not the time of the year, but our minds taking us to memories of cooler temperatures and *sweaters*. I was always so happy when it got cooler so I could hide my undisciplined body. Hiding meant I could eat more and after all, "The holidays are here and I'll worry about my weight in January." Has anyone other than me ever felt like that?

The problem with that type of thinking is that our internal organs and cells have no calendar to remember it is the holidays and *they are now required to filter and digest three times more than normal.* They have the task of trying to metabolize, detox, filter, distribute, and store those extra calories they do not need and cannot process. No one ever asked their opinion.

Have you ever been given so much to do and you know there is no way you can handle all of the assignment? Your response sometimes could be "take the easy route—just quit." This attitude is exactly what happens within our bodies when pushed beyond their designated boundaries. Sometimes our organs simply quit functioning due to extreme overload. And disease is more than willing to become the taskmaster. I can tell you this is true more than we care to know.

Our organs and cells cannot think for themselves and are limited in what they absolutely can do. Let us not push them to the brink of quitting. I suggest we offer our bodies what they need and not necessarily what we want. They are depending on us.

September 11: Today We Remember

Today marks a special day in the journey of our nation. On September 11, 2001, a devastating and historical event occurred—the terrorist bombing of the twin towers in New York City. I would imagine that many of us can remember exactly where we were and the shock and horror we felt. I remember feeling hopeless and scared. I remember being numb as the realization of so much death shook me. And yet I remember the heroic acts, the touching final moments so many shared, and I remember how our country unified for a brief moment.

On the Wednesday and Sunday following the event, our church was packed. I imagine so was yours. However, as the event's memory faded, so did those who, out of fear, ran to the hope and comfort of the church. In their minds, they escaped death and catastrophe. I remember the sadness I felt that so many came and left really not knowing that God wanted to be a part of their lives in the good and the bad.

I want to stop and remind each of us today to remember even in our lowest day, our day of total failure (in our minds), our day(s) of never moving ahead and feeling that our health is a nagging chain that always tugs at our attention, that the one who created us, knows the number of hairs on our heads and the names of every star knows that we are constantly having to fight for our health. He knows.

He also knows that the enemy of our soul never rests and never quits. Satan's number one goal is to cause enough pain in our lives to create distrust and cause us to lose hope that God is who He says He is and will do what He says He will do. Let us stop today and still our minds, our hearts, our souls and say, "Yes, God knows, God cares, and with God's help I will finish my life in health and wholeness." Speak that out today and slaughter the voice of the one who brings you torment. God never changes in our seasons whether they are good or bad. Our souls wrestle for an answer and many times God simply says, "Trust me. I am the answer."

Today we remember.

September 12: Sing It!

I am a wee bit tired as I have been singing off and on through the night. I find when my spirit needs to be strengthened, I head into seasons of worshiping in my spirit while I sleep. Every time I rolled over from deep within me the words form a particular song were on repeat. Have you ever experienced this? It is a song of declaration that God was before the world began and He is unstoppable and unshakable.

Why bring up singing? I do want us to remember the power behind singing. Oftentimes in history, during very difficult circumstances, men and women could be heard lifting their voices in song. How many of you know that singing that powerful, or happy, or fun song just puts a "groove" in your move, a smile on your face, a joy in your heart? It does. Get your favorite song playing on the stereo and record your reaction. People move, snap, laugh, and wiggle their neck. Get a picture.

So many times when living in a healthy world, it seems as if denial is our portion. Continual denial can bring sadness and a feeling of isolation and dejection. But singing, even for a moment, can take our minds off what seems to be a daunting task and release a vibe of joy. It does for most people I know. Could I go one step further? Smile while you sing, or lift up your face toward heaven, or move your body and release those endorphins. Those little guys play a huge part in our mental status, and I need all the help I can get. I especially need the help when I am hungry. How about you?

Today, no matter what is in front of you, simply take a few minutes and sing. I cannot prove this, but perhaps singing throughout the day could help at the scale the following morning? I'm not sure, but we do know that stress releases cortisol, which stores fat around our belly and backside. That affects the scales. Right? Maybe singing, which lowers stress and reduces cortisol, can help in the other direction? I am not saying that is a fact, but I know singing is a great comfort to my soul and brings a warm smile to my face. Sing a lot, sing out loud, and sing for joy.

Singing releases those happy endorphins, which in turn keeps the cortisol down. Keep singing and let me know if you lose like a million pounds. We can start a revolution. I really believe that simple things can make such a profound difference and that God gave us simple things to keep us living at our best for as long as He intends.

Life is short, so sing!

September 13: Granola

Yield: 16 servings

Ingredients

- 2 cups rolled, old fashioned oats
- ½ cup pecans
- ½ cup raw almonds
- ½ cup raisins
- ½ cup dried cranberries
- ½ cup pumpkin seeds
- ¼ cup flax seeds
- 1 container blueberries
- 1 stick light butter
- 1 cup xylitol
- ½ cup water

Procedure

1. Preheat oven to 300°F.
2. Boil the water, butter, and xylitol for about 5 minutes.
3. Mix all of the above ingredients except the blueberries. They will go in last.
4. Cover a 9x13 baking dish with parchment paper and lightly spray. I usually only cover the bottom, but you can try the sides.
5. Spread the dry ingredients in the baking dish.
6. Pour the liquid over the dry, mixed ingredients and mix well.
7. Bake for a couple of hours, stirring about every 30 minutes. When your mixture is as crunchy as you like, add the blueberries and cook an additional 20 minutes. The granola will not be extremely crunchy, as the xylitol doesn't harden like regular sugar, but the taste will be amazing.

Per Serving:
Calories 209.6
Total Fat 10.3 g
Cholesterol 7.5 mg
Sodium 65.7 mg
Potassium 157.2 mg
Total Carbohydrate 30.7 g
Dietary Fiber 4.9 g
Sugars 9.5 g
Protein 4.1 g

September 14: Chicken Alfredo with Spaghetti Squash

Yield: 6 servings

Ingredients

- 1½ tablespoons olive oil (I prefer the light tasting)
- 2-3 cloves minced garlic
- 1½ cups heavy whipping cream (you can use regular cream, but the taste will vary)
- ¾ cup *fresh* grated Parmesan Reggiano cheese (taste is better)
- 4 tablespoons light butter
- 1 tablespoon fresh or dried parsley
- Salt to taste
- 4 chicken breasts boiled, cooled, and cut in chunks

Procedure

1. Heat the olive oil and sauté the garlic over medium heat.
2. Add the cream and Parmesan cheese and stir well. Watch carefully as this burns and sticks.
3. Add the butter and spices and blend well. Mixture should be nice and warm, but not boiling.
4. Add the chicken chunks about 10 minutes from serving, so they heat thoroughly without becoming tough.
5. Serve over warm spaghetti squash. Top with grated Parmesan.

Per Serving:
Calories 425.3
Total Fat 27.3 g
Cholesterol 158.1 mg
Sodium 397.3 mg
Potassium 343.4 mg
Total Carbohydrate 1.9 g
Dietary Fiber 0.1 g
Sugars 0.1 g
Protein 41.9 g

September 15: Oil Changes, Part 1

I do not know about you, but I have often said to the Lord, "I want to live to the age of one hundred if I am healthy." I sat beside a woman at the retina specialist office last week who was ninety-six years old and whose best friend was a hundred and four. It really blessed me. I can honestly say I never set living to one hundred years old as a goal when I was younger and I certainly never ate properly as an investment into this plan (better late than never, right?). I have contemplated on many occasions lately exactly what it takes to live to 104 years old and be healthy. As you know, I am a schemer and a planner. I think the Lord showed me something about this the other day.

My husband is a stickler for keeping the oil changed, tires rotated and balanced, and all the fluids clean and filled in my car. He is really obsessive about it. I see the correlation to my own health these days. His routine maintenance on my fifteen-year-old vehicle means she drives amazingly well. She is beginning to show some wear and tear and body dings, but she drives nicely. Why? It is certainly not because I am an amazing driver or have a magic formula. It is because my husband keeps the oil changed and never allows it to go beyond the suggested boundary. He is adamant about the oil thing. My husband continues to remind me, "One simple thing will ensure the life of this car." How simple, and yet how profound.

We have talked a lot recently about changing the "one" thing, living a simple life, and being diligent with the "one." If you are joining our family on this journey, first of all I want to say, "Congratulations!" Secondly, don't commit to change everything all at once. Decide to modify your eating first and then add the movement. Getting a win under your belt without the added pressure of accomplishing the whole package is a safe start. After a couple of weeks of choosing fabulous foods, set a hydration goal. Then start to move those muscles. Take one thing at a time. Here is an example, again, to prove that often it is not the complicated things that keep us going but the simple.

September 16: Oil Changes, Part 2

When I was first married and realized my husband had this obsessive issue with the oil in my car, I just shook my head. It was almost an *emergency* when the mileage marker indicated the time of change was near. I thought, *Nothing could be that serious to the life of a car.* I was wrong. Today my car still runs well, and it is a living declaration that Terry's diligence to adhere to the truth works.

For us, the simple truth is what we place in our mouth has everything to do with our long-term health. There are other factors such as rest, stress, hydration (we've covered most of them), but the day-to-day process of nutrition (food and drink) is what gives us the best chance at great health until we are one hundred years of age. However, this process must be maintained; it cannot be hit and miss. Terry has been faithfully doing the "oil thing" for twenty-six years and reminding me every time, "If you allow this to go beyond a certain point, all the internal parts to the engine will be affected and eventually the engine is gone." I have been told this so much I can recite that statement in my sleep. But, he stays right on top of it to ensure the life of my car.

My car may go a couple of months without his intense scrutiny, but inadvertently I will see him start the watchful eye again. He never forgets; he never tries a different route; he never misses the appointment; he never allows me to be the "responsibility person for oil changes." Why? So that our vehicle serves our family to the best of its ability for as long as it can. Do you see this as it relates to your health? I do.

While I may get frustrated that Terry is so particular about this, my car bears the beauty of it. Let us commit to stay on top of our health maintenance and do not put off for months, or years, those essential things that give us long life. How many of you would like to be my 104-year-old friend? I would like that.

September 17: Giving Hope

Did you ever have to do stuff as a kid that you detested? Mom tried to make me eat beets, asparagus, and floss my teeth. Sometimes I felt like she was the "nag squad." Today, I see things differently. She was amazing, but I never really appreciated her efforts until I became a mom. It is amazing how time has the ability to focus our sight on the realities of life.

When I am tired or frustrated, eating cucumbers just do not bring me comfort. I know it is supposed to bring me hope of a great future, but as it touches my lips, I am not feelin' the love. It is in those times I have to remember that being tested and tried purifies my resolve and strengthens something within me. I have to remember that while healthy eating was not part of my journey until a couple of years ago, *it is my life now.*

Someone came to me recently and said they know a woman in ministry whose husband is battling cancer. One of the first things the doctor instructed her to do for her husband was delete all sugar from his diet. I know I sound like a broken record, however I feel God is training each of us to offer hope when we hear statements like that. Being told to delete sugar, when sugar is your best friend, can send many into a spasm. But God has allowed us a head start so we can be that life-line of hope to others.

This devotional cookbook is filled with "sugar-type" recipes that offer hope to someone who is experiencing sugar withdrawals. And I prefer the term *sugar-type recipes* to *sugar-free.* People can live in a world void of sugar and starch, even if they feel they cannot. Our healthy family is proof of that.

I would like to think that my difficulty to break free of food addictions could actually benefit someone other than me. If I can help someone else with an encouraging word or a sugar-free pound cake and a smile, that lights up my day. Continue to pray for God's insight into your health and His direction as you are trendsetters in your office, home, and family.

September 18: My Personal Best

I have been studying Cain and Abel for one of my illustrations in Virginia at the end of the month and have carefully dissected portions of their story. I imagine that growing up they played four square and video games together. Maybe? As they were the first and only children, I am certain they spent a lot of time together. They each had their own talents and interests, as many of our children do. Not a problem. However, Cain's decision to not bring his best to God initiated a jealousy pocket and eventually led him to kill his brother and perhaps best friend. How could that happen?

Cain looked at his brother, who had done what pleased God, made a comparison, and opened the door to sin. Comparison is a curse. When questioned by God about Abel, Cain's response was, "Am I my brother's keeper?" Did he mean to respond to God in that manner? Not only had he embraced sin, he now wanted to deny, cover up, and be sarcastic. The effects of sin are ravaging and we must consider all the insight God places in His Word as weapons in our own journey.

For us, we must fight the urge to look at someone else who is having a *seemingly* better journey with their health and compare. We each have a daily choice as to what we eat and do. We need to do our personal best each day and celebrate as others do their personal best. We are not comparing, we are complimenting. These two different responses yield two different results. Comparing led to a violent death and circumstances Cain was not prepared to handle.

We can all admit that judging and comparing causes such inner turmoil. Being healthy is not about how we look though; we have discussed that often. It is about living life to the fullest and giving our daily personal best to our body, so it can give its personal best to us. The fastest way to break the comparison trap is to ask God to heal the inner hurts that are in our hearts and those wounds that are hidden often from childhood. These hurts can cause us to see life from a wrong perspective.

Make good choices today and celebrate a good day. Tomorrow, hit the repeat button. Keep your eyes on the finish line, which is a healthy body. That is the prize for which we reach.

September 19: Back to the Basics

I think one of the things I hate the most is being afraid. How about you? I went to the county fair this past Saturday with some family and precious friends and I remembered a time when I used to ride all the high, fast rides and loved the excitement of being scared to death cresting the first huge hill of the old, wooden roller coaster. Those days are definitely over. Whether out of maturity, or the "fear" of a chiropractic bill—it's over. I used to watch horror movies—that's over. Those fears are legitimate. But how about the fear that seems small and insignificant? It can be still bothersome. Right?

You know that creeping, nagging, unstable place that occasionally each of us deals with? That is where I understand and embrace Psalm 23 and Psalm 91. Those passages are my anchors. Sometimes on my health walk there are days where I will gain a few pounds and immediately there is a fear of returning to my past state of obesity. I have to grab that emotion and remind myself I have not cheated, I have not opened any doors, so let's slow down and see what the truth is. I no longer react out of emotion, but respond to my body.

I start going through the list, "Did I get my water in? Have I rested properly and allowed my cells to deliver nutrients and water to my organs? Have I been too generous with my portions?" Somewhere in those questions lies the truth. So, I answer and adjust. I correct the problem and usually within a few days the scales reflect the correction. It is critical in our journey to be able to operate not from fear or legalism but in truth. That is how we roll.

We were created in the image of God and given dominion over the earth and our bodies. We cannot blame our bodies when we willingly overstep the truth. All that blame shifting started in the garden of Eden and was based in fear and disobedience. And once fear is rolling, it often causes us to do stupid things—drastic things—like trying to live on water for a week or working out seventeen hours a day to eliminate those extra pounds.

Stop and go back to the basics. Humankind was created using basic things like dust and bones. Go back to the basics. I am very aware of every commercial offering the next quick fix. Unfortunately, there are none. I tired every one possible. Stop the fear and embrace the truth by returning to the basics. Evaluate your meals for today. Are they reflective of the proper tools your body needs to produce life minus your candy bar?

September 20: Strawberry Jam

Yield: 16 servings

I like to use this jam on top of a slice of my cheesecake recipe. Sometimes I serve it as a side to my cheesy, cheddar biscuits. You can eat a spoonful when needing a taste of something sweet and you're really deleting the chocolate bars. Also try it as a topping for the almond flour pancakes.

Ingredients

- 2 large containers fresh strawberries, washed and cut lengthwise in half.
- 1-2 cup(s) xylitol depending on how sweet you prefer your jam
- 1 cup water

Procedure

1. Mix all the ingredients and cook on medium heat until all the liquid is evaporated and the jam forms. Stir occasionally at the beginning, but as the liquid reduces stir more frequently to prevent burning, but give allowance for maximum reduction of the water. This stores well in the refrigerator for several weeks.
2. The container used for cooking needs to be fairly large as a foam forms on the top and can bubble out of the container.

Per Serving:
Calories 43.4
Total Fat 0.2 g
Cholesterol 0.0 mg
Sodium 0.4 mg
Potassium 74.1 mg
Total Carbohydrate 15.1 g
Dietary Fiber 1.0 g
Sugars 2.3 g
Protein 0.3 g

September 21: Squash Casserole

Yield: 16 servings

Ingredients

- 8-9 large, yellow squash
- 1-2 large Vidalia onions
- ½ stick light butter
- ¼ cup Duke's mayonnaise
- 1 large jar pimentos, drained well
- 3 large eggs
- 2 cups sharp cheddar cheese
- Salt to taste
- 1 box melba toast
- 5-6 dashes of TABASCO®

Procedure

1. Wash and slice the squash.
2. Chop the onion and add to the squash. Boil with the butter until the squash is tender. Drain the liquid and cool.
3. Preheat oven to 350°F.
4. When the squash is cooled, add the mayo, pimentos, eggs, half the crumbled melba toast, 1 cup of cheddar cheese, TABASCO® and salt to taste. Reserve the other cup of cheese and melba toast for the top of the casserole.
5. Spray a 9x13 baking dish and spread the squash mixture evenly.
6. Distribute the remaining cheese and melba toast evenly over the top.
7. Bake for approximately 35 minutes or until the cheese is melted and browning and the sides are bubbly.

Per Serving:
Calories 159.3
Total Fat 11.3 g
Cholesterol 58.3 mg
Sodium 199.7 mg
Potassium 421.8 mg
Total Carbohydrate 8.9 g
Dietary Fiber 2.4 g
Sugars 0.4 g
Protein 7.7 g

September 22: Rolling through the Stop Signs

I asked the Lord what He would like to say to each of us this morning. I heard Him say, "rolling through the stop sign." Wow, okay Lord, what about that? Many times (and I would imagine many of us do this), we approach a stop sign and perhaps slow down but never fully stop. Or perhaps we stop only if a police officer is adjacent? Even if we stop, sometimes it's more like a pause. That is called rolling through a stop sign, as I am certain you are well aware.

In our health journey I would imagine we do the same. Perhaps some of us come to the "stop sign" and roll right through it. Stop signs are designed with an emphatic purpose. Often, we do not care about their purpose; we care about our agenda. I want us to consider several reasons to stop today—really stop—along our journey to health:

1. Have you stopped long enough to have a physical lately? These stop signs are critical. Have your blood checked every six months, as it reveals the inner truth.

2. Have you stopped long enough to have your eyes examined recently? The blood vessels in your eyes give clear indication of certain maladies that are directly related to our health.

3. Have you taken a day simply for yourself with no agenda and no plans? Our minds need pockets of intense rest. Put your project down and allow your body to breathe.

4. Have you stopped long enough to send a card to someone special, a meal to someone in need, or given your family your undivided attention? These random acts of kindness bring a smile.

5. Have you stopped long enough to prepare the meals you need for your health, or are you simply grabbing the burger from the dollar menu with your kids and rolling through life?

6. Have you stopped long enough to lift your head toward heaven and thank God for His love, faithfulness, and plan of salvation?

I could journey awhile here, but maybe you get my point? Our health journey is more than apples and twelve cups of water. Rolling through the stop signs will eventually bring consequences that could be unpleasant. Stop today—really stop. Let's not "roll through" this day and miss the majesty of God and all the wonderful things in place to keep us safe during our journey toward our one-hundredth birthday.

September 23: Striving to Be Perfect

I was watching a movie yesterday about a woman who created another person, graphically designed her own picture on the woman's body, and started writing an advice column under a pseudonym. Immediately, as she was a great writer, the column exploded. She lied and created this false person, as her editor never allowed her an opportunity to advance as a writer because of her weight and appearance. It was horrible, but often this scenario is a reality.

I remember being ridiculed as a child because I was heavy. It was not pleasant. The first part of the movie was difficult to watch as it brought me to a painful time in my past. The good news is that I am finally moving beyond that challenging period in my life. And as with my life, this movie had a happy ending as the main character started a healthy eating and exercising plan, found her way into her normal weight range, fell in love, and finally exposed the truth.

What prompted the lying, deception, and loss of identity? The struggle we often battle—to be perfect. What are some of the truths that each of us could use to confront the lies we face repeatedly? First, we were not created perfect, nor will we ever be until we reach heaven. Next, God chose us and loves us in our imperfect state. Finally, we must confidently rest in the person God creates us to be, make the changes necessary to be the best healthy person we can be, and stop striving. Striving makes me tired, how about you?

Let's keep asking the Holy Spirit to show us the foundation of our striving to be perfect. Then, let's forgive others and ourselves for rejecting *us,* especially in relation to our appearance. God has never rejected us ever. He chose us, adopted us, paid a high wage for us, sings over us, and He never leaves us alone. He never intended for us to strive for his affection or approval.

Today, receive the truth from God's Word, reject the lies from your wounded heart, and never feel you have to lie to be perfect.

September 24: Pickin' and Lickin'

Here is a word of caution today, *keep watching the small things you consume unknowingly out of boredom.* They all add up. Remember the Bible says, "the little foxes spoil the vine" (Song of Solomon 2:15). For us that could mean a bite of this, a spoon of this, or a pinch of these counts as nothing. Right? Wrong.

How many times have you snacked an entire day only to declare you have not had one meal? In the south, they call it "pickin' and lickin'." I wish I had a dollar for every time I made that statement. Calories add up no matter how small. I was taught to always taste what I was cooking and adjust. The bad part of being instructed in that manner was I was never satisfied with one taste. In fact, I could eat almost an entire meal just "tasting" to determine if what I was serving *was appropriate for my guests.* Was I trying to be funny or what? Now, because I cook only lean proteins, vegetables, and fruits with no sauces, the pre-meal tasting has almost stopped. I just felt that nudge of the Holy Spirit to remind us all to watch out for the "little foxes" today. Here is my prayer for you:

> *Father, in Jesus name, I declare that our family will walk in strength and health. We will choose to eat only those things that bring life to our bodies and we will reject those that bring death. I ask for Your help, Holy Spirit, for each of us that days of wandering off and on will cease and we will be filled with power from on high to choose and enjoy healthy foods every day. We are free and healthy to live for You and are not depressed, rejected, or walking in condemnation where our focus is on our failure.*

> *I ask You, Father, to touch those in critical need today and bring divine wisdom. Your Word says if we ask for wisdom, You give it liberally. I ask for our family and our biological families as well that health will rest over us. Let joy be our portion while our stomachs, and the lust of our eyes, be restored to perfect health. Lord, we honor You with our confession of love and in humility we come and say, "Thanks for helping us walk in freedom. We cannot do this alone. We need the restraining hand of the Holy Spirit, and we appreciate that You have freely supplied that."*

I am proud to journey with you and I want to personally thank you for caring enough to make a difference right where you are.

September 25: Our Truth Clothes

I am reminded this morning that as the cooler temperatures are coming we often start adding layers of clothes and usually layers of fat. That is not going to be the case for us this year, right? Usually, we wear layers of clothes for warmth, but in my case it was to hide the fact that the lust of my eyes caused me to stuff my face, be depressed, say ugly things about myself, hide again, and start all over.

When we think of Adam and Eve in the garden, some think the clothes God made for them simply hid their nakedness. I do not agree. The clothes were the outward reminder of their freedom. God sacrificed an animal to cover their sins and in that they were free from the eternal consequence of their sin. Our team verse (Galatians 5:1) addresses this so beautifully; "It is for freedom that Christ came to set me free."

When we bring Christ into our daily food choices and ask the Holy Spirit to give us wisdom, courage, and strength, we no longer hide food, sneak and eat, access the drive-thru before going home. We no longer have that need to hide. We confidently walk in open freedom in God's declaration together as a family.

Our confessions and encouragements give me (us) wisdom and strength coupled with the Holy Spirit's voice and nudge. What a great package. Keep layering the truth of God's Word on your body and not those clothes. Say out loud, "I am more than a conqueror. I can do all things through Christ. It is for freedom that Christ came to set me free." Put these "clothes" on and let us not walk in fear and cower down.

We are free to be all that God has purposed us to be. Do not confess, "Well, the winter is coming and I always put on weight." No, we now put on truth. Our *truth clothes* do not have anything to hide. Our lives proclaim victory!

September 26: Jesus Is in the Boat

I know that I could not have made this victory trip with all its storms without Jesus. I know it beyond a shadow of any doubt. I see myself as one of His disciples, and sometimes I find myself living inside their stories that God shares with us from His Word. I have been reading in Matthew chapter 8 about the disciples as they were on the boat with Jesus and often wondered what that must have been like. When I reach heaven someday, I will understand.

The disciples were in a storm, in a small boat. No stabilizers—just Jesus. We have to fully embrace that Jesus is in our boat, not intimidated by our issues, and that He will not jump ship and abandon us at the first sign of trouble. He told the disciples very assuredly they were going across the lake. Their response indicates their doubt in His instruction and quite frankly shocks me a bit. Why did they doubt? Because the storm came. In their minds, the storm trumped Jesus' words. Really? *But this is Jesus.* I was giving the disciples a tongue lashing when I came to another truthful realization.

Am I not every bit as guilty? I know Jesus as my Lord and Savior and still sometimes in the storm I doubt. My doubt does not change who Jesus is or His intentions. I want you to remember when you get discouraged about your weight or health, Jesus will get us to the other side. I cannot get myself over, but He is in my boat.

I still fight for freedom daily, which is mostly a fight in my mind. I have to be honest; I stood yesterday and thought, *Okay, these past several years have been great, but when will it be over? When will the past grab me again?* For about three seconds I reverted and then the Spirit of the Lord thumped me. Quickly I confessed, "No way. I am not going back. This is the real me, the healthy me, and I choose life. Why does the past ever have to clothe me again?"

Jesus is in the boat. My encouragement to you this morning is this: Do not look at the storm, look at Him.

September 27: Gourmet Low-Carb Burger

Yield: 8 servings

Ingredients

- 2 pounds lean ground beef
- Grill Mates® Montreal Steak seasoning
- 8 thick slices sharp cheddar cheese
- 8 eggs
- 16 pieces sugar-free bacon
- Romaine lettuce

Procedure

1. Patty your hamburgers and grill with steak seasoning to your desired interior color.
2. Place your bacon on a cookie sheet and bake it in the oven until crispy. (I usually bake on 350°F until crispy.)
3. As the hamburgers are coming off the grill and the bacon is crispy, fry your eggs and leave them firm but runny.
4. Prepare your gourmet burger:
    - Take the burger from the grill and place on a Romaine lettuce leaf.
    - Top with the cheddar cheese slice.
    - Add three strips of crispy bacon.
    - Top with your fried egg.
    - Sprinkle with sea salt and fresh ground pepper.
    - May serve with cheesy, cheddar biscuits (recipe in this book) or slices of avocado.

Per Serving:

Calories 457.2
Total Fat 32.3 g
Cholesterol 303.2 mg
Sodium 785.5 mg
Potassium 450.3 mg
Total Carbohydrate 2.4 g
Dietary Fiber 0.3 g
Sugars 1.1 g
Protein 35.5 g

September 28: Chunky Guacamole

Yield: 12 servings

For a great low carb "chip" to go along with this, I use baked pork skins. They contain no carbs and are usually low fat.

Ingredients

- 5 ripe, firm avocados (dark in color, but indents slightly when you press with your finger)
- 2 soft limes or the juice of one small naval orange
- Duke's mayo (optional, but sometimes I use a tablespoon)
- 2 jalapeños
- Seasonings to taste (listed in the procedure section)
- ¼ cup of finely chopped red onions
- 2 Roma tomatoes (optional)

Procedure

1. Cut the avocados in half length-wise and remove the seed.
2. Score the fruit with a sharp knife into small squares. Invert and dump into a large mixing bowl.
3. Add the juice of the limes or orange. If you are not a lime fan, add the juice of one only to keep the avocado from turning black.
4. Add the jalapeños that you have halved, seeded (or leave a few if you like things spicy), and chopped finely. Then, the onions.
5. Add the following seasonings: salt, pepper, garlic salt, onion salt, chili pepper, jalapeño powder, and cumin. I use about a ½ teaspoon of each and 2 teaspoons of cumin. Sometimes I will use 2 teaspoons of chili powder as well. If the chili powder is too spicy for you, opt for paprika.
6. Stir the above well until seasonings are blended.
7. Add the mayo if you desire.
8. Very important: when you are pleased with the spice taste of the guacamole, add the diced tomatoes and fold. You do not want to add the tomatoes and keep blending the mixture and playing with the spices as the tomatoes are easily crushed and add additional liquid to the guacamole.

Per Serving:

Calories 150.4
Total Fat 12.5 g
Cholesterol 2.5 mg
Sodium 21.5 mg
Potassium 388.7 mg
Total Carbohydrate 11.3 g
Dietary Fiber 3.0 g
Sugars 1.3 g
Protein 3.0 g

September 29: A Picnic

I love big social gatherings like weddings, ball games, and church picnics. As a child, when I knew there was a church share-a-dish or picnic, I knew we were "gonna be chowin." The mothers of the church, you know the ladies who run all the dinners, spent hours preparing the most decadent of all dishes. Occasionally someone would be on a diet, *but not during the church picnic.* It was almost as if it were a sin. I did not realize until much later that the only sin manifesting at the picnic was gluttony. But when you're ten years old, who cares?

Have you ever noticed all the various foods that can be placed on one paper plate at a picnic? I never really paid any attention to that until recently. I can guarantee you that I probably won the prize for the largest configuration of food and desserts ever on one plate. I never understood those people who placed a ½ teaspoon on their plates and pushed it around. Why get a plate and why waste time? Eating is serious business to me.

Recently, while preparing to attend a picnic, I realized I could not take the chance that food items which served my plan would be readily available. I made a plan prior to the picnic and ate ahead of the gathering so when the crowds arrived, I was fueled and ready to party. This plan saved me a lot of calories and afforded the opportunity to socialize in exchange for the eating. That is a win-win combination in my mind. What was interesting though was how many people asked why I was not eating. At first it was hard to respond. Awkward. But finally I simply said, "Too many choices and not too many of them healthy." I grabbed an apple from my purse and the questions calmed down. Ah, another trick.

Here is your recipe focus for this morning: As we enter the fall apple season, let us be creative with our recipes. I was thinking that almond flour pancakes with stewed apples would be yummy. We could add some maple syrup (recipe included) and this combo might just be a winner. But remember that sugar-free does not mean calorie free. You cannot consume as much as you want and still not throw your scales down the toilet in the morning. We are breaking free of obesity and the lust of our eyes. You *can* say no as often as you need to. I give you permission.

September 30: September Reflection Page

As you are completing the September devotions, are there things you wish you had highlighted or which you had written down? Do the cooler temperatures cause you to wander to the county fairs and mountain excursions? Remember, cook ahead and be prepared for sugared items everywhere at the county fair.

_____

_____

_____

_____

_____

_____

_____

_____

_____

_____

_____

_____

_____

_____

_____

_____

_____

_____

_____

_____

_____

October

This is going to be our real planning month for the "holiday" over-eating extravaganza. Already the Halloween candy is on the shelves and you need a plan now so your children have alternatives. Almond flour brownies sound good. Yes?

302 | Apples, Brownies, or Both? A Devotional Cookbook

October 1: The Great Physician

I had a very interesting talk yesterday with a friend who recently discovered their adrenal glands were compromised. Their symptoms were extreme tiredness, decreased mental acuity, weight gain, bouts of insomnia, and even occasional mild depression. Multitudes of tests were administered and still no clear diagnosis. Finally a blood test pointed the doctor in the right direction. He suggested poor nutrition could play a critical role in causing the adrenal glands to function improperly. Maybe you are experiencing some of these symptoms and perhaps you need to have your family doctor test your blood? I have listed a few of the doctor's suggested treatments as a means of reminding us we are on the right track.

Remedy #1: eight+ hours of sleep. My friend was encouraged to be in bed by 10:00pm as a manner of training the body that it is "sleep time." This routine should be followed regardless of whether we go to sleep. The doctor then suggested that kids need over ten hours of sleep and we are doing our children a medical injustice when we allow them to stay up and not fulfill this commitment to health. Neglecting this directive, long-term, can be detrimental.

Remedy #2: a healthy eating plan. This plan included no starch and no sugar. The doctor informed my friend that sugar is so destructive in our bodies it may be one of the leading causes in adrenal failure. He went on to say that most diseases can be avoided, and some cured, by simple nutrition. The doctor suggested that as a whole we should consume 70 percent vegetables and 30 percent protein when first needing to heal our adrenals.

Remedy #3: detox. The doctor recommended an Epsom salt bath twice a day. I do this almost daily and it is fabulous. If you take one cup of Epsom salt and add this to a hot tub of water, soak for fifteen minutes, and examine the color of the water, you may be surprised. I was. Pulling toxins from our bodies is actually beneficial and should be included in our regular routine.

These were just a few of the suggestions, but after a couple of weeks my friend's body began to respond. It does not take long for our bodies to react to the proper adjustments. After just two weeks of choosing health, I was off medications for reflux and arthritis.

God is the greatest physician and I never mind talking with Him about my health issues as He knows my body better than I do.

October 2: Internal Trumps External

One of my greatest joys is hearing from so many people on a weekly basis and realizing that they are doing so well living in their new bodies. It just brings me smiles every time I look up. My life's message is hope, and for many of us being freed from our *sick and trapped* bodies makes such a bold statement about hope to many others. I applaud each of you for living your life in such a way as to bring others the courage to fight for their right to live.

I heard a message again recently about the curse of comparison. Jealousy is a wicked emotion right out of Lucifer's heart and DNA. His jealousy of God caused him to sin and be kicked out of God's presence, along with his band of jealous followers. The curse of comparison began right there, and Satan perfects that jealousy scheme daily. We have to genuinely fight against these feelings sometimes. Can we be honest? The truth is we are going to all lose weight differently and look differently in our clothes. But those are merely external factors. The real measure of health comes when our blood tests report that our blood sugar, cholesterol, and triglyceride levels are all normal to perfect. These indicators are internal, and that is exactly where the *real* truth abides. The external is driven by what the media portrays as perfect and often what we have been taught since childhood. And for a lot of us, these external signs are the measure of winning. That is dangerous on many levels.

The Bible says in Philippians 4:8, "And now, dear brothers and sisters, one final thing. Fix your thoughts on what is true, and honorable, and right, and pure, and lovely, and admirable. Think about things that are excellent and worthy of praise" (NLT). Let's look at each other and celebrate victory. Let's ask for help when we are struggling. Let's keep offering food ideas, stand and fight when one of us is weak, and intercede when one of us wants to throw in the towel. Tossing that towel into the circle of defeat may relieve the pressure of feeling that everyone is doing better than you, but it does not relieve the pressure of sickness from our body. Freedom, for us, is not just about gaining control over our body weight. It is also freedom from comparing, which often leads to a sincere desire to quit.

Examine your overall weekly picture from the scale, not the daily snapshot. Refrain from cheating and making excuses for it. If you are hungry, then eat, but fill your body with whole foods that enrich your cells. A candy bar or another fast food burger is not going to do that. Remember, the external us vividly reflects the internal us.

October 3: My Big Pajamas

The book of Jude closes with a doxology that I love:

> "Now to Him who is able to keep you from stumbling, and to present you faultless before the presence of His glory with exceeding joy, to God our Savior, who alone is wise, be glory and majesty, dominion and power, both now and forever. Amen" (Jude 1:24-25 NKJV).

That is a concrete declaration that God is able to keep us from falling, and He is! God is able, but humankind was given a free will. Just because I stand on the truth that God is able to keep me from stumbling does not mean God is going to shut my mouth and keep that next brownie from being swallowed. I used to get upset with God and others when everyone but me seemed to have breakthroughs and deliverance in gaining their health.

On this side of victory, I have a different perspective about God's part of the journey. Knowing that God could absolutely keep me from falling became another excuse for me. I would reason, "If my health really mattered to God, He would help me. God does not really care if I am fat, so why do I care?" God's love for me has nothing to do with my weight. Right? God does want the best for each of us, however, and being obese is not His best.

When I was obese, I was too tired, sluggish, depressed, and self-loathing to really be effective. I was glad to get home, get in my slouchy clothes, eat to comfort myself, and find the next excuse to eat another piece of cake. I had no energy for God, my family, or myself. I was grateful for the evening so I could hide in my big pajamas.

John 10:10 declares Satan's purpose for each of us:

> "The thief does not come except to steal, and to kill, and to destroy. I have come that they may have life, and that they may have it more abundantly" (NKJV).

I believe the enemy will use food as a weapon if we are not careful. While I accept the first half of the verse, it is the second half, the part "b," that truly brings me life. My new level of health has given me stamina, joy, passion, and a renewed sense of purpose. I can stand on that. I like standing on firm things. And in my opinion there is nothing more stable than the Word of God.

October 4: Giants in My Land

Last night I was talking with someone about the mammoth availability and abundance of food. While we are eating healthy, we still must monitor our foods closely. Just because we got delivered from food addictions does not necessarily guarantee we are delivered from overeating. I have watched so many people make great choices to eat fruit instead of cookies and then consume three peaches at one sitting! While peaches are better, they are still high on the glycemic index (I'll save that truth for another day).

I was thinking about this scenario and began to see the connection to the children of Israel. They came out of bondage—out of slavery—out of chains, and weeks later were complaining. God help us! Leaving Egypt and going into the Promised Land, for them, represented relocating from their house of bondage (Egypt) to their house of abundance (spiritually speaking). For us, this a picture of leaving our cell of obesity and walking down the health road to our freedom. But, as in the biblical story, the new land contained giants. God never promised to destroy the giants. He left some of the work for us to do. But He did promise to give us the land.

For us, those giants can be tiny excuses to cheat that lead to paths we never need to travel again, false expectations, overeating a little here and there and not weighing (remember you can gain ten pounds before your clothes show it), getting tired of doing what is right, and reverting to fast foods. These are just a few of the giants that await each of us. I wish that was a maybe, but it is a definite reality.

Each of us may have differing daily struggles, but if we are honest, we would each have to admit we occasionally still wrestle with some form of giant in our healthy land. When I get tired of drawing my sword again, I go back to my altar of remembrance and remind myself of the countless times God has fought for me in my weakness.

Giants, I serve you notice this day that God is my shield and my strength. I will stand and see His deliverance in my land. Can you declare this with me today?

October 5: Foods Plus Everything

It is hysterical to me that one of the first words we learn to say as little bitty people is *no*. For those who are parents, you know we are the recipients of that term, matched with numerous expressions on various occasions. I am always amazed at parents, though, who laugh when their infant makes a face and screams, *no*! Laughing is not my suggested response in this situation, although I cannot say I have not done it. The more rebellious the yell, the more we laugh. Not good.

Where does the *no* word go as we begin to progress and discover the taste of food? As infants, eating carrots from the baby food jar is usually met with a frown and a negative response. As an adult, eating carrots often does not elicit the same response. What happened? The answer is easy—butter, sugar, salt, ranch dressing, brown sugar, to name a few. In the baby food jar, we find carrots plus nothing. Have any of you ever tried food from those jars? I have, and on more than one occasion "no way" was my response. However, raw foods plus nothing kept us growing as infants. But how ironic that foods plus everything keep us growing as adults? And often growing in ways we wish it did not.

God created a simple plan for us that really does not require all the extras. Let us consider the three Hebrew boys in Daniel 1:8-15:

> "But Daniel was determined not to defile himself by eating the food and wine given to them by the king. He asked the chief of staff for permission not to eat these unacceptable foods. Now God had given the chief of staff both respect and affection for Daniel. But he responded, 'I am afraid of my lord the king, who has ordered that you eat this food and wine. If you become pale and thin compared to the other youths your age, I am afraid the king will have me beheaded.' Daniel spoke with the attendant who had been appointed by the chief of staff to look after Daniel, Hananiah, Mishael, and Azariah. 'Please test us for ten days on a diet of vegetables and water,' Daniel said. 'At the end of the ten days, see how we look compared to the other young men who are eating the king's food. Then make your decision in light of what you see.' The attendant agreed to Daniel's suggestion and tested them for ten days. At the end of the ten days, Daniel and his three friends looked healthier and better nourished than the young men who had been eating the food assigned by the king" (NLT).

Daniel was certainly no infant, but a man who knew how to infuse his body with health and vitality by simply saying no. I am not saying that a lifestyle of eating only vegetables and water is perfect of all of us. But Daniel's courage to say no is an en*courage*ment to me this morning. How about you?

October 6: Healthy 4 You Turnip Greens

Yield: 12 servings

Ingredients

- 2 bags pre-washed turnip greens
- Water to cover the greens
- Salt to taste
- Grill Mates® Montreal Steak Seasoning
- Olive oil (optional)
- 1 ham hock (optional, but great flavor)

Per Serving:
Calories 37.5
Total Fat 2.4 g
Cholesterol 0.0 mg
Sodium 192.0 mg
Potassium 162.8 mg
Total Carbohydrate 3.9 g
Dietary Fiber 1.8 g
Sugars 0.4 g
Protein 0.8 g

Procedure

1. Place all ingredients in a large double boiler on the stove. The greens are really bulky out of the package, but they will reduce in size as they cook.
2. Cook on medium high for 60-90 minutes or until the greens are tender. They take a while to tenderize.

October 7: Cranberry Relish

Yield: 16 servings

Ingredients

- 2 bags whole cranberries
- 2 large Honeycrisp apples (or you can use Granny Smith if you prefer a tart taste)
- 1 to 2 teaspoons lemon extract (optional, but yummy. You can use a couple of tablespoons of fresh lemon juice if you prefer.)
- 1 large can sugar-free mandarin oranges
- 1 cup English walnuts or pecans, chopped
- 1+ cup xylitol (if you like it sweeter, give an extra sprinkle of sweetener)
- ½ teaspoon sea salt
- 1 large naval orange, for zesting

Procedure

1. Wash the cranberries and chop well in the food processor.
2. Wash, core, and chop the apples finely. Can use the food processor as well, but I prefer another kitchen utensil to chop. I like the small chunks for texture.
3. Zest the skin of one orange and retain.
4. Add mandarin oranges to the cranberries.
5. Add the remaining ingredients and blend well. Now, sprinkle the orange zest and give one more stir. Be careful to *not* crush the mandarin oranges.
6. Place in the refrigerator for 6-8 hours, or overnight, before serving.

Per Serving:
Calories 172.5
Total Fat 10.1 g
Cholesterol 0.0 mg
Sodium 2.4 mg
Potassium 141.7 mg
Total Carbohydrate 25.5 g
Dietary Fiber 3.7 g
Sugars 6.9 g
Protein 2.5 g

Variation: Cranberry Sauce

Ingredients

- 2 bags cranberries
- 2 cups water
- 1 cup xylitol
- 1 capful lemon extract

Procedure

Mix all ingredients together and boil on medium high until the liquid is completely reduced. This takes about 45 minutes. The mixture will thicken, but will not congeal as store bought. The berries do pop while cooking, so do not be alarmed by the sound.

October 8: I Look at Food Differently

I know this month features candy on every end cap and aisle close to the cashier and when I pass them, I usually wink and comment, "You're not the boss of me." And, as I usually say it out loud in a sarcastic tone, I wonder just what the other patrons are thinking. *Bratty girl*, I bet that is what they are really thinking. Oh well, I know how sugar metabolizes and stores on my body and talking to the candy aisle helps me. Yes it does.

I heard a commercial recently and thought, *Have they been reading my devotionals*? The woman on the television said, "Hi, my name is Michelle, and I look at food differently." Amen! I immediately copied that and proclaimed, "Hi, my name is Kathy, and I look at food differently." Refueling is a simple concept, although probably not very appealing. But it works and that is good enough for me. Refueling, as we have discussed, is the process by which we really look at food and eating differently. We have come to understand that food no longer is our passion, but serves our purpose, which is to tank our bodies and allow them to perform at optimal condition for the remainder of our lives.

Embracing the concept of refueling confronts our availability to view food as an idol. Once we reach this point, most of us are okay with eating the same thing at every meal for days if the options are not plentiful. In my old self, I would pout and whine if my meals did not offer me what I felt they should. Today, I see things differently. Meals refuel my cells, not my desires. That is a big difference. I am not saying that food should not be fun, creative, and packed with taste. But it can't be the thing we run to in every crisis. Our meals cannot be the thing we dwell on during the day. We eat, but we eat for the correct reason, that is the simple principle of refueling.

Hi, my name is Kathy, and I look at food differently. Start now and make that statement personal for you.

October 9: Theater Popcorn and Butter Are from the Devil

I know many of you have never met me, or if you have you probably do not know me well, but I love going to the movies. Watching a film for two hours allows my brain to rest and that is great. However, one of the other great loves of my life is theater popcorn. When my husband would ask, "Wanna see a movie?" I heard, "Would you like some popcorn and extra butter?" Yes. As we would draw close to the theatre I would always ask, "So, would you like a popcorn, too?" And my husband, who for most of our lives has eaten like a bird (hard on a girl who knows how to chow), would always respond, "Sure, I will have some of yours."

Now for those who share easily, perhaps this poses no problem for you. And while I share most everything with no issues, I am horribly bratty when it comes to certain foods. Did I really say that? But I have to be honest, *when he asked if we could share the popcorn, my face always contorted.* My comment was, "You have two options. One, get your own. Two, refill the huge, large one that I plan to purchase that cost a million dollars. You pick." Normally he chose to get the enormous one, which really served my greater purpose. Get it? My love affair with butter-laden popcorn ended a couple of years ago, but a girl can reminisce. Right?

I went to see a movie yesterday and it was fabulous. However, the smell of popcorn and butter filled the air and that was not fabulous. It was a huge fight for me. I had just eaten a really healthy lunch and had some hot tea, but it was still a battle. The Scripture comes to mind from 1 Corinthians 6:12, "You say, 'I am allowed to do anything'—but not everything is good for you. And even though 'I am allowed to do anything,' I must not become a slave to anything" (NLT).

Popped corn in itself is not a huge, bad thing for us, but I cannot eat it plain. I love the butter in abundance. So since I cannot eat a little butter on my popcorn, I choose to pass on the popcorn altogether. Keeping that door shut is important to me. I will not be defeated by a huge container of popcorn drenched in butter. I will not.

October 10: Some Say

Life Group last night was "off the chain." We had a great fellowship laced with new people who were checking out the *eating healthy journey*. I appreciate people who are willing to explore new things and consider making life-long changes to improve their health. I think they were pleasantly surprised. They were amazed that we had healthy stuffing with the turkey as well as healthy pumpkin spice muffins with pumpkin spice cream cheese icing. Then we tasted a cranberry relish made with xylitol and millet flour flatbread with no starch or sugar. Are you kidding me? The encouraging factor was that all the contributed foods were quite tasty.

Laughter is always good with a meal; and as we laughed last night, we shared stories of how we had purchased items labeled healthy, only to discover they tasted like cardboard. However, our group has proven that we can live life, eat healthy, and not sacrifice taste. That is a "win-win" scenario for us. One of the pillars of our group is creating and sharing great tasting foods. I really encourage you to try starting a healthy eating club with your friends. I promise the benefits will far outweigh the costs.

This morning I was reflecting on how people can view the same journey so differently. *Some* see our fight against obesity as denial with a whole list of things that we can and can't eat, and more on the can't list than the can. *Some* see our fight against obesity as a passing fad. *Some* see our fight against obesity as a genetic condition we will never conquer. *But some* see this as a journey that offers life, hope, and endless possibilities. I imagine it depends on how you choose to view the situation. Our healthy eating group is choosing to see the journey as limitless. We cook it; we share it; and we love it.

October 11: Judge Well

I was reading about Ezekiel this morning during my devotional time. For Ezekiel, God was asking him to evaluate and discern. He needed to help judge the people. The word *judgment* can be used in a couple of ways. God allowed Ezekiel to see clearly the situation in order to bring a word of correction and wisdom to the people. I thought about how as a family of healthy trendsetters (that is our code name) we are sharpening our skills to discern whether foods are supportive of our plan or not.

We really need to clearly evaluate all new food items. This requires carefully reading each of the listed ingredients then judging wisely. Yes or no? It is handy to have a phone ready to look up words you cannot pronounce. Recently I learned some new things to avoid from the diligence of those around me to look these things up. I do not want even a small portion of some of those chemicals in my body.

I have heard people say, "A little bit of (insert whatever) is not going to hurt you." For most of my life I bought into that philosophy, but not now. A small amount of poison could hurt me terribly. It is critical that we judge well when consuming processed foods. Manufacturers are getting quite tricky with their labels aren't they? For example, someone recently made me a cup of coffee, which contained some "no sugar added" hazelnut coffee flavoring.

One sip proved that it was *too sweet for no sugar added*. After the second sip I asked to see the container. While there was no *sugar* added, the second ingredient was corn syrup and the sugar content was high. I had to gently hand the coffee back and I felt horrible. I loved the taste and wanted it so desperately, but God has given us the Holy Spirit to help our eyes *see*, judge, and then make a tough call if needed. I applaud you for making the tough calls on a daily basis.

When we celebrate our one-hundredth birthdays and our bodies are still walking two miles a day and we are leading the senior workout class, we will all smile and know we judged well. God is for you and you can do all things through Christ who strengthens you.

October 12: Can Halloween Look Different?

I know many of us are planning our Fall Festivals and gathering our candies for the big Halloween event. I am really proud of my granddaughter, Kailey, who is now living life sugar-free. She told my daughter recently that she did not want to "do" Halloween because of all the sugar contained in the candies. How many nine year olds do that? I know many adults who cannot go a day without sugar, let alone an event. I am so proud of her.

One of our greatest challenges is to continue to look for an alternative to candy for our young ones as well as ourselves daily. I was thinking we could give out small tubes of gum sweetened with xylitol for Halloween. If we lived in another era, we could bake almond flour brownies or distribute apples. But not today. While handing out sugar-free gum, we can make a treat for ourselves. If you like vanilla yogurt, take a small container of plain Greek yogurt (fat free, sugar-free, 100 calorie, plain) and add 2 teaspoons of Truvia® and a teaspoon of clear vanilla extract. Stir well and return to the refrigerator for about 15 minutes so the Truvia® can dissolve and mix well. If you like banana splits, add some blueberries, strawberries and bananas and get ready to shout and dance. Yummy.

Can we declare this Halloween as a sugar-free day? Remember, however, that does not mean we grab a host of aspartame-sweetened products. No, simply grab an apple and natural peanut butter, or make a trail mix that is healthy. When the kids arrive at the door, give them some xylitol gum. God has given us wisdom in the area of our health, so don't be afraid to share that wisdom, especially during holidays. By this time next year, perhaps we can create sugar-free candies that are natural and explode with great taste.

I leave you with this today: your life is a gift, your body is a gift, and your mind is a gift. When someone gives us a gift, how do we treat that gift? Do we place little to no value on it and re-gift it? Do we place *some* value on it and place it in a box in our closet? Or, maybe if it is a special gift we display it for all to see, as we are proud to be the recipient of such an amazing gift. Where are you today? Where am I? Can we take the gifts given by God and keep them in perfect condition and display them proudly as a testimony of the gift given and the amazing Giver of the gift?

Lord, we rejoice today in the gifts You have given each of us and we will use our creativity to breeze through this Halloween.

October 13: Chili with Portabella Mushrooms

Yield: 8 servings

Ingredients

- 2-2 ½ pounds 93% low fat ground beef (very lean)
- 2 Vidalia onions
- 2 tablespoons olive oil
- 3 large cans fire roasted, diced tomatoes
- 1 regular container medium salsa
- 1-2 containers portabella mushrooms (optional, but I use these as a texture filler in place of the beans)
- 1 cup water
- ½ bunch cilantro (optional. I remove the stems and chop finely.)
- 1 pkg. chili seasoning (Make sure there is no sugar, or use my recipe below.)

Procedure

1. Heat the olive oil and add the chopped onions. (I leave the onions in larger pieces for the texture.) Sautee until onions are tender and turning brown.
2. Add the beef and brown well.
3. Add the seasoning package (or spices listed below) and stir well.
4. Add the remainder of ingredients and bring to a boil, then reduce heat. Allow to cook on medium low for approximately an hour.
5. Serve with Mexican blend cheese and sour cream.

Per Serving:

(Includes 3 tablespoons of cheese and 2 tablespoons of sour cream)
Calories 396.4
Total Fat 23.1 g
Cholesterol 78.2 mg
Sodium 151.1 mg
Potassium 681.6 mg
Total Carbohydrate 23.1 g
Dietary Fiber 4.2 g
Sugars 8.3 g
Protein 24.2 g

Kathy's Chili Seasoning

- 2 tablespoons of salt
- 1 teaspoon coarse ground pepper
- 2 tablespoons cumin
- 1 teaspoon red pepper flakes
- 1 tablespoon garlic powder
- 2 tablespoons paprika
- 1 tablespoon onion powder
- 1 tablespoon jalapeño powder
- 1 teaspoon of chili powder
- 2-3 tablespoons of TABASCO®

October 14: Sautéed Mushrooms and Onions

Yield: 6 servings

Ingredients

- 2-3 tablespoons olive oil
- 2 containers portabella mushrooms
- 1 large Vidalia onion
- 2 tablespoons teriyaki sauce
- 2 tablespoons sesame seeds (optional)

Procedure

1. Heat the oil and sauté the onions until tender.
2. Add the mushrooms and allow to cook for 5 minutes before adding the remaining ingredients.
3. Lower the temperature to medium and allow to cook until the liquid is reduced completely. As the liquid evaporates, watch the mushrooms as they can burn easily. Serve with your favorite grilled meat, either steak or chicken works well.

Per Serving:
Calories 99.4
Total Fat 8.4 g
Cholesterol 0.0 mg
Sodium 232.5 mg
Potassium 176.5 mg
Total Carbohydrate 5.0 g
Dietary Fiber 1.2 g
Sugars 1.5 g
Protein 2.2 g

October 15: The Fruit of My Mouth

"Words satisfy the mind as much as fruit does the stomach; good talk is as gratifying as a good harvest. Words kill, words give life; they're either poison or fruit—you choose" (Proverbs 18:20-21 MSG).

How many of us need to be reminded every day that our words are powerful? They can bring a smile to someone's face so quickly or tears to the eyes of someone *feeling* slapped. I would love to say I had never done the latter, but I have. My heart breaks when I look at someone's eyes as my words have conveyed something that pierces their hearts. Sometimes it is unavoidable as we are required to deliver a message that can shake even the most solid foundation. That does not make it easier. Does it?

Recently I realized that sometimes I am very careful about the words spoken to others, while giving no account to the horrible words I speak about myself. I have a bad habit of making ugly personal comments about myself, even as a healthy person. This is an old habit that needs to die. I have said this one million times, "I might be fat, but I'm not stupid." While people have always laughed, I never really did. Those negative words became part of my actual journey. My husband and my long-time friend, Shelly, both remind me that this phrase brings a cloak of darkness to my life. Shelly constantly points out my struggle with this, as she is my cheerleader. She is the *happy me* and is always quick to encourage me to grab my words. Thanks, Shel. Everyone needs a Shelly in his or her life.

I know as soon as that stupid phrase rolls off my tongue, it is not good. But it really is a bad habit. Great news: habits can be broken and redirected. My husband is really challenging me in this. So today, every time we consume a piece of natural fruit, let us pause and say something uplifting about our health journey and ourselves. Let's speak life and smile with our eyes. And the next time we start to make some negative comment about ourselves, or someone else, let us remember that Proverbs teaches us that our words have such power.

Declare that your body is healthy. Declare that your cells are operating at maximum capacity and fulfilling their God-given assignment. Declare that you shall live and not die to declare the works of your God. Declare it today. Eat your natural and spiritual fruit with a smile.

October 16: Humility to Ask

Sometimes it is just a good soaking God-rain that brings life to areas of death in our spirit. How many of you know there are those *suddenly* moments in the Bible? One soaking rain and suddenly the ground becomes tender again. The flowers are parched and suddenly God responds. I love it.

I truly believe that sometimes God allows a period of time before He answers our prayers so we don't become spoiled and accustomed to snapping our fingers and seeing the answer. I also believe that there is always an answer. It may not be the answer we seek, but there is always an answer. It will either be yes, no, or not now. We can count on that. What father do you know who refuses to answer when asked a question by his adored child?

We know that God is all-knowing and trusting Him is centered within undeniably knowing His truth and comprehending that He hears, He cares, and He has a plan for each of us. But often that basic comprehension is easily challenged. We know God desires for us to be free, and for those of us who are believers in Jesus, we are eternally free from the point of salvation. Many times, though, our daily freedom (sanctification) is confronted and requires a response from us. Sometimes we get out of balance and start "working" on our own, in our own power and might. Maybe we feel like God is tired of helping us in this one area. Can I tell you that belief is not true? God knows us; He knows our hearts. He knows we desire to walk in health and that we struggle with remaining free at times.

I want to reaffirm to you that God is ready every day to help each of us. God never gets tired of us coming and asking for help. Let me ask you this, if Jesus came and said, "I will grant all your prayer requests from yesterday," what would be answered? Let us ask the Lord for wisdom, help, care for others, laughter, passion for the lost, and total healing. Smile during the day knowing He heard every word. Thank God at night for His help and when we awaken tomorrow ask again. My prayer for each of us is that Jesus would help us be the best we can be in Him this day.

Never get tired of asking for help. It shows humility and not weakness. Proud folks would never ask.

October 17: Talking to Myself

Does anyone in this group ever talk to yourself as I do? While in the grocery store yesterday, I was having this conversation about the healthy contents of jicama and whether or not I could justify the price of the crab legs (even though they were 40 percent off). Then, last night I caught myself having quite the conversation with *someone* all by myself. I was giving "this person" my best arguments and then I caught my husband staring at me.

I thought, *What a waste of time—what a distraction.* It is hard enough to have a difficult conversation once, but do I need to practice it on the air and myself? I am sure all of you have an opinion. Our bodies do not need any extra tension; they need to relax and enjoy life. Life is too short to have the same intense conversation twice. Maybe too short to do it once? Being healthy for us has to encompass all areas—food, hydration, attitude, and issues. It just does. I wish the journey was not quite so complicated, but it is.

The Bible says in Romans 12:18 (AMP), "If possible, as far as it depends on you, live at peace with everyone." And guess what, most of the time it actually does depend on us. Stress is a bi-product of tension and often causes a response that most of us do not like which is either anger or hunger. Neither is good. But it is our choice. In the long run, living in peace and finding joy in the journey is the real winner. The older I get the more I seek peace above all else.

I don't know, maybe there is something to be said for fighting a battle in your mind's eye, solving the issue, and never having to have a tough conversation. What is good about talking out loud and battling in my mind is that I always *win*. Winning does not mean I actually have to confront the offender; sometimes I need to win the battle with my mouth and heart that needs to be quiet and run to the cross.

Winning in the arena of obesity is never a compromise. I will win every time. I am passionate and determined. Winning the battle against obesity is critical. Winning in an argument is often not that important.

October 18: Cotton Candy, Part 1

Do you love going to all the county fairs that are being held this month? I love the people, the pomp, the circumstance, the color, and all the fun things that remind me of my childhood. One thing, however, that was always such a disappointment to me was the cotton candy. Can I hear a *yes* from somebody else? I loved the color, the "melt in your mouth" texture, the taste, but there was no substance. It was sticky, but no substance. Within seconds this huge mound of prettiness was gone.

On our journey to health, sometimes we choose the fluffiness of, "In January I am going to get serious about my weight." This is just cotton candy. Or we might say, "Well, I know I should make some changes to my diet, but there are just certain things I cannot live without." Cotton candy. Or yet we could say, "My family has always been heavy and I am doomed for that same journey." Cotton candy.

I spent most of my life talking about being healthy, talking about learning to eat vegetables without frying them, and declaring, "In January of next year I am going to really get this." Cotton candy. My talk was never really intended to stick. It was just a comforting word to me in my obesity. Somehow it gave me false hope.

The Bible states in Proverbs 18:21 (NLT), "The tongue can bring death or life; those who love to talk will reap the consequences." I loved talking about what I thought I wanted, but my actions never represented my words well. I find so many people have difficulty in this area. We want change, but we do not want it bad enough to maneuver through every obstacle and never quit.

When I was young and battling obesity, the words of change were simply motivated by the desire to look good in shorts, jeans, or a swimsuit. I had no clue that the foods I ate would someday play such a critical role in my long-term health. There is something blissful about being young. But as my body began to display that my words and actions were not on the same page, my body started demanding my attention and cotton candy answers were no longer allowed. I vote we leave the cotton candy to others.

October 19: Cotton Candy, Part 2

As you know, I finally confronted the lies about my health and began confessing that God's best for me included great health. I murdered the negative thoughts and words that I had allowed to define who I was for many years. I quit making excuses and giving myself false hope. I quit eating the cotton candy and grabbed the apple with an intense passion to never grab the cotton candy again. It did not happen overnight, but when we confess something long enough and passionately enough, it begins to take root. Then life can begin.

In our journey, there are a lot of choices daily. Speaking life to our bodies can just be a ritual or false hope (cotton candy) if our hearts and the Holy Spirit are not helping us to walk in reality. Have you heard the cliché, "It is better to walk the walk than talk the talk?" Our health journey is a prime example.

We will all have a bad day sooner or later, even while being healthy. I had one Sunday when exhaustion took over and all I thought about was food. I did overeat, but it was foods on plan. I ate all day, in fact, and then realized how strong and raw my emotions were and that I was still vulnerable. But praise God I never crossed the line with food selections. Portions went out the window, but health was still in my heart. I admit it—I stumbled. But I hit the ground with enough fortitude to bounce right back to my feet.

I also had gone for two days under my normal water intake. It was as if craziness overtook my mind. But Monday came, as did thirteen cups of water and a refreshed commitment. And might I happily share that I never said, "Well, in January I will really start working on getting healthy." I let my tongue bring life, as I did not default to a negative confession. I knew I was on the roller coaster, but I never ate the cotton candy.

Find something you did right today and be proud of *you*. The cotton candy has no stability, but you do. Congratulations.

October 20: Mahi Mahi Grilled with Tarrago

Yield: 4 servings

Ingredients

- 2-3 fillets Mahi Mahi
- 1 lime juiced
- Fresh tarragon
- Greek salad dressing
- Sea salt to taste

Procedure

1. In a large baggie, place the Mahi Mahi fillets and ½ bottle of the salad dressing. Allow to marinate in the refrigerator for several hours.
2. Create a pouch for the grill by cutting a large square of aluminum foil. Place one fillet in a pouch.
3. Squeeze some of the juice of the lime onto the fish, and top with fresh tarragon leaves. Lightly sprinkle with sea salt to enhance the flavor.
4. Fold the corners of the pouch toward the center and over lap. Crinkle in the center to tighten. Follow the above procedure for all the fillets.
5. Place on a medium-hot grill for approximately 20 minutes. When done, the fillet will flake easily. Don't burn.
6. If you like the grill marks, remove from the pouch and place on a hot grill for a minute on each side.

Per Serving:

Calories 233.6
Total Fat 12.5 g
Cholesterol 116.7 mg
Sodium 348.1 mg
Potassium 70.4 mg
Total Carbohydrate 6.1 g
Dietary Fiber 1.0 g
Sugars 1.6 g
Protein 27.2 g

ctober 21: Dressings for Salads

vinegar alone is a great dressing, as is white balsamic. No calories, but a lot of taste.

Honey Mustard

Ingredients

- 2 tablespoons yellow mustard (sugar-free)
- 1 pkg. Truvia® Natural Sweetener
- 1 teaspoon apple cider vinegar (could increase or decrease depending on your taste)

Procedure

Mix well and serve.

Vinegar and Tarragon

Ingredients

- 2 tablespoons white Balsamic vinegar
- ¼ teaspoon dried tarragon

Procedure

Stir together and serve. (You could add some light tasting olive oil to this mix.)

Healthy 4 You French

Ingredients

- 2 tablespoons Duke's mayo
- 1 tablespoon ketchup (use a low sugar variety or try my recipe for ketchup on page 61)
- 1 teaspoon Worcestershire sauce
- Garlic salt to taste

Procedure

Mix well and allow to sit for about 10 minutes for the flavors to blend. You can make ahead and keep for a couple of days.

For a Thousand Island variation, add ½ teaspoon of no sugar added sweet pickle relish.

Asian Orange

Ingredients

- 2 tablespoons olive oil
- 1 tablespoon white balsamic vinegar
- 1 pkg. Truvia® Natural Sweetener
- Juice of one orange
- ¼ teaspoon dried ginger
- Dash sea salt

Procedure

Mix well and serve.

October 22: Priceless

I was thinking yesterday about the word *priceless*. The word basically defines itself—*that to which no price can be ascribed.* I was thinking about the things in my house and life that are priceless—my relationship with God, my Bible, my husband, my family, my close friends, pictures of my family, my mother's engagement ring, letters from my daughter and granddaughters, a cassette tape of my oldest granddaughter singing at the age of two (although I am not certain I can still find a machine on which to play it). These are just a few things that, if threatened by destruction, a murderous spirit would arise from within me (not really that bad, but close). How about you? Can you make your list?

My question to be answered by us all is, "Do we see our health and ourselves as priceless? Do we really place great value on being healthy or on ourselves?" I venture to say, from many years of pastoring, countless people really do not love anything about themselves. Shame, guilt, un-mended wounds, hurts, and failures all seem to remind us that we are certainly not priceless. And yet God saw each of us as having such great value, He was willing to give His one and only Son, Jesus, that we might have eternal life. That is priceless to me.

Is our health worth guarding? Absolutely. Is it worth placing in a safe place? Again, I say yes. Ask yourself honestly right now, is your health as valuable as one of your most priceless possessions? In my very humble opinion, it should be very close. For many, however, I fear the answer would be "not so much." And while I understand the long-range implications of valuing our health as it contributes to the condition of our "golden years," the real reason is not centered in a physical manifestation at all. The foremost reason for guarding our health is that our bodies house the Holy Spirit. We actually house the Spirit of the Lord. That is profound to me! I never want to feel as though I have not done my best to provide the best possible house for God's Spirit (go ahead and read John 17 again this morning).

Sometimes we must remind ourselves repeatedly of our value and worth. Today, move yourself to the priceless list and do whatever it takes to maintain your best health. God sees each of us as priceless. Let that truth invade your life today.

October 23: The One

Our church hosted a women's conference recently. We had a wonderful conference, and for me the highlight came at the conclusion when we water baptized twenty-two women. In my entire life, I am not certain I have ever experienced that feeling before. It was powerful. I want to share a very tender moment I had with the Lord concerning the conference and then bring this into our world of being healthy.

Our women's ministry team worked for seven months on this conference. I knew it was going to be amazing. But for whatever reason, the attendance did not build early on as I thought it would and I was a bit discouraged. I felt that God was going to do amazing things and I wanted to share it with as many ladies as possible. On Thursday morning when the conference started, I was praying and asking God to move on the last few who had not registered and bring all those who were supposed to attend. I felt the Lord speak to me in that place in my belly and ask me a very profound question. He asked, *Would you do all this elaborate planning and creating of the conference for just one person?* That question shook me. God would have done it all "for the one." That is how He rolls. He wanted to know if I had the same feelings concerning *the one.*

God is so amazing to bring balance to everything. Why am I bringing this up today? Sometimes when God does not answer our prayers quickly and we are still battling with those last few pounds, we can become discouraged and even reason that God has "more important things" to accomplish than helping us be healthy. Stop that noise. God cared about *the one* at the conference. He is intimately concerned with our lives, and according to the Scripture, He knows how many hairs are on our head and every thought in our heart. He cares about *the one.*

Stop today and thank Him for giving you great health according to His plan for your life. Ask Him to remind you to hydrate and give you the power to say yes and no as you should throughout the day when stress may cause your natural eyes to fix on a solution other than something healthy. I promise, God loves and cares about each of us at that level.

Are you grateful to be *the one?*

October 24: Tricks and Treats

The arctic blast has certainly shouted loudly that it is tired of being confined. It has not been this cold in almost a year. All that cold air, which is so dense and heavy, must be clapping with joy as it has been released to descend, as it loves to do. Anyway, what a busy week this is for me with our Fall Family Festival on Halloween evening and a wedding I am directing for a precious couple in our church whose son belongs to my covenant friend, Shelly, whom I mentioned earlier.

There are lots of opportunities for eating wrong foods this week with such a busy schedule. Therefore, I am devising a plan for success before the week begins. I really feel that victory resides in the planning. In my past life, Halloween was my "open the gate" starting point to the holiday season. I started eating candy as soon as it arrived on the shelves in early October, as well as making the excuse that January was only eight weeks away from Halloween. Even as I type this I am shaking my head. No wonder I was so unhealthy and sick.

The week began with a bridal party at my house, and I planned a menu that worked for me, including a sugar and starch free pumpkin pound cake with pumpkin spiced whipped cream and "sugared" pecan pieces. Sounds yummy, huh? Being the hostess provided me the opportunity to honor my sweet Daniela and eat healthy too. It was a fabulous connection.

On Halloween Day, I packed a large lunch with grilled chicken, a salad, and extra apples to lightly dip in my natural peanut butter before the Fall Family Festival. I also included some healthy brownies to help me smile as all the chocolate was being consumed around me. I will not be denied. I chose this journey, I am healthy because of this journey, and I am happy because of this journey. However, in order to remain in this happy state, I have planned ahead of time to say, "No thank you."

There will be many people who offer me unhealthy choices this week, but none of them control my destiny. I am strong enough to smile and say, "No thank you" without justifying, defending or explaining. I want to encourage you that these next eight weeks do not have to be times of denial or failure. Say no ahead of time; practice if you will, with no explanation, and bring your own foods to the parties, which bring a smile to your body. Say no early and never deal with the frustration of feeling you failed following Halloween. We know the *tricks* to healthy eating because we create our healthy treats. So for us it is not "trick or treat," it is tricks *and* treats. Cool, huh?

October 25: Turn It Around

In Genesis 50, the story of Joseph reminds us that God is able to take our mess and create a message. God is able to take our desperation and give someone else hope. Joseph commented to his brothers that what they had intended for evil, God intended for good (verse 20). As we journey though this day, we need to remind ourselves that Satan wants to discourage and trap each of us. He can use the large obstacles in our lives or the simple things like candy, Halloween cupcakes, and issues that may serve to seemingly place us in a pocket of hopelessness.

I cannot even imagine what being betrayed by my family and left to die really feels like. As many of you know, Joseph not only escaped the entrapment, but also secured hope for others needing a route of escape. Let us make that life-long pledge. Life will often betray us, but how we handle the betrayal is the gift we hand ourselves as well as others.

I remember the years of eating so much sugar on Halloween that I would be literally sick by the end of the night and looking for a release. Unfortunately, many people will experience the same journey. For me, the worst part was looking in the mirror and confessing failure once again. My heart hurts even now as I think of the prison I endured for years. Maybe you are thinking, *Really, it's not that serious*. But sugar is so addictive and extremely difficult to overcome. Have you actually tried a sugar-free week? Usually within a couple of days the release of toxins causes some yucky symptoms and many often return to sugar as their remedy. If sugar is such a good substance, why then the bad reaction upon deletion?

God is taking the mess of my past and giving me creative energy in the kitchen as His tool to help rescue me. And guess what? He will do that for you as well. I promise. Joseph endured and then conquered. That is going to be our testimony. Can I encourage you today? No candy or sweets for Halloween. It may be hard, but later you will thank me. Make a pledge with me—no sweets—not one bite. No aspartame either, please. We cannot exchange one prison cell for another.

October 26: The Freedom of Laughter

Have you ever been with a friend and gotten tickled and laughed until your side hurt? That happened one day as I actually laughed with two friends for almost an hour. I promise we had consumed no alcohol, but we could not stop laughing. We would get calmed down and then one of us would look at each other and it would start rolling out again. Honestly, we laughed so hard my side was sore for the next couple of days.

After we were done with our laughter visit, and I was on my way home, I felt such elation and yet almost tired from laughing that hard. Have you ever done this? It was at that moment I realized endorphins were more than a term I could not spell and laughter was definitely great medicine. I do not like the slapstick comedy, but at certain seasons of devastation and prolonged confrontation, I will find anything to watch to evoke laughter. The more I laugh, the less paramount my issues seem. And you know what is so great? God created the whole mechanism as a blessing for us. God wants us to trust Him. Sometimes we need to just laugh at our issues and "make 'em take a number."

Laughter is free, contagious, sometimes uncontrolled, and even as we speak I can reminisce of times in the car as Kailey would laugh so hard that none of us were immune. That feeling and release breaks things in our spirits. But I am amazed at how we lose the freedom of laughing the older we get. Have you ever thought about that? Kids laugh loud and often. When tickled, their laughter fills the house. But adults, not so much. That is actually sad to me.

We often have a predetermined composure that is expected of us and uncontrolled laughter does not work at meetings, bridal showers, or the doctor's offices. I get it. But if we strongly consider that laughter really is a powerful healing force, then why do we laugh so little? I vote in our battle, we schedule a period of laughter. I would imagine that the more that occurs, the easier it would become. And who knows, eating well and laughing deeply could cause us to sleep better, be better companions, and live to the age of a hundred and fifty.

Anybody know a great comedy we can watch?

October 27: Meaty Spaghetti Sauce

Yield: 16 servings

This makes a very large pot of sauce, but is a crowd favorite and usually doesn't last long. Also, it freezes well if needed for two family dinners. This sauce is great on spaghetti squash topped with Parmesan Reggiano cheese.

Ingredients

- 2 lbs. of lean, ground beef (I use 93% lean)
- 4-5 pieces of chicken breasts, cut into small chunks
- 2 packages of smoked sausage (or 3 if you like sausage as we do) cut into small chunks.
- 1 large onion
- 3 large containers of your favorite, sugar-free spaghetti sauce (plain)
- 2 teaspoons of Italian seasoning
- 1 teaspoon of ground basil
- 1 teaspoon of sea salt
- 1 container of fresh, portabella mushrooms
- Parmesan Reggiano cheese to taste

Procedure

1. Spray a large pot, as the lean ground beef does not release much fat.
2. Add the ground beef and begin browning. After it browns, add the onions and continue to cook until they are tender.
3. Add the remaining two meats and cook for about 5-6 minutes. Add the seasonings and still well.
4. Add the spaghetti sauce and allow to heat thoroughly for about 45 minutes. This also allows the flavor of the meats to infuse the sauce. You may serve as is *or* to thicken the gravy and infuse a different flavor, add 1 cup of Parmesan Reggiano and allow to cook an additional 20 minutes. The cheese will adhere to the pot and sometimes cleaning is more difficult, but the flavor is worth the effort.

Per Serving:

Calories 496.3
Total Fat 21.3 g
Cholesterol 93.3 mg
Sodium 433.2 mg
Potassium 362.8 mg
Total Carbohydrate 37.3 g
Dietary Fiber 7.7 g
Sugars 6 g
Protein 36.9 g

October 28: Spaghetti Squash Bake

Yield: 8 servings

What do you do when you have a leftover bowl of spaghetti squash and some sauce from a meal a couple of days ago? Re-purpose it. Or you can make it from scratch and include the meats in the dish. It bakes somewhat like lasagna without the noodles. This makes a great side dish for grilled chicken or boneless pork tenderloin.

Ingredients

- Medium bowl of spaghetti squash (could be fresh, mine was leftover)
- Spaghetti sauce (my meaty sauce listed in this book)
- 3 eggs
- Sea salt to taste
- Garlic to taste
- 1 small bag 2% mozzarella cheese
- Grated Parmesan Reggiano for the top

Procedure

1. Preheat oven to 400°F.
2. Combine the spaghetti squash and three large eggs that are beaten well.
3. Add the sea salt, garlic salt, and the remainder of the spaghetti sauce (about 5-6 cups). Stir well to blend. (As these were leftovers, all of this was cold so the eggs weren't stringy. If you are making this hot, the squash mixture must cool well before adding the eggs or they can begin to cook and you will have white, stringy egg whites in your mixture.)
4. Add a small bag of 2% skim mozzarella cheese. I mixed all this well and placed in a baking dish sprayed with cooking spray and started baking it on 400°F. After about 30 min, I turned the temp to 450°F and added the grated Reggiano and let the cheese crisp and brown a bit (maybe another 15 min).
5. Let this cool for about 15 minutes before serving.

Per Serving:

(The following data only reflects the value for the eggs, garlic, and 2 cheeses. The calories from the spaghetti squash and meaty sauce are listed on those recipe pages)

Calories 94.2
Total Fat 6.0 g
Cholesterol 82.5 mg
Sodium 209.0 mg
Potassium 56.4 mg
Total Carbohydrate 1.4 g
Dietary Fiber 0.1 g
Sugars 0.3 g
Protein 8.5 g

October 29: The Rainbow

Following the summer, the pockets of colder air begin their decent. Cold air masses are denser, which means they are looking for a place to settle, and when they encounter the warm air, sparks can fly and storms erupt. I can just imagine the people in Noah's day as the storms began and rain fell from the sky, which they had never seen. Prior to this, the earth watered itself from the ground level and not the sky. There was no water cycle and for a season, no need for one. Today, however, I want to focus on the rainbow and not the rain. I love rainbows. I love the manner in which they are created. I love the beauty of their colors and the power of the message they convey—God's first promise.

How many of you know that God absolutely recognizes that we all learn differently. He created us that way. Statistics indicate that 20 percent of us learn by hearing, 50 percent by seeing, and 80 percent by doing. Big differences. I am the visual person. I can imagine God thinking like this, *Kathy will need a picture in the sky at certain times to remember I always keep My promises.* And even though I consistently read in God's Word of His covenant to keep His promises throughout the generations, it seems that when I need it most, a rainbow will appear to reinforce the written Word.

God has provided everything our body needs for health and long life. He is an abundant provider and never leaves us without a window. Think about it—He provides different fruits and vegetables that can endure the different seasons, airplanes to transport foods from various places, and the Sunday paper with its abundance of coupons to gain the maximum "bang for the buck" at the grocery store all for us because He said He would provide. Do I really believe God did that for us? Absolutely.

So, why do we worry about rising food costs? Why are we fearful that our budget is heavy on the food side and healthy eating may need to be adjusted? Why? Here is what I pray for us all: *let there be rain today followed by a rainbow that will re-emphasize God always honors His Word.* While He created the rainbow for those of us who are visual learners, let the auditory learners read God's Word aloud. Sorry tactile learners, rainbows cannot be touched. Maybe today the visual is your best learning option.

Whether displayed in the sky or explained via text, God absolutely wants us to know that He always keeps His promises.

October 30: Watching the Policeman in the Rearview Mirror

Have you ever noticed that when you pass a law enforcement officer in your vehicle, most of the time you check the rearview mirrors? Sometimes we know we are speeding and as the blue lights spin, checking the mirror allows us time to determine where we put our insurance card.

But most of the time I am not speeding and yet I always check the mirror to determine if they are pulling out, cutting on the lights, or laying low. Have you ever thought about that? On the way to church recently, I passed not one, but five law enforcement cars and *every* time I checked the rearview mirror. Praise God, not one time was I speeding. Finally I thought, *this is as bad as texting*. Well, not really. But I actually paused long enough to ask myself why and what insight was I to gain from this continued response.

Here is what I think: In this case, looking back is based in fear. Even when we are not speeding, we have probably been stopped before and there is always that chance we could be wrong. I considered that if I had never been stopped, I would have no past experience to cause me to operate in fear and look back. There would be nothing in the past to motivate that reaction. I wonder how much of our lives are spent looking back in fear that drastic outcomes could reappear? Probably more than we wish to honestly convey. That is why I think the rainbow devotion from yesterday is so critical.

I would like to suggest that each of us find the promises from God's Word about our health, memorize them, and when tempted to look for the blue lights in the mirror, (indicating failure or distress) we quote the promise out loud. This will help you look forward and not back. And especially when you are navigating in a vehicle, that is a great thing. I hope you see the implications in all this. It was a vivid picture to me yesterday.

October 31: October Reflection Page

As you are completing the October devotions, are there things you wish you had highlighted or which you had written down? Can you use the space below to list the "tricks" you used to have a healthy Halloween? It wasn't so bad, was it? Each holiday will get easier as you continue to make the commitment to never open the wrong doors again.

_____

_____

_____

_____

_____

_____

_____

_____

_____

_____

_____

_____

_____

_____

_____

_____

_____

_____

_____

_____

_____

November

A month of saying, "Thank you." I think it is odd for an entire month to be designated to something we should do daily. But I am grateful that whoever created this monthly emphasis allowed us a period of time to slow down and genuinely focus on telling others we appreciate them.

November 1: It Takes Time, Part 1

Okay, we cleared one hurdle and got through Halloween. How did you do? Did you get through the day sugar-free or at least low sugar? If not, today is a new day in a new month. Perhaps you can handle a small Halloween cookie or a couple of M&M's. That is okay if you can; I cannot. A small amount of sugar for me opens doors to places I plan to never revisit. Just having a little is not the same as having none, is it? Sometimes we tell people we have not eaten anything sweet in days when actually every day we had embraced a chocolate "kiss" or two. Ask God to show you the balance needed.

Each of us should identify what our health triggers are. If you are uncertain what causes an increase in your weight and blood sugar level, start keeping great notes. I followed this routine for six-week periods and identified mine quickly, fortunately. Also, as we have discussed, each of us should be using regular blood tests to determine the internal health of our bodies. Please remember, just because your clothes fit does not mean you are at maximum health. Many use that as their "test" for being healthy. Being healthy is composed of several elements, and zipping our jeans is only one of those.

I was thinking about how busy our lives get and sometimes I wonder if people are not healthy because it takes *time* to be healthy. I am amazed at how many people share with me they do not have enough time to "do what I do." Well, if I can master the time constraints, with the time issues that I face daily, anyone can. I would match my daily schedule to the best of them. But, I had to confront illness face to face and realize no lack of time was worth dying for. Yes, cooking and shopping take time, but so does fighting cancer. Guess which one I would pick?

As I have started to really live this life, not simply because I lost so much weight, but because I gained my health and in turn my life, I realized that one component is probably never discussed and yet critical in the success of this journey...*time*. Tomorrow we will discuss time again.

November 2: It Takes Time, Part 2

As we concluded yesterday's devotion, we were examining the critical, and often under-discussed, topic in our journey of *time*. It takes *time* to shop and find the healthiest foods, as well as *time* to explore different, new items so we do not get bored with the eating plan. (Let me interject that while a 100 calorie snack bar is easy, it is full of sugar and chemicals.) It takes *time* to stop and drink water all day. It takes *time* to prepare and cook real foods. It takes *time* at a restaurant to examine the menu, ask for modifications, and choose the healthy items. It takes *time* to go for a walk. Come on, this journey takes *time*.

But let's be honest, we all make *time* for the things that are important to us. I spend hours on Sunday and Monday preparing foods for lunches and quick-fix dinners after a long day at work. I try at least once a week to prepare something special for my granddaughter who has lost over twenty pounds recently choosing to eat healthy. This takes *time*. It would be easier to buy Kailey a box of candy. But the candy would lead her back to a place of being diabetic. I would much rather give my *time* to assist in her journey than see her debilitated from diabetes.

The moral of this morning's devotion: being healthy does take time, but you and I are so worth it. Where can you take some time from another venture that may not have the same long-term benefits of great health? I realize we cannot create time, but we can delegate our time. Maybe you could take one television show a week—perhaps an hour—and give that to your health? Pull out some of the recipes from this book and make those, freeze some, and do something wonderful for you. I watch some television too, but not before I prepare my foods and invest my time in the future of my health.

Have an awesome day!

November 3: Keep It Simple

I am resting from a long couple of months—pajamas on, coffee cup warm, and movies about to start. I need to rest my brain. Do you ever need to rest your brain? If not, pray for me, it could be my age.

Last night's Life Group was amazing again. Linda wowed us with several salads, some baked pears, and a little chocolate ball made with chia flour. It was good. We also had breakfast frittatas and cheesy garlic biscuits for Christmas breakfast joined by a scrumptious dessert pizza. Why am I sharing this with you? So when you start your Healthy Connection Group, you can see what the sister groups are preparing. No pressure though.

As we were discussing alternatives for sweets at Christmas parties, I was reminded that we cannot over indulge with healthy foods simply because they are declared "legal." We must remember that portion size helps the scale to be friendly during the morning weigh-ins. I had to laugh as a friend asked last night, "So, I guess I'm gonna have to cook?" Yes, sweet girl, that is absolutely a critical component on our journey.

I know that those of us who work are pressed for time (yesterday's devotion), but *simple meals work.* They really do. Life Group is our time to explore fun foods for weekends and events, but the day-to-day eating regimen can be very simple. I like to cook six to eight pieces of chicken, six turkey patties (or whatever meat is on sale that is lean), and vegetables once a week to prepare for my lunch and dinner meals. I do the same thing with my raw, cut vegetables. I keep everything pre-portioned and ready to go. Then, I can always add a fruit or steam another veggie and be really happy. *If I'm lighting the grill, I'm loading the grill* (that is a great saying and works at our house). I believe in being a good steward across the board, even with the gas in my grill.

Are you struggling with keeping things simple? Being healthy is about refueling, not grueling hours of preparation. Let your natural foods provide the nutrition and you provide some creativity. That is a recipe for success. I would encourage you to stray from the smorgasbord of products that are processed, and choose whole foods as often as possible. Peel and eat; it's simple.

I'm going to go peel some jicama right now and follow my own advice.

November 4: The Sifter

I have been especially stirred of late as several people have contacted me with a cry from their hearts that somewhere they opened a "wrong" door and being healthy has "gone the way of all flesh." I totally understand. I have been there and done that. That is one of the hardest things from which to recover. Failure can be so devastating, can't it? And sometimes simply the fear of failure alone can sabotage any small success we might have with our health.

We must be reminded that Satan desires to sift us (test, test, and test again) to break us down, and eventually have his way. Do any of you remember baking with your grandmothers? My Nanny had a sifter; you know those, right? She placed her baking flour inside and sifted it sometimes three to four times so that it was broken down into fine pieces. The flour was so soft and Nanny pushed it around easily and made it become what she wanted. She could do with the sifted flour *as she wished*. Get that picture in your mind.

Remember the Bible teaches that Satan comes only but to kill, steal, and destroy (see John 10:10). He has the same agenda every day and never grows weary of working the plan. The worst part is he never sleeps, eats, or vacations. But neither does my powerful God. Okay, back to the sifter explanation we go.

For me, my weight was such a huge component through which I filtered everything. Not being able to zip my pants meant a bad day. Gaining six pounds in one month meant a bad month. Looking at the fatness of my face in photos meant a look at failure and a stab in my heart again. Anybody been there? I totally understand your frustration and still face that myself on occasion. Let me encourage you, as I told someone last week, congratulations for reaching out to someone and admitting you have gained weight. I always tried to hide and make jokes about being a failure. It became easier to laugh at obesity than try one more time to conquer it. I hear you, and my heart wants to bring you hope.

Do some serious investigation. Get out of Satan's sifter by deleting the sugar and starchy foods and take a deep breath. Remember, some doors may have to remain closed forever. I have several.

November 5: Tune Your Ears

When you find that you have gained weight for several days in a row, it is time to stop and ask God where the breech is and make a repair. You cannot let one day roll into a week, then into a month and *hope* you can stop gaining. No, you need to determine *why* you gained weight and fix that issue. Is it sugar? Is it lack of preparation? Is it boredom? Is it an issue with saying no? These are fixable issues. I promise.

I believe Proverbs 2:1-11 holds the key:

> "My child, listen to what I say, and treasure my commands. *Tune your ears* to wisdom, and concentrate on understanding. *Cry out* for insight, and *ask* for understanding. *Search for* them as you would for silver; *seek them* like hidden treasures. Then you will understand what it means to fear the Lord, and you will gain knowledge of God. For the Lord grants wisdom! From his mouth come knowledge and understanding. He grants a treasure of common sense to the honest. He is a shield to those who walk with integrity. He guards the paths of the just and protects those who are faithful to him. Then you will understand what is right, just, and fair, and you will find the right way to go. For wisdom will enter your heart, and knowledge will fill you with joy. Wise choices will watch over you. Understanding will keep you safe" (NLT, emphasis mine).

Here is what I believe the Lord showed me this morning. Sometimes we have our stations on the wrong frequency. Tune your ears back to the truth. Somewhere along the way, the "truth frequencies" got bumped, stifled, confused, or something. You must tune it back. Ever been in a car where the radio is not "quite" on the station—close but not quite? Sometimes we can find ourselves in this same type of situation with our health—close but not really. We know what to do, but sometimes another frequency (voice) questions our reality and unless we are firmly established on the real truth about our health, we could question the principles we have adopted. That creates a platform for excuses and cheating.

We must tune our ears back to wisdom. I do not believe it is a one-time event either, sorry. And the word *you* in the verse above means no one can do this for us. As we enter the holiday gauntlet, let's tune our ears to truth and remember food is simply for refueling. Do not make it more than it is. Look at verse 10 again, "When wisdom is tuned back into our heart (follow the plan) then knowledge (truth) will fill us with joy." Is a piece of chocolate cake worth the feeling of failure the day after? Tune your ears to wisdom that proclaims healthy foods will give you long life while chocolate cake can steal it. Sharpen that frequency, family.

November 6: Almond Flour, Buttermilk "Cornbread"

Yield: 24 servings

Ingredients

- ½ cup oil (half in batter and half in 9x13 baking dish, heating while constructing batter)
- 2 eggs
- 1 ¼ cups buttermilk
- ½ teaspoon baking soda
- ½ teaspoon baking powder
- 3 pkgs. Truvia® Natural Sweetener (optional)
- 2 ¾ cups almond flour
- ¾ teaspoon sea salt

Procedure

1. Preheat oven to 400°F.
2. Spray 9x13 pan along the sides and add ¼ cup oil. Place in oven while batter is being constructed.
3. Mix all ingredients (dry first, then add wet), stirring well, and add to the hot pan with oil.
4. Bake 26-32 minutes, or until golden brown and toothpick inserted comes out clean.

Per Serving:

Calories 114.4
Total Fat 10.3 g
Cholesterol 15.9 mg
Sodium 75.4 mg
Potassium 25.1 mg
Total Carbohydrate 4.2 g
Dietary Fiber 1.1 g
Sugars 1.0 g
Protein 3.2 g

November 7: Dressing for Thanksgiving

Yield: 24 servings

Ingredients

- 1 complete recipe of Almond Flour, Buttermilk Cornbread from page 341
- 1 box sea salt melba toast
- 4 eggs
- ½ carton 99% fat free chicken stock (start w/ half carton, not too soupy as the almond flour does not absorb as much as white flour. Watch this liquid addition carefully—less is more right here)
- 2 cans cream of chicken soup
- ½ large Vidalia onion, chopped very fine
- 3 stalks celery, chopped very fine
- 1 tablespoon sea salt
- Seasonings to taste (I use poultry seasoning and some black pepper)
- Pecans (optional)

Procedure

1. Make cornbread and break into pieces in big bowl.
2. Crumble melba toast in medium pieces and add hot chicken stock. Let sit for about 20 min. to soften the melba toast and absorb.
3. Preheat oven to 400°F.
4. Combine the cornbread and melba toast mixture. Stir well.
5. Add the remaining ingredients and stir well.
6. Check the taste for additional seasonings.
7. Spray a 9x13 baking pan liberally with no-stick cooking spray before adding the dressing.
8. Bake for 1 hour.
9. Let sit for a few minutes to cut in squares or serve by the spoon while hot.

Per Serving:

(The following nutritional value does not include the value from the cornbread on page 341. Please combine for complete nutritional values.)

Calories 69.8
Total Fat 1.9 g
Cholesterol 34.4 mg
Sodium 389.3 mg
Potassium 65.9 mg
Total Carbohydrate 10.5 g
Dietary Fiber 1.1 g
Sugars 0.4 g
Protein 2.9 g

November 8: Seed Time and Harvest

I wanted to point out that once a seed has been planted (you make a commitment to follow a healthy life-style plan) you must nurture that seed as its roots fight for their space in the ground. This takes *time* (refer to the devotions about time in October for a refresher). The ground actually represents uncharted territory with the hope of producing fruit, which is evidence that the truth has taken root.

If our real motive is to be healthy, then we will do whatever we can to protect the seed (our health plan) and eliminate as many of the variables of opposition as possible. There are storms of life that come to uproot the seed and pull it away from the goal of positive life change; we all know these too well. But if we are consistent and patient, sticking with a healthy lifestyle against all odds, there is a great chance that a harvest of life will come. A seed (a new lifestyle) is placed in a cold, dark environment and it must fight to push its roots down into the soil deep enough to sustain the ability to produce life-giving fruit or flowers.

I am certain the little seedlings struggle, want to quit, fail on occasion, but eventually fight for their purpose and in *time* produce a harvest. That is a vivid picture of our health family. We must accept the work and *time* it takes to produce a life change. It does not happen overnight or without opposition, but if we keep pressing and reaching into a deep place within our resolve, it can happen. We declared at work yesterday, "No diet—only real life change."

So keep allowing this life-change journey to take hold of your heart and mind. Embrace the concept that it is no longer a seed, but a real change. Eating healthy has its challenges but in the long run, overcoming those obstacles produces a beautiful, colorful "life" that gives hope to others. I hope you see the analogy today. And remember, give yourself *time* to see the evidence of a new lifestyle. Genesis 8:22 states, "While the earth remains, seedtime and harvest, cold and heat, winter and summer, and day and night shall not cease" (NKJV). Confess it again: "I planted the seed. It will take time, but I will see a harvest!"

November 9: The Smell of Victory

I have been thinking about Thanksgiving morning and my favorite part is the smell of Tom Turkey baking in the oven. To me, there are not many scents that fill the entire house, every inch, and are proud of it. When I think of *that scent*, I immediately travel to past years of family mornings of watching the Thanksgiving Day Parade by the fire. Then, *that scent* reminds me of setting the table with tiny pumpkins as Mom prepared a feast that none of us could fathom. And *that scent* brings the flashbacks of watching my father carve the bird, delicately collecting the skin that we fought over as children. *That scent.*

I was thinking about how powerful that fragrance and all the memories that flood my soul are. They are so real to me, and yet are more than fifty years old. Sometimes I will cook a turkey breast and I am convinced that I just need the smell. There are places in our lives where we experienced joy, family, happy memories, and peace. Where is that for you? Can you see it? Is there a scent attached? For me, the smell of Thanksgiving morning is one of my "happy places."

Along our freedom journey, there are going to be times when giving up may seem the easiest choice. Returning to the prison of obesity may seem to be the only "easy" thing to do. When you have those days, can you find a place, a scent, or a family tradition (not related to food) that brings a smile and releases some endorphins? Sometimes we must remember the good and victorious spots and we must encourage ourselves, and each other, that life is good.

Negativity and failure seem to suck the life from our will to be free. Then the excuses begin to flow. I challenge each of us to be real. Certainly there will be bumps, daily, but as long as we continue to do what is right in the face of wrong options, we win. God told Cain that sin was crouching at the door, but he simply needed to do what was right. I like to remind people that *making excuses for weaknesses means you get to keep them.*

Sometimes we need to light a candle that reminds us of Thanksgiving morning and smile. Or bake a turkey and smile. Stop and find the thing that makes you smile and remember the good; stop focusing on the failure. Put the cookie down and grab an apple. Burn the candle and make a new sensation connection. Our minds and memories are amazing. I challenge you today, no matter where you are on your journey, find the victory scent and smile.

November 10: Thank You to the Veterans

This weekend was filled with giving honor where honor is due. Many men and women have boldly defended the freedom that I sometimes take for granted. I repent right here. As we had our veterans stand yesterday in church so the congregation could honor them, I felt a real tugging on my heart and a sense of honor. I was proud of their accomplishments and sacrifice. I doubt I will ever fully comprehend their journey, but I am proud that I live in a country where they were willing to take a risk for me and so many others they would never know.

There is really something to fighting for freedom. We certainly recognize that in "non-war" times, the preparations for war are not as intense. But our military still prepares. They participate in combat simulations, PT, and all the educational experiences to become proficient with the latest technology. While war may not be occurring, the threat is always a reality.

On our health journey, this should serve as a reminder that we must always remain alert and be prepared. Sometimes internal weaknesses in our bodies can lie quietly for years without our attention. Poor diet, lack of exercise, and improper rest can actually be aiding the illness in its silent development. Then, at a most inopportune time, the "enemy" surfaces like a military submarine lurking under the water. Our response is often fear, and rightly so. All creation houses a desire for life. I do not know too many people, or animals, who give up without a struggle when confronted with death.

When the *submarine* of illness emerges and we are unprepared, our options may be limited. I like the proactive approach; how about you? We recognize that food, water, exercise, and rest are our best weapons against poor health, right? We accept that. However, I find that often we wander from the correct path or begin to make excuses for side excursions. It does not take long to find we are lost and our compass is no longer active.

For our military, I am certain PT at 5:30 a.m. (without being at war) is not pleasant. However, being physically fit at the exact moment needed is crucial. The submarine of disease is always lurking, but we have our own weapons and victory strategy. Let's stay on top of being physically fit and remember that preparing for a battle with the enemy standing over you is too late. The outcome of that encounter requires a miracle. Yes, we know a Miracle Maker, but let us do our part to always be prepared.

November 11: Thanks

I am so excited to be sitting in Brentwood, Tennessee, which is a beautiful city located right outside Nashville. This morning there is a thick layer of frost on the car. It really feels like winter here. I made some God connections yesterday and will wait to see what doors God opens. I have told God for years, "I'm available." Having said that, God has always held me to my word. He has moved me and done things in my life I never imagined. I always tell people, "If you're available to God, you can count on the ride of your life."

Sometimes God made changes in my life that were not easy, but I know God shifted me as He needed to. My heart is always to please Him. I reflected this morning about the extreme value of being in a group who are walking the same path, understanding the day-to-day issues that challenge each of us, and knowing that we are better together.

I do not tell you enough, "Thanks!" Thanks for being my friends and helping me choose health. My whole life it seems I have always lost my way somewhere. Thanks for sharing your recipes and insight with a girl who gets bored easily and always looks for the next best thing. Thanks for the hugs, smiles, and gritting teeth experiences we have shared via these devotions and email conversations. God knew I needed a group in order to experience life-long success and He sent you to me. Thank you, God!

As we are planning our family dinners for next week, can we challenge each other? Have we planned foods that are healthy, that taste good, and will allow us to enjoy the holidays without guilt? God doesn't want any of us to be guilty. Jesus came to bring freedom to our lives. Let our hearts be refreshed and make that declaration as we approach next week. Never plan to cheat; plan now to eat healthy. Do not plan to fail, but create a great plan that excludes the possibility of failure. Do not allow family to coax you into a place of compromise. It is time for our families to follow *our* lead.

November 12: Look on the Bright Side

Our journeys have a lot to do with how we view our life. I am amazed at how many times gaining weight or failure on my health journey affected my attitude. Many times it was my own intense battle for success that dictated the face my friends and family "saw" daily. I hear from so many people as to how this day-to-day battle for health affects everything. I understand. Often the enemy of our soul wants people to embrace the lie that they are the only one struggling and there is no hope for victory. The Word of God declares in Psalm 34:19 (NLT), "The righteous person faces many troubles, but the Lord comes to the rescue each time." If we could only come to fully trust this promise it would absolutely affect our attitude.

Our families do not need to bear the brunt of our *bark*, which really says, "I'm hurting." When we respond in a negative manner we must grab that attitude, that face, that *bark* and sit back and let God's Word recalibrate our hearts and minds. Who wants to be the recipient of barking? Not me.

Yes, our health is important, but sometimes it becomes such a motivational drive that everything else suffers. This is not good. No, God's Word and His love have to be the driving force of our journey. God's Word brings a smile to my heart and a joy like none other.

I picked a Scripture today to share that made me smile. I like starting the day with a smile and I plan to remind myself of this verse every time I am tempted to allow life's journey to draw me away from this internal pocket of joy.

> *"And therefore the Lord [earnestly] waits [expecting, looking, and longing] to be gracious to you; and therefore He lifts Himself up, that He may have mercy on you and show loving-kindness to you. For the Lord is a God of justice. Blessed (happy, fortunate, to be envied) are all those who [earnestly] wait for Him, who expect and look and long for Him [for His victory, His favor, His love, His peace, His joy, and His matchless, unbroken companionship]!"* (Isaiah 30:18 AMP).

God expects, looks, and longs to be gracious to each of us. That is worth a smile. So today, when you are tempted to see your failures and start barking, choose to re-read the above verse and look on the bright side. Keep saying the second half of the verse and smile, "That is me. I am happy, fortunate, and to be envied because this day I earnestly wait for God and expect, look, and long for His joy, his favor, his love, his peace, his matchless, unbroken companionship." There is another, brighter side available. Choose well.

November 13: Healthy 4 You Green Beans

Yield: 12 servings

Ingredients

- 4 large cans Allen's green beans* (not the seasoned variety)
- 8 beef bouillon cubes
- 1-2 large Vidalia onions
- 3 tablespoons bacon bits (optional)

*Registerd trademark of Allen's, Inc.

Procedure

1. Place the green beans and juice in a large container on the stove. Start the beans on high.
2. Add the bouillon and whole, peeled onion. After the beans boil for about 5 minutes, lower the heat and continue cooking until the liquid is reduced, almost gone. I prefer only a small amount of liquid, but you may prefer more. If so, reduce the cooking time. Resist stirring until most of the liquid is gone, as the green beans and onion will get mushy. This takes about an hour.
3. If you are adding the bacon bits, do that the remaining 10 minutes.
4. As you serve, you could add a chunk of the cooked onion. It is sweet and flavor filled.

Per Serving:

Calories 54.7
Total Fat 0.4 g
Cholesterol 1.3 mg
Sodium 851.9 mg
Potassium 19.6 mg
Total Carbohydrate 9.7 g
Dietary Fiber 2.2 g
Sugars 4.0 g
Protein 2.6 g

November 14: Scalloped Jicama Au Gratin

Yield: 16 servings

Ingredients

- 2 large jicama
- 8 oz. cream cheese (room temperature)
- 1 16-oz. container light sour cream
- 1/2 regular container 99% fat free chicken stock, no MSG
- 4 oz. chopped ham (no sugar)
- TABASCO® to taste (I used 6-7 shakes)
- Salt to taste
- 1 medium onion, diced well
- 4 cups four blend Mexican cheese

Procedure

1. Peel the jicama.
2. Boil the jicama for an hour.
3. When completely cooled, shred the jicama with a potato peeler or mandolin into thin slices. I used a mandolin.
4. Preheat oven to 350°F.
5. Mix the cream cheese, sour cream, chicken stock, TABASCO®, ham, salt, and 2 cups of Mexican cheese.
6. Spray a large casserole-baking dish. Place ½ the jicama in the baking dish. Then add ½ the onions and cover with half the liquid cheese mixture. Repeat.
7. Add the remaining Mexican cheese to the top.
8. Bake for 45-60 minutes. The cheese needs to be browning well and bubbly. The jicama will remain crunchy; do not wait for it to become tender, it will not.

Per Serving:
Calories 228.5
Total Fat 18.1 g
Cholesterol 59.5 mg
Sodium 450.8 mg
Potassium 181.9 mg
Total Carbohydrate 5.4 g
Dietary Fiber 1.1 g
Sugars 1.0 g
Protein 11.2 g

November 15: Thank You, Lord

As we approach this large thirty-day window of parties and food preparation, thank the Lord for several things:

1. HIS help to bring restraining discipline when we want to taste someone's best cookie recipe.

2. HIS provision of healthy choices for us. I wonder sometimes if it is easier to bless our meal when it is unhealthy? Just asking? When it is what we want to eat as opposed to fish, which is rich in Omega 3's, is it easier to rejoice and be grateful?

3. HIS desire for us to walk in health and not our own motivation to be skinny so we can look like someone we want to be. Remember Psalm 139.

4. HIS creativity in the kitchen as we create recipes that are healthy, hearty, and yummy.

5. HIS provision to purchase healthy foods, as they tend to be more expensive.

6. HIS blinders that prevent us from accessing the fast food joints and allow us to head home for some lean protein and vegetables.

7. HIS taste for fruits daily that provide fiber and help lower our cholesterol.

8. HIS wisdom in all areas of our health journey.

These are just a few of the areas that came to my heart this morning. Can we confess these truths for the next thirty days and allow truth to encourage us? God's ways are higher than our ways and His thoughts are so much higher than ours. He is seated in a place far above and can see things we cannot. Let us embrace His perspective and allow it to bring success to us in this upcoming month. Remember, food is about refueling. It is not our source of pleasure, God is. Choose life these next thirty days and eat to live.

November 16: Smile Passages

There are many people who can speak into my life during times when I need to be steadied. How about you? But nothing stabilizes my soul like the power and truth that comes from reading the Bible. Sometimes people feel they cannot connect with certain facets of God's character and what they fail to do is view the entire Bible and see Who God really is. We can never make God be who we need; He is who He is. Yes, there are passages that seem scary or firm, but the Word is filled with redemption and God's desire to include us in His plan. It's not His intention to keep us in the dark or uninformed. This often breeds fear. His Word teaches that He did not give us a spirit of fear, but of power and love and a sound mind. Then God included this truth in His Word so that those of us like me who are visual learners could read and re-read to reconnect with that truth when the storms of life try to grab our peace.

The following passage is one of my smile passages. Do you have those? There are certain verses that cause me to lift my head, hands, and heart and say again, "Thank you, Father God."

> "Now concerning how and when all this will happen, dear brothers and sisters, we don't really need to write you. For you know quite well that the day of the Lord's return will come unexpectedly, like a thief in the night. When people are saying, "Everything is peaceful and secure," then disaster will fall on them as suddenly as a pregnant woman's labor pains begin. And there will be no escape.
>
> But you aren't in the dark about these things, dear brothers and sisters, and you won't be surprised when the day of the Lord comes like a thief. For you are all children of the light and of the day; we don't belong to darkness and night. So be on your guard, not asleep like the others. Stay alert and be clearheaded. Night is the time when people sleep and drinkers get drunk. But let us who live in the light be clearheaded, protected by the armor of faith and love, and wearing as our helmet the confidence of our salvation. For God chose to save us through our Lord Jesus Christ, not to pour out his anger on us. Christ died for us so that, whether we are dead or alive when he returns, we can live with him forever. So encourage each other and build each other up, just as you are already doing" (1 Thessalonians 5:1-11).

If you simply read verses 1-3 perhaps you might be fearful. But that picture is God giving a glimpse into the eternal plan in order that we are not in fear. But my smile passage comes in verses 4-11. Can you actually read that and not smile? God is declaring who we are and promising that when the world is suffering, we will be drawn to His side. Love that!

Be encouraged as this week ends to find your smile passages and write them out for those times when you need to stand firm.

November 17: Let God Pick Your Clothes

I pray this morning that you feel "chased down and overtaken" by the Spirit of the Lord. I know that God has great plans for each of us, to do good by us and never harm us (see Jeremiah 29:11). That is a great reason to give thanks this day. Can you stop for five minutes right now and start thanking the Lord for all your blessings? Do not ask for anything, just offer thanksgiving. Does that feel great?

Now, back to our devotion.

This morning I was thinking about how we clothe ourselves differently depending on seasons, activities, or the way we feel about our body. God's Word in Psalm 3:3 teaches that God is the shield around us. I immediately thought of Him being my clothing. When He is the shield wrapped around me and He becomes my clothing, any choice of personal clothing I might consider seems below par.

God clothed Adam and Eve in the garden when their choice for clothing was not a great one. They were hiding and ashamed. Sometimes when we have a bad day on our journey, we want to hide and are ashamed that we failed. We can become discouraged and everything around us is affected. My heart is always moved when the Lord will reveal that someone is hurting so badly due to poor health choices. I empathize to the one million mark. Psalm 3:3 concludes by saying that He is the glory and lifter of our head. I realize totally that we have a real choice in our health journey, but I also realize that God always desires to clothe us with His Spirit regardless of what we weigh or how we see ourselves.

We must do our part, yes, but we must never forget that the Holy Spirit is always ready to give us strength when we are weak and lift our heads when we feel we are trapped in this body of flesh. Be encouraged this day, family. God has your clothes picked out. Wear them well.

November 18: Braid It Three Times

As I was reading this morning in Ecclesiastes, this jumped out at me:

> "A person standing alone can be attacked and defeated, but two can stand back-to-back and conquer. Three are even better, for a triple-braided cord is not easily broken" (Ecclesiastes 4:12 NLT).

I know how critical being in a group and having someone as an accountability partner is to my health journey. Writing keeps me accountable to those who read my blog and devotions and perhaps they are not even aware that they served in that capacity. But what about this new twist? What if the three-stranded cord is us, the scale, and our blood reports several times a year? I like that. None of us really wants to be the one to announce, "You have gained a couple of pounds" to our best friend or sister. Awkward.

We will often do the good friend stuff which is bring some water, make a salad to share, comment when you look "thin," but the real truth tellers are the scale and the lab reports. Let me remind everyone to find a solid place within your journey where embracing truth is actually your friend and not your foe. In the past, when I knew I was having lab work done I prayed for any catastrophe that would keep me from having the exam. I knew what my mouth had consumed and I feared what that lab report was about to confirm. Failure—again.

Today, my perspective has forever been altered. Lab work—bring it on. Scales—bring it on. Smaller portions—bring it on. Truth—bring it on. These have now become my new best friends on my health journey.

As we think about being a strong cord let us repeat: "It is us, the scale, and the blood report." Yep, that is accountability and truth at its finest. I can always do better with the truth than a lie. Come clean, lay the cards on the table, and let me deal with the truth. If I never have an encounter with the truth, there is a chance real-life change is only a fleeting thought.

November 19: No Obligation

I especially love mornings while I have my Christmas tree decorated and lit. I love to read my Bible, drink coffee, and look at the lights. I guess the little girl in me lives on.

I am a firm believer that the journey of our health has a lot to do with our attitude—you know this. So many people live their lives with such a lackadaisical attitude that never compels them to stop settling for average. We know the routine. Successfully shed a few pounds, keep it off until the next feeding frenzy, and cave in. Repeat. Repeat. Repeat. Maybe you never did this, but if you find my picture in the dictionary, you will find this as part of my definition. And rather than admit I was undisciplined, I blamed this cycle on my body. Have you ever confessed, "Some people got the 'skinny gene' and I am destined to be fluffy." That was my regular retort (my close friends have heard this before).

My attitude said failure, my actions created failure, and my heart cried over failure. I had finally come into agreement with my flesh that this was my plight in life. But one phone call from my brother, Chip, turned my attitude around that January day in 2011. That call pointed me forward to this day. I want to speak to you again to quit settling. Your hope could be one phone call, one blog, or one revelation away. I wrote this morning in my notes, *"Eating healthy is our choice. The consequences of choosing to not eat healthy are not our choice."* Oh my goodness, such a divine revelation. Ponder that for a little while.

Our attitude often requires an adjustment, though, and we have to realize that our flesh is always at war with our spirit. Our spirit is being bombarded with an attitude of death. The Scripture says in Romans 8:12-13:

> "Therefore, dear brothers and sisters, you have no obligation to do what your sinful nature urges you to do. For if you live by its dictates, you will die. But if through the power of the Spirit you put to death the deeds of your sinful nature, you will live" (NLT).

This holiday season why don't we determine to have no obligation to our flesh with its sinful urges, making us free to choose health instead of death? Anyone with me? I am looking at this flesh today, as I have a party tonight, and saying, "I owe you no obligation. You will not be overfed, you will not be fed inappropriately, and you will not be allowed to dictate to me." This is war and I will win.

November 20: Pumpkin Cheesecake

Yield: 16 servings

This cake tastes better even the second and third day!

Crust:

Ingredients

- 2 cups almond flour
- 1/3 cup finely, chopped pecans
- 5 tablespoons butter melted
- 3 tablespoons xylitol

Procedure

1. Preheat oven to 325°F.
2. Mix together and press into the bottom of a 10-inch spring form pan.
3. Bake for 10-12 minutes.

Cake:

Ingredients

- 4 pkgs. light cream cheese
- 1 ½ cup xylitol
- 5 large eggs
- 1 teaspoon vanilla extract
- 1 ½ cups pumpkin
- 2 tablespoons pumpkin pie spice

Procedure

1. Beat cream cheese and xylitol.
2. Add eggs one at a time and beat thoroughly.
3. Add remaining ingredients and pour on top of crust.
4. Bake at 325 degrees for 70 minutes or until knife comes out clean in center. Make certain you bake this in a water bath. Often I will turn the heat off, open the door slightly and allow to cool for 30 minutes.
5. Cool an additional hour or two, then wrap and cool in refrigerator for 8-24 hours.

Per Serving:

Calories 284.9
Total Fat 22.7 g
Cholesterol 44.7 mg
Sodium 328.9 mg
Potassium 83.3 mg
Total Carbohydrate 19.0 g
Dietary Fiber 2.1 g
Sugars 3.0 g
Protein 7.5 g

November 21: Pumpkin Spice Cake

Yield: 24 servings

Ingredients

- 1 stick light butter
- 1 8-oz. pkg. light cream cheese
- 1 cup xylitol
- 5 eggs
- 2 ½ cups almond flour
- 1 can pumpkin (no spices or sugar)
- ½ cup chopped pecans
- 2 tablespoons pumpkin pie spice
- 2 tablespoons baking powder
- 1 teaspoon lemon extract (optional)
- 1 ½ teaspoon vanilla extract

Procedure

1. Preheat oven to 350°F.
2. Cream butter and xylitol.
3. Add eggs, one at a time, beating after each.
4. Mix flour with baking powder in separate bowl.
5. Add flour a little at a time to liquid mixture while beating.
6. Add pumpkin, pecans, and spices.
7. Add extract(s), beat again.
8. Pour or scrape with spatula into 9x13 greased baking pan.
9. Bake 30-35 min. or until cake is firm in center and toothpick inserted in center comes out clean.

Pumpkin Spice Cream Cheese Frosting

Ingredients

- 2 8-oz pkgs. light cream cheese at room temperature
- 1 cup xylitol
- 2 tablespoons pumpkin pie spice
- 1 teaspoon vanilla extract
- 1 cup pecans

Procedure

Whip the cream cheese and xylitol together. Add the pumpkin pie spice and vanilla. Frost a cooled cake and top with pecans. If this is not sweet enough for you, increase the xylitol by half a cup.

Per Serving: (Cake)
Calories 171.0
Total Fat 13.9 g
Cholesterol 50.2 mg
Sodium 137.1 mg
Potassium 86.6 mg
Total Carbohydrate 10.4 g
Dietary Fiber 1.9 g
Sugars 1.3 g
Protein 4.8 g

Per Serving: (Frosting)
Calories 95.1
Total Fat 7.6 g
Cholesterol 13.3 mg
Sodium 73.5 mg
Potassium 21.9 mg
Total Carbohydrate 7.5 g
Dietary Fiber 0.5 g
Sugars 0.9 g
Protein 1.8 g

November 22: Build That Wall

I appreciate all of you who work diligently each day to read labels, menus, and check vitamins. Who knew some vitamins have sugar and starch in them? I know it seems like a big task sometimes, but when you successfully complete your first year of health, it will be worth it. I promise. I know that Nehemiah must have thought building a wall in fifty-two days was impossible, but he trusted God and was not intimidated by the masses. He never allowed obstacles to keep him from seeing his vision completed. I wonder if we genuinely have a vision of ourselves being healthy? In the beginning of 2011, before I had my life-changing breakthrough, I put post-it notes everywhere that read, "What does a size ten look like?" Guess what size I am today?

People will tell you that life cannot be lived successfully without cheating. I hear it all the time—"everyone cheats." Does that have to be true of us? Cannot *everyone* refer to everyone *else*? If someone opens the door one crack and looks at a pornographic site, it may push them into a journey they never intended to walk. Is that one cheat worth it? That is why we guard our virtue, guard every day against that one cheat.

It is not fear that motivates us to protect our health, but the truth that our bodies are the temple of the Holy Spirit and He deserves the best we can give Him. He cannot use us *as effectively* when we are riddled with weight-induced diseases. Right? I am determined, like Nehemiah, to see my life rebuilt and restored to the fullest. I will post guards, put up safety boundaries, and fight for my life to be the best it can be. Our bodies were designed by God to repair themselves, but we must give them every opportunity to do so.

Start rebuilding your wall today and refuse to listen to one negative thought. Rebuild it and rebuild it better.

November 23: What's in Your Cell?

I imagine being a pastor has everything to do with me loving testimonies. Revelation 12:11 (AMP) reveals, "And they have overcome (conquered) him by means of the blood of the Lamb and by the utterance of their testimony, for they did not love and cling to life even when faced with death."

I feel we can gain some helpful insight from this passage this morning. First, in Jesus we are overcomers. The passage reminds us that the blood of the Lamb, which gives us our personal relationship with Jesus, also gives us victory over the enemy, as well as victory over the power of sin and death. Second, by declaring the word of our testimony, which is an out loud experience, professing that we accept Jesus as our personal Savior, we deepen the overcomer's journey. The truth of God's Word spoken over our circumstances brings victory. This includes rehearsing the fact that God has never been late, been deficient, lied, or failed us. We recite our victory testimonies, or the testimonies of others, because it gives us strength and renewed confidence in our relationship with God. I feel like preaching this morning!

One Sunday morning I told a young woman I am mentoring that she better open her mouth and declare her testimony so that every demonic weapon coming against her can hear the truth about being an overcomer. Our words are powerful. I wonder if we really understand or believe that confessing and declaring God's Word from our mouth is as powerful as if it were proceeding from His mouth. It is the same Word-His Word! The Word has life; the Word has hope; the Word has power. Open your mouth, speak the truth, and remind yourself that God has never failed you and never will. That is what overcomers proclaim.

When you walk out of that prison cell, put your excuses and your ability to cheat in that same cell, lock the door, and destroy the key. We overcome because Jesus' blood gives us the right to open the cell, leave the cell, and never return, whatever the cell is. I know this book is about health, but pastorally, Jesus' blood gives us victory over sin and death in whatever cell we need. Amen.

November 24: God Is Always Merciful

"Give thanks to the LORD, for he is good! His faithful love endures forever. Let all Israel repeat: 'His faithful love endures forever.' Let Aaron's descendants, the priests, repeat: 'His faithful love endures forever.' Let all who fear the LORD repeat: 'His faithful love endures forever.' In my distress I prayed to the LORD, and the LORD answered me and set me free. The LORD is for me, so I will have no fear. What can mere people do to me? Yes, the LORD is for me; he will help me. I will look in triumph at those who hate me. It is better to take refuge in the LORD than to trust in people. It is better to take refuge in the LORD than to trust in princes. Though hostile nations surrounded me, I destroyed them all with the authority of the LORD. Yes, they surrounded and attacked me, but I destroyed them all with the authority of the LORD. They swarmed around me like bees; they blazed against me like a crackling fire. But I destroyed them all with the authority of the LORD. My enemies did their best to kill me, but the LORD rescued me. The LORD is my strength and my song; he has given me victory. Songs of joy and victory are sung in the camp of the godly. The strong right arm of the LORD has done glorious things! The strong right arm of the LORD is raised in triumph. The strong right arm of the LORD has done glorious things! I will not die; instead, I will live to tell what the LORD has done" (Psalm 118:1-17 NLT).

I don't know about you, but when I read that passage I get excited. As I talked about in yesterday's devotion, the Word of God has such power. I would be shocked if any of us could read this and not feel encouraged. And, when you read the word *nations* listed above, I want you to insert *anything*—any obstacle that is surrounding you trying to keep you from being healthy. What are *your* nations that surround you? List them somewhere on this page.

I had a list of nations, but one by one they were destroyed as my body repaired and I began to stand on the foundation of health. I give thanksgiving to God for His steadfast help. I encourage you to read the passage again every time you feel you are going to fail. What does the passage say happened to the nations? You must come to know this truth intimately. And remember, it is not true for me alone, but for each of you as well. Close those doors and declare, "God is always merciful."

November 25: Big-Boned People

I got another great report from my OB/GYN doctor yesterday and also some eye-opening news. As you know my weight is stable and if I gain a pound or so, I jump on the losing wagon until that is gone. But I still have not been able to get that last ten off. At the doctor yesterday, my blood pressure was excellent (110/70) my iron count was excellent (15) but my weight, according to their charts, was still four pounds in the overweight category for my height. At first I was very bitterly disappointed.

When the physician's assistant came in to examine me, she was one happy lady. She kept congratulating me and finally I said, "I really thought I was not overweight any longer." She flipped back to my chart and smirked, "Listen, this time last year you were at the top end of obese for your height and now you are at the bottom end of overweight. That is unheard of for us." So, I perked up a wee bit. I am really determined now to get myself to the normal range.

After she and I discussed the ranges and how each contributes to medical health, I felt validated for a minute. The medical profession (according to what she told me yesterday) opts for the bottom end of the groupings (obese, overweight, normal) as they believe that weight has so much influence with regard to chronic illness and disease. (I also believe that.) But for me to be at the bottom end of the normal range for my height, I would have to lose forty additional pounds. Did I really just type that? I have determined doctors must see skinny as healthy and have no compassion for "big-boned" people.

The bottom line is that I want to be healthy and if I have a few pounds to go to get to the "normal" range, I simply do. I had to remind myself that the days of making excuses are over. I hope you are all going to the doctor and having those check-ups regularly. Especially as we age, it's important to stay on top of everything. Today I will set my scope on those four pounds and wrestle those boys to the mat. Yes I will.

November 26: Eating at the Royal Palace

I was reading in Daniel chapter 1 yesterday and could see our lives lived out through that story. The Hebrew boys were given the choice food and the King's portions. For us that could be Thanksgiving dinner and eating whatever we want. Daniel could have agreed to do that for a season, but from the beginning he knew it was not the best choice for them. How many of you know that sometimes we have to make a stand among the *royalty and expectations* of the household? Daniel asked permission to eat differently and the results amazed everyone.

It is okay for us to say to our families, "I have made a decision to eat more healthy, and is it okay for me to bring_____?" Some people will understand, some will be threatened because you are challenging their meal plan, and some may be jealous because they wish they had your strength to make healthy choices. Remember, some may be in prison, as I was, and desperately desire freedom, but have abandoned all hope of life beyond the torture of obesity. There could be a number of responses and it is okay. Nobody can fight for your health more valiantly than you.

I heard someone comment yesterday, while I was at a huge luncheon, "Overeating is what I live for. I plan to gain ten pounds between now and the end of the year. I do it every year and I will deal with it in January." I did that for many, many years, but as I got older I never made it out of that ten-pound bondage suit I added by stuffing the hole in my face. It seemed that following every holiday season I was older, less active, riddled with affliction, depressed, and a complete failure. No, never again. This Thanksgiving I chose turkey, almond flour stuffing, celery, pumpkin pecan spice cake with cream cheese icing (all sugar-free), and water. I was so happy. I met a friend at a coffee shop and skipped the large, extra hot pumpkin spice latte with extra whip. I actually had a bottle of water. And guess what, I had a great time without the sugar and calories!

We can have a healthy life—every ounce of it—and not feel guilty. I can have Thanksgiving and Christmas dinners with my family and choose life. I can attend parties and choose life. I can meet at a coffee shop and choose life. How about you? Can we do this together? Yes, we can.

November 27: Pumpkin Pound Cake

Yield: 12 servings

Ingredients

- *1 stick light butter
- *1 8-oz pkg. light cream cheese
- *1 cup of xylitol
- 5 eggs at room temperature
- 1 15-oz can plain pumpkin
- 1 teaspoon baking powder
- 1 teaspoon pumpkin pie spice
- 2 tablespoons vanilla, butter, and nut extract (That is a combo extract, not individual extracts. If your grocer does not carry this, use one teaspoon each of vanilla, butter, and black walnut flavorings.)
- 3 cups almond flour
  * Room temperature

Procedure

1. Preheat oven to 350°F.
2. Cream together top three items.
3. Add eggs one at a time, beating well after addition.
4. Add extract and blend.
5. Add dry ingredients and mix well.
6. Spray a 9 x 13 inch baking dish or Bundt pan and pour batter into pan.
7. Bake for 50-55 min.
8. Use a toothpick placed in the center to determine if cake is done. Cool completely before cutting.

Per Serving:

Calories 267.1
Total Fat 20.6 g
Cholesterol 100.4 mg
Sodium 273.5 mg
Potassium 124.7 mg
Total Carbohydrate 18.6 g
Dietary Fiber 2.7 g
Sugars 2.0 g
Protein 8.7 g

November 28: Strawberry Cake

Yield: 24 servings

You could also use this recipe to make 12-16 cupcakes.

Ingredients

- *1 stick light butter
- *1 8-oz. pkg. light cream cheese
- *1 ½ cup of xylitol
- 5 eggs at room temperature
- 2 teaspoons baking powder
- 3 teaspoons almond flavoring
- 16-oz. bag frozen, sugar-free strawberries (thawed, drained, and mashed)
- 1 regular box sugar-free strawberry gelatin
- 3 cups almond flour
  * Room temperature

Procedure

1. Preheat oven to 350°F.
2. Cream together top three items.
3. Add eggs one at a time, beating well after each addition.
4. Add extract, mashed strawberries, and blend well.
5. Whisk dry ingredients and add to strawberry mixture.
6. Spray a 9x13 pan and add cake mixture
7. Bake for 45-50 min.
8. Use a toothpick placed in the center to determine if cake is done. Cool completely before cutting. Watch the cake as almond flour burns easily.

Strawberry Icing

Ingredients:

- 2 pkgs. light cream cheese
- 1 small container fat free plain Greek yogurt
- 1 container fresh strawberries, washed, dried, and chopped
- 2 teaspoons strawberry extract
- 1 ½ cups xylitol

Procedure:

1. Cream the xylitol and cream cheese.
2. Add the yogurt and extract. Blend well.
3. Gently fold in the strawberries to reduce the addition of liquid from them.
4. Frost cake when completely cooled. Store in refrigerator until used.

Per Serving:
(Includes the cake and icing)
Calories 221.5
Total Fat 13.7 g
Cholesterol 32.7 mg
Sodium 211.2 mg
Potassium 71.1 mg
Total Carbohydrate 26.1 g
Dietary Fiber 2.1 g
Sugars 3.3 g
Protein 5.5 g

November 29: A Size Ten?

What a great morning to not have to go outside. I was reading a little devotional for women this morning and the woman writing said when she was young her father used to do an exercise with her where he would start a phrase and she would complete it. One of her favorites was, "A wise woman…" and she would say, "has a servant's heart." I know we are not all women in this family, but I do know we could all rehearse statements that encourage and shape us. For example, what if we were to train our children and ourselves to say, "Eating healthy…" and their reply, "is not an option." Or we say, "Choose life…" and they reply, "and eat to live."

Sometimes silly little statements are just that to us—silly. I remember on January 1st of 2011, while at my heaviest weight, I started writing sticky notes and asking myself for days, *"What does a size ten feel like?"* I mentioned this in a recent chapter and when I first started scripting, it was a very silly statement. I wrote that question in ten different places. I had no clue what I was to do, how to start, or what the plan was? I simply knew I was in prison and desperate. However, God knew. And the more I confessed, the more confident I became that God had a plan. Three weeks later, my brother, Chip, and I made the determination to break free together, and the rest is not just history but victory.

All of us wage war in our minds. That is often where the most intense battles occur. However, I could not just ask myself about being a size ten. I had to believe, confess, confess again, bring my thoughts under subjection, remind my flesh, "You're not the boss of me," determine that cheating was not an option, and fight and claw my way to a place of touching truth and gaining my freedom. I also had to be realistic about my health. I am never going to be a size two. Ever. I had dieted enough to know what the real picture was for me. Being healthy cannot be about what size we wear. This was a hard battle for me. Somehow I determined if I could reach a size two, it would mean victory. That was based off vain imaginations, not reality.

Can one statement really declare freedom? Absolutely, yes. "I believe that you are the Christ, the son of the living God" is one statement that proclaims freedom for generations (see Matthew 16:16). For us, "Choose life and eat to live" is only one statement. However, if we understand that eating is a choice—our choice—and that eating correctly promotes health and not "being skinny," there is dynamo-type power in that one statement.

November 30: November Reflection Page

As you are completing November, are there things you wish you had highlighted or which you had written down? Can you write out the many thanks you owe God at the conclusion of this month?

_____

_____

_____

_____

_____

_____

_____

_____

_____

_____

_____

_____

_____

_____

_____

_____

_____

_____

_____

_____

December

It is the close of this year and you did it! You worked through twelve months of devotionals and recipes. My prayer is that you have gained freedom and your hope has been restored. God is the answer.

God was the answer, He is the answer, and He will forever be the answer. I pray your Christmas is healthy and the best ever.

December 1: The Most Wonderful Time of the Year

Christmas songs always produce smiles and laughter as people toss fake snow in the air and take rides on sleighs drawn by white horses. Yes, Christmas is wonderful. And yes, Christmas is my most favorite time of the year. However, Christmas was the season where I was the most out of control and looked daily for places to hide.

I am grateful to have now completed my first sugar-free Christmas, and might I say, "It was glorious." I was not certain what to expect, as this is a season of sharing the best of the best desserts, the richest of the candies, and journeying from one party to the next one hundred. With every passing event that I navigated successfully, the holiday became even more my favorite. I do not think I ever really connected with just how powerful the feeling of success can be.

Each successful encounter provided enough challenge to draw from creative inspiration I never knew I had. I took healthy desserts to parties that amazed my friends and were consumed while the *real* ones remained on the tables. What? For the first time I was reprimanded for making excuses about bringing healthy foods. What? Why was I defending my food? I had no clue, but my friend reminded me that I am free and no justification for my holiday contributions was necessary. I almost cried. Can life be this good? Absolutely. This time next year, you will be sending me testimonies of your Christmas victory dances.

God's Spirit is alive in us and He holds the keys to life, success, creativity, and all else. He offers His best plan for each of us when we really do not deserve it. I have never been so in love. I love God dearly and I love my new life. Can you tell? This can be you in a short period of time; I promise.

I pause this Christmas, with tears as I type, to give honor to my heavenly Father who has allowed me to create, share, invite others into my story, and be so faithful to offer me His hand again and again. Every recipe and every devotion was inspired by God and He allowed me to share them with you. Merry Christmas, family!

December 2: A Christmas Announcement, Part 1

I have heard the proclamation by Gabriel of the birth of Christ labeled as the *Christmas Announcement*. But it was so much more and so far reaching. Following the book of Malachi, God remained silent with no communication to humankind for four hundred years. God chose to break the silence by speaking to Zechariah through the angel as recorded in Luke 1, "Do not be afraid, for your prayer has been answered" (see Luke 1:12). However, Zechariah refused to believe and was silenced by God until the birth of his son.

God reaches out again in Luke 1:30-31 as He directs the angel to speak to the Virgin Mary, "Do not be afraid, Mary, for you have found favor with God. And behold, you will conceive in your womb and bring forth a Son, and shall call His name Jesus" (NKJV). Although Mary had questions as to how this miracle would occur, she trusted God when the reality of her faith could cost her very life. Her response to the announcement was quite different than Zechariah's had been. She replied, "Let it be to me according to your word" (Luke 1:38 NKJV). Finally, with Gabriel's announcement to the shepherds in Luke 2, God not only speaks to humankind once again, but ushers in a new covenant through the birth announcement of His only Son, Jesus. This glorious encounter declared good news and joy for people everywhere and for all generations.

Can you stop and smile as you really connect with the announcement that God, the Creator of the universe, sent a message of good news, joy, and hope that would include all of our names? Gabriel was speaking our names in that revelation. Before God created the world, He knew us (see Psalm 139). He knew He would have Gabriel announce to *all people,* and God knew we would be comforted knowing we were included.

The shepherds were afraid; you know the story, but I would probably be afraid also. I do not imagine, however, it took those boys too long to realize they were engulfed by something they could not explain nor dared to try—God's purpose and eternal love. They, too, responded well to the announcement and left immediately to find the promised joy. Can you imagine what their hearts must have felt?

I want to tell you that God sent that announcement as a decree of freedom—their freedom and our freedom. God knew we would need a plan for freedom and He created one. Take that today on whatever level you need. We will finish the story tomorrow.

December 3: A Christmas Announcement, Part 2

For us, Galatians 5:1 declares our freedom from the chains of past addictions, bondage, and wrong thinking. Paul makes a grand announcement in this verse, minus the "fear not." His message was one of great encouragement and hope as well. In fact, the entire Bible is a book of announcements, isn't it? God's heart has always been to fellowship and dialogue with His creation. We see this clearly through His visitations with Adam in the garden in the cool of the night. Can you imagine walking with God in a garden of paradise? Heaven will be our turn for such splendor.

Sometimes we can be fearful about getting through the holidays and doing well on our health journey. These six weeks often pose such a challenge. I am so proud of one of our group members as she announced the other day, "I'm losing weight over the holidays." Now that is a Christmas announcement, too, with no fear involved! That statement says, "I am free to enjoy the holidays and I have a plan." Do not wait until January 2nd to renew your commitment to health. Be careful as six weeks of undisciplined eating can equate to a deep hole as the New Year begins.

This Christmas I want to bring forth *this* announcement (a Kathy paraphrase), "Fear not, for behold I bring you a good message of great hope. There is freedom for you, which is found in Christ alone. The Holy Spirit will come and live within you and He shall assist you in making healthy choices and walking in freedom." I am always grateful to receive messages that offer help and assistance.

Following the announcement, we have an opportunity to respond. Will we respond as Zechariah did and deny the power of God, or will we accept, by faith, God's help and respond as Mary did? Let us each rejoice this Christmas that we are stronger than obesity, and may we respond that we will "stand firm, then, and will no longer allow ourselves to be burdened for the hundredth time with a yoke of slavery."

Enjoy Christmas, love your family, attend all the parties, and take your food. That is the beginning of Christmas presents for you.

December 4: A Masterpiece on My Plate

I love color; how about you? One of the reasons I love Christmas so dearly is all the color, the lights, and the decorations. Color, color everywhere. Beyond Christmas, I love color on my body, clothes, in my house, in my yard, and now on my plate. Remember, you cannot eat the same exact veggie or fruit every meal even though you love it. Our bodies need differing nutrients from a variety of fruits and vegetables.

I challenge you to examine your plate before every meal. Is it colorful? Is it a repeat of last meal? Yesterday? That is not your best health plan. God gave us beautiful foods with rich colors, so let us explore some different ones. For example, I found a purple potato. While I do not eat potatoes, I know some of you do. According to my research these purple creatures are low in sugar and rich in antioxidants. Great combo. Keep reading, searching, and asking God to place you in the markets carrying the freshest and most colorful foods.

I am trying diligently to have the most colorful plate at each meal to reflect my Christmas decor. It is a personal challenge to me. However, there are some foods I simply cannot eat regardless of their beautiful colors. Beets. What was God thinking? I know beets are such a beautiful color and packed with great nutrition, but I cannot go there. Sorry, I did not get that anointing. While we are working diligently to add color though, let us not forget to vary our textures as well. I also try to vary cooked and non-cooked vegetables on a daily basis simply as a matter of change. Change is good; it helps to keep us from getting bored.

Change things up, create a masterpiece on each plate, and explore all the beautiful foods God gave you. Just as you would never feed an infant the same food all the time, we need to feed our cells (which feed our organs, which keep us healthy) various colors so they maintain their health and accomplish their purpose. Perhaps our Christmas gift to our cells would be beautifully crafted and colorful plates each meal. Merry Christmas, cells.

December 5: Be It unto Me

I want to take another look at the Virgin Mary's story from the aspect of addressing fear.

In the first chapter of Luke, the angel Gabriel says, "Fear not" three times. Why? Perhaps because our flesh is weak and we are very familiar with our own failure and the multitude of times we have failed to trust God's words. The fear of failure, fear of man, and fear of rejection live at the top of our lists for most of our lives. We must remember that the emotion of fear is not stronger than we are. Our plans, our resolve, our information, and our trust in God are really more powerful than fear. The problem occurs when fear is the loudest voice we hear, as it is often the one being fed most frequently.

I find that when I understand the circumstances that often provoke fear, I am less likely to allow this emotion to gain control. Understanding does not mean I will never battle fear, but it allows me to stand firm more times than not. I find that when my resolve is steady and I have not broken trust or strayed from the path, I am stronger and less afraid that I could return to my old, unhealthy habits. How about you? Fear is real and powerful, always provoking a response. And if we do not respond well, it can control the outcome of our journey. God shared with me once, *"Courage is not the absence of fear; it's trusting God in the presence of fear."*

Can you imagine the fear Mary must have felt? *A baby...a virgin...the Holy Spirit will over shadow me?* She was most likely very afraid. Yet her response, "Behold the maidservant of the Lord! Let it be to me according to your word" (Luke 1:38 NKJV), suggests that her trust in God was greater than her fear. I wonder how many of us would have responded in the same manner? I may have run at the sound of Gabriel's voice but definitely asked a few more questions as death was certainly in the realm of Mary's possibility.

Many events are positioned in front of me the next three weeks, and sometimes I feel myself getting a little fearful about trying to navigate three events in one day and fuel my body well during this season. However, I refuse to let my emotions control me. Mary was basically saying, *my emotions do not understand, but my spirit will submit to your plan.* We cannot live by our emotions or the parties that entice us to eat. No, the Holy Spirit gives us wisdom to make the right choices and follow the plan one day at a time. When He says no, we say, "Let it be to me according to your word."

December 6: Cheesy Cheddar Drop Biscuits

Yield: 12 servings

Ingredients

- ½ cup light butter, melted
- 2/3 cup almond flour
- 4 eggs
- ¼ teaspoon salt
- ¼ teaspoon onion powder
- ¼ teaspoon garlic powder
- ¼ teaspoon baking powder
- ¼ teaspoon cayenne pepper
- ½ teaspoon parsley
- 1 cup sharp cheddar cheese, shredded (white or yellow)
- ½ cup Parmesan Reggiano

Per Serving:

Calories 136.7
Total Fat 11.7 g
Cholesterol 68.6 mg
Sodium 215.5 mg
Potassium 59.4 mg
Total Carbohydrate 2.0 g
Dietary Fiber 0.9 g
Sugars 0.3 g
Protein 7.2 g

Procedure

1. Preheat oven to 400°F.
2. Blend together eggs, butter, salt, and all spices.
3. Combine flour with baking powder and whisk into batter until there are no lumps.
4. Fold in cheeses.
5. Grease mini-muffin tins or larger ones if preferred and distribute the batter. I prefer the minis.
6. Bake for 15-18 minutes. The biscuits should be brown and bubbly.

December 7: German Chocolate Cake

Yield: 24 servings

Ingredients

- 4 ounces unsweetened chocolate (4 squares)
- ½ cup water
- 2 cups almond flour
- 1 teaspoon baking soda
- ½ teaspoon salt
- ½ lb. light butter at room temperature
- 1 teaspoon clear, vanilla extract
- 1 ½ cups xylitol
- ½ cup brown sugar (Whey Low® for diabetics)
- 4 eggs, separated
- 1 cup buttermilk

Procedure

1. Preheat the oven to 325°F.
2. Melt the chocolate squares in the microwave. (Be extremely careful as I burned myself badly when the chocolate melted through a small plastic bowl I used, which *was* microwave safe.) Blend well, add the water, and blend again. Allow to cool as you continue.
3. Mix the almond flour, baking soda, and salt in a separate bowl.
4. Cream together the butter, vanilla extract, xylitol, and brown sugar (Whey Low®) until light and fluffy.
5. Add egg yolks one at a time, beating well after each addition.
6. Blend in the melted chocolate and add the flour mixture and buttermilk, alternating, until just combined.
7. Beat the egg whites until stiff peaks form. Gently fold the whites into the batter.
8. Pour the batter evenly into a greased 13x9-in. baking dish.
9. Bake until a toothpick inserted into the center of the cake comes out clean, about 70-75 minutes.

Per Serving:
Calories 277.1
Total Fat 22.1 g
Cholesterol 46.7 mg
Sodium 192.1 mg
Potassium 123.4 mg
Total Carbohydrate 23.4 g
Dietary Fiber 3.1 g
Sugars 5.6 g
Protein 5.8 g

Frosting

Ingredients

- 1 cup xylitol
- 1 cup evaporated milk
- 1/2 cup butter
- 3 egg yolks, lightly beaten
- 1 teaspoon vanilla extract
- 2 1/2 cups flaked, unsweetened coconut (I used 2 bags frozen.)
- 1 1/2 cup chopped pecans

Procedure

1. Combine the sugar, milk, butter, and egg yolks.
2. Cook and stir over medium-low heat until thickened and a thermometer reads 160°F or is thick enough to coat the back of a metal spoon. Remove from the heat.
3. Stir in vanilla, fold in coconut and pecans.
4. Allow the frosting to cool for about 15 minutes and distribute on the cooled cake.

December 8: Kailey's Story

I have been studying the book and character of Philemon this morning and lost track of time. It's a great book if you need some words of encouragement. It caught my attention that Paul writes in Philemon 1:7 (NLT), "Your love has given me much joy and comfort, my brother, for your kindness has often refreshed the hearts of God's people." Would you love that to be said of you? Maybe this story will refresh your heart today.

In late July 2012, my granddaughter Kailey's blood sugar level was very high and she had gained seventeen pounds in four months. We were told she would either need to lose a good amount of weight and modify her foods, or perhaps start insulin. This was difficult news for our family. But God had a plan. Kailey, who was only nine at the time, started mirroring my health plan. She was my first child to coach and I am *over the moon* proud of her. I do bake yummies for her every couple of weeks, cook a big, healthy meal once a week, and talk her through some tough situations. But Kailey has embraced this journey and is committed to being a healthy teen. Her mom makes healthy lunches now, and Kailey is so disciplined. She never strays—never.

After only four short months, Kailey got to do the victory dance. Yesterday she went for her check-up and since the 29th of July, she has lost and kept off twenty pounds, her blood sugar level was back to normal (although still on the high end of normal so we still need to tweak a few things), and her body fat ratio was significantly diminished. Again, she was only nine. Can you say *proud*?

There were tears at times, and it does require that Teree and I cook special, shop special, and buy special. But here is another life that has been rescued from insulin. Her birthday is in this month and she is asking for a sugar-free cake. What child does that? *A child who has learned early that her health is more critical than any birthday cake.* Helping Kailey Noel achieve success with her health goals is my greatest birthday gift to her for this year. It brings tears to my eyes. Kailey, if you read this, Nina is so proud of you. I could ride the tallest roller coaster and smile the whole time because you are my hero.

If you have kids, they can change. Kailey even challenges me now. Sometimes I might want to offer her additional food, as her plate had a lot of empty spaces before dinner began. I might ask if she wants something else and often she responds, "No Nina, I have had enough." Go Kailey!

December 9: Christmas Lights

Do you love it when everyone has their Christmas lights up and the neighborhood is flooded with beautiful, colored lights that pierce through the darkness? I am such a light girl. Keep the darkness, give me the light. As we were driving home last night, it was easy to spot the lights in the dark. The lights make a bold statement from deep within the trees and proudly from the rooftops as they shine and bring a smile to my face. However, until they have been powered up, they remain hidden. That is basic science.

With no power or energy source, the lights never fulfill their purpose. I like to apply that to us. Often when we experience negative emotions about ourselves or about the fact that we have made poor health choices, we want to hide. I was comfy in my house, on my sofa, in my baggy clothes. Those were days when it was easier to stay in the cave and feel good about myself, as opposed to being in a group and being slapped with the reality that I was obese and sick.

I am a realist; I'm sorry. One bad gathering seemed to fuel the lie that I would never be free and send me into hiding. *Lights unplugged.* Eventually though, I had to stand strong on the truth of my new health, which caused me to start illuminating at parties and events, as opposed to making excuses as to why I could not attend. *Lights plugged in.* We all face opportunities to make excuses. Occasionally we can start to rationalize that it could be okay to remain *unplugged* for a couple of weeks during the holidays. Is it really? Remember, our lights help everyone else smile, see the truth, and feel the warmth. We can never tell how many people are really looking for the beautiful lights in "our health yard."

Have you ever considered that taking healthy lunches and healthy snacks to events and functions could remind your friends and families that *someone* is lighting the path to health, and if they choose to start down that long, often unlit path, your light could be their path maker? That is a really deep thought today, I know. Anyway, let your light shine this season. Make a stand for health and offer those who are suffering and in prison real hope that they can enjoy the holidays and parties while eating nutritious, tasty foods.

Have you ever thought of your successful health journey as Christmas lights? Come on, get *plugged in* and let your light shine.

December 10: Getting My Rain On

I was thinking about the devastation that lack of water is bringing to our nation. I read somewhere that it would take nine feet of snow in some portions of the north to begin to support the spring run-off needed to bring health to the land. As I drove to south Georgia this past Saturday to take my mom to Historic Westville for her birthday, my attention was dragged time and time again to the destitute plight of the land suffering due to a lack of water. Ponds and small lakes were dried almost completely. Docks were sitting on the dry ground and ugly, parched land with pitiful weeds peeked out to inform me that death was near.

I looked and wondered, *Is that what our internal organs do when starved for water? Does my body shrivel and die from the inside out, longing for one small hydration pocket?* I would say absolutely yes. Here is the bad part of the story: our bodies cannot hydrate themselves any more than the dried and dying ponds can rain on themselves. They are totally dependent on water to arrive from an outside source. I wonder if a lack of hydration causes our internal organs to fight for their lives as they sense death as well. Do they display the same picturesque symptoms as the dying lakes and ponds?

Have you noticed the way the ponds and lakes around you appear when in a deep season of drought? If not, try to summon an image. If yes, then use that mental reminder to remember that God created our bodies utilizing 75 percent water. When we fail to water our bodies, they become shriveled, dry, and pitiful, which is comparable to what we are experiencing around us today.

We cannot create rain, nor can we make the heavens release rain to the earth. But, we can water our bodies. We do have control over that situation. Take a look today and ask the Lord to allow the natural pictures of the earth to remind you that watering your body changes everything. I pray these *real* pictures of a drought-stricken land make a real and lasting impression on each of us. I am getting my rain on as we speak by flooding my body with water all day long.

December 11: The Gift of Health

When I walked into the staff meeting yesterday there was a huge box. Although it was my birthday, I certainly never assumed it was for me. Did I mention it was huge? Anyway, when I was instructed to open the box the water began to run from my eyes. I had been considering one of these mixers for several months and there it was in my favorite red. After the tears slowed down, the *real* truth emerged. The gift was purchased for me, but was for the benefit of the staff, as they know I love to cook *for them*. I get it.

Since then I have been continuously baking, as it is so much easier with my new toy. The first recipe I created and utilized with my gift is actually in this book. It is the strawberry cake with cream cheese icing. I considered naming it after the staff who so richly blessed me. However, I could not find a cool name that combined the terms strawberry and staff.

Anyway, 'tis the season of gift giving, yes? I don't know about you but I spend a lot of resources on gifts each year during this season. Some of those gifts serve nothing more than for me to see the smile in the eyes of my family. I get that. But I have begun to long for more from the gifts I give. I want the smile, but I want the gift to have meaning. I want the gift to have a legacy. Perhaps that is due to my age?

Can I recommend a legacy gift for you and your family? What about the gift of health? Perhaps you could consider making a healthy cake with which to bless someone? Could you make some sugar-free whipped cream, purchase a pound of coffee, and add a small box of Truvia® to create a fabulous gift bag? You can never tell who will grab that creative, healthy gift and decide that you are their hero. Wouldn't it be hilarious if every gift under our tree were a healthy food item? Maybe *unpopular* would be a more realistic term? Years ago healthy foods were given as gifts, but I think my grandchildren would revolt if I was to experiment with this concept during Christmas. Great thought though.

As you wrap those gifts to make your family and friends smile, remember a toy may break, new clothes will wear out, but helping someone realize that eating healthy may add years to their life could be the single greatest gift they ever received. Does that make you feel good?

Happy gift giving! And by the way, thanks to my staff for giving me a birthday gift that benefits my health. I will share with you from my bounty!

December 12: Merry Christmas to Us!

I often wonder why the "holiday creator person" (whoever lines up the holidays) would link Halloween, Thanksgiving, and Christmas within a six-week period? That is just wrong. I have considered that whoever made this determination must have never battled the "Christmas ten." When I say battle, that may be a wrong phrase. Many never aspire to battle their weight through *any* holiday of the year. They simply embrace the cliché, "Eat today, for tomorrow may never come." I have decided *skinny people* write that kind of stuff. Not only do *skinny people* write crazy stuff like that, they lie. Eating today absolutely affects tomorrow.

Of course we have two ways to consider how our eating affects tomorrow. On one side, making poor health choices ensures the gyms are packed in January, which the fitness companies love. Staying with poor choices, the "Christmas ten" sometimes becomes the "New Year ten," and those added pounds wait patiently for the next "Christmas ten" to appear. It appears the extra pounds have an agenda and vacating our bodies is not it. I always had great intentions of dropping that extra weight starting on the second day each year. However, January is a long month and my good intentions never made it to January 31st.

On the other side are those who choose to enjoy the holidays in a perfectly healthy manner. Have you ever considered that you *can* enjoy Christmas without eating beyond the health boundaries? You can. News flash: being healthy during the holidays ensures that your jeans will zip and the clothes Aunt Sandra gave you (which you told her were your sizes) actually can remain in your closet and not be re-gifted. Yes, they can.

Merry Christmas to us!

December 13: Roasted Vegetables

Yield: 8 servings

Ingredients

- 3-4 carrots
- 1 large onion (I prefer Vidalia for that sweet flavor)
- ½ head of broccoli
- ½ head of cauliflower
- Chunky portabella mushrooms
- Snap peas (optional)
- Garlic cloves (optional)
- 2-3 tablespoons olive oil

Procedure

1. Preheat oven to 400°F.
2. Wash and prepare all the vegetables, slicing the carrots and onion, while chopping the others. Try to keep the vegetables about the same thickness. Using a mandolin helps with this.
3. Place all the vegetables in a baggie and add 1/3-1/2 cup of olive oil, depending on how many vegetables you are roasting. Add kosher salt, fresh ground pepper, garlic salt, dried thyme,and dried rosemary (about ¼ teaspoon of each). Allow the vegetables to marinate with the flavors for about 60 minutes. I continue to turn the bag upside down every 10 minutes.
4. Place the vegetables on a large, rectangular baking sheet in the oven. The vegetables will cook better if spread out and not layering on top of each other. This will help to ensure they are crisper. Sometimes I use parchment paper underneath.
5. Bake for 30 minutes. When removed from the oven, sprinkle with a dusting of grated Parmesan if desired.

Per Serving:

Calories 96.2
Total Fat 5.5 g
Cholesterol 0.0 mg
Sodium 55.8 mg
Potassium 491.9 mg
Total Carbohydrate 10.7 g
Dietary Fiber 4.4 g
Sugars 1.7 g
Protein 3.5 g

December 14: Hot Spiced Cider

Yield: 16 servings

Ingredients

- 1 large container natural apple juice (no sugar)
- 10 pkgs. Truvia® Natural Sweetener
- 3 large naval oranges
- 4 bags apple cinnamon spice tea
- 3 tablespoons pumpkin pie spice seasoning
- 4 cinnamon sticks
- ½ teaspoon salt

Procedure

1. In a large container on the stove, mix all of the listed ingredients. I wash and slice the oranges and give a slight squeeze before placing in the pot.
2. Allow the cider to brew on medium heat for at least an hour. This will allow the juices to blend flavors.
3. I often lower the temperature to warm and keep on the stove throughout a party, as the scent is as delicious as the cider.

Per Serving:

Calories 117.2
Total Fat 0.4 g
Cholesterol 0.0 mg
Sodium 6.1 mg
Potassium 290.7 mg
Total Carbohydrate 30.5 g
Dietary Fiber 1.2 g
Sugars 5.3 g
Protein 0.5 g

December 15: Trash Talk

This morning the chimes are ringing boldly on my front and back porches from the force of the wind. While we cannot see the wind, it definitely makes its presence known. In my case, all this strong wind is filling my yard again with a heavy load of leaves. You know what that means? I am about to embark upon an upper body workout with the rake. I would rather break a nail. Anyway, while *I see* the yard being covered with leaves, the leaves *instinctively know* they must fall to the ground in preparation for the new growth on the trees in the spring. Same scene—two different perspectives.

I wonder how often we allow a negative perspective to overshadow the good that is intended for a particular situation? As soon as the negative statement proceeds from our mouths, I wonder just what type of power it has? We cannot see the wind, but we can certainly see the effects of its power. Making negative statements about our day, our situation, our weight changes nothing. Or does it?

Many people will often give a new health plan a *try* with the escape route of, "If this does not work in a week, I am over it," tucked in their back pockets. Often I hear, "I will *try* this, but nothing works for me. I have tried everything and I promise, nothing works."

You know what that is to me? Trash talk. I suggest we leave the trash talk buried deep within this past year and boldly march into our new year declaring, "God plans to do good by me and not harm me. He provides a good hope and good future for me." Let us commit to allow the dead leaves of negative statements about our futures to be blown away by the power of the Holy Spirit.

I am not claiming that just because we *confess* things, they happen. Consider this: I have stuffed myself at events and parties, gone home and declared how beautiful I was as well as a multitude of other promises from God's Word, and gained weight. Go figure. And to make a bad situation worse, I would be mad at God. Can I be real? I am not saying that declaring God's truth gives us the liberty to live beyond reason. I am saying that we often cloak the morning with our negative declarations, and in that pocket of self-pity we comfort ourselves with extra layers of food throughout the day.

Stop the trash talk, claim God's talk, and take the health walk. That works.

December 16: The Greatest Gift

Isaiah 61 speaks about proclaiming. I want to offer this for consideration though—*proclamation without action is simply words in the air with no feet.* You know that is right. I never want to say again, "Next year I am seriously going to try to get healthy." Nope, I am getting healthy each and every day. Even one day of delay is too many. I am hopeful you feel the same as you are reading this book and finally solidifying your new North Star. Good job.

There is something to be said for aligning our actions with our declarations and watching our bodies come back to the health God purposed for us. The world offers every excuse for failure—fast foods, processed foods, sugared foods, too much food. Let it be said of us that we choose to not take the offer. We have chosen to be healthy and for our families to be healthy. Our lives are offering success instead of failure to those around us. As I type this, I am smiling. Someone has to blaze the trails. I have spent so much of my life snarling at the trails that the thought of starting another one was very scary. But I did it and you can also.

This Christmas, the greatest gift to anyone is Jesus Christ, and I believe the second greatest is our health. Ask anyone who is suffering physically. Let's be honest, when we eat good, drink good, feel good, and look good, we often are good. It is amazing how extra weight and tight clothes can bring out the worst in us all. If we are honest, when we feel good about ourselves, the rest of the world is smiling. I like it when the world is smiling. I like it when I am smiling, but often my undisciplined life cheated me of that.

This Christmas, my best gift for each of you is encouragement. I hope this devotional cookbook has given you the courage and the determination to be continually healthy. Health is at the core of our being. It contains the seeds of our future, much like the apple core contains the future of the apple. Be kind to yourself this Christmas and remember that your future does not have to look like your past. Put some feet to those words and never look back.

Health is a gift.

December 17: What Gift Are You Unwrapping?

As I opened some of my gifts early yesterday, I could not help but wonder, *What new gifts can be opened for our health family this coming year? What are the new foods, the new recipes, the new adventures sitting in front of us?* I know there are new adventures for me as well as many of you. Are you making your requests known to God? Are you dreaming big and asking God to use you totally? I was reflecting on this past year about how God has brought some fabulous recipes to us. God is the Eternal Iron Chef.

As I unwrapped those gifts, I began to see beyond the natural paper. Unwrapping the gift of health has been one of the greatest blessings of my life. For so many years I would *unwrap* the next diet plan, the next miracle, diet pill, the next "give me a chance" food journey. Then by February, when the Valentine's candy would emerge, off the wagon I would fall. I would quickly try to re-package the program and start again only to decide "This is really not the plan for me." Can anybody else identify with this?

How about we purpose today to unwrap a healthy eating plan for the remainder of our days on earth? I just mention that, as I am not certain what we will be eating in heaven, so I cannot use the time frame of eternity. But I pray that it is pizza. Let us unwrap a mindset that allows no cheats—not a smidgen. Let us make a declaration of no more re-packaging, no more excuses, no more failure. The next package you unwrap would be a healthy blood report that gets rewarded with a new shirt. Then, and from hence forth, you unwrap healthy, new foods and recipes as God shares them with you and you re-gift them to this team who knows that we can live healthy in an unhealthy world. We know we can eat food that tastes amazing and is packed full of great nutrients.

Now that is a gift I want to unwrap. How about you?

December 18: Law versus Grace

While reading this morning from James, I was reminded again that compliance with the law could not save me. I do realize the consequence of sin, but I am most grateful for the saving grace of Jesus. I also read again that all of the commandments were summed up in only two—love God with all that I am, and love others *as I love myself*. That is easy, only two.

I challenge you to look at those two again. Can we start with the second half? *As I love myself.* Do I *really* love myself? Do you love yourself? Can I love others as God desires if my only thoughts concerning myself are loathing? You really need to stop and ponder that. I really tried to reconcile that concept for years. I totally loved God, but did I really love others as I loved myself?

We need to conquer those nagging thoughts of failure and low self-esteem. There is no good in that manner of thinking. *What about this: if the law cannot save us, then can a diet plan filled with regulations rescue us from an unhealthy future?* (Great question, right?) For a season, maybe yes; but we will eventually falter and break the restriction laws because our flesh is so powerful at times.

Loving yourself enough to choose health and healthy eating is a much better plan than the legalistic journey of "do's and don'ts." Filling my house with healthy choices is grace to me, not law. I eat protein, vegetables, and fruits because I want to and the consequences are good to my body. To me, this is such a deep parallel to the contrast between law and grace.

So, enjoy your day, choose well, and reap the consequences of great choices.

December 19: Lessons from Sticks of Butter

I was lying in bed last night thinking about the difference one year can make. This time last year I was baking like a fiend with as much sugar as I could load into every recipe. I was buying tons of candy and eating to the point of sickness in preparation for my *diet* in January. I spent hours planning elaborate food items for parties that would definitely clog the arteries. Then, I would stare in the mirror and ask myself how I ever allowed this to happen. Was that my consolation question? I tried not to answer because I did not want to lie and neither did I want to really change. Ever been there?

I remember one night when my grandkids were all coming for dinner and stockings. I had more candy than most stores carry, but a quarter of what I purchased had *surprisingly* found its way to my mouth. I could hardly get my pants buttoned and my leather jacket could only hide so much. I looked at pictures recently of that Christmas family gathering and while I am smiling in the photos, I was weeping on the inside. No one knew the torture I was enduring. What a difference sixty-five pounds can make. Can you imagine filling a trash bag with sixty-five pounds of butter—that is sixty-five boxes—that is 260 sticks. If you do not believe me, do the math. Can you imagine trying to carry that around, hide that, and work around that? No wonder I was miserable.

I want you to consider the following visual. If you want to lose ten pounds, think about that being forty sticks of butter. Gather those forty if you like and carry them in a sack for fifteen minutes. Or, get a ten-pound weight and attach it to your body somewhere and never take it off. It is a challenge to work with that much weight for fifteen minutes, let alone weeks and months at a time. Often, ten pounds is at the bottom end of what we really need to lose to be within our healthy range. Maybe you are a visual learner like me. Two hundred and sixty sticks of butter is a lot of weight for one person to carry. Think about it. Maybe not if you are Santa Claus!

I may never see a stick of butter in the same fashion again.

December 20: Zucchini Lasagna

Yield: 16 servings

Ingredients

- 1½ pounds lean ground beef
- 2 large cans organic fire roasted diced tomatoes
- 1 small can tomato paste
- 1 medium onion, chopped finely
- 2-3 tablespoons olive oil
- 4 large zucchini squash
- 1 large container ricotta cheese
- 1 large container 2% cottage cheese
- 1 regular container sour cream
- 4 eggs
- 4 cups part skim mozzarella
- 1 cup Parmesan Reggiano cheese
- 2 tablespoons Italian seasonings (You can buy the blend or use ¼ teaspoon of oregano, basil, thyme, rosemary, garlic, and sea salt. You can increase the spices if you like more flavor as I do. Sometimes I definitely increase the basil and garlic.)

Procedure

1. In a large skillet, heat the oil and add the onion. Cook until the onions are tender. Add the ground beef and brown. If the fat content is low enough, there will be no need to drain. However, if needed, drain the meat and set aside.
2. Using a mandolin, or a very sharp knife, slice the zucchini into long planks about ¼ to ½ inch thick.
3. In a large pot of salted, boiling water blanch the zucchini. Remove from the water after 5 minutes and allow to drain in a strainer for about 30 minutes.
4. While the water is draining from the squash, combine the ricotta and cottage cheeses and add the sour cream. Beat the four eggs and blend into the cheese mixture.
5. Add the spices as well as 2 cups of the mozzarella. Blend well.
6. Spray a 9x13 baking dish and preheat the oven to 375°F.
7. In the bottom of the baking dish, place 1/3 of the zucchini, followed by 1/3 of the meat mixture and 1/3 of the cheese and spice mixture. Repeat 2 additional times. Top with the 2 reserved cups of mozzarella and 1 cup of Parmesan Reggiano cheese.
8. Bake for 40-45 minutes or until the cheese is browning well and bubbly on the sides.
9. Allow to cool for about 20 minutes before cutting.

Per Serving:
Calories 417.9
Total Fat 25.2 g
Cholesterol 124.8 mg
Sodium 1,057.2 mg
Potassium 596.5 mg
Total Carbohydrate 16.0 g
Dietary Fiber 2.3 g
Sugars 5.9 g
Protein 31.5 g

December 21: Jalapeño Sausage Balls

Yield: 50 servings

Ingredients

- 2 pkgs. sausage (one hot and one regular)
- 1 cup almond flour
- 2 large eggs
- 2 teaspoons baking powder
- 3 cups four blend Mexican shredded cheese (can use sharp or pepper jack)
- 1 medium onion, chopped finely
- 3 large, fresh jalapeño peppers, chopped finely (without the seeds)
- 5 cloves minced garlic
- 1 teaspoon chili powder
- 1 teaspoon cayenne pepper (optional)
- TABASCO® to taste (5-6 splashes)

Procedure

1. Preheat oven to 400°F.
2. Mix all ingredients in large bowl just until blended. (I use my hands, but the mixer on low speed would work.) Shape into 50 (1-inch) balls or 100 smaller.
3. Place on 2 lightly greased baking pans. Spread them apart so they brown evenly. I prefer to line a large pizza pan (with holes) with parchment paper. Using the paper allows for easier clean-up and requires no turning.
4. Bake 20-25 minutes, turning them over after 15 minutes if you do not use parchment paper, or until brown and as crisp as you like.

Per Serving:

Calories 70.1
Total Fat 5.7 g
Cholesterol 19.5 mg
Sodium 166.1 mg
Potassium 50.9 mg
Total Carbohydrate 1.3 g
Dietary Fiber 0.4 g
Sugars 0.1 g
Protein 3.7 g

December 22: A More Opportune Time

Let us talk today about temptation. I am convinced that our eyesight plays a part in the struggles we face with our health. What? We do not eat with our eyes. That is true; but our eyes are often stimulated and communicate to our stomachs that we are *starving* even if we have eaten recently. Anyone know this to be true?

Part of the temptation lies in the fact that our eyes lust for things we do not really need sometimes. Do we need another biscuit? No, but we see it lying on the platter and do not want to *waste* it. Do we need another pair of sandals? No, but our new dress would look better with a coordinating pair of shoes. Can you see where I am going with this? Commercials are notorious for displaying food items, which serve as visual stimulants, so we will rush to the kitchen and grab a bag of chips whether we are hungry or not. On a side note, I believe that advertisers increase the volume of commercials to ensure as you are running to grab the chips you hear the information about their latest products. Does anyone other than me find that to be true?

Luke 4:13 communicates that Jesus was tempted immediately following His baptism. His encounter with Satan did not go the way the evil one intended. The verse includes the "rest of the story" which I believe gives us hope that we *can* overcome temptation no matter when it occurs. Satan saw this as a very opportune time to tempt the Lord following forty days with no food. That was totally a wicked scheme. When success was not gained, I believe Satan simply removed his plan of temptation until another time—a *more* opportune time. What time was that? Perhaps it was in the garden of Gethsemane?

Submission to temptation often perpetuates the cycle of failure. Jesus knew this and He came to give us a win, not see us fail. There was no room for failure in the wilderness or the garden. Jesus never allowed what He was shown to gain victory over the truth. We can never allow the yeast rolls with butter or the second bowl of ice cream to tempt us to re-enter the cycle of failure again. Can we keep our eyes on the truth of being healthy and off the foods we feel we need? Our weakness often manifests at the most *in*-opportune times, does it not? Remember, no temptation is greater than the victory we have in Jesus.

December 23: Delivering the Puppy

I love the Christmas season. However, I hate it when I realize Christmas is almost over and all the grand displays of lights and fun parties are about to close for this year. I believe that is the reason I decorate my house for the holidays in June. I am kidding, but realistically by Thanksgiving. The older I get, the sooner I decorate, and the longer I allow the lights to remain in the yard.

One of the things I love most about Christmas is watching everyone open their gifts. My family goes around the circle and each one in turn opens a present. I get such a delight when people scream over something I have gotten them. One of my love languages is *gifts*, so giving gifts really stirs me. It makes my heart smile. I love searching for the perfect gift and I start months in advance watching for the gift, planning for the gift, securing the gift and creating that unique delivery of the special gift. Can you tell I love this?

My granddaughters wanted a puppy last year and they started months in advance sending pictures via email, reminder texts, and photos posted in my office. Mackenzie, my oldest one, did all the research for me. She offered prices and made it very clear as to which puppy was the "best" deal. When Papa and I purchased the puppy without their knowledge and delivered it on Christmas morning, they screamed so loud it rattled the neighbors' windows. I have the entire event recorded and have watched it multiple times. They cried and I cried. Have you ever been a part of that type of scenario? Consider this:

God looked at our lives from start to finish and said, "They need a special gift." Have you ever seen someone in passing or standing in the market and you *knew* they needed a touch? God saw us and knew we needed a *special* gift. Not just any gift but a gift that we would unwrap daily and enjoy hour by hour. Jesus—the gift of eternal life—given to us when we did not deserve such an amazing gift. I don't know about you, but I feel Jesus is the best gift giver ever.

December 24: How Hard Is Impossible?

Two days and counting and then we can all do the victory dance as we clear Christmas Day with a healthy check.

As I study the Christmas story in Luke, the birth of Jesus was not just a difficulty. It was an impossibility. Mary and Joseph knew that. However, the angel of the Lord instructed Mary that the Holy Spirit would come and bring life to her impossibility "for nothing is impossible with God." I want to shout!

I wonder what situation in your life looks like an impossibility right now? I am not talking about being unrealistic. Is there a God-dream in your heart right now and it seems impossible? Perhaps you desire complete health and you have only known failure? Perhaps you want to be completely free of all medications by the end of this year, but being healthy is "probably not going to make a difference." Perhaps you would love to embrace health if you knew you could remain strong in the face of opposition? Do any of these seem like impossibilities? Absolutely. But with God all things are possible.

In reading Luke 1:35-37, the power of the Holy Spirit overshadowed Mary and changed her circumstance. That is what we all need. I need the Holy Spirit hovering on my flesh reminding me that fruits and vegetables are amazingly beneficial to my body. I need the Holy Spirit reminding me of how destructive sugar can be. I need the Holy Spirit helping me to choose life every day by embracing a healthy lifestyle. His intervention is critical. I may not understand the whole "overshadowed" scenario, but I can certainly observe Mary's life and see the end result. Amazing.

So let us take our impossibilities before the Lord, stand in faith, and watch God do the miraculous.

December 25: A Christmas Song

Merry Christmas, my sweet family. I cannot write long today as I have prime rib baking in the oven and lots of healthy sides to construct for my family lunch, which will be concluded with a sugar-free cheesecake that is to *live* for (get it?). But I do want to stop briefly and tell you I appreciate the fact that we are on a journey together.

The Word of God says in Amos 3:3, "Can two people walk together without agreeing on the direction?" (NLT). I often mention that we are walking together, and yet I have not met many of you. That is okay. When you try my recipes and share healthy meals with your families, we are, in essence, walking together as well as in agreement. I do not have to stand beside you to walk beside you. Well maybe, but I am trying to have a real tender moment here.

Anyway, this Christmas, I pray you did it differently. If not, it is okay. *Make the small changes that can lead to the **big** changes and keep going.*

How about I sing a song for you as your Christmas gift?

> *I'm dreaming of my fruits and vegetables,*
>
> *Steamed, grilled, and raw or else sautéed.*
>
> *Even when I'm hungry, I'll drink my water,*
>
> *And live my life for all to see.*
>
> *I'm eating all these healthy recipes,*
>
> *I won't give in or trash my scale,*
>
> *And I'll show my family that I am healthy*
>
> *And live within the boundaries.*

I know that is exceedingly silly, but you must admit that someone cares for you if they would write a goofy song and actually type the lyrics. Companies make millions of dollars from jingles and visuals. But I think they pay millions for people, unlike me, to make them sound amazing.

That is enough. Merry Christmas!

December 26: Joy, Joy, Joy

My spiritual son in Africa sent pictures of a family he and a friend helped this Christmas. It was far from the extravagance that we sometimes use as our measuring rod of a *great* Christmas. These people were excessively poor, poorly clothed, living on mud floors, and yet smiling so warmly as my son and his friend provided fruit, a pair of used shoes, and a few other small items given to this family. I examined that picture closely last night and thought, *I am not certain I really understand how blessed I am.* I am blessed my son has the heart of Jesus for his people.

This family displayed joy that I often do not see on the faces of many around me. This has been a tough year for several families I know, but it cannot compare to what I saw in that picture. You know the saying, *a picture is worth a thousand words?* That picture served as my reminder that joy and happiness really are different emotions. One is a choice and one is not.

If I never lose another pound, never change another size, never buy another article of clothing—touching lives in a sacrificial way is the real joy for me. I think we could all agree that life cannot be totally focused on our own desires or needs. However, we like getting *our* gift as well and none of us can deny that. I got my gift (Jesus), have made my choice to serve Him, am taking care of the Holy Spirit's house (my body), and now I turn my attention to sharing the gift of joy with as many as I can. It is not about *my* understanding, *my* feelings, or *my* desires. At this stage of my life, it is about being available to God. That brings me everlasting joy.

I look forward to exploring new things with you next year. I pray you find encouragement and a deep sense of awe as you share joy with those around you. Bring Jesus into every situation and allow His star (see Numbers 24:17) to remind you that He shatters yokes, destroys the lies and excuses we choose to believe, and came to set us free (Galatians 5:1).

Eat your vegetables and fruits and say "joy" one hundred times today—unspeakable, uncontainable joy. Joy, joy, joy!

December 27: Greek Salad with Grilled Chicken

Yield: 4 servings

Ingredients

- 2 stalks romaine lettuce washed and chopped
- 1 container tomato and herb feta cheese (or whatever variety you prefer. To skinny the recipe, use light cheese.)
- 1 small red onion
- 3 Roma tomatoes
- 1 small container sliced, black olives
- Pickled banana peppers (optional)
- Greek seasoning
- ½ container Greek salad dressing
- 4 grilled chicken breasts (grilled with Grill Mates® Montreal Steak Seasoning)

Procedure

1. Chop and wash the lettuce. Allow to dry for about 20 minutes in a strainer.
2. Prepare the onion by slicing into very thin rounds and then cutting in half.
3. Slice the tomatoes in rounds, about 5-6 pieces per tomato.
4. After the lettuce has dried, combine everything except the dressing.
5. Sprinkle with a good dose of Greek seasoning.
6. Add the dressing and toss.
7. Take the grilled chicken and cut it into strips.
8. Arrange the salad on a plate and add the hot chicken before serving.

Per Serving:

Calories 519.9
Total Fat 25.3 g
Cholesterol 189.3 mg
Sodium 785.3 mg
Potassium 663.9 mg
Total Carbohydrate 11.4 g
Dietary Fiber 2.4 g
Sugars 1.5 g
Protein 60.7 g

December 28: Creamy Ambrosia

Yield: 8 servings

Ingredients

- 4 large, naval oranges
- 1 can pineapple tidbits (in its own juice)
- 1 pkg. unsweetened coconut (I use the one in the freezer.)
- ½ cup xylitol
- 1 pkg. light cream cheese (room temperature)
- 1 cup sour cream (light)
- ½ cup pecans (can use regular, toasted, or cinnamon roasted)
- Red grapefruit (optional)

Procedure

1. Zest one of the oranges and reserve.
2. Peel the oranges and grapefruit, then remove the skin from each section. I prefer the miniature oranges and only use the red grapefruits.
3. Drain the pineapple well and combine with the halved orange sections.
4. Blend together the cream cheese and xylitol. Add the sour cream and mix well.
5. Add the oranges, pineapple, coconut, and pecans and blend well.
6. Refrigerate for at least four hours or overnight.

Not So Creamy Variation:

Delete the cream cheese and sour cream.

Per Serving:
Calories 308.6
Total Fat 20.1 g
Cholesterol 31.8 mg
Sodium 125.4 mg
Potassium 356.9 mg
Total Carbohydrate 32.9 g
Dietary Fiber 4.8 g
Sugars 17.4 g
Protein 4.9 g

Per Serving: (Variation)
Calories 197.7
Total Fat 10.5 g
Cholesterol 0.0 mg
Sodium 3.0 mg
Potassium 317.9 mg
Total Carbohydrate 29.7 g
Dietary Fiber 4.8 g
Sugars 16.4 g
Protein 2.0 g

December 29: Salad Times Three

New Year's Eve parties are right around the corner, and that takes some grocery shopping for us. Let all the trendsetters lock and load, pack and carry, laugh and enjoy. Remember as you pack for the party, cover your bases. If you are not certain what is being served, plan a meat, some finger-food vegetables you can nibble while socializing, and your own sparkling water. No one needs to know you are packing. I do it all the time!

Last night at a party, when some saw I was not eating the bread or the croutons and "picking" on the prepared salad, several of them refused to eat their bread as well. I think they felt I was on some weird, hard diet and they were assisting me by their denial. I hate for people to act awkward when I am being a good girl. I simply said, "I am not very hungry at *this* point." (Remember, I usually eat something small before parties so I am not caught in a panic.) At a party is not the easiest or best time to uncover our health plan unless we are asked the right questions. However, if someone needs to know, I need to share.

When I finally decided to eat and asked for a third bowl of salad however (I know—I was hungry now), people were smiling and looking oddly at me. This time I replied, "I just love salad," which is actually more true as the months progress but not my real food love. Then I thought, *Why do I need to comment?* If I were asking for a third piece of bread, I would have to say nothing. Or if I were grabbing a third piece of cake, the cheers and jesting would come, but it would probably be accompanied with laughter and not scrutiny.

I did not eat dessert or take one (poor planning on my part) so when we got home, I cut a big apple and consumed it with some natural peanut butter. I made a cup of peach tea and Truvia® and it was double treat. At the end of the day, I was not mad at myself or angry that I had eaten too much. I like feeling that way.

Anyway, the phrase for today is lock and load—pack and carry.

December 30: It Is My Choice

What do we do together on the *next to the last day* of this year as a family? We look back and thank God that we are not where we were at the beginning of this year. Looking back is not always the best option, but when we come to the close of one year I like to reflect and gather my memories. I have many "gathered" truths peppered throughout my journals and Bibles. I love it when truth sticks. *I have learned if truth does not stick, then a lie is always an option.* I believed so many lies about my life and health for so many years. But once the truth really stuck, my freedom came.

Thank God that He brought us together as a group of trendsetters who absolutely are convinced that being healthy is not a fad. It is a choice, and we choose life. We choose what foods we eat. We choose what we use for hydration. We choose to rest. We choose to laugh at our lives and ourselves on a regular basis. We choose to create a healthy home for the Holy Spirit and our families and above all else we *choose to live our lives to the fullest.*

We learned this year that freedom from obesity is something worth fighting for. We learned that refueling is a better choice of words than eating because it takes less fanfare to simply refuel our cells. We are not driven to plan the next extravagant meal. We simply refuel our cells and they provide us with a healthy lifestyle that allows us to be used by God in a better way.

We do not choose to overeat, nor do we choose disease and depression. We do not choose excuses and hiding our weaknesses as we drive through the fast food lane and grab another cheeseburger. We do not choose isolation and we do not choose compromise. We choose life!

Thank you for choosing to walk with me. Your words have encouraged me to keep writing. I pray God's Word encourages you to fight for your freedom and choose the apple *and* the brownie!

December 31: December Reflection Page

You did it! You completed twelve months. As you are completing December, are there things you wish you had highlighted or which you had written down? Use the space below to summarize the major insights you gained this year.

_____

_____

_____

_____

_____

_____

_____

_____

_____

_____

_____

_____

_____

_____

_____

_____

_____

_____

_____

_____

_____

Conclusion

As you have traveled through the past twelve months, perhaps you have gained a new perspective on the power of Jesus to bring freedom into your life in all areas. God's Word is filled to overflowing with His encouragement for His creation that He adores. My prayer is that His truth became your truth and your ultimate reality.

Perhaps there are those who have never connected with Jesus or made Him their personal Lord and Savior. This is God's best plan for everyone. John 3:16-17 (AMP) reads:

> "For God so greatly loved and dearly prized the world that He [even] gave up His only begotten (unique) Son, so that whoever believes in (trusts in, clings to, relies on) Him shall not perish (come to destruction, be lost) but have eternal (everlasting) life. For God did not send the Son into the world in order to judge (to reject, to condemn, to pass sentence on) the world, but that the world might find salvation and be made safe and sound through Him."

I would like to conclude this devotional cookbook with a personal invitation to anyone reading and cooking with me, who may not have accepted God's love, to read the verse again and make an eternal connection. Living outside of Jesus' sacrifice never brings forth life. Accepting the salvation of Jesus, on the other hand, always produces life. We all have a need for a savior.

If this conclusion is meant for you, consider the following:

Accept the fact that we are all sinners in need of a Savior. All of us have fallen short in many areas (Romans 3:23; Ecclesiastes 7:20; 1 John 1:8-10).

Believe that Jesus came and died that you might be free. Freedom from eternal judgment of sin and abundant life while upon the earth are both critical components to God's redemptive plan (John 3:16-17; John 10:10; John 6:40; John 11:25).

Confess that you need Jesus' sacrificial gift and plan of salvation and ask Him to change your heart. We call these simple dialogues, prayer. God always wants to hear from His creation (Romans 10:9-10; Acts 16:31; Matthew 10:32).

Once you have completed your ABC's, find a Bible and begin to read the gospel of John. It will share with you the magnitude of God's love. Then, find a local church where you can grow with other believers in your knowledge of God's Word and work in your life. Finally, share your good news with everyone. Matthew 28 gives all believers a charge to go and tell. If you have accepted God's plan of salvation today, please contact me through my website so that I can touch base and pray with you. I would love that.

And, while you are going and telling, bake something sugar and starch free and share your personal journey to freedom in the area of your health as well. "It is for freedom's sake that Jesus came."

Choose life,

Kathy

About the Author

When you meet Kathy Hill, you immediately feel a connection so genuine and strong it will probably surprise you. She is an example of what happens when southern hospitality combines with the supernatural personality of the Holy Spirit. She is fiercely independent and at the same time totally reliant on the transforming power of a dynamic heavenly Father.

Kathy's manner is inclusion. "You're welcome." Not as the expected response to, "Thank you," implying that a thoughtful deed has been performed. Instead, Kathy's welcome should be translated, "You belong here. I have been expecting you." Regardless of what your past looks like or where you find yourself today, she encourages you to pull a chair up to the table and join in just like you're family—because you are family.

Her method is service to others because she loves people. Kathy has a heart for those who find themselves victims of human trafficking, locked in the prison of obesity, bound by the chains of past mistakes, or living in despair, having given up any hope of enjoying a life beyond their current circumstances. Kathy loves getting real with people, spending time with them, loving them, and introducing them to the God of the Universe who cares about them individually.

Kathy's motivation is teaching; she's an inspirational communicator. Since she was a child she has felt the call to teach, and today she regularly instructs through her personal and poignant blog posts. Kathy shares how she and her biological family, as well as her extended family consisting of kindred hearts seeking God's plan for physical wellness, were able to break free of the chains of obesity and poor health and how you can as well. Kathy's teaching often extends well beyond her blog and into the local church where she shares how to walk in freedom in all areas and the importance of making yourself available to God. Indeed, her story is a dynamic testament to the power of availability and the freedom that comes through obedience.

Kathy's message is hope. Whether teaching a group, conducting personal coaching, speaking before a packed auditorium or on the mission field, or writing her blog—and now a book—Kathy's message remains strong: there is always hope. God has cared about you from the beginning of time and regardless of what decisions you have made, He has never changed His mind about you; He wants you to be victorious.

Currently, Kathy serves as Executive Pastor at New City Church in the Atlanta, Georgia area and oversees staff, ministry teams, weekend services, and events. She is also a prolific blogger, personal coach, wife, mother, grandmother, and speaker.

Equal parts inquisitive student, inspirational teacher, and persistent coach, Kathy eagerly shares personal experiences, practical examples, and Biblical truths to encourage us to live a victorious Christian life. You can follow Kathy's writing via her blog Coffee with Kathy at www.freedomconnection.org.

Recipe Index

More Titles by 5 Fold Media

The Transformed Life
by John R. Carter
$20.95
ISBN: 978-1-936578-40-5

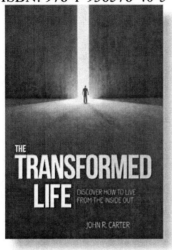

Personal transformation requires radical change, but your life will not transform until you change the way you think. Becoming a Christian ignites the process of transformation.

In this book, John Carter will teach you that God has designed a plan of genuine transformation for every person, one that goes far beyond the initial moment of salvation. More than a book, this ten week, forty day workbook will show you how to change.

Letters from Heaven
The Passion Translation
by Brian Simmons
$12.95
ISBN: 978-1-936578-56-6

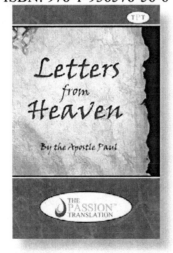

Some of the most beautiful and glorious truths of the Bible are found in the letters of the apostle Paul. Paul's letters are now available in The Passion Translation. Reading through these letters is like having Paul sitting in your living room personally sharing his experience of the power and majesty of God's Word for His people. Be ready to sense the stirring of the Holy Spirit within you as you read *Letters from Heaven by the Apostle Paul.*

I highly recommend this new Bible translation to everyone. ~ Dr. Ché Ahn, Senior Pastor of HRock Church in Pasadena, CA

Like 5 Fold Media on Facebook, follow us on Twitter!

"To Establish and Reveal"
For more information
visit:
www.5foldmedia.com

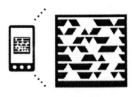

Use your mobile device to scan
the tag and visit our website.
Get the free app:
http://gettag.mobi

CPSIA information can be obtained at www.ICGtesting.com
Printed in the USA
LVOW09s2025040614

388583LV00012B/375/P